LGBTQ INTIMATE PARTNER VIOLENCE

The publisher gratefully acknowledges the generous support of the Barbara S. Isgur Public Affairs Endowment Fund of the University of California Press Foundation.

LGBTQ INTIMATE PARTNER VIOLENCE

Lessons for Policy, Practice, and Research

Adam M. Messinger

UNIVERSITY OF CALIFORNIA PRESS

University of California Press, one of the most distinguished university presses in the United States, enriches lives around the world by advancing scholarship in the humanities, social sciences, and natural sciences. Its activities are supported by the UC Press Foundation and by philanthropic contributions from individuals and institutions. For more information, visit www.ucpress.edu.

University of California Press
Oakland, California

Library of Congress Cataloging-in-Publication Data

Names: Messinger, Adam M., 1982- author.
Title: LGBTQ intimate partner violence : lessons for policy, practice, and research / Adam M. Messinger.
Description: Oakland, California : University of California Press, [2017] | Includes bibliographical references and index.
Identifiers: LCCN 2016033165 (print) | LCCN 2016033522 (ebook) | ISBN 9780520286054 (cloth : alk. paper) | ISBN 9780520961357 (Epub)
Subjects: LCSH: Intimate partner violence. | Sexual minorities—Violence against.
Classification: LCC HV6626 .M475 2017 (print) | LCC HV6626 (ebook) | DDC 362.82/92—dc23
LC record available at https://lccn.loc.gov/2016033165

Manufactured in the United States of America

25 24 23 22 21 20 19 18 17
10 9 8 7 6 5 4 3 2 1

CONTENTS

ILLUSTRATIONS

FIGURES

TABLES

BOXES

PREFACE

"Is that a thing?" my friend inquired, somewhat doubtful.

I had been explaining that the book I was writing was focused on intimate partner violence (IPV) among lesbian, gay, bisexual, trans*, and queer (LGBTQ) people. "Yes," I assured him, "LGBTQ IPV is *definitely* a thing."

I explained that LGBTQ people are actually *more* likely to experience abuse in a romantic or sexual relationship than heterosexual-cisgender (HC) people. LGBTQ IPV is similar in many ways to HC IPV. Still, there are also key differences: LGBTQ IPV exhibits unique causes, abusive tactics, and barriers to receiving help. Sadly, there are often systemic failings in how societies address LGBTQ IPV—such as pertinent laws and policies that exclude certain LGBTQ IPV victims from coverage, a lack of training for key personnel working with victims and abusers, and a trend toward providing LGBTQ IPV victims with ill-fitting services designed for HC IPV victims.

My friend's eyes widened. This was news to him, but I assured him that he is definitely not alone. Studies suggest that many people—even some who work in law enforcement and shelters—do not consider LGBTQ IPV to be "real" IPV. This misunderstanding has in part been fueled by global efforts to address IPV that have historically focused on male-to-female abuse. While this focus is understandable given that the majority of people are heterosexual-cisgender, mounting evidence suggests that the pendulum may be swinging too far, to the point of rendering LGBTQ IPV nearly invisible.

While the emerging movement to address LGBTQ IPV takes many forms, research is arguably one of its most important tools. Research has the capacity not only to improve public understanding of LGBTQ IPV but also, and just as important, to offer invaluable suggestions for perfecting future policy, practice, and research on the issue. Thankfully, the LGBTQ IPV research literature that began in 1977[1] has massively expanded over the past forty years—to the point that by 2016 we now have reached over *six hundred* research publications on the subject. Unfortunately, it is too often the case that excellent research of the past gets buried, never to be discussed again after its initial publication. This can be exacerbated both by the sheer size of this literature and by the fact that scholars often do not read publications from outside their core discipline, such as when articles in medical and legal journals do not get read and cited by social science scholars. How can we benefit from past research when no one is aware of it?

Nearly a dozen excellent books have been written on LGBTQ IPV research to fill such a need, to bring to light this treasure trove of research-based information. In each instance, though, these books have been limited in scope, by excluding either key LGBTQ subpopulations (e.g., trans* people, gay men, etc.) or entire decades of research. As a consequence, no book has yet to attempt to review the entirety of this literature. It might be time for that to change. Rather than being expected to read hundreds of research publications on the subject, policymakers, practitioners, and researchers should have one book available to them that will synthesize the literature and draw out evidence-based tips for taking on LGBTQ IPV.

My hope is that this can be such a book. At once highly detailed and yet accessibly written, *LGBTQ Intimate Partner Violence: Lessons for Policy, Practice, and Research* is intended for all the key players in the movement to address LGBTQ IPV. This includes both academic audiences (e.g., researchers, teachers, and students who are interested in IPV or LGBTQ populations) and nonacademic audiences (e.g., victims and their supporters, activists, LGBTQ organizations, IPV shelter and hotline staff, IPV government agencies and community organizations, mental and medical health-care providers, law enforcement, attorneys and court personnel, and policymakers). This book is ultimately written for anyone who is tired of societal ignorance and discrimination permitting batterers to go unchallenged in their control over victims.

This book offers a thematically organized and engaging overview of nearly every English-language journal article, book chapter, and book on LGBTQ IPV, supplemented by a number of research reports from well-known organizations. Wherever existing research permits, topics are examined with an eye toward uncovering ways in which IPV differs not only between LGBTQ and HC individuals but also *within* LGBTQ populations, such as differences by sexual orientation, trans*-cisgender identity, gender identity, social class, age, race-ethnicity, immigration status, and nationality. Chapters conclude with specific, research-informed tips for future policy, practice, and research.

It is my sincere hope that, by learning from our past, we can help spur on an evolutionary leap forward in how societies address and prevent LGBTQ IPV. Welcome to the movement.

ACKNOWLEDGMENTS

Perhaps more so than any other project I have ever worked on, this book would literally have been impossible without the help of others. In particular, I want to thank the countless researchers, practitioners, activists, and allies who have built this vibrant research literature. I am humbly aware that I stand on the shoulders of numerous scholars, without whom such a book could not exist. We are forever indebted to the trail you have blazed. On a more technical level, I would also like to thank my publisher and reviewers for your expertise and time spent shepherding this project to completion. This project was also made significantly happier by the interlibrary-loan department at Northeastern Illinois University, which processed likely hundreds of journal article requests for me. Finally, to my family: thanks for your love and humor, and for keeping me sane through this sad yet uplifting process. I couldn't be luckier.

INTRODUCTION

Making the Invisible Visible

At age 14, love struck. Jai Dulani was beginning ninth grade in northern India, eight thousand miles from his home in America. *She* was a new student at Jai's school, incredibly smart and beautiful. Jai learned that she, too, felt out of place, having moved many times for her father's job. They began confiding in each other their secrets, hopes, and fears. Soon came a flurry of love letters, secret hand-holding under desks, a quick kiss during study hall. Jai fell hard. Adding to the excitement was that no one knew. They were very careful. They had even worked out a special code to say "I love you" without their parents knowing. As Jai puts it, they were living "a secret underground love story."

Jai does not recall when the fights began, but he learned that losing was the only option. In part because his girlfriend was a victim of child abuse, she came to rely on Jai for emotional support. She insisted on knowing where he was at all times, in case she needed to talk. She felt particularly hurt when he was busy with anyone else. One time, furious that Jai was meeting up with friends, she called his home phone over . . . and over . . . and over again. Jai was deeply embarrassed. Challenging her only seemed to hurt her more, and he soon found it easier to lie and be late when meeting up with friends, family, or teachers. Over the next two years, her anguish and anger flourished. When she was especially upset, she might yank his hair, scratch him, grab his face, push him, or hit him with the back of her hand. She eventually turned to cutting herself and overdosing, often in front of Jai, who would cry and plead for her to stop. She seemed to be sending a clear message: *you are failing me, and this is what you have driven me to.* What could he possibly say to anyone? After all, their relationship did not officially exist.

Just before he turned 16, Jai and his family moved back to the United States. His girlfriend sent countless letters. *"Why did you leave? I need you. Everything got worse when you left. When are you coming back? I can't take it anymore."* When Jai finally stopped talking to her, she unfortunately was not prepared to stop talking with Jai. One day, she picked up the phone, dialed his grandmother, pretended to be a friend, and acquired his new contact information.[1]

To anyone who has worked with or knows someone like Jai, his story may sound eerily familiar. That is because Jai's story is one of many that involve intimate partner violence: psychological, physical, or sexual abuse or homicide between romantic and sexual partners. It can begin, seemingly innocuously, with jealousy. Jealousy is often perceived to be a sign of love, as in, *I care about you so much that I want to spend all my time with you.* To avoid conflict and emotionally hurting the abuser, victims may be pushed to see friends and family less and less. When victims are blamed for angering the abuser and "causing" the abuse, no one is left in the victim's life to cry foul, to remind the victim that no one deserves to be abused. By the time abuse escalates, no one is left to help the victim escape. In a very real way, IPV flourishes when it is most invisible to the world.

Jai's story is unique, though, in one key way: today a trans* man who uses the pronoun "he," Jai identified as a girl at the time of the abuse. The context of discrimination and stigma had a devastating effect on this relationship from the very beginning. Cisgender people (i.e., those whose current gender identity matches their biological sex at birth in a way expected and privileged by society) and heterosexuals very often share the exciting news of a first date or a budding relationship, unconcerned that doing so makes their gender identity and sexual orientation more visible. By comparison, for those who identify as a sexual minority (i.e., lesbian, gay, bisexual, or queer) or trans* (i.e., those whose current gender identity does not match their biological sex at birth in a way expected and privileged by society), discussing a relationship with friends or family may be out of the question, since doing so requires being open about their gender identity and sexual orientation in a world that so often rejects them. Thus, whereas cisgender and heterosexual IPV victims often feel trapped by virtue of the abuse being hidden within a visible relationship, for IPV among lesbian, gay, bisexual, trans*, and queer (LGBTQ) individuals, the relationship itself may be invisible. How do you ask for help with a relationship that supposedly does not exist? In the instances when victims choose to make the relationship visible, IPV has historically been stereotyped as solely occurring within the realm of heterosexual-cisgender people, leading many to downplay or ignore the seriousness of relationship abuse among LGBTQ people. For these same reasons, even LGBTQ abusers and victims may not fully recognize what is happening.

LGBTQ IPV has thus been rendered largely invisible to our friends, families, schools, communities, medical and mental health providers, policymakers, law-enforcement agencies, courts, and scholars. This remains the case despite research repeatedly concluding that LGBTQ people are more likely to experience IPV.[2] An important step in bringing LGBTQ IPV out of the shadows would be to shed light on what we already know about the issue and how we can use this knowledge *today* to bring about change. This book helps bring together in one place the vast majority of published research and information about LGBTQ IPV, along the way helping identify key lessons and implications for future policy, practice, and research. This is a book that aims to make the invisible visible.

THE FIVE MYTHS OF LGBTQ IPV

IPV victim agencies play a valuable role in helping victims of both LGBTQ IPV (IPV relationships involving at least one LGBTQ partner) and HC IPV (IPV relationships involving two heterosexual-cisgender partners). They can offer short-term counseling and emergency shelter, along with operating telephone hotlines to connect victims with needed services. More fundamentally, their positive and affirming response can send a message to victims that they are indeed experiencing IPV and that they deserve better. Researchers Michael Brown and Jennifer Groscup had a very basic question: Do IPV victim agency staff take same-gender IPV as seriously as they do different-gender IPV? To answer this question, Brown and Groscup asked 120 staff members at a U.S. suburban IPV victim agency to read a fictional IPV story. In this story, the police arrive at a home after a neighbor has heard screaming and breaking glass. The police first interview one partner, who describes the incident as involving both partners trying to physically hurt one another—what is known as short-term bidirectional IPV. Then the police interview the other partner, who describes this being just one of many incidents in which their partner attacked them without resistance, or long-term unidirectional IPV. The fact that this story was a blank slate with room for multiple interpretations meant that staff had to rely on their intuition to guide them in evaluating the seriousness of the case. The researchers wanted to test whether the staff's intuition could be influenced by one key factor: the gender of the partners. One-fourth of the sample received a version of the story with two female partners, one-fourth received exactly the same story but with two male partners, one-fourth read about a male and female partner, and one-fourth likewise read about a female and male partner with the roles reversed. In other words, Brown and Groscup were testing whether deeply held gender- and sexual-orientation-based assumptions about IPV might influence how seriously the crisis-center staff took same-gender IPV.

What the researchers found was rather astounding. As compared with different-gender IPV, the IPV victim agency staff members rated both male-male and female-female IPV as less serious and less likely to worsen over time. Moreover, regarding the character who was reporting ongoing unidirectional IPV victimization, the staff was less likely to recommend that the victim leave the abuser if the victim and the abuser were of the same gender.[3] Unfortunately, with rare exceptions,[4] research suggests that Brown and Groscup's findings are not limited to IPV victim agencies. Several studies similarly suggest that same-gender IPV is perceived to be less serious than different-gender IPV by IPV shelter service providers in the United States, by M.A. and Ph.D. counseling psychology students in the United States, and by college students in the United States and Sweden.[5]

One can only begin to imagine the catastrophic implications for same-gender IPV victims. If the people they turn to first for help refuse to validate their experiences as legitimate abuse, if they refuse to help, victims may begin to doubt whether they are true victims, whether they deserve help, whether they should try to leave, and whether help will be there for them if they do leave. The experience of Susan, a 37-year-old lesbian woman, sums up what this apathy regarding LGBTQ IPV might look like through a victim's eyes:

> My mom didn't believe me—when I told her she didn't believe that she—her reaction was that doesn't happen with other women. Women don't do that to each other. And I think it took her actually seeing me bruised to have her realize the [sic] yeah, I wasn't just blowing this out of proportion. It hurt. It made me feel like she didn't believe what I was telling her. When I called her and asked her to come over and get me because Greta had hurt me, she stopped at a sewing machine place on the way because she had an errand to run. So, I mean that—that, I think hurt more than Greta's fist.[6]

Note that Susan's mother was not apathetic regarding IPV generally, just LGBTQ IPV. Simply put, her mother—like many IPV victim agency staff, counselors, students, and others—does not believe LGBTQ IPV is that serious. Therein lies perhaps the largest hurdle for improving policies, services, and research in this movement. If LGBTQ IPV is not taken seriously, it is rendered invisible.

There are many reasons LGBTQ IPV is ignored or not taken seriously, but many of them can be boiled down to five widely held myths, or erroneous assumptions that undercut the legitimacy of LGBTQ IPV as a real phenomenon worthy of societal attention: (1) "LGBTQ IPV is rare," (2) "LGBTQ IPV is less severe," (3) "LGBTQ IPV abusers are masculine," (4) "LGBTQ IPV is the same as all other IPV," and (5) "LGBTQ IPV should not be discussed." (See box 1.) To make the invisible visible, we must begin by pulling back the curtain on these myths.

Myth no. 1: LGBTQ IPV Is Rare

It is difficult to take LGBTQ IPV seriously if it is perceived to be rare.[7] This myth is likely owing at least in part to the small size of the LGBTQ global population. According to a study pooling data from large-scale surveys in Australia, Canada, Norway, the United Kingdom, and the United States, anywhere from 1.2% to 5.6% of people in these nations identify as lesbian, gay, or bisexual, and U.S.-based

BOX 1. THE FIVE MYTHS OF LGBTQ IPV

1. LGBTQ IPV is rare.
2. LGBTQ IPV is less severe.
3. LGBTQ IPV abusers are masculine.
4. LGBTQ IPV is the same as all other IPV.
5. LGBTQ IPV should not be discussed.

research hints that less than 1% of people identify as "transgender."[8] There are of course limitations in these studies that might imply that the numbers could be higher in reality, and even these small-sounding percentages actually tally up to quite a few people. For instance, there are an estimated nine million LGBTQ adults in the United States alone.[9] For a sense of scale, that is just under the size of the entire population of Sweden.[10] In any case, there are far more heterosexual-cisgender people in the world, and as a direct result, the majority of IPV abusers and victims are heterosexual-cisgender as well. However, this is a far cry from saying that LGBTQ IPV is rare.[11]

The myth that LGBTQ IPV is rare has been largely debunked by research. Among LGBTQ people, the risk of IPV is quite high. Certainly, variations in study design—such as whether sexual orientation is assessed by asking for the respondent's self-identified sexual orientation or same-gender relationship history, as well as whether IPV is assessed in an inclusive or narrow manner—influence prevalence rates. (See chapter 2 for a discussion of how study designs influence estimates.) For this reason, it can be difficult to boil the many available prevalence rates down to a single number. That said, when examining the most accurate estimates available from large, randomly sampled studies, beyond two exceptions finding equivalent rates,[12] research has repeatedly concluded that sexual minorities and those with a history of same-gender relationships are at a *higher risk* of experiencing psychological,[13] physical,[14] and sexual IPV[15] relative to heterosexuals and those with a history of only different-gender relationships. Just as one example, the most recent nationally representative estimates from this crop of studies come from the National Intimate Partner and Sexual Violence Survey (NISVS), a 2010 cell-phone and landline telephone survey of 16,507 adults from across the United States. NISVS reveals disturbingly high lifetime victimization rates: nearly *one-third* of sexual minority males and nearly *one-half* of sexual minority females in the United States were victims of rape, physical violence, or stalking by an intimate partner at some point in their lives. Additionally, over *half* of sexual minority males and nearly *three-fourths* of sexual minority females were victims of psychological IPV by an intimate partner at some point in their lives. (See table 1.) By extrapolating from research estimating the size of the U.S. sexual minority

TABLE 1   Lifetime IPV victimization prevalence in the United States

	Gay men	Bisexual men	Heterosexual men
Psychological IPV	59.6%	53.0%	49.3%
Physical IPV, rape, or stalking	26.0%	37.3%	29.0%
Physical IPV	25.2%	37.3%	28.7%
Partner rape	*	*	*
Partner stalking	*	*	2.1%

	Lesbian women	Bisexual women	Heterosexual women
Psychological IPV	63.0%	76.2%	47.5%
Physical IPV, rape, or stalking	43.8%	61.1%	35.0%
Physical IPV	40.4%	56.9%	32.3%
Partner rape	*	22.1%	9.1%
Partner stalking	*	31.1%	10.2%

SOURCE: Data reported from M. L. Walters, J. Chen, and M. J. Breiding, *The National Intimate Partner and Sexual Violence Survey (NISVS): 2010 Findings on Victimization by Sexual Orientation* (Atlanta: National Center for Injury Prevention and Control, Centers for Disease Control and Prevention, 2013).

*Not reported by study authors due to relative standard error > 30% or cell size < 20.

population and applying sampling weights, the study authors estimate that there are over *4.1 million* lesbian, gay, and bisexual individuals in the United States alone who have experienced physical IPV, partner rape, or partner stalking in their lifetimes.[16] Like NISVS, all large, randomly sampled studies on this issue have thus far been conducted in North America—so how does prevalence vary in other parts of the world? As compared with rates in North America, studies with smaller or non-random samples generally find either similar or higher rates of IPV among sexual minorities in Australia,[17] China,[18] South Africa,[19] and the United Kingdom.[20] Indeed, in the only study directly comparing IPV victimization rates of sexual minorities in different nations, past-year sexual IPV victimization rates were found to be nearly identical inside and outside North America, and past-year physical IPV victimization rates were actually found to be either the same or higher outside of North America, including in Australia, Brazil, South Africa, and the United Kingdom.[21]

Data is extremely limited on IPV among trans* individuals. Studies comparing trans* and cisgender people are mixed on whether IPV risk differs between these populations.[22] Still, as with sexual minorities, lifetime victimization rates are incredibly high for trans* people. According to available nonrandom (and thus less accurate) studies spanning Australia, Scotland, and the United States, 57% of trans* people experience psychological IPV,[23] 43–46% experience physical IPV,[24] and 8–47% experience sexual IPV[25] in their lifetimes. While no general-population, representative survey has inquired about IPV victimization from trans*-

identified individuals in any nation, the aforementioned studies strongly suggest that IPV is not purely a cisgender problem. (For a detailed examination of LGBTQ IPV prevalence, see chapter 3.)

In sum, LGBTQ IPV happens, and it happens *a lot*. Why, then, is there such a disconnect between these research findings and the persistence of the myth that LGBTQ IPV is rare? A key reason why some believe LGBTQ IPV to be rare may be due to an assumption that LGBTQ people are inherently nonviolent. This may be particularly the case for sexual minority women. In contrast to the aggression often associated with culturally prominent masculinity norms, many lesbian women are socialized to perceive relationships involving two women as a peaceful and ideal "lesbian utopia." Unfortunately, this powerful stereotype can impede lesbian female victims' ability to recognize that a partner's behavior is in fact abusive rather than normal.[26] For example, in reflecting on her same-gender IPV victimization back in the 1990s, Julie describes the ubiquity of the lesbian utopia ideal in the United Kingdom that prevented her from discussing the abuse with anyone: "Well it was during a period where everyone was just raving about erm how brilliant woman-to-woman relationships were and also I don't think anyone believed that one woman could do that to another woman—there was just no, no sense of reality around that at all. There was sort of a political euphoria about lesbianism at the time; well not even lesbianism, just woman-to-woman relationships."[27] Echoing these sentiments, a victim of female same-gender IPV in the United States explains the powerful influence the lesbian utopia ideal had on her ability to recognize the abuse: "No—I thought, well, I just thought that it was fine because we were girls, like, and girls don't hurt each other like that. So I just thought that it was the way it was supposed to be."[28]

Although considerably less research has been conducted on the process of recognizing abuse among sexual minority male and trans* IPV victims, some evidence suggests that these victims may at times make a similar assumption—that LGBTQ people are inherently nonviolent. For instance, in a study of fifty-two gay-identified male victims of IPV, 44% reported that a major reason they remained with the abuser was that they "didn't understand there was such a thing as 'gay domestic violence.'"[29] Some scholars speculate that this stereotype of sexual minorities being inherently nonabusive is tied in part to the belief that two people of the same gender are presumably of similar size and strength and therefore cannot dominate one another.[30] The problem with this theory, of course, is that not all IPV is physical: psychological and sexual IPV are largely unrelated to physical size or strength, and even victims of same-gender physical IPV may find challenging an abuser difficult when that abuser is someone whom the victim loves and who justifies their violence as somehow being the victim's fault.

A similar assumption of nonviolence among some trans* partners may be influenced by a variety of factors. On the one hand, trans* individuals who are male- or female-identified may be impacted by the same assumptions of nonviolence in lesbian, gay, and bisexual cisgender communities. On the other hand, the particularly high levels of marginalization and discrimination experienced by many trans* individuals may make it more difficult for their partners to view them as anything but victims of a transphobic society, even when those same individuals perpetrate IPV.[31] Sherisse, a cisgender sexual minority woman who was abused by a male-identified trans* partner, explains:

> I'd feel like being on the receiving end of emotional abuse that I believed I never would have taken from a non-trans man and I never would have taken from a woman. . . . I spent a lot of time . . . educating myself on *his* oppression and [thinking of him as] so powerless in a societal sense that there would be no way he could have enough power to be abusive, so I didn't recognize it in a way that I would have otherwise . . . but I know that he used his various identities—trans included—to reinforce that myth for me.[32]

The difficulties that Sherisse faced in recognizing abuse are not unique to LGBTQ IPV. It is well documented that heterosexual IPV victims often excuse the abuser's behavior or fail to recognize it for what it is.[33] At the same time, because the dominant public discourse on IPV tends to omit LGBTQ people and their relationships, recognizing that LGBTQ IPV happens, and may even be happening in your relationship, can become that much more challenging.

Myth no. 2: LGBTQ IPV Is Less Severe

Even if one accepts the unfortunate fact that LGBTQ IPV is common, it would be difficult to take it too seriously if one assumes that consequences for victims are minor.[34] Research has not directly assessed whether the general public perceives different-gender IPV to result in more severe consequences for victims than same-gender IPV. However, evidence does indirectly point to this being a pervasive myth. For instance, with few exceptions,[35] studies in the United States have found that college students rate a fictional story of IPV victimization as more likely warranting leaving the victim alone, not calling the police, and not pressing charges if the story includes same-gender rather than different-gender partners.[36] The assumption that police involvement is unnecessary for LGBTQ IPV is likely in part derived from a belief that LGBTQ IPV is not severe enough to rise to the level of an emergency. Another study on Californian adults found that different-gender physical IPV, such as beating up or slapping one's partner, is far more likely to be perceived as illegal than same-gender physical IPV.[37] If physical IPV is more likely to be viewed as legal in some same-gender relationships, this may be due to an assumption that victims can effectively defend themselves if they and their abusers are of similar size and strength. Research also indicates that people are more likely to presume that same-gender IPV involves two abusers purposely trying to hurt one another rather than unidirectional IPV with one abuser and one victim.[38] This may contribute to a stereotype of same-gender IPV being a low-level spat between equals rather than a severe crime. Finally, scholars have speculated that the public perceives same-gender relationships to be less committed and less intimate than different-gender marital relationships, particularly in societies where same-gender partners cannot legally marry. As a result, perhaps same-gender IPV will be assumed to be less tangled up with love, children, and legal barriers that would prevent a victim from successfully escaping[39]—an argument that, for instance, has been used by some politicians to argue against enhanced legal protections for same-gender IPV victims.[40] Each of these assumptions feeds into a dangerous myth that the consequences of IPV are less severe for LGBTQ people than for heterosexuals.

This stereotype of LGBTQ IPV being less severe has indeed been proven by research to be a myth rather than reality. For example, NISVS, the previously mentioned nationally representative study of over sixteen thousand Americans, found female sexual minority IPV victims to be either just as likely as or more likely than heterosexual female IPV victims to experience fear, concern for safety, and post-traumatic stress disorder symptoms as a result of IPV. Bisexual female victims were also more likely than heterosexual female victims to experience injury, require medical care, need legal services, and miss work or school as a result of IPV. Likewise, gay male victims were just as likely as heterosexual male victims to experience at least one of these negative outcomes. As previously discussed, sexual minority men and women were also either just as likely as or more likely than heterosexuals to experience all forms of IPV. Moreover, certain particularly trauma-inducing tactics were more likely to be perpetrated against sexual minorities: bisexual women were more than twice as likely as heterosexual women to experience intimate partner rape, sexual coercion by a partner, and severe forms of physical IPV, including being hit with something hard, slammed against something, or choked and having a knife or gun used on them. Severe physical IPV was also slightly more likely to be experienced by lesbian than heterosexual women and by gay than heterosexual men.[41] The general conclusion that sexual minorities are either just as likely as or more likely than heterosexuals to experience negative IPV consequences has been supported by several other large representative research studies.[42] While data on outcomes of IPV victimization among trans* individuals is sorely lacking, there are reasons to suspect that the picture is similarly bleak. According to a 2013 study of predominantly LGBTQ crime victims seeking help from one of several Canadian and U.S. LGBTQ IPV victim agencies, as compared with cisgender IPV victims, trans* IPV victims were nearly twice as likely to experience physical IPV, two and a half times more likely to experience an IPV incident in a public space, and nearly four times as likely to experience discrimination such as transphobic verbal abuse by an intimate partner.[43]

The implication here is that trans* IPV victims may be at particular risk of physical injury and the psychological consequences related to experiencing controlling tactics.

Indeed, several studies suggest that a substantial portion of trans* and sexual minority IPV victims experience fear (10–13% of trans* victims[44] and 13–48% of sexual minority victims[45]), mental health consequences (76% of trans* victims[46] and 3–46% of sexual minority victims[47]), and physical injury (16–42% of trans* victims[48] and 3–47% of sexual minority victims[49]). (See chapter 3 for a detailed review of LGBTQ IPV outcomes.) It would appear, then, that contrary to expectations, victim outcomes are just as severe for LGBTQ IPV as they are for HC IPV, if not more so.

Myth no. 3: LGBTQ IPV Abusers Are Masculine

In addition to myths that minimize the prevalence and severity of abuse in LGBTQ relationships, some myths contribute to particular types of LGBTQ IPV relationships being more invisible than others. One such myth that is especially troubling is the assumption that LGBTQ IPV abusers are more masculine than their victims.[50] This myth undoubtedly arose from research on and public perceptions of different-gender IPV. While scholars continue to debate whether men are more abusive than or just as abusive as women in different-gender relationships, considerable evidence suggests that women's physical violence is motivated by self-defense more often than men's violence, and men are more likely to injure, rape, stalk, and kill their female partners.[51] One prominent theory of "male-to-female IPV" perpetration (i.e., IPV perpetrated by a man against a woman) is that male abusers are often performing traditional masculinity norms of aggression and dominance.[52]

This emphasis in research and public discourse on male-identified and masculine perpetrators of male-to-female IPV may have inadvertently fed into a myth that same-gender IPV perpetrators are similarly more male-looking and masculine-acting than their victims. For example, a study found that undergraduate students rate a fictional female-female IPV story as more realistic and probable if the accompanying photos of the fake partners depicted one masculine-looking (i.e., "butch") and one feminine-looking (i.e., "femme") partner in the relationship, rather than two masculine-looking partners or two feminine-looking partners.[53] The danger of this myth is that LGBTQ IPV victims who seek help may be taken less seriously if they are perceived to be too masculine or if their abusers are perceived to be not masculine enough. Some scholars speculate that victims may be perceived as more masculine if they are racial-ethnic minorities, who are often stereotyped as hypermasculine regardless of gender identity.[54] One particularly disturbing consequence of this myth is that some in law enforcement rely on these gender stereotypes to determine who is the "true" victim and who should be arrested.[55] When gender stereotypes of same-gender abusers and victims do not map onto a heterosexual masculine-feminine template, law enforcement may arrest both the abuser and the victim or, in some instances, just the victim.[56] This in turn may negatively affect the victim's coping process as well as their access to legal protections and other services.[57] It is unfortunately not surprising that gender stereotypes can influence arrest patterns, since research indicates that officers rarely are provided with the educational training on same-gender IPV that is needed to undercut this myth.[58] Additionally, drawing on erroneous assumptions that masculinity can be manifested only by men, evidence suggests that some presume that male same-gender IPV is more prevalent and severe than female same-gender IPV.[59]

The belief that LGBTQ IPV abusers are especially masculine has been shown to be a myth. Research has not consistently shown that same-gender IPV abusers are more masculine or more feminine than their victims.[60] In fact, sexual minorities tend to perform relationship roles and gender stereotypes that are different from those of heterosexual people.[61] No research has been conducted on the relative physical size and strength of same-gender IPV abusers and victims,[62] but in any event physicality is often not a factor in psychological abuse or sexual coercion. Physical violence may also be particularly difficult to defend against when the victim loves the abuser and when the abuser has made the victim feel responsible for inciting the abuser. Notably, among studies that include both men and women in their samples, the vast majority find among sexual minorities that women are more likely than men to experience psychological, physical, and sexual IPV.[63]

Myth no. 4: LGBTQ IPV Is the Same as All Other IPV

Another myth that contributes to LGBTQ IPV being taken less seriously is the assumption that LGBTQ IPV and HC IPV are largely the same. While there are many similarities, as this book will demonstrate, LGBTQ IPV is a social problem that also has unique causes, dynamics, and outcomes. For example, homophobia and transphobia—factors largely irrelevant to HC IPV—are theorized to play integral roles in LGBTQ IPV, from motivating abusers and weakening the resolve of victims, to presenting unique IPV tactics such as threatening to out victims, to creating powerful barriers for both abusers and victims to seek needed help. Conversely, gender norms and societal gender inequality, which have been heavily implicated in facilitating HC IPV, may not have the same impact on LGBTQ IPV.[64] (See chapter 4 for an examination of causes of LGBTQ IPV perpetration and barriers to help-seeking.)

There is a particular danger inherent in this myth of a universal IPV experience. Specifically, if HC IPV and LGBTQ IPV are erroneously presumed to be by nature the same, it might also be presumed that a one-size-fits-all approach is best for addressing all IPV. In reality, this often means taking HC IPV-tailored policies and services and making them available to LGBTQ people. This strategy may be particularly appealing given that it involves using existing societal responses rather than expending resources and energy to develop new ones. Certainly there are many similarities with HC IPV, so HC IPV-specific policies and services will to some degree be helpful for people involved in LGBTQ IPV. Where they fall short, though, is in failing to address the many unique aspects of LGBTQ IPV.

The influence of this one-size-fits-all approach to addressing IPV can be seen in various arenas, one of which is service provision. For instance, in 1991 Claire Renzetti surveyed a selection of 566 U.S. service providers listed in the *National Directory of Domestic Violence Programs*. When asked whether their organizations welcome lesbians as clients, a nearly unanimous 96% responded that they did. When pressed for details on how they achieved this, the majority indicated that they welcomed lesbians primarily through a nondiscrimination policy. "Volunteers are trained to care for the people involved, not to question lifestyles," a typical service provider reported. "We won't turn them away," offered another provider. On the surface, a nondiscrimination policy may be vital in signaling to LGBTQ victims that they do not need to fear homophobia or transphobia at these organizations. Upon closer inspection, though, solely relying on these policies to adequately draw in and serve LGBTQ IPV victims may be masking a significant flaw in some organizations: IPV is often being treated as an experience that is identical across genders and sexual orientations. Indeed, only one in ten providers in Renzetti's study could point to specific efforts taken to tailor services or advertising to lesbian women. Instead, services largely designed for HC IPV victims were being made available to lesbian victims without any efforts to address the unique aspects of LGBTQ IPV.[65] Research hints that this trend has not entirely disappeared in the United States and throughout the world.[66] (See chapter 5 for an exploration of the many nongovernmental resources responding to LGBTQ IPV.)

Abuser interventions serve as another example in which a universal IPV experience is often assumed and a one-size-fits-all response has been applied. As part of sentencing, it is not uncommon in many nations for courts to order convicted abusers to partake in a multisession education program designed to lower the risk of their committing IPV in the future. Sometimes referred to as "batterer-intervention programs," or BIPs for short, their programs are often based on one of two main models. Cognitive behavioral therapy (CBT) focuses on unlearning violent tendencies and building healthy conflict-resolution skills. Conversely, the Duluth model places emphasis on unlearning patriarchal attitudes that encourage men to feel entitled to control over women.[67] Some evidence suggests that the Duluth model, either on its own or in conjunction with CBT, is the most widely employed approach for BIPs.[68] While elements of both CBT and Duluth BIPs are relevant to LGBTQ IPV, they largely ignore the unique aspects of LGBTQ IPV and the role of homophobia and transphobia.[69] In the case of the Duluth model in particular, with its emphasis on patriarchal ideology, the treatment was originally designed for HC IPV, and LGBTQ IPV abusers now may partake in the same exact program. Often in the United States, for instance, states require separate BIP groups for HC abusers and LGBTQ abusers, but the BIP program content itself will be largely identical. In other states, HC and LGBTQ abusers will be placed into the same BIP group. In both cases, the sexual orientation and gender identities of LGBTQ abusers are often effectively ignored.[70] No study to date has examined whether Duluth BIPs are as impactful for LGBTQ abusers as for HC abusers. Although BIPs more generally have been shown to be limited in their effectiveness,[71] it is conceivable that they will prove even more ineffective for LGBTQ abusers if ideology and experiences unique to LGBTQ IPV are never raised. (See chapter 6 for a review of government-based responses to LGBTQ IPV.)

LGBTQ people are of course not the first—nor likely the last—minority group in history to be pushed to the margins of the movement to address IPV. In 1991, Kimberle Crenshaw wrote passionately about the invisibility of racial minority female victims in the IPV intervention movement. To Crenshaw, simply reshaping the language and imagery of the movement to appear inclusive of racial minority women does nothing to acknowledge and address their unique concerns. As she puts it, "Tokenistic, objectifying, voyeuristic inclusion is at least as disempowering as complete exclusion."[72] Tokenistic inclusion—such as welcoming LGBTQ people to HC IPV-focused victim services—should not be entirely discounted, since it helps to address the aspects of LGBTQ IPV that are shared by HC IPV. This is a good beginning, but it is only a beginning. LGBTQ IPV and HC IPV are not identical. Continuing to treat them as such in policies, services, and research risks potentially serious consequences for those involved in LGBTQ IPV.

Myth no. 5: LGBTQ IPV Should Not Be Discussed

Arguably the most troubling myth of LGBTQ IPV is that it should not be discussed by the communities, service providers, and researchers working to prevent and address IPV. The consequences of this should be clear by now. Because LGBTQ IPV is prevalent, severe, and distinctive enough that it is often inadequate to simply use HC IPV responses, silence on the issue can only further embolden abusers and trap victims. In spite of this, three powerful rationales contribute to the myth that LGBTQ IPV should remain out of the spotlight of public discourse. More specifically, some believe that the acknowledgment of the existence of LGBTQ IPV may further stigmatize LGBTQ people, divert funding away from addressing HC IPV, and be misconstrued as evidence that gender is unrelated to IPV.

One understandable reason that some do not wish to discuss LGBTQ IPV is out of concern that doing so may further stigmatize an already stigmatized group. This concern is particularly salient for many victims, whose abusers may have already heightened their sense of stigma by making them feel ashamed for being LGBTQ and being victimized. In an interview study of forty-seven sexual minority women in the United States who had been victims of same-gender IPV, one participant reflected on how a concern about further stigmatizing sexual minority women deterred her from seeking help: "I was in this fishbowl, and if I was to tell somebody what was going on, then . . . they'd look at the whole lesbian thing and, 'See, it's not supposed to be that way, because look what happened to you.' And it really added a lot of pressure . . . because I really felt like I had to represent a good relationship. And prove that I made the right choice."[73]

For this individual and many like her, a healthy-appearing relationship can be one valuable way to normalize and destigmatize being LGBTQ. If that relationship begins to turn abusive, the need to combat potential homophobia and transphobia can generate substantial pressure to mask the abuse and present to the world a facade of a healthy relationship. This pressure can result both in victims not seeking help and in LGBTQ friends they might seek help from not providing it. In a personal account of her experience with female same-gender IPV victimization, Adrienne Blenman notes that other lesbian women to whom she disclosed her experience urged her to not seek further help and to not tell others about the victimization because they feared that doing so would increase society's homophobia.[74] Another author, Kimberly Balsam, recounts a personal experience in the 1990s when she worked for a feminist, lesbian-oriented bookstore that in part served as a resource and information hub for the community. When she put brochures about IPV among lesbian women on display in the store, her manager confronted her angrily. To Balsam, "[t]he message, loud and clear, was that making this issue visible would portray lesbians in a negative light."[75] This fear of enhancing LGBTQ stigma by acknowledging LGBTQ IPV is not baseless, of course. One unfortunate consequence of greater awareness of LGBTQ IPV has been that some have used this as a justification for discouraging same-gender marriage.[76] This is an argument put forth by several conservative policy and lobbying groups, one of which is the Family Research Council, based in the United States. Their website as of the writing of this book stated the following:

> There are . . . key reasons why the legal rights, benefits, and responsibilities of civil marriage should not be extended to same-sex couples. . . . [H]omosexual relationships are harmful. Not only do they not provide the same benefits to society as heterosexual marriages, but their consequences are far more negative than positive. . . . Do homosexuals have higher rates of domestic violence? Yes. . . . [M]en and women in heterosexual marriages experience *lower* rates of domestic violence than people in any other living arrangement.[77]

The extension of this argument—that the high prevalence of HC IPV would presumably be proof that marriages of all heterosexual-cisgender people should also be discouraged and banned—has of course never made because the original argument at its core is both illogical and arguably rooted in homophobia. Hurtful actions are taken by people of all ages, races, religions, cultures, genders, and sexual orientations, but research and common sense dictate that those actions do not define an entire demographic group. One solution to avoid these types of stigmatizing conclusions about LGBTQ IPV is to simply avoid discussing LGBTQ IPV. The major drawback of this approach, though, is that it largely leaves victims trapped and abusers not held accountable.

Another common rationale for keeping silent about the issue of LGBTQ IPV is based on a concern that the issue may draw funding away from addressing HC IPV. Historically, activism and government intervention to address IPV emerged from the broader movement to end men's violence against women.[78] Although the modern "battered women's movement" in much of the world began in the 1970s with the building of the first victim shelters,[79] national policies on violence against women were slower to follow, not being ratified in most nations until the 1980s and 1990s.[80] Although policies have become more inclusive of IPV perpetrated by women against men and of LGBTQ IPV over time, the movement is rooted in a distinctly heterosexual and cisgender focus. Even current IPV-related publications and subdivisions of the United Nations[81] and World Health Organization[82] largely address HC IPV. With such a short history and understandable concerns over maintaining momentum and funding, some working in the IPV prevention and intervention movement have questioned whether raising the issue of LGBTQ IPV risks derailing focus and financing for addressing HC IPV.[83] For instance, in a study of feminist-oriented mental health counselors in Canada, one counselor discussed fears that shifting discussion away from solely male-to-female IPV can have negative consequences for the battered women's movement: "Where I find the language frightening is that working in a shelter with male violence, there are a lot of people in the population who would like to say 'Hey this happens to everyone,' so they can just defuse it. So I don't want to talk about this and that's why. I don't want to lose the funding, lose the momentum."[84]

Other studies suggest that funding sources exert pressure on shelters and other IPV victim resources to exclude LGBTQ IPV victims.[85] While these concerns over funding and staying on message are valid, when taken to an extreme they generate an either-or debate: either LGBTQ IPV must be ignored, or HC IPV will be ignored. In reality, there is room in public discourse and funding for both, and, more to the point, no IPV victim is any more worthy of compassion and assistance than any other IPV victim.

An additional rationale for minimizing discourse on LGBTQ IPV is a concern that LGBTQ IPV may be misconstrued as evidence that gender is unrelated to all IPV. Much of the global battered women's movement has been shaped by feminist-rooted theories that argue that masculinity gender norms and societal gender inequality both encourage and enable men's violence against women.[86] These theories are given particular credence in light of research suggesting that HC IPV— particularly regarding sexual IPV, injurious physical IPV, partner stalking, and partner homicide—is predominantly perpetrated by men against women.[87] Since the 1970s, research has emerged suggesting that men and women are equally likely to use physical violence in different-gender relationships.[88] Although this "gender symmetry" finding has been hotly contested—most especially on the grounds of women being more likely to use violence in self-defense, more likely to be injured by male violence, and more likely to be victims of nearly every other form of IPV[89]—it has given rise to a group of scholars who argue that gender is irrelevant to IPV and that female-victim-oriented shelters, services, and policies need to become more gender-neutral to help the presumably large and overlooked population of male HC IPV victims.[90] One of the supporting arguments that some scholars use to bolster claims that gender norms and inequality do not cause IPV is the high prevalence of same-gender IPV. If two people of the same gender identity can experience IPV, presumably this implies that gender inequality is not a prerequisite for IPV to occur. Likewise, if female same-gender IPV is highly prevalent, it would imply that the influence of (heterosexual) masculinity norms is not a prerequisite for IPV, either.[91] For instance, in arguing that male victims of female abusers are often overlooked, Donald Dutton and colleagues put forth same-gender IPV as evidence that gender does not matter and that IPV can happen to anyone: "Further evidence of women's use of abuse in relationships, men's risk for victimization by intimate partners, and data to refute patriarchal explanations of partner abuse to the exclusion of other theories, has been gleaned from research on homosexual male and female relationships."[92]

John Hamel makes a similar argument: regarding feminist theories predicting male-to-female IPV, Hamel feels that "[p]atriarchal explanations are also contradicted by other research findings. . . . [W]omen are as victimized in same-sex relationships, where patriarchal structures should not exist."[93] The same case has been brought forth by some antifeminist "men's rights" organizations, such as in regards to many of the contributors to the non-peer-reviewed online publication *Everyman: A Men's Journal*. For instance, in a book review published in *Everyman*, Jason Bouchard writes, "He even has the rates of domestic violence in lesbian relationships (31%) and gay male couples (12%)—so much for the idea that patriarchy is the root of domestic violence!"[94] Even several researchers who focus on LGBTQ IPV have questioned whether feminist-based theories of IPV can be accurate if same-gender IPV is prevalent.[95] Thus, same-gender IPV has become a form of ammunition for some looking to discredit feminism, the battered women's movement, and the belief that male-to-female IPV is prevalent.[96] Therefore, for some scholars working to maintain funding and policies for addressing male-to-female IPV, there may be concern that the inclusion of LGBTQ relationships in the public discussion of IPV may result in funders and policymakers viewing HC IPV as gender-neutral. Even the very term *intimate partner violence*—one that is more inclusive of abuse among LGBTQ people than gendered terms like *woman abuse* and *wife battering*—has been criticized for masking the reality that the majority of HC IPV victims are women.[97] This rationale is certainly understandable, in that the issue of LGBTQ IPV can be and has been used for political purposes such as attacking the battered women's movement. At the same time, from the perspective of movement building, the terms *intimate partner violence* and *domestic violence* (and their equivalents translated into other languages) have global meanings that provide instant legitimacy for the experiences of historically overlooked LGBTQ IPV victims. These survivors and everyone else invested in the movement to address LGBTQ IPV should not be held back or partitioned off simply because this issue complicates methodological and theoretical debates.

Clearly there are many pressures to keep public awareness of LGBTQ IPV at a minimum. Regardless of concerns over further stigmatization of LGBTQ people, diverting funds away from addressing HC IPV, and providing ammunition to attack the battered women's movement and the gendered nature of HC IPV, there is one main reason *not* to keep silent on LGBTQ IPV: silence makes IPV worse. Silence hurts the victim who is not taken seriously because no one has heard of LGBTQ IPV. Silence hurts the abuser who may not even realize they are being abusive because there is little public awareness of LGBTQ IPV. Silence hurts policymakers who may be poorly informed about the extent and nature of the problem. Silence hurts service providers who may be inclined to apply ill-fitting HC IPV victim services to LGBTQ IPV victim clientele. Silence hurts.

HOW WE ARE FAILING LGBTQ VICTIMS

The year 2007 was a good one for the holy trinity of salt, grease, and potatoes. That year, McDonalds had over 31,000 restaurants worldwide. If you happened to be traveling through Asia, you did not have to look far for your fries fix. For instance, India tallied 128 McDonalds, while China had an impressive 876. Not to be outdone, Japan offered 3,746 different McDonalds venues in which to be convinced that wasabi dipping sauce is a viable alternative to ketchup.[98] Of course, fries may not have been a top priority for the many gay men who became IPV victims that year. Although LGBTQ IPV research is absent throughout much of Asia, a recent study estimated that 33% of gay men in China have experienced some form of IPV in their lifetimes.[99] With this in mind, in 2007 Monit Cheung and colleagues initiated a comprehensive global review of government and community agencies serving male IPV victims of any sexual orientation. What they found in three Asian nations—India, China, and Japan—is astounding: a grand total of *zero* places to turn to for help.[100] Have a hankering for a quick snack, some fries perhaps? Not a problem. You need help because your partner is beating you? Sorry, please try another country.

We are failing LGBTQ IPV victims. In many parts of the world today, victim services are nonexistent for LGBTQ people. Given the global emphasis on addressing male-to-female IPV, access to services are often most limited for sexual minority men and trans* individuals. For example, in a recent study of a nationally representative sample of U.S. IPV agencies, it was found that nearly all types of victim services were provided to sexual minority women, whereas only one- to two-thirds of agencies provided access to certain services for sexual minority men.[101] Access is often similarly limited for trans* individuals, particularly for those who do not identify and present as female. For example, Timothy Colm, a trans* man and IPV survivor, recalls being closeted about his gender identity in a female IPV survivor support group out of fear that he would otherwise be evicted from the group:

> In the support group, I found comfort and solidarity, but I also had to sacrifice pieces of who I was to access the space. Statements were regularly exchanged about how we were all women and that made the space so safe, while I bit my lip and stared at my hands. It took me a full year after coming out as trans to tell the group. I didn't think I could be there anymore if they knew I was a guy.[102]

Even for cisgender sexual minority women, although they often have greater access to services, the quality of services suffer when they are not tailored to LGBTQ IPV.[103] For instance, some evidence suggests that battered women's shelters may not be cognizant of the possibility that female abusers may present themselves to a shelter as a victim in order to stalk a partner living at the shelter.[104] This would also suggest that many people with opportunities to assist LGBTQ IPV victims craft their responses by relying upon their understanding of HC IPV, inaccurate LGBTQ IPV myths, and at times homophobic and transphobic attitudes. While it is important to remember that there are numerous medical, mental health, and emergency service providers as well as law-enforcement officers who create a safe and positive experience for LGBTQ IPV victims,[105] research suggests that discriminatory beliefs and dismissive views regarding LGBTQ IPV are still rampant.[106]

In many ways, the struggle to legitimize LGBTQ IPV as a genuine public-health concern is rooted in the struggle to legitimize LGBTQ human rights. After all, if LGBTQ people are not afforded equal rights in many parts of the world, it should come as no surprise that policies, services, funding, and research do not adequately reflect the concerns of LGBTQ people. To put it mildly, the world is not a very hospitable place for LGBTQ people. According to a 2014 report published by the International Lesbian, Gay, Bisexual, Trans, and Intersex Association, of the nearly two hundred nations in the world, same-gender sexual acts are illegal in seventy-eight of them, five of which impose the death penalty in such cases.[107] Merely sixteen years ago, in 2000, same-gender marriage was illegal in every corner of the world. As of the writing of this book, only twenty-two nations plus sections of Mexico have fully legalized same-gender marriage.[108] While these laws hint at the depth of global homophobia, they are also undeniable barriers for LGBTQ IPV victims: when IPV laws protect only married couples in a nation that does not permit same-gender marriage, or when seeking help requires admitting to the "crime" of being LGBTQ, remaining silent may be the only option. Additionally, just fifteen nations have legalized joint adoption by same-gender couples.[109] For victims living in one of these nations or any of the several nations that also prohibit second-parent adoption, often only the biological parent can acquire legal parental rights. If that parent is also an abuser of a same-gender partner, victims risk losing access to their children if they choose to escape the abuser.

On a more fundamental level, though, societal discrimination is such an important force in these abusive relationships because it can indirectly lead family, friends, service providers, law enforcement, and policymakers to take LGBTQ IPV less seriously or to ignore it entirely. Societal discrimination can shape a nation's IPV laws and service-provider attitudes. Societal discrimination can fuel an abuser's anger. Societal discrimination can lead victims to not recognize abuse. Societal discrimination helps make LGBTQ IPV invisible. As one indicator of societal homophobia, according to a 2014 *Gallup World Poll* report, only 28% of adults in the 123 nations surveyed answered that their city or area is "a good place to live for gay or lesbian people." Homophobia is universally embraced in certain parts of the world, including large swaths of Africa, where over 95% of adults in Gabon, Malawi, Mali, Niger, Senegal, and Uganda answered that their city or area is *not* a good place for gay or lesbian people to live.[110] According to a 2013 nationally representative study of 1,197 LGBTQ adults in the United States, 39% reported at some point in life being rejected by family or a close friend because of their sexual orientation or gender identity.[111] A recent survey of 354 U.S. agencies providing homeless-youth services suggests that rejection at home and in schools can unfortunately also contribute to homelessness. Findings revealed that approximately 40% of homeless youth and those at risk of becoming homeless are LGBTQ-identified, with family rejection and family abuse serving as key factors in their leaving home.[112] The workplace may be another force contributing to LGBTQ poverty and homelessness. Only sixty-one nations prohibit discrimination in employment based on sexual orientation,[113] and only forty-seven prohibit discrimination against trans* people.[114] Additionally, many nations including the United States can make it difficult for trans* people to change the gender identity listed on their driver's licenses, birth certificates, and passports, with some nations requiring sex-reassignment surgery, sterilization, or psychiatric evaluation. This is particularly problematic given that identity documents are often relied upon to validate credit-card purchases, fill medication prescriptions, sign contracts, travel through airports, cross international borders and police checkpoints, and so on.[115]

Compounding the problems posed by these numerous legal and attitudinal barriers are the untold acts of discrimination and violence beyond IPV that LGBTQ people experience. In their meta-analysis of 164 studies from 1992 to 2009 reporting on these experiences among 503,826 individuals spanning multiple continents, Sarah Katz-Wise and Janet Hyde concluded that sexual minorities are significantly more likely than heterosexuals to experience discrimination and violence victimization both generally and within families, schools, and workplaces. In sum, 41% of lesbian, gay, and bisexual individuals experienced discrimination in the workplace, health care, or elsewhere; 55% encountered verbal harassment; 37%, threats; 24%, property violence; 40%, stalking; 28%, physical assault; and 27%, sexual assault.[116] One of the few studies of trans* discrimination and victimization found similarly disturbing results. According to the *National Transgender Discrimination Survey*, of 6,450 trans* people surveyed from across the United States, 63% had experienced discrimination, 71% had hidden their gender identity and 57% delayed transition specifically to avoid discrimination, 78% experienced harassment in school, 35% experienced physical assault and 12% sexual assault in school, 57% encountered significant family rejection, and 41% attempted suicide. To put that final powerful statistic into context, just 1.6% of the general U.S. population has attempted suicide.[117] Unfortunately, only twenty-seven nations recognize hate crimes based on sexual orientation.[118] Beyond the obvious harm incurred by a lifetime of victimization, it is possible that these experiences normalize abuse for LGBTQ IPV victims and magnify its negative effects.

These barriers to helping LGBTQ IPV victims appear so overwhelming that it may be tempting to say that nothing can be done. When we look at the course of history, though, so much has already improved. In many nations, LGBTQ people are being written into existing IPV laws and protections. Shelters are slowly opening their doors to male and trans* victims. Legalized homophobia is not nearly as widespread as it once was. This is not to say, though, that our work is over. A key question then is, If we are to make this a safer world for LGBTQ people who are in unhealthy and abusive relationships, what steps can we take to strengthen LGBTQ IPV policy, practice, and research?

CHAPTER ORGANIZATION

Each remaining chapter of this book explores a different section of the LGBTQ IPV research literature. Chapter 2, "How Do We Know What We Know?," critically examines the tools used to collect information on LGBTQ IPV: current challenges in designing studies on LGBTQ IPV and IPV more generally. Chapter 3, "What Is LGBTQ Intimate Partner Violence (IPV)?," unpackages the lived experience of LGBTQ IPV: the common forms of abuse, prevalence estimates for each, the typical number of "abusers" in relationships, what is known about sequencing of abuse, and outcomes for victims. Chapter 4, "Why Does LGBTQ IPV Happen?," reviews competing explanations of why LGBTQ IPV happens: causal theories common to HC and LGBTQ IPV, causal theories unique to LGBTQ IPV, the controversial role of gender performance, and the barriers that keep victims in IPV relationships and empower abusers. Chapter 5, "How Can We Improve Nongovernmental Responses?," examines the strengths and weaknesses in nongovernmental responses to LGBTQ IPV: responses by friends and family, mental and medical health providers, IPV victim organizations, and other related services. Chapter 6, "How Can We Improve Government Responses?," discusses responses by governments to LGBTQ IPV: particular attention is paid to the role of legal protections, law enforcement, courts, and batterer-intervention programs. Each of these chapters concludes with concrete recommendations for future policy, practice, and research. Wherever the literature allows, an intersectional lens is adopted throughout the book, emphasizing ways in which LGBTQ IPV experiences may differ by sexual orientation, trans*-cisgender identity, gender identity, social class, age, race, ethnicity, immigration status, and nationality. The final chapter, "Conclusions: Where Do We Go from Here?," draws on the preceding chapters to provide a review of overarching lessons of this book.

A NOTE ON TERMINOLOGY

In 2005, C. J. Pascoe published an ethnographic study on the use of the words *fag* and *gay* in the everyday discussions of male students in a California high school. Findings confirmed what many already suspected. These words unfortunately are being regularly used as a substitute for *stupid,* as in "That's a gay laptop! It's five inches thick!"[119] Fearing the implication that the researcher, Pascoe, would think they were homophobic, several of the boys attempted to clarify that they never think about sexual orientation when they use the words *fag* and *gay* as negative slurs. Said one student, "It has nothing to do with sexual preference at all. You could just be calling somebody an idiot you know?"[120] Even if these boys are given the benefit of the doubt—that they do not use these words *because* they are homophobic—is it conceivable that the reverse is true: Do people become more homophobic *because* they are using these words in this manner? A study published in 2012 suggests that this is actually a very real possibility. Researchers Gandalf Nicolas and Allison Louise Skinner asked sixty college students to read one of two versions of a fictitious conversation between friends. In one version of the story, the words *stupid* and *lame* are used periodically, and in the other, these words are replaced by the word *gay.* They found, amazingly, that exposure to negative uses of the word *gay* led students to hold more antigay attitudes.[121] This notion that the words we use shape the way we think is not entirely new, of course, dating back to 1930s research on "linguistic relativity" by linguists Edward Sapir and Benjamin Whorf.[122] Likewise, in social science surveys, researchers have long been aware that the language they use in questions has the power to influence respondents, particularly when the wording implies that certain answers are more or less societally accepted.[123] All of this is to say that our words matter: they limit how we and others around us view the world.

For this book, several choices were made regarding terminology. These terms are often imperfect in capturing the entirety of the human experience, but they were viewed as preferable to known alternatives. "**Sexual orientation**" is defined inclusively in this book as any combination of romantic or sexual *attraction* to, *behavior* with, *relationships* with, and *self-identity* regarding people of the same or different gender identity. "**Gender**" is similarly defined in a broad manner as a combination of *gender performance* (i.e., thinking and acting in a manner that either falls within or goes against "gender norms," the unwritten societal rules of behavior and thought associated with your gender identity group) and *gender identity* (i.e., self-identity as male, female, or "genderqueer," the latter of which is an umbrella term for gender identities other than male or female). "**Sex**" is defined as the *societal label* (i.e., male, female, or intersex) assigned to a person based on biological markers like chromosomes and reproductive organs. Importantly, the subcomponents of sexual orientation do not always neatly align in a societally expected and privileged manner, nor do the subcomponents of gender, nor do sexual orientation with gender and sex. Moreover, sexual orientation, gender, and (with the assistance of medical interventions) sex can change over time for individuals.

Since the term *homosexual* is often associated with outmoded and stigmatizing mental health disorder diagnoses, and since it has often been used as a negative epithet unto itself, the terms "**lesbian**," "**gay**," and "**bisexual**" are used instead. Likewise, although the term *straight* is still regularly used in everyday discourse, the linguistic opposite of *straight* is *crooked*, which simultaneously normalizes heterosexuality and renders lesbian, gay, and bisexual (LGB) people as deviant. In place of *straight,* therefore, the term "**heterosexual**" is used. While "**sexual minority**"—an LGB or queer person—is a somewhat problematic term as it focuses on the negative aspects of the lived experiences of LGB people, it is used at times in this book because of the very fact that it highlights that LGB people are often targets of homophobia, which is key to understanding their experiences with abuse.

"**Cisgender**" people are defined as those whose current gender identity matches their biological sex at birth in a way expected and privileged by society (e.g., those who were labeled at birth as being of the male sex and currently self-identify their gender as male, or those who were labeled at birth as being of the female sex and currently self-identify as female). "**Trans***" people are defined as those whose current gender identity does *not* match their biological sex at birth in a way expected and privileged by society (e.g., those who were labeled at birth as being of the male sex and currently self-identify their gender as female or genderqueer, and those who were labeled at birth as being of the female sex and currently self-identify their gender as male or genderqueer). Many activists, scholars, and trans* individuals add an asterisk after the prefix *trans* to connote the numerous gendered suffixes individuals may most identify with, such that the asterisk might be replaced by *man, woman, genderqueer, agender, sexual,* and so forth. Although *transgender* is often used synonymously with *trans**, to many, *transgender* has come to more narrowly refer to those whose current gender identity is male or female (not genderqueer, unlike with some trans* people) and does not match their biological sex at birth in a way expected and privileged by society (i.e., those labeled as male at birth and currently identify as female, and vice versa). In this sense, "transgender" people may be viewed as a subgroup of the umbrella group of "trans*" people. Bear in mind that both "cisgender" and "trans*" are labels researchers might apply to people based on the aforementioned definitions, some of whom may not personally self-identify as "cisgender" or "trans*." Note also that this definition of *trans** compares sex at *birth* with current gender identity—current sex is not factored into this definition, meaning that sex-reassignment surgery and other forms of medical interventions are not required, as long as one's gender identity does not match in a societally expected way with sex at birth. Sexual orientation is also not a part of this definition, meaning that both cisgender and trans* individuals may land anywhere on the full spectrum of sexual orientations.

Research on IPV often includes both LGB people and trans* individuals, or LGBT people. The term "**queer**" has historically been used as a negative slur against LGB people, and to this day in many nations it is unfortunately still being used in this manner. At the same time, the term has been reclaimed by many young sexual minorities as a positive self-identity. Moreover, it is often used as a positive umbrella term that includes not only people who self-identify as LGBT but also people who are noncisgender or nonheterosexual but do not like any of the existing labels within the LGBT acronym. It is with this definition in mind that the term *queer* is employed in this book. Collectively, LGBT and queer individuals are often labeled as "**LGBTQ**" people.

At face value, it may appear problematic for IPV researchers to study sexual minorities and trans* individuals simultaneously. After all, although there is much overlap, many of the causes, dynamics, and outcomes of IPV differ depending on whether sexual orientation or gender is the focus. At the same time, it is important to keep in mind that sexual orientation necessarily implies that there is a gender identity for people and their partners. While it is often assumed that this gender identity "matches" their sex at birth, sexual minority and trans* identities are not mutually exclusive: sexual minorities can be either cisgender or trans*, just as cisgender and trans* people can be either a sexual minority or heterosexual. These are not distinct groups but often intersecting groups.

As previously noted, "**intimate partner violence**," or "**IPV**," refers to psychological, physical, or sexual abuse or homicide between romantic and sexual partners. At times researchers have focused on abusive relationships with two people of the same gender identity. Surveys often ask "What is your gender?" or "What is your sex?" Using the terms interchangeably without definitions provided likely leads many respondents to assume the researcher is asking about how they currently identify—that is, their gender identity. Abuse in these relationships has typically been called "same-sex IPV," yet, because these labels are typically based on gender identity, a slightly more apt label might be "**same-gender IPV.**" The comparison group in research consists of people involved in what is often termed *opposite-sex IPV* or *opposite-gender IPV*—yet the word *opposite* inaccurately implies either that there are only two gender identities (when there are in fact more) or, at the very least, that other gender identities are less important. Therefore, when discussing IPV relationships involving a male-identified and female-identified partner, this book applies the label "**different-gender IPV.**" Because the gender identity of partners is not the same as their self-identified sexual orientation, popular but misleading labels like *gay IPV, lesbian IPV,* and *heterosexual IPV* will not be used in this book unless it is to refer to their usage in past research. Last, although same-gender IPV is a major emphasis in this book, this book will focus more broadly on "**LGBTQ IPV**"—IPV relationships involving at least one LGBTQ partner—and its similarities with and differences from "**HC IPV**"—IPV relationships involving two heterosexual-cisgender partners. This definition of LGBTQ IPV is more inclusive than same-gender IPV for two reasons: first, the issue of LGBTQ IPV includes IPV involving at least one trans* partner (i.e., "**trans* IPV**"), and, second, it includes IPV involving at least one sexual minority partner (i.e., "**sexual minority IPV**"), even when occurring in different-gender relationships.

GOALS OF THIS BOOK

The sheer quantity of published research on HC IPV dwarfs publications on LGBTQ IPV, making it at times feel that LGBTQ IPV research must be nearly nonexistent. In reality, while still evolving, research on LGBTQ IPV dates back to the late 1970s[124] and spans hundreds of journal articles, books, and research reports. Like any substantial body of information, the size of the literature presents a barrier for those who cannot afford the time to pore over thousands of pages of dense text. If this information could be synthesized in one place, golden nuggets that might have otherwise remained buried could be unearthed, dusted off, and used to help build new ways of addressing LGBTQ IPV in the world.

Offering a metaphorical flashlight, foundational books emerged in the 1980s and 1990s that reviewed the earliest research on same-gender and sexual minority IPV.[125] This was followed by several excellent books in the 2000s that primarily provided research updates on key subtopics regarding female same-gender and female sexual minority IPV[126] and rape,[127] as well as key subtopics regarding LGBTQ IPV.[128] (This is in addition to several books and bound reports[129] that predominantly reported on a single study and were not designed to review the literature.) Notably, only one book[130] in the 2000s reviewed portions of the male same-gender IPV literature, although not all of it, and that was also the only book to review portions of the trans* IPV literature. A slew of journal articles and reports have taken a similar path by offering bite-size overviews of key subtopics regarding same-gender IPV[131] and LGBTQ IPV.[132] If there is one unavoidable limitation to highlighting key subtopics, though, it is that the nooks and crannies of the literature remain in the shadows, unable to impact society.

Of course, it may not actually be possible for a book to cover the *complete* LGBTQ IPV research literature; there will always be a report or article missed, new studies emerging every day, and research in other languages that cannot be easily translated. (This latter point is of particular importance because the scope of this book is limited to English-language publications on LGBTQ IPV. As a consequence, the majority of research discussed here emerged from English-language-centric nations such as Australia, Canada, the United Kingdom, and the United States, with a significant North American focus in this published literature. For a description of the methodology used to locate the journal articles, book chapters, books, and research reports included in this book, see the appendix.) All the same, this book aims to be one of the first to bring *nearly* every piece of English-language published research on LGBTQ IPV into one place. In doing so, this book offers up an easy-to-use road map in our unending journey to more informed policy, practice, and research. Ultimately, by looking to our past, this book begins answering a vital question: What next?

2

HOW DO WE KNOW WHAT WE KNOW?

Professors Joseph Catania and Ron Stall had a problem. For IPV among sexual minority men to be taken more seriously in the United States, it was important to determine its prevalence. However, to do so accurately is harder than it may seem. One major barrier has been the small size of the **population** (i.e., all people with one or more shared characteristics, such as all gay- and bisexual-identified men in the United States). According to the nationally representative *2008 General Social Survey*, only 2.2% of American adult men identify as gay (1.5%) or bisexual (0.7%). This number jumps to 9.7% when we include those who do not identify as either but have experienced same-gender sexual behavior (7.5%).[1] Still, this would mean that for every one hundred men a researcher approaches, on average only ten would meet this loose definition of a sexual minority. Reality is actually even bleaker for the researcher, though. Two to eight of those sexual minority men will likely decline participation for a variety of reasons,[2] and one or more may pretend to be heterosexual due to fear of being outed or stigmatized.[3] Of those who do consent to participate, a portion may never have experienced a romantic or sexual relationship, precluding even the possibility of IPV for those individuals. Catania and Stall undoubtedly asked themselves the same question researchers had been asking for decades: How do you find a needle in a haystack?

One solution is to recruit subjects from venues with a high concentration of LGBTQ people, like gay pride parades or gay bars.[4] This approach has the benefit of saving time and, as a result, decreasing the number of months that expensive research-staff salaries must be paid. However, there is a major drawback to taking this quick route to finding subjects: less-accurate study results. By recruiting gay and bisexual men only from specific venues, anyone who does not visit those venues at the time of recruitment or at all will never have a chance of being selected for a study. For example, people who attend a gay bar may be more likely to be out of the closet, have expendable income, and be younger. Similar limitations apply to other LGBTQ-centric venues. As a result, key portions of the population may never have a chance of being selected for the **sample** (i.e., people to be studied who are drawn from a population). Any results will reflect the lives only of people in the sample, not the entire population. When a researcher's goal is to accurately learn about a population, this is a significant problem.

An alternate solution to locating a sample from a difficult-to-find population is the long, expensive route. First, a **sampling frame** (i.e., a list of names and contact information for most or all of a population) that includes the target population must be identified. Since no national registry of sexual minority men exists, this means finding a broader listing of Americans that includes all sexual orientations, such as a telephone book. From there, **sampling** (i.e., the process of selecting a sample) can involve randomly selecting people from the sampling frame. Random sampling, also known as **probability sampling,** gives everyone in a geographic region a chance of being selected (unlike **nonprobability sampling,** or nonrandom sampling, such as recruiting the first people a researcher meets at, say, a gay pride parade). On the downside, nearly all people the researcher contacts will be heterosexual. Therefore, initial conversations with potential study subjects will involve **screening** (i.e., preliminary questions to determine eligibility for a study sample) by asking about the individual's sexual orientation. Only those who are screened as eligible will then be invited to participate in the study. However, because sampling begins with a comprehensive sampling frame such as a telephone book, the sample will include all sorts of people—some older and some younger, some out and some not, some in high-income and some in low-income neighborhoods, and so forth—and therefore the sample will be representative of the sampling frame. This means that, whatever a study reveals about a sample, researchers can say with a high degree of certainty that these findings are also likely true for the population.

Exactly how hard is it to find a needle in a haystack? Catania, Stall, and their team of researchers would find out in their *Urban Men's Health Study.* From 1996 to 1998, the team randomly called phone numbers in Chicago, Los Angeles, New York City, and San Francisco. As a compromise to speed up the time it might take to find their sample, they predominantly limited their sampling frame to phone numbers from neighborhoods known to have a high concentration of sexual minority men. Additionally, the researchers made the assumption that certain regions outside of known gay neighborhoods may have amenities that draw numerous sexual minorities to live nearby. Since similar phone numbers often share the same geographic regions, when calling certain phone numbers proved successful in finding sexual minority men, the researchers decided to call a greater number of phone numbers beginning with the same sequence of digits. Likewise, when many phone numbers beginning with the same sequence of digits proved unhelpful, numerically adjacent phone numbers were less likely to be called. By keeping track of which types of phone numbers were more or less likely to be called, the researchers were able to apply **sampling weights** in analysis (i.e., mathematical calculations that can adjust study results to show what the results would have likely shown had certain portions of a sampling frame not been oversampled or undersampled), thereby preserving the probability-sampling technique and the greater accuracy in their findings.[5]

Catania and Stall's research group was ultimately able to recruit 2,881 sexual minority men for their sample. Because the size of the sample can assist in increasing the accuracy of findings, and because probability sampling does as well, the team, in collaboration with Gregory Greenwood, was able to learn with some degree of certainty that an astounding 39% of American sexual minority men had experienced at least one form of same-gender IPV in the previous five years.[6] The research team had been hard at work for three years, and they finally had the statistic that could validate the concerns of sexual minority IPV victims.

To put the scale of this achievement into context, though, consider how many different phone numbers they needed to dial in order to arrive at their final sample: 195,152.[7]

Like any study, this one was not without limitations. Because sampling had focused on neighborhoods and regions with a high concentration of sexual minorities, sexual minority men who lived outside of those areas were far less likely to be selected. Likewise, sampling was limited to four metropolitan cities, and sexual minority men who lived in smaller cities or more suburban or rural areas were omitted. These regional differences may matter if, for instance, sexual minority men are more likely to be out of the closet if they live in a more accepting neighborhood or city. Additionally, like any neighborhood, people in gay neighborhoods may be more likely to share a similar economic class and racial category, so diversity may suffer in the final sample. Moreover, the population studied was somewhat limiting: in addition to including men who self-identified as gay or bisexual, the researchers also included men who had had sexual intercourse with other men since age 14 regardless of their self-identified sexual orientation. This emphasis on men who have had sex with men, or **MSMs,** is understandable given the study's primary focus on sexually transmitted infections and sexual risk-taking behaviors. At the same time, this is an incomplete definition of sexual minority men, as it excludes men who neither identify as a sexual minority nor have had sexual intercourse with other men but *have* engaged in other sexual activities with men such as oral sex, have had romantic relationships with men, or are predominantly attracted to men. Even those who were recruited for the study because they had had sex with other men may not meet even a loose definition of a sexual

minority because of how MSMs were defined. To qualify as an MSM for the purposes of the study, a respondent had to have had sexual intercourse with another
man since age 14. It is conceivable, therefore, that at least a portion of the sample
may have not self-identified as a sexual minority but did have sexual intercourse as
a minor with another male adult. As a result, those particular subjects would have
been selected for the sample effectively because they had been the victims of child
sexual abuse. Last, sexual orientation is not static: our identities, sexual behaviors,
and romantic and sexual preferences and relationships can shift over time. There
certainly is value in including in the sample MSMs who do not self-identify as gay
or bisexual, given that sexual orientation can be expressed in a variety of ways
beyond self-identity—yet many of these individuals may have had sex with another
man many years ago, no longer do so, and today may even identify as heterosexual.
Whether it is accurate and just to label such individuals as "sexual minorities" or
even MSMs is a difficult question that researchers often struggle with.

Beyond limitations pertaining to sampling and defining the population, this
study, like others, faced challenges in accurately measuring IPV. Questions were
adapted from the widely used Conflict Tactics Scale.[8] Specifically, subjects were
asked whether a same-gender partner had perpetrated "unwanted physical or emotional violence" in the previous five years, including verbal threats against the subject, demeaning the subject in front of others, ridiculing the subject's appearance,
forcing the subject to get high or drunk, stalking the subject, destroying or damag-
ing the subject's property, hitting the subject with fists or an open hand, hitting the
subject with an object, pushing or shoving the subject, kicking the subject, throw-
ing something at the subject, or forcing the subject to have sex. Although fairly
inclusive, this definition of IPV, like most, is not comprehensive. For instance, it
excludes IPV that occurred prior to five years earlier, it excludes IPV by a different-
gender partner where either the subject or the partner is a sexual minority, and it
excludes a variety of IPV tactics such as forced sexual activities other than intercourse, coerced sexual activities, burning, pulling hair, controlling the subject's
bank account, demeaning the subject in private for reasons other than the subject's
appearance, and so forth. Just as significant, the IPV questions focus solely on victimization. Because many people in abusive relationships fight back in self-defense,
without the inclusion of questions about IPV perpetration and motivations like
self-defense, it is quite possible that many of the "victims" in the sample are in fact
abusers whose victims hit the subject solely to defend themselves. Thus, some victims will be misidentified as nonvictims, and some abusers will be misidentified as
victims.

Piling up these limitations, it may appear that this study was fatally flawed from
the beginning. In reality, Catania and Stall's *Urban Men's Health Study* is one of
the finer examples of researchers working tirelessly to find accurate results. All
social science research has its limitations. Research involves so many difficult

choices—whom to learn about, how to find them, what to ask, and how to interpret results. Each choice comes with its own benefits and drawbacks. Simply put,
there is no such thing as the perfect research study.

Still, some studies are *more* perfectly designed than others. A number of excellent review articles have been published dissecting the research methodology of
certain portions of the literature,[9] but no review has assessed methodologies in the
complete literature. This chapter explores how we know what we know about
LGBTQ IPV . . . and how we can improve our research designs to learn even more.

THE LIMITS OF RESEARCH

An old man is driving down the highway when his phone starts buzzing. It's his husband. "Herman, be careful! I just heard there's a crazy person going the wrong way
on the highway." To which the old man responds, "What do you mean ONE crazy
person? There are hundreds of them!"[10]

Poor Herman. This joke has been retold so many times, in so many different
versions—usually with a wife rather than a husband, not surprisingly—that, all
these years later, Herman is alive and well in our imaginations as the perpetually
inept driver. Why not add to his imaginary embarrassment a bit more, though, for
old time's sake? Let us try a thought experiment, then, in which Herman's story is
real. Pretend for a moment that Herman's story catches the attention of the national
media, who soon descend on Herman's small town.

Three news reporters lead the charge to report the incident. The first reporter
believes in **positivism,** which is to say that she believes there is a single truth out
there about the highway incident, and that only carefully planned and unbiased
research will unlock that truth. Positivists often prefer large samples with standardized questions, such as rounding up as many eyewitnesses as possible and asking them the same questions: What was the orientation of Herman's car relative to
other cars on the road? What time did you see Herman's car? And so forth. The
most commonly given answers must be the truth. The second reporter believes
instead in **standpoint theory.** He feels that, while there may be a single truth about
the incident, everyone has a different perspective shaped by personal biases, and
therefore they each can offer only slivers of the truth. An officer on the scene may
view the incident from a legal perspective and therefore sees only a lawbreaker. A
local resident may note that the on-ramp signs are poorly lit at night, making it
particularly difficult for those without perfect vision to see they are heading the
wrong way. A reporter who asks only one of those eyewitnesses for an interview
will get only a small piece of the truth. Therefore, it is important to have a diverse
group of people in a sample and on the reporter's research staff. Just as important,
since the complete truth will likely never be knowable no matter how carefully

data is gathered, a standpoint theorist may suggest that interviews are more ideal than questionnaires. Interviews may introduce the potential for new biases—the reporter's positive or negative tone of voice and body posture may influence people to alter their answers—but, since bias is inevitable according to standpoint theory, at least interviews open the door to collecting far more detailed data. By comparison, a multiple-choice questionnaire question will never provide as much information as an interview question that permits someone to give a long, detailed answer. Finally, the third reporter believes strongly in **postmodernist theories** that question the very notion that there is one truth. Who is to say that one perspective of Herman's highway incident is any more correct than another. Since traffic laws are socially constructed, agreed upon by many but not necessarily all, it may be more fruitful for the reporter to simply document the different views in high detail, without attempting to identify a nonexistent truth.

Imagine, now, that researchers are studying LGBTQ IPV instead of a highway incident. Even if researchers are in general agreement today that IPV is morally wrong regardless of the partners' trans*-cisgender identities and sexual orientations, what exactly is LGBTQ IPV? Is there one or multiple ways of thinking about whom it happens to, why it happens, what occurs in these relationships, and their outcomes? Is bias in such research avoidable—perhaps through questionnaire-based studies with large samples—or is bias inevitable, such that interview-based studies with smaller samples may introduce additional biases, but at least the information collected is of much higher detail? These questions are ultimately about **epistemology,** a debate about what is possible to learn through research. How a researcher answers these questions—particularly whether the researcher is aligned more with positivist, standpoint, or postmodernist theories—can deeply affect the types of studies the researcher conducts and, therefore, the types of results collected.

The issue of epistemology quietly colors LGBTQ IPV research. One effect of differing epistemologies of researchers is the types of research that are viewed as valid. For example, some have suggested that much of LGBTQ IPV research has thus far been inaccurate due to using predominantly small, nonrandom samples.[11] This of course begins with positivist assumptions that there is a single truth about LGBTQ IPV that is knowable through carefully designed, unbiased research. Positivists often lean towards **quantitative research,** studies that result in low-detail data for which responses from a sample can be easily compared, such as answers to a multiple-choice questionnaire question. Because quantitative data can be quite easy to collect—sometimes as simple as posting a questionnaire online—and can be fairly quick to analyze using statistical computer software, it is not much harder for a researcher to quantitatively study one thousand people than it is to study ten people. The benefit of studying one thousand people is that a larger sample will presumably better represent the population it came from. If selected at random, the sample should be even more representative, and therefore the results can be assumed to reflect what is actually happening with the rest of the population.

On the other end of the spectrum, some postmodernist researchers suggest that LGBTQ IPV does not have a single truth: "abusers" have one perspective, "victims" have another, clinicians and researchers have others, and readers of research reports may add their own interpretation of study findings that neither the researcher nor the sample intended.[12] In other words, research is a bit like a giant game of telephone, with much rich detail lost in translation. One solution to this problem may be for researchers to eschew quantitative research for **qualitative research,** studies that result in high-detail data for which responses from people in a sample cannot be easily compared, such as answers to open-ended interview questions. Qualitative data can be time-consuming to collect. Each individual interview may take upward of an hour, and longer-term ethnographic studies can entail interviewing and observing a community for weeks or even years. The resulting data can be so detailed and have so many gaps—such as when one subject is asked different follow-up questions than another subject—that analyzing for common patterns in the sample can be similarly time-consuming and challenging. As a result, it is difficult to have very large samples in qualitative studies. However, from a postmodernist perspective, the size and representativeness of the sample may be less important than the rich level of detail that qualitative research can provide. While many positivist and standpoint theorist researchers may search for the most common patterns in qualitative data, a postmodernist researcher might instead present all views—such as those of abusers and victims—as equally valid and truthful, even when those views do not appear to agree or even when they hint that partners do not fit neatly into "abuser" and "victim" roles.[13]

Another way in which epistemology silently shapes LGBTQ IPV research is in debates about what types of people should be able to conduct research on the topic. Standpoint theory suggests that researchers may be taught by friends, family, and the media to think differently if they are heterosexual or cisgender rather than LGBTQ, and as a result non-LGBTQ researchers may be at an initial disadvantage. For example, Joan McClennen has poignantly described her sense of being an "outsider" as a heterosexual woman studying LGBTQ IPV—from feeling apprehensive about studying a population she previously knew little about personally, to encountering objections by some that heterosexuals should not study sexual minorities, to encountering homophobic responses from fellow professors, family, and friends who questioned the legitimacy of LGBTQ IPV research as well as the researcher's own sexual orientation. To overcome these outsider disadvantages, McClennen highlights several strategies, including challenging one's own hidden biases, immersing oneself in LGBTQ cultures, collaborating with LGBTQ researchers, drawing from LGBTQ communities for advice on how to best design research studies in the first place, and mastering knowledge of past research on LGBTQ IPV.[14] Researchers Robert Peralta and Jodi Ross add an intriguing point to this discussion about outsider status: there is no singular LGBTQ experience. LGBTQ people can be quite different from one another, varying by social class, race, ethnicity, national origin, and so forth. As a consequence, even LGBTQ-identified researchers may not be able to perfectly relate to the experiences of their LGBTQ subjects if those subjects differ from the researchers in other ways, such as in terms of their gender, race, or other factors. Therefore, Peralta and Ross question whether it is possible for even LGBTQ researchers to be true "insiders" for everyone in their samples.[15] In some ways, perhaps we are all simultaneously insiders and outsiders.

Which brings us back to Herman. If reporters began with different assumptions about what can be learned about the highway incident, they may have chosen to go about their investigations in very different ways. When a news report finally hits your television screen later that night, it is important to keep in mind that the story you hear is a carefully filtered one. Likewise, the choices that researchers make in how they collect information about LGBTQ IPV can have a profound impact on what the results show—and in turn, these results may shape local and national responses to LGBTQ IPV. A lot rests on the methodological choices of researchers.

CHALLENGES IN STUDYING LGBTQ IPV

With the rare exception of studies that entail analyzing annual crime reports from law enforcement, research on LGBTQ IPV has been conducted almost exclusively through "survey" methods. That is to say, whether quantitatively or qualitatively oriented, most LGBTQ IPV research collects data through questionnaires, individual interviews, or focus-group interviews. To learn from one another and improve the accuracy and detail of future LGBTQ IPV research, it will be valuable to review two key challenges in studying LGBTQ IPV: issues pertaining to (1) measuring IPV and (2) defining and sampling the population. (See figure 1.)

Challenge no. 1: Measuring IPV

Research on LGBTQ IPV shares many of the same potential methodological pitfalls as HC IPV research. Many of these issues deal with how to best measure IPV in survey research. In particular, LGBTQ IPV researchers should be cognizant of several specific challenges in assessing IPV: differentiating IPV from other types of interpersonal crimes, sensitivity versus specificity in IPV survey measurement, not omitting or merging distinct types of IPV, choosing an appropriate time frame in which IPV may have occurred, adequately distinguishing victimization from perpetration, and adequately designing IPV measures for LGBTQ populations. This section will review each of these potential pitfalls.

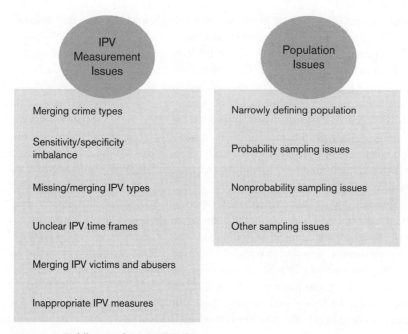

FIGURE 1. Pitfalls in studying LGBTQ IPV.

Differentiating Crime Types   IPV, child abuse, and peer victimization: each is an interpersonal crime, they involve similar abusive tactics, and they often occur in the lives of the same people, but the relationship between the perpetrator and victim differs significantly. In IPV, the perpetrator is a romantic or sexual partner, in child abuse an adult harms a minor, and in peer victimization the perpetrator usually knows but is not in a familial, romantic, or sexual relationship with the victim. Not surprisingly, the theorized causes, dynamics, and consequences of these types of crimes differ,[16] suggesting that researchers should be careful to measure these separately. These distinctions are not always easy to draw in research, though. For example, Naomi Freedner and colleagues conducted an important and much-cited study of sexual minorities ages 13 to 22 years, who were attending an LGBTQ youth-rights rally in the United States. Subjects were asked whether a "date or partner" ever perpetrated a variety of IPV forms against them.[17] However, this very specific request for information only on IPV assumes that the respondents can correctly identify their abuser as a date or partner. If any of the minors—13- to 17-year-olds in the sample—were victims of ongoing abuse by adults, the criminal justice system in the United States would likely define this as child abuse, not IPV. All the same, some of these subjects may have been led to believe by their abusers that they were in a romantic or sexual relationship with the abuser, and they might be describing their child-abuse victimization in response to these IPV questions. The same issue might arise if researchers ask about lifetime IPV victimization and do not specify that they want IPV reported to the researchers only if it occurred after the subject became a legal adult. In IPV studies that sample only minors, one solution might be to place additional qualifications into a survey's description of the types of relationships the subject should report on, such as by specifying that the partner cannot be an adult or a relative.

In rarer cases, researchers may unintentionally confuse peer victimization and IPV. Christine Barter suggests that in the United Kingdom, young people who are romantically or sexually involved may prefer to call each other "friends" rather than "partners."[18] While these differences in partner titles may reflect actual differences in how seriously these people view their relationships, abuse in romantic or sexual relationships should still be analyzed by researchers as IPV even if partners call each other "friends." This creates a challenge for the many IPV studies that limit survey questions to relationships between "partners" or "couples." For instance, arguably the most widely used sets of survey questions measuring IPV are the Conflict Tactics Scale (CTS)[19] and its revised version (CTS2),[20] which in a March 2015 search of Google Scholar (scholar.google.com) were listed as having been cited 5,420 and 3,767 times, respectively. In both sets of questions, the terms *couple* and *partner* are used to describe the relationship the subject must have with another person in order to be eligible to answer the IPV questions. As a result of this qualifier, much peer victimization will rightly be omitted from studies of IPV that use the CTS or CTS2—but, conversely, some IPV may go unreported where the subject labels a partner as a "friend." Likewise, studies that appear to be about peer-violence victimization may actually unintentionally include IPV victimization. One study professing to be about "bullying and sexual harassment victimization" among adolescents asked, "During this school year, have one or more students at school," followed by a series of abuse tactics like "scared you" and "pushed, shoved, slapped, or kicked you."[21] The reality is that the types of tactics involved in peer victimization are quite similar to those in IPV. In the case of this particular study, the fact that the perpetrator is a fellow student should not preclude the possibility that the perpetrator is dating the victim, changing the nature of the crime from peer victimization or bullying to IPV. Even if the researchers had specified that subjects should report victimization only from friends, as Barter notes, the term *friends* appears to have the potential to be code for *partner* for some youths.

Perhaps the distinction between IPV, child abuse, and peer victimization is a cultural one. For instance, in the United Kingdom there is a major service-providing organization and charity called the National Society for the Prevention of Cruelty to Children. On their website, they list several forms of what they call "child abuse," including "domestic abuse," "bullying and cyber bullying," and "child sexual exploitation," among other forms. Thus, in some cultures, labels like "child abuse" may be used to refer to victimization of minors regardless of whether the perpetrator is a nonadult intimate partner, a nonadult, non-intimate-partner peer, or an adult. While there are commonalities in these types of interpersonal victimization, they are not identical,[22] and researchers should consider attempting to clearly delineate between them.

Sensitivity versus Specificity.   What looks like IPV, sounds like IPV, but is not actually IPV?

This is an issue that raises concerns for many IPV researchers: the possibility that they have accidentally labeled relationships as abusive that in fact are not. A playful or even flirtatious push or shove between partners may not qualify as IPV by most definitions, but research—particularly quantitative survey research—often lacks the level of detail needed to see the full context of these actions. Is there a way to avoid including these "false positives," subjects that are labeled by researchers as victims who are not in fact victims . . . and are the costs of doing so too high? Should IPV survey questions have higher **sensitivity**—that is, capture all actual IPV in a sample, even if some play fighting is added in by accident; or should they have higher **specificity**—that is, ensure that all the IPV that is captured is actually IPV rather than play fighting?

To avoid false positives and increase specificity of IPV survey measures, some researchers choose to ask survey questions about IPV in such a way as to more clearly communicate with subjects that they are inquiring only about IPV. For instance, a study from the 1980s of sexual minority and heterosexual women asked if someone "you were dating ever *raped* you";[23] a study in 2000 of lesbian and heterosexual women asked if "you have ever been a *victim* of non-sexual *violence*" and if you "have . . . ever been physically *attacked*" by a "sex partner";[24] and a secondary analysis of a 2008–2009 study of heterosexual and sexual minority undergraduate students asked, "[H]ave you been in a relationship that was: Emotionally *abusive*? Physically *abusive*? Sexually *abusive*?"[25] (emphasis added). In such studies, terminology is used that the average person will likely associate with crimes, immoral actions, and, more specifically, IPV.

Many researchers have pointed out, though, that high specificity comes at the cost of decreased sensitivity. That is, while surveys using terminology closely associated with IPV will increase the chances that only true IPV victims respond, other IPV victims may be dissuaded from reporting because of this exact approach. This is in part due to a social science research phenomenon called **social desirability bias.** Social desirability bias occurs when a researcher implies that there is a morally right or wrong answer to survey questions.[26] This often happens unintentionally on the part of the researcher, and the influence on subjects can be so subtle as to operate on a subconscious level. Nonetheless, research suggests that survey-question wording really can influence participants to on average shift their true answers to appear more morally acceptable.[27] IPV research is particularly vulnerable to this type of bias because many of the terms researchers might normally use to describe IPV—such as *violence, abuse, assault, victim,* and *batterer*—tend to carry strong negative connotations, both for IPV victims and abusers. Some terms like *rape* and *domestic violence* may even appear in a nation's criminal statutes, so survey questions that use those terms in particular would be asking subjects to align themselves with behaviors that are not only socially stigmatized but, for perpetration, also illegal. Moreover, research suggests that abusers often self-justify their behaviors to the point that they might not always self-label as abusers,[28] and victims are often convinced by abusers that they have somehow motivated the abuser to the extent that victims might not self-label as victims.[29] When considering that many victims and abusers do not want to admit to researchers, let alone themselves, that they have been involved in IPV, it may be important to ask subjects about IPV in a way that does not require them to label their relationship as abusive.

For this reason, many IPV scholars recommend decreasing specificity and increasing sensitivity, by avoiding the use of value-laden terms in research and instead relying on specific behavioral definitions of IPV.[30] For example, instead of asking a subject if a partner ever "perpetrated physical violence," a researcher might instead ask if a partner ever "hit, kicked, slapped, punched, pushed, burned, or threw objects" at them. Although not completely destigmatized, such behaviorally specific language may avoid added social desirability bias. Some of the most widely used IPV questions in survey research—including the previously mentioned CTS[31] and CTS2[32] as well as the youth-focused Conflict in Adolescent Dating Relationships Inventory (CADRI)[33]—not only use behaviorally specific language to destigmatize IPV tactics but also include instruction paragraphs that attempt to destigmatize the context around IPV. For example, the CTS2 instruction paragraph begins with the following information on the relationship environment that can result in IPV: "No matter how well a couple gets along, there are times when they disagree, get annoyed with the other person, want different things from each other, or just have spats or fights because they are in a bad mood, are tired, or for some other reason. Couples also have many different ways of trying to settle their differences. This is a list of things that might happen when you have differences."[34] The introductory paragraph of the heterosexual-female version of the CADRI similarly begins with the following: "The following questions ask you about things that may have happened to you with your boyfriend while you were having an argument."[35] Note that terms commonly used in publications by researchers to describe the context of IPV—*abuse, coercive control, cycle of violence*—never appear in these introductory questionnaire paragraphs. Instead, the CTS, CTS2, and CADRI avoid criminal labels and judgmental terminology, and they even describe potentially abusive relationships as "spats" and "arguments" that may result from very normal conditions like "a bad mood" or being "tired." For victims and abusers who want to distance themselves from stigmatized and criminal IPV labels, such language may decrease social-desirability bias and increase the likelihood that they report IPV on a survey. On the other hand, as some scholars have noted, IPV incidents might occur outside the context of an argument, suggesting that even the CTS, CTS2, and CADRI may artificially exclude some IPV.[36]

The specificity-sensitivity debate can also be seen at work in qualifiers added into IPV survey questions. For example, Naomi Freedner and colleagues asked people at an LGBTQ youth-rights rally, "Has a date or partner ever *hurt* you physically?"[37] (emphasis added). Likewise, Scott Rhodes and a team of researchers asked sexual minority and heterosexual male undergraduate students, "Has a date or boyfriend or girlfriend ever *started* a physical fight with you?"[38] (emphasis added). In both cases, it is likely safe to assume that being physically injured by a partner or being in a physical fight initiated by a partner increases specificity and decreases false positives. However, it is also likely true that sensitivity suffers as a consequence. Consider first injury: most IPV victims never experience physical violence, let alone physical injury, and those who do experience particularly minor injuries may not always self-describe themselves as being injured. Indeed, some research on HC IPV suggests that heterosexual masculinity norms leave men less likely to interpret physical pain inflicted by a female partner as consequential or serious.[39] Next, consider initiation of physical IPV: setting aside for a moment the reality that, again, IPV is not always physical, some IPV victims may feel that they were the ones who initiated the fight if they define initiation as starting a verbal argument that the abuser uses to justify a physical attack.[40] Thus, while qualifiers in IPV survey questions—such as being injured or the abuser initiating attacks—likely increase specificity, they almost certainly also decrease sensitivity. A similar issue can arise in analysis of collected data. For instance, some recommend combining collected data on IPV frequency and outcomes to create threshold cutoffs with which to categorize subjects as having experienced extreme IPV.[41] As a result, researchers may bring certain types of IPV victims more into focus than other types.

Which is more vital for IPV research: sensitivity or specificity? The former will result in surveys that show higher rates of IPV and that are more inclusive of the full range of IPV experiences, whereas the latter will result in surveys that show lower rates of IPV but will be able to assert with greater certainty that these subjects have actually experienced IPV. In many ways, how societies respond to LGBTQ IPV in terms of services, interventions, and policies may hinge in part upon whether they are based on research cataloguing a wide range of IPV experiences or a narrowed and particularly severe IPV experience. It is difficult to make a survey 100% sensitive and 100% specific, which is why researchers often need to make a choice about which is more important to them. IPV research appears to be moving more toward sensitive questions in recent years, and the widespread use of sensitive IPV questionnaires like the CTS have had the added benefit of making it easier to compare results across studies using the same IPV questions. Nonetheless, the sensitivity-versus-specificity debate remains a vital one, both in HC IPV and LGBTQ IPV research.

Missing or Merged IPV Types. Whereas the experience and consequences of other forms of IPV may be more difficult for a nonvictim to imagine, physical violence is easy for anyone to understand. A fist can hurt, and from a young age we learn that hitting is morally wrong. Still, physical IPV is not the only form of IPV. Research indicates that other forms of IPV—psychological and sexual abuse—can have similarly scary effects on victims,[42] yet they are often less likely to be studied. As will be reviewed in greater depth in chapter 3, certain IPV tactics also appear to be understudied in LGBTQ IPV research, particularly threats of violence, partner stalking, and LGBTQ-specific forms of IPV victimization. More generally, perpetration appears to be measured far less often than victimization. Perhaps understandably due to fears of prosecution for subjects and ethical concerns for researchers, LGBTQ IPV partner-homicide perpetration is rarely studied, and when it is, it is based on official police records rather than self-report surveys. On occasion, no specific forms or tactics of IPV are distinguished, with a single generic question being used to encompass all types of IPV.[43]

Even when researchers include the same specific IPV tactics in surveys, they often disagree about how to best combine or merge those tactics into umbrella forms of IPV for the purposes of analysis. On rare occasion, LGBTQ IPV researchers have subsumed sexual IPV under a physical IPV label.[44] However, arguably, the form of IPV that has had the most nebulous definition is what is often termed "psychological" or "emotional" IPV.[45] Often treated as *everything else*—that is, every IPV tactic that is not physical IPV, sexual IPV, or partner homicide—it can include combinations of what might be called verbal abuse (e.g., verbal slurs, verbally making the victim feel inferior or inadequate, embarrassing the victim privately or publicly, or verbally spreading negative rumors about the victim), threats (e.g., threats against the victim, the victim's family, or the abuser in the form of self-harm, in order to coerce the victim into an action or to prevent the victim from leaving the abuser), monitoring and stalking behaviors (e.g., learning where the victim is going or what the victim is doing, either directly by asking or indirectly by checking their recent phone log, email messages, and social media accounts), isolation behaviors (e.g., efforts to isolate the victim from friends and family through direct commands or indirectly through jealous comments and accusations), and other controlling behaviors (e.g., dictating what clothing the victim can wear, hiding hormone-therapy medications).

These psychological or emotional IPV tactics can be combined in various ways in analysis into multiple umbrella forms of IPV. How to combine these tactics into umbrella IPV forms, though, has never been standardized by researchers.[46] For instance, are threats examples of tactics of different IPV forms? Are threats in order to have sexual intercourse—as was the case in an analysis of IPV among sexual minorities in the *National Intimate Partner and Sexual Violence Survey*[47]—a tactic of sexual IPV? Perhaps physical and sexual threats should be subsumed under a verbal IPV umbrella form, as was the case in Eric Houston and David McKirnan's study of IPV among MSMs?[48] Maybe instead threats should be treated as a distinct umbrella IPV form, as was the case in Gregory Merrill and Valerie Wolfe's study of IPV among sexual minority men?[49] Going in a different direction, many LGBTQ IPV researchers opt to merge verbal abuse, isolation behaviors, monitoring and stalking behaviors, threats, and other controlling behaviors into a single psychological or emotional IPV umbrella form. On the surface, the decision of how to categorize psychological IPV tactics, whether as a single IPV form or multiple forms, appears to be simple semantics.

One could argue that abusers use whatever tactics will achieve their goals, regardless of whether they cross IPV form boundaries socially constructed by researchers. At the same time, there may be different causes and outcomes of, say, being stalked versus being publicly embarrassed versus threats of suicide. To ignore these possible distinctions may be to miss out on key information that can assist service provision and improve intervention design. Likewise, if forms of LGBTQ IPV get omitted entirely from survey research, the risk becomes that those forms of IPV will be similarly overlooked in future policy, practice, and research.

IPV Time Frames

Friend: "How about we have dinner next Tuesday."

   Me: "Do you mean *this* Tuesday, as in two days from today?"

Friend: "No, *next* Tuesday."

   Me: "As in not the very next Tuesday but the Tuesday *after next?*"

Friend: [*Looks confused.*]

         END SCENE.

Does this conversation sound familiar? When it comes to understanding social existence, time frames matter. In the case of a dinner date, clearly defined time frames may mean the difference between eating with your friend versus an empty chair. In IPV research, clearly defined recall time frames may similarly mean the difference between useful and unintelligible findings.

For instance, one study of IPV among self-identified lesbian women was important to the research literature in many ways, but it might have benefited from a clearer IPV time frame. Researchers inquired about the subjects' experiences with IPV victimization in different-gender "past relationships," "the most recent past" same-gender relationship, and "the current" same-gender relationship.[50] One issue subjects may have had to consider is whether different-gender "past relationships" include current relationships, as in lifetime IPV victimization, or whether instead the researchers were really asking about lifetime IPV victimization minus current relationships. If the subject is currently in a same-gender relationship, should they report about it twice, first as "the most recent past" same-gender relationship and then a second time as their "current" same-gender relationship? Moreover, if we were to try to see how IPV experiences and rates differ for these subjects in different-gender and same-gender relationships, what variables would be comparable: are different-gender "past relationships" the same exact time frame as "the most recent past" plus "current" same-gender relationships, or, for the reasons just stated, is this potentially an apples-to-oranges comparison? This is by no means the only study that has used unclear language to describe IPV time frames. Like "this Tuesday" and "next Tuesday," it is possible that the meaning of such time frames was lost in translation with some subjects. Being clear about time frames, both to subjects and to readers of research publications, is of critical importance because these time frames directly influence IPV prevalence rates and subsequent analyses with IPV covariates.

To avoid such confusions, researchers tend to limit survey questions to IPV experiences that occurred within a specific time frame or period, and any IPV that occurred outside of that time frame is not inquired about. Even if a current or recent relationship is inquired about, it may be useful to layer on top of that a month-based or year-based time frame, such as the past year within a current relationship. Which exact time frame to select depends on the researcher's goal. Particularly when LGBTQ subjects are few, researchers may wish to increase the odds of identifying IPV experiences by focusing on lifetime IPV. Given that sexual minorities typically experience their first same-gender attraction prior to age 18,[51] it may be useful to ask about IPV not just in adulthood but also beforehand, as long as efforts are made to avoid mixing reports of child abuse and IPV. On the opposite end of the spectrum, IPV researchers often purposely limit the time frame to the past year because subjects will recall recent events with the greatest accuracy. This may enable the collection of finer-grain detail through questions such as how frequently very specific IPV tactics were used or received.

Perhaps reflecting these common research goals, most LGBTQ IPV research appears to lean toward using past-year and lifetime IPV time frames. Still, a multitude of time frames in between and beyond have also been used, such as the subject's lifetime since turning 18 years of age,[52] lifetime excluding the past year[53] or excluding the past five years;[54] during the past six years,[55] past five years,[56] past two years,[57] past eighteen months,[58] past six months,[59] past five months,[60] or past four months;[61] during college;[62] in the most recent relationship,[63] the current relationship,[64] or the "worst" relationship;[65] and over an unspecified time period.[66] While there is no inherent reason why one time frame is better than another—for instance, the recall accuracy is likely very similar for the past six versus five months—researchers tend to reuse the two most popular time frames, past year and lifetime, in part because it makes it considerably easier to compare results across studies.

Distinguishing IPV Victimization and Perpetration.   LGBTQ IPV victimization and perpetration are clearly related, yet they have different causes and outcomes that are equally worthy of study. To provide better services to victims, victimization needs to be studied, while to prevent or to stop ongoing IPV it is important to study perpetration. Unfortunately, in some cases, studies have failed to distinguish between victimization and perpetration. For example, a secondary analysis of the 2008–2009 *National College Health Assessment* examined IPV among heterosexual and sexual minority undergraduate students. However, because the questionnaire asked, "Have you been in a relationship that was" abusive, it is unfortunately not possible to determine if subjects who experienced IPV were the victims, perpetrators, or both.[67] Similarly, one study sampled HIV-positive MSMs who had a "history of" IPV, without any clear indication of whether subjects were victims, perpetrators, or both.[68] Yet another study asked subjects, "Have you or your partner" used various IPV tactics, never asking whether it was the subjects, their partners, or both who perpetrated IPV.[69] Such approaches make it nearly impossible to understand what is happening in these relationships and why.

When LGBTQ IPV victimization and perpetration are not merged, LGBTQ IPV studies appear to be far less likely to study perpetration than victimization. The obvious problem with this disparity is that societies are left with considerably less information on LGBTQ IPV abusers, information that may prove vital in designing prevention programs and batterer-intervention services. A less obvious but equally important drawback is that, in the absence of perpetration data, some subjects may be inaccurately labeled by researchers as "victims." As will be discussed at greater length in chapter 3, research on HC IPV and some research on LGBTQ IPV suggests that at least some portion of subjects who are recipients of IPV tactics are also users of IPV tactics. Complicating matters further, in relationships where both partners have used IPV tactics, it is possible that one partner is the primary "victim" and uses IPV tactics like physical violence only in self-defense. Therefore, it is particularly important that researchers measure both IPV victimization and perpetration within the same studies, along with contextualizing factors like motives and outcomes.[70]

It certainly may be fruitful to study individuals who at some point in their lives have perpetrated IPV and at another point in their lives were victims of IPV. However, when researchers aim to learn about "directionality"—that is, whether subjects are victims only, perpetrators only, or victim-perpetrators within a given relationship—it is helpful to narrow questions to a specific relationship, such as the past year of the most recent relationship. Studies that have failed to do so have in some instances resulted in researchers drawing conclusions about relationship-level directionality without adequate supporting data. For example, a secondary analysis of the *National Longitudinal Study of Adolescent Health* examined same-gender IPV perpetration and victimization in the past six years. Another study of sexual minorities attending sexual minority community events assessed IPV victimization and perpetration in the past five years. In both studies, subjects who had experienced both victimization and perpetration at some point during the assessed time frame—but, importantly, not necessarily in the same relationship—were labeled somewhat misleadingly by the researchers as having experienced "bidirectional IPV" for the former study[71] and "mutual partner violence" for the latter study.[72] Without narrowing questions to a particular relationship and instead just using a time frame, it becomes impossible to state with any certainty whether subjects who both used and received IPV tactics did so in the same relationship.

To study IPV perpetration and victimization within the same relationships, it is only in very rare cases[73] that both partners from the same relationship have been recruited for a study. Instead, most often researchers ask only one half of a relationship to report both what IPV tactics they received and used. This is partially because it is often challenging to recruit the partner of a subject: the partner may not want to spend time on the study, may no longer be with the subject, and may not wish to disclose stigmatized or illegal behaviors. Equally as important, though, is that recruiting both partners in an abusive relationship together may pose a safety risk for the victim. Particularly when an abuser receives a survey that is identical to the one received by the victim, the abuser knows exactly what stigmatized and illegal actions they perpetrated that the victim may report to the researcher. Suspicion and fear that the victim will disclose victimization experiences to the researcher may lead some abusers to attempt to silence or retaliate against the victim. It is for this particular reason that it is often recommended that researchers make every effort to sample only one partner in a relationship, even if that means, for instance, recruiting only one subject per household in a telephone survey.[74]

Of course, while there will always be inaccurate reporting in surveys to some degree—whether because subjects do not recall what happened with perfect clarity, or because the subjects do not wish to disclose socially undesirable experiences—it can be assumed that the accuracy of reporting will suffer even more when a subject is asked to indicate what their partner did to them. For this exact reason, researchers Liz Margolies and Elaine Leeder suggest that it would be valuable to recruit both partners in the same relationship. Doing so allows researchers to determine whether abusers' and victims' perspectives differ. They highlight one particular issue that might be clarified by such research: victims often can perceive that their lives are being controlled by the abuser, whereas research indicates that, ironically, some abusers view themselves as powerless.[75] Learning about these differences could have a number of important implications, such as in helping to create mental health services and intervention programs that specifically target the rationalizations used by victims and abusers to downplay the existence and severity of IPV in their relationships. Obviously, as mentioned previously, there are serious risks to IPV victims when their abusers are included in the same study, so, in the absence of extreme precautions, it is generally recommended that researchers rely on one partner to report both victimization and perpetration experiences.

Appropriateness of Measures for LGBTQ IPV.   Clearly there are many potential pitfalls in designing accurate survey questions about LGBTQ IPV: from being sure the questions do not confuse IPV with other crimes like child abuse and peer victimization, to striking the right balance between sensitivity and specificity, to not omitting or merging distinct IPV types, to deciding which time period in the lives of subjects the IPV questions should focus on. Once a researcher has run this gauntlet to successfully create a series of survey questions on different IPV tactics—collectively referred to as an IPV **measure**—ideally the measure would then go through a series of rigorous diagnostic tests with a small sample of subjects before being used in a full-scale, more expensive study. These tests can catch problems such as question wording being unclear (which can be discovered when subjects directly tell this to the researcher, as well as when the survey is answered very differently by two demographically identical samples, suggesting that the question wording can be interpreted in multiple ways), wording being overly judgmental to the point that subjects appear to underreport certain IPV behaviors as compared with past research findings, clear and nonjudgmental questions that nonetheless result in certain IPV tactics never being reported by subjects (which may mean that such items could be removed to decrease the time it takes to complete the survey), IPV tactics that are known from previous research to often coincide with other key variables (such as similar IPV tactics or related causes and outcomes) that for some reason are rarely co-occurring when using a certain measure with a small sample of subjects (which may hint that your questions are not worded correctly), IPV tactics that seem to co-occur almost every single time (which in some cases may mean you have included two almost identical questions and that one can be removed), and so forth. These diagnostic tests are not simple to do, and it often takes both significant time and research funding to complete them correctly. Simply put, creating an IPV measure is *hard.*

Fortunately, several IPV measures have been carefully designed, rigorously tested, and made available to other researchers to use in their own studies. The two most widely used examples of this are the previously mentioned Conflict Tactics Scale (CTS)[76] and its revised version (CTS2),[77] each of which has been cited in thousands of publications. Not surprisingly, the CTS, the CTS2, and similar measures have been heavily relied upon in research on not just HC IPV but also LGBTQ IPV. In the case of measures that have used gendered pronouns under the assumption

BOX 2. EXAMPLES OF LGBTQ-SPECIFIC IPV TACTICS INCLUDED
IN PAST SURVEY STUDIES

- Abuser threatened to out partner's sexual orientation to people the
  victim knows.
- Abuser forced public displays of affection (e.g., hand-holding).
- Abuser questioned whether the victim is a "real" lesbian/gay/bisexual/
  man/woman.
- Abuser withheld medications (particularly relevant for trans* victims using
  hormone medications).

that the sample has experienced only different-gender relationships, some LGBTQ
IPV researchers have simply adjusted the language to become gender-neutral and
then used the measure in their studies.[78] There are just two problems with these
measures and others like them: they are rarely tested diagnostically with LGBTQ
samples, and they almost always exclude tactics unique to LGBTQ IPV.[79]

To date, neither the CTS nor the CTS2 has ever been fully diagnostically tested
with an LGBTQ sample. As Bonnie Moradi and her colleagues have noted about
the broader LGBTQ research literature, the fact that a measure has been diagnostically tested with a heterosexual-cisgender sample does not mean that it would pass
the same diagnostic tests with an LGBTQ sample.[80] Likewise, a measure that was
tested with gay and lesbian cisgender subjects may not be appropriate for bisexual
or trans* subjects, and a measure tested with cisgender women may not be appropriate with cisgender men.[81]

The inappropriateness of a measure may stem from a variety of sources—from
the use of heterosexual-based assumptions about the varieties of sexual IPV that
can occur to a less streamlined list of questions that includes tactics that are
uncommon or unclear for this population. Only a handful of IPV measures have
been diagnostically tested with sexual minority populations, including measures
examining IPV in the relationships of LGBTQ people and same-gender relationships,[82] the relationships of sexual minority men,[83] male same-gender relationships,[84] female same-gender relationships,[85] and male and female same-gender
relationships,[86] often achieved by making minor edits to the CTS or CTS2 without
substantively reevaluating whether the core of the IPV questions should be altered
or added to. No diagnostic tests of an IPV measure with a trans* sample or subsample have been published thus far. Several ideas for LGBTQ-specific IPV tactics
to include in future IPV measures can be found in published questionnaire-based
studies that used IPV measures never diagnostically tested. Although by no means
an exhaustive list, these examples from past research may be a good starting point.
(See box 2.)[87] Many additional ideas are available in chapter 3.

Challenge no. 2: Defining and Sampling the Population

The issue of whom to include in a study of LGBTQ IPV is not a trivial one. When certain types of people and relationships are excluded from IPV studies, the findings may not be applicable to all LGBTQ people, leaving policymakers and service providers with less information about how to better aid certain subpopulations. Moreover, when certain types of people and relationships are systematically excluded in IPV research, the unintended symbolic message may be that researchers and society view these people and their relationships as less important. Finding a way to be as inclusive as possible of all LGBTQ people and their romantic and sexual relationships in research studies is therefore an important goal. Herein lies the second great challenge facing researchers of LGBTQ IPV: defining and sampling the population.

Defining the Population. If we are to study the people experiencing LGBTQ IPV, to whom exactly does that refer? More specifically, should IPV researchers focus on same-gender relationships regardless of the sexual orientation of partners, or should IPV researchers focus on relationships involving at least one LGBTQ person regardless of whether it is a same- or different-gender relationship? And what does it even mean to be "LGBTQ"?

Historically, LGBTQ IPV researchers have focused their attention on IPV in same-gender (often also called "same-sex") relationships, thereby excluding from studies the IPV experienced by LGBTQ people in different-gender relationships. This may be the case for a number of reasons. For instance, in nations and time periods where sexual orientation has been viewed as a taboo topic and a potential barrier to receiving research funding, studies may have omitted sexual orientation self-identity from questionnaires, leaving researchers to rely upon gender-identity questions to cobble together a faux measure of sexual orientation that relies on same-gender relationship history. In other cases, some scholars may assume that self-identified lesbian and gay people are almost entirely involved in same-gender relationships, and vice versa, despite evidence to the contrary.[88] (For instance, in one review of past research on "female same-sex intimate partner violence" or "FSSIPV," the authors write, "While research on IPV among heterosexuals has progressively expanded over the past 30 years, a similar increase has not occurred with regard to addressing FSSIPV."[89] They appear to imply here that being heterosexual-identified and experiencing same-gender relationships are mutually exclusive, with likely a similar assumption being made about nonheterosexual identity and different-gender relationships.) In fact, a number of studies have found that a substantial portion of IPV among sexual minorities occurs in different-gender relationships.[90] (For instance, one researcher found that just over half of gay male victims and one-fourth of lesbian female victims have a different-gender abuser.[91] Likewise, according to a nationally representative U.S. study, while same-gender

IPV is almost nonexistent among heterosexual men, over 10% of heterosexual-identified female IPV victims have a same-gender abuser.[92])

It is also possible that this research emphasis on IPV within same-gender relationships can be viewed as part of a broader historical erasure of bisexual identity, such as in LGBTQ activist leadership ranks, where bisexuals have been noticeably less visible.[93] The relative invisibility of bisexual identity has historically also been an issue in social science and public health research more generally (where bisexual identity may be omitted from sample recruitment and survey questionnaires entirely, or instead subsumed under umbrella categories like MSM or "homosexual").[94] Perhaps indicative of a disinterest in bisexuals and the different-gender relationships of sexual minorities, many researchers have called and today still call male same-gender relationships and IPV "gay relationships" and "gay IPV," respectively; female same-gender relationships and IPV are often likewise called "lesbian relationships" and "lesbian IPV," just as male-female relationships and IPV have been termed "heterosexual relationships" and "heterosexual IPV."[95] When using such terminology—which infers sexual orientation from the gender of partners—the implication is that bisexual-identified individuals must be gay or lesbian when in a same-gender relationship and must be heterosexual when in a different-gender relationship, thereby denying the reality that bisexuality is a stable and unchanging self-identity for many people regardless of the gender of their partners.[96]

Each of the above justifications for focusing on same-gender IPV is based on inaccurate myths about LGBTQ people and their relationships. Arguably the most compelling reason to focus on same-gender IPV, though, is an assumption that homophobic attitudes held by partners, law enforcement, and service providers are more likely to impact IPV in a same-gender relationship, where the sexual minority status of partners is particularly visible and therefore more stigmatizing. While this is undoubtedly true, the reach of homophobia may still extend to different-gender relationships. Most notably, research has consistently found that those who identify as bisexual (relative to those who identify as gay, lesbian, or heterosexual) as well as those who have experienced both at least one same-gender and at least one different-gender relationship (relative to those who have experienced only same-gender or only different-gender relationships) are most likely to experience IPV. It is less clear whether abusers are typically of the same or different gender as bisexual victims.[97] (See chapter 3 for further discussion.)

In other words, the sexual orientation of the victim seems to influence IPV even in different-gender relationships—whether because sexual minority victims fear being outed, feel stigmatized, or fear a homophobic or biphobic response by friends, family, service providers, and the criminal justice system. Perhaps this is why many researchers have moved away from studying just same-gender IPV and are now studying IPV among all LGBTQ people, both in same- and different-gender relationships.

More rarely, some researchers have even taken the approach of simultaneously relying upon both sexual orientation and the gender of partners in current or past relationships to define the target population, enabling more-detailed research conclusions. In some cases,[98] this results in a sample of sexual minority–identified subjects who have experienced a same-gender relationship. An ideal extension of this would be to study IPV in same-gender relationships (regardless of sexual orientation) *and* IPV in the relationships of LGBTQ people (regardless of whether the relationships are same- or different-gender). This solution has three major benefits: it includes same-gender relationships involving two self-identified heterosexual people, it allows for a comparison of findings on how IPV varies in the same- and different-gender relationships of LGBTQ people, and it is more directly inclusive of IPV among trans* people.

If indeed it is important to study IPV in all relationships of LGBTQ people, the next question is this: What does it mean to be lesbian, gay, or bisexual, and, likewise, what does it mean to be trans*?

Being lesbian, gay, or bisexual—that is, a "sexual minority"—can be defined in multiple ways: sexual minority *self-identity, romantic-sexual attraction* to at least people with the same gender identity, and *romantic-sexual interactions or relationships* with at least people with the same gender identity.[99] Each of these components of sexual orientation can shift independently over time, not always neatly aligning in stereotypical fashion.[100] At the heart of the struggle among researchers to define sexual orientation is the question of what most fundamentally makes someone a sexual minority: actions or self-labels.

Researchers Robert Peralta and Jodi Ross argue that behaviorally based sampling requirements, like being "MSM"—men who have had sexual intercourse with men—are preferable to sampling people who identify as "gay" or "bisexual," because same-gender IPV may occur among people of a variety of sexual orientations, including heterosexuals.[101] (Terms like *MSM*—and its counterparts, *MSMWs* [men who have sex with men and women], *WSWs* [women who have sex with women], and *WSWMs* [women who have sex with women and men]—first emerged in the 1990s from epidemiological research on the spread of sexually transmitted infections, and therefore such terms may also continue to be particularly relevant for studies with this as a primary focus, even when they happen to also include IPV in questionnaires so as to examine its role as a cause or outcome of sexual risk-taking behaviors.)[102] On the other side of the debate, some researchers have criticized such behaviorally based sampling criteria in that they overlook the possibility that self-identified sexual orientation has a very real impact on the lives and relationships of people, including IPV relationships.[103] At a symbolic level, one could also take issue with researchers applying labels (often "gay" or "lesbian" based solely on the gender identity of relationship partners[104]) that LGBTQ people do not use to describe themselves, unintentionally implying a lack of respect for a key aspect of their identities. For instance, one study went so far as to label women in its sample as either lesbian or heterosexual based solely on the gender of their current partner, regardless of whom they had been romantically-sexually involved with previously and regardless of how they self-identified.[105]

Likewise, researchers are divided on whether it is best to define being trans* (or transgender) in terms of actions or self-identity. Measuring trans* status in terms of actions—that is, gender identity relative to birth sex—requires, of course, a clear definition of being trans*. There are two ways this is often done, both of which define being trans* as having a gender identity that is different from one's biological sex at birth. A commonly used version of this definition requires that one's gender identity be male or female, and likewise that sex at birth must be male or female.[106] A less widely used but more inclusive definition of *trans** permits one to have had any type of sex label at birth (male, female, intersex) and any type of gender identity (male, female, genderqueer), just as long as they differ from one another. In either case, a behaviorally based definition of being trans* can be measured through two survey questions, one about sex at birth and the other about current gender identity.[107] This approach is particularly beneficial since many people who meet one of these behavioral definitions of being trans* do not self-identify as trans* but instead view themselves as solely male, female, or genderqueer, yet their trans* status still may influence experiences with transphobia and IPV. Conversely—or in addition to this behavioral approach—some researchers directly ask subjects whether they self-identity as trans* or transgender. As with sexual orientation, one can argue that measuring trans* self-identity should be important to researchers, both because self-identity may impact experiences with discrimination and other factors and because ignoring self-identity may be considered a sign of disrespect. For a more comprehensive understanding of trans* IPV, researchers may wish to include both behaviorally defined and self-identified measures of being trans* in their studies.

Whether a study measures sexual orientation and being trans* through self-identifications, preferences, or behavioral histories, there are two practical issues that researchers must contend with: time frames and labels.

Time frames are particularly important for researchers to consider because sex, gender identity, and sexual orientation can change independently over time.[108] As a consequence, a subject may have experienced IPV at a time in their lives when their sex, gender identity, or sexual orientation differed from what it was at the time of the study's data collection.[109] (For instance, what may be the earliest study in the literature describes a currently lesbian-identified adult who experienced different-gender sexual IPV as a 17-year-old youth.[110] Without additional information about the sexual orientation of the victim at the time of victimization, it is difficult to determine whether it is appropriate to categorize this as LGBTQ IPV.) While identity shifts may be less likely when assessing IPV that was experienced in the past year, this may be a particular concern for research assessing IPV in the subject's lifetime—a vast period in which many subjects will have seen shifts in personal identity. Survey studies often strive to have few questions, so as to encourage more subjects to participate in a study and complete a survey—and for this reason it is tempting to inquire only about how the subject currently identifies. Nonetheless, to more fully understand how IPV intersects with identities, sexism, homophobia, and transphobia, it may be valuable for researchers to begin asking about how their subjects identified at the time of relationships, whether by asking them to recall those periods in their lives or by collecting data longitudinally from the same subjects over a matter of months or years. Moreover, because IPV experiences, risk factors, and outcomes may differ depending on the trans* status, gender identity, and sexual orientation of both partners, researchers might begin asking about these factors for both the research subjects and, based on their recollection, those of their partners—a practice that is quite rare still.[111]

Labels or categories, particularly for trans* identity and sexual orientation, are another practical methodological issue for LGBTQ IPV researchers. An unavoidable truth is that many LGBTQ people will fear identifying with any trans* or sexual minority label provided in a survey, either because they are closeted or because they fear being further stigmatized. As a result, on surveys, an unknown portion of sexual minorities will self-identify as heterosexual, an unknown portion of genderqueer subjects will identify as male or female, and an unknown portion of trans* subjects will self-identify as cisgender.[112] That said, if a survey forces subjects to select from a limited list of identity labels (known as **closed-ended questions**), failure to include the identity that the subject prefers may result in the subject choosing an inaccurate but listed identity.[113] Often, researchers will include a variety of identity labels (e.g., trans*, bisexual) to select from with no doubt positive intentions to be inclusive and respectful of how their subjects choose to self-identify—but then in key analyses and results, these variables may be entirely omitted.[114] However, as Bonnie Moradi and her colleagues aptly point out, even when researchers make their best efforts to include a variety of identity labels in surveys and then use them in analyses, researchers are often out of touch with the latest identity labels that are being used in society. More problematic is the possibility that, as labels begin to multiply and continuously shift in meaning, having people choose from a short list of self-labels may not tell researchers as much as they think about the lived experiences of their respondents.[115] Therefore, researchers may wish to also include a blank space in which subjects can write their preferred identity label (known as an **open-ended question**) if they do not like the listed options.

A final key issue regarding defining the population is at once obvious and yet a common pitfall: researchers must be clear to potential subjects about what types of people they wish to recruit for their study samples. As previously discussed, the term *lesbian relationship* (along with gay and heterosexual relationships, and lesbian, gay, and heterosexual IPV) is unclear because it could have multiple defini-tions: a female-female relationship, a lesbian-lesbian relationship, a relationship with two sexual minority women who might identify as bisexual or lesbian, or a relationship with at least one lesbian or sexual minority woman regardless of whether the other partner is heterosexual or male. When such vague terms are used by researchers—as they often are[116]—this has the potential to confuse not only readers of their reports but also potential subjects responding to study recruitment advertisements. A similar confusion can arise when a researcher uses the term *lesbian* to mean sexual minority woman and *gay* to mean sexual minority man, when in fact sexual minorities who do not identify with these specific labels may assume the researcher is not interested in including them in the study. For example, one study's recruitment advertisements stated, "Lesbians needed for rela-tionship study" for "research examining dynamics and conflict resolution in les-bian relationships." Only those who contacted the researchers after seeing this advertisement were then asked a series of screening questions to verify their eligi-bility for the study, including questions "asking them to verify that they were les-bian or bisexual."[117] In other words, based on the screening questions, the researchers were clearly interested in recruiting both lesbian and bisexual women for the study, but many bisexual women may have ignored the study because the advertisement clearly stated, "[L]esbians needed." Even among lesbian-identified women viewing this advertisement, many may have decided to not respond because they assumed that their previous relationships were not "lesbian relation-ships," perhaps because their intimate partner was a man, a heterosexual woman, or a bisexual woman. Another study report used the term *same-sex relationships* interchangeably with the terms *gay relationships* and *lesbian relationships,* suggest-ing that the researchers assumed that all same-gender relationships involve either gay- or lesbian-identified partners, and vice versa. Their sample recruitment advertisements described the study as being about "conflict between gay and les-bian partners," which to the researchers may have been code for same-gender rela-tionships but could have easily been interpreted by potential respondents as requiring that both they and their partners identified as either gay or lesbian (and not, say, bisexual).[118] Such details may appear inconsequential when a sample is either small or nonrepresentative in some other way, and a case could even be made that using these terms in this way is respectful because many LGBTQ people themselves use them to describe their relationships. Some study reports[119] have even stated that all subjects were LGBTQ but then failed to explain how they knew this, perhaps implying that it does not really matter how sexual orientation or trans* identity are defined in a study. That said, there are two major reasons for researchers to be clearer about sample eligibility requirements in their study-recruitment materials, even with nonrepresentative samples: first, doing so will ensure that service providers and policymakers know to whom the study results apply (rather than erroneously assuming that results apply to a subpopulation not included in the sample), and, second, it becomes less likely that certain subpopulations are unintentionally excluded from studies (e.g., bisexual women who do not identify as "lesbian" and do not identify their same-gender relationships as "lesbian relationships").

Sampling the Population.   With rare exceptions, "populations" (all people of a certain type that a researcher wishes to learn about, such as LGBTQ people) are large and geographically spread out, making it difficult for researchers to include everyone from a population in a study. When factoring in that study subjects often get paid a small financial incentive to encourage study participation, populations that include tens of thousands of people or more tend to become cost prohibitive to study in their entirety. Instead, as previously discussed, social science researchers almost always study just a "sample" (i.e., a subset of people drawn from the population, who will be included in a specific research study). The goal of "sampling," or the process of selecting a sample from a population, is to create a sample that is almost identical to the population, both demographically and in most other factors such as attitudes, past experiences, and so forth. When a sample is representative of a population in this way, researchers can say with a high degree of certainty that the study results for a particular sample are similar to what the results would have been had the entire population been studied. In other words, by studying just several hundred people or thousands of people selected from a population, researchers hope to learn about patterns in the broader population. As previously mentioned, sampling can be accomplished through either of two basic approaches: "probability sampling" or "nonprobability sampling." Unfortunately, both sampling approaches come with their own challenges for researchers of LGBTQ IPV.

Probability Sampling Issues.   Probability sampling entails randomly selecting people from a "sampling frame," or a list of people's names and contact information, and those selected people are then contacted to recruit them to participate in the study. If the sampling frame includes nearly everyone from the LGBTQ population, the sample drawn from it should be very similar to this population, causing the study's results to be much more accurate. This might be the case if, for instance, names were randomly selected from a city telephone book. If the researcher recruits everyone who was randomly selected from the sampling frame, the sample would of course be predominantly heterosexual-cisgender. On the rare occasions when researchers can afford to construct mammoth samples, while the LGBTQ subjects will be only a small fraction of the overall sample, there may be enough LGBTQ subjects to enable accurate analyses. Indeed, this sampling technique will arguably provide the most accurate results of all sampling approaches.[120]

Plus, it has the benefit of enabling the accurate comparison of HC IPV with LGBTQ IPV. Too often researchers are left comparing the results of a study on just LGBTQ IPV with a study on just HC IPV, and it becomes difficult to know if any differences in results are artifacts of differences in the sampling and methodologies of the studies. When LGBTQ and heterosexual-cisgender people are sampled in exactly the same way and asked exactly the same questions in the same study, it becomes much clearer that any differences between the two are real and accurate.[121] Additionally, unlike samples based in higher-education institutions, if the sampling frame is instead drawn from a city or nation, the resulting sample will reach both highly educated and less educated LGBTQ populations.[122]

The "accuracy" of results from such studies—or, more specifically, being able to say with a high degree of certainty that the findings of a study are nearly identical to what the results would have shown had the entire population been studied—is incredibly valuable because service providers and policymakers hope to apply what is learned from studies to the broader LGBTQ population that was not studied. As recently as the 1990s, large-scale probability-sampled studies with data on LGBTQ IPV were nonexistent, leading some researchers[123] to question the accuracy of all existing (nonprobability) LGBTQ IPV studies up until that point.

Still, there are three potential limitations to this traditional probability-sampling approach for LGBTQ IPV research. First, because the vast majority of subjects would be heterosexual-cisgender, researchers in such general IPV studies often are less interested in the dynamics of LGBTQ IPV. Therefore, issues that are highly relevant to LGBTQ IPV (such as degree of outness, internalized homophobic and transphobic attitudes, etc.) are almost always omitted from such studies, greatly limiting the utility of this body of research. Second, the sample must be enormous (usually in the thousands if not tens of thousands of subjects) for there to be enough LGBTQ IPV relationships for the results to be accurate.[124] (Even when there are several hundred LGBTQ people in a sample, only a percentage of them will have experienced an intimate relationship, only a percentage of that subset will have experienced IPV, and any additional survey questions of interest—such as whether they reported to law enforcement and, of that subset, how were they treated—will further narrow the number of subjects that can be analyzed, often to the point that certain analyses would become wildly inaccurate because they would be based on only a handful of subjects.) The larger the sample, the more financial incentives need to be offered to subjects and the more time and research-staff salary need to be budgeted for.[125]

A common solution[126] is to delete data on LGBTQ subjects from IPV studies when there are too few of those subjects for accurate analyses. Another common solution is to merge all sexual minorities into one group in analyses for comparison with all heterosexuals[127] or, more rarely, to merge all sexual orientations among just women to compare with gay men and bisexual men.[128] Both solutions are problematic—the former because it eliminates the chance of learning about LGBTQ IPV and the latter because it eliminates the chance of learning about how IPV differs among LGBTQ subgroups. At the same time, the most ideal fix—to simply continue sampling more people to boost LGBTQ subject numbers—is off-limits to some researchers who are on a fixed budget and timetable. It is perhaps for this reason—the massiveness of the amount of time and resources needed to gather an LGBTQ probability sample—that some researchers as recently as within the past decade claimed that this was an impossible task.[129] That is clearly not true, since there have been a number of probability-sampled IPV studies to assess sexual orientation and gender identity,[130] but the challenges are undoubtedly substantial.

One variant of probability sampling that avoids these pitfalls entails randomly selecting potential subjects from a general sampling frame (e.g., telephone book), asking "screening questions" of these individuals to determine if they fit the target population description (e.g., LGBTQ-identified), and then inviting potential subjects to participate in the study only if they pass the screening questions. This setup is beneficial because the entire sample will be LGBTQ, which means that there should be enough subjects to conduct all LGBTQ IPV-related analyses, and researchers will feel more inclined to also include survey questions that are particularly relevant to IPV among LGBTQ people. As detailed previously in this chapter, the *Urban Men's Health Study* (UMHS) illustrates the primary drawback of this approach. With LGBTQ people consisting of only a small percentage of the general population, many people—hundreds, thousands, or, in the case of the UMHS, hundreds of thousands—will need to be screened who will turn out to be not eligible for the study (e.g., heterosexual-cisgender). Whether recruiting by phone, mail, email, or some other method, research staff need to be paid salaries for many weeks of work. Screening is a time-consuming and expensive process when done at such a scale. While all LGBTQ IPV research should warrant consideration for grant funding, studies that involve massive samples and lengthy sampling procedures are at greatest risk of extinction without financial support. It is therefore of the utmost importance that grant-giving organizations and governments continue to expand research funding opportunities for this vital line of inquiry.[131] Additionally, government-funded studies that include IPV questions should at the very least begin adding sexual orientation and trans* self-identity questions,[132] which appears to be more the case these days than in the past. National census studies should also include sexual orientation and trans* self-identity questions to make it possible for probability-sampled studies on LGBTQ IPV to verify if LGBTQ subjects are representative of their LGBTQ census counterparts in other respects, such as race, ethnicity, class, and so on.[133]

Nonprobability Sampling Issues.   Conversely, "nonprobability sampling," or nonrandom sampling, entails selecting people from the population without a sampling frame, without any way of calculating the probability that a person is selected from the population.[134] That is, likely many people in the population have lower or zero odds of being selected because the researcher does not even know they exist. As a result, the sample may be unrepresentative of the population, with certain types of LGBTQ people unintentionally excluded. Moreover, nonprobability sampling often results in a sample that is "homogeneous" (i.e., predominantly sharing the same characteristics) on variables of interest—for instance, most of the sample may be White, middle-class, out about their sexual orientation and trans* identities, and with a low degree of internalized homophobia and transphobia. Comparing this large portion of the sample with the handful of subjects who differ makes results on those variables inaccurate (e.g., comparing ninety-seven White subjects to three racial minority subjects on IPV victimization experiences will be inaccurate because those three racial minority subjects may all be men, or homogenous in some other way, and therefore not representative of LGBTQ racial minorities in the population).[135] Even though larger samples are typically more diverse than smaller samples, when nonprobability sampling is used, diversity—and therefore the accuracy of many analyses—tends to suffer.

This might occur in **venue-based sampling,** where the researcher recruits people who happen to be present at an event or organization at the same time that the researcher is there (e.g., selecting anyone the researcher can find in the waiting room of an HIV clinic, people who pass by a table at a gay pride parade, people at an IPV victim shelter, etc.).[136] While technically probability sampling can be performed at venues—for instance, by conducting time-space sampling, a technique that randomly selects venues from a comprehensive listing of local venues and then randomly selects days and times during which the researcher will physically go to the venue to recruit participants[137]—sampling in venues is typically done in a nonprobability manner, where the researcher visits the venue at times that are convenient to them to recruit venue visitors or to ask venue staff to refer potential subjects. Whether performed in a probability or nonprobability manner, the primary limitation of venue-based sampling resides in the venue itself not being representative of the target population. If an LGBTQ-focused organization is sampled, chances of finding LGBTQ people quickly are high—yet the types of people who do not tend to belong to such organizations (e.g., closeted, higher internalized homophobia, biphobia, and transphobia, older, etc.) have a low chance of selection.[138] The same limitation has been noted to exist for sampling from IPV-victim-centric organizations: chances of finding IPV victims are high when sampling from shelters, counseling support groups, emergency rooms, or courts, but victims who do not realize they are being abused, are still with their abusers, or have not sought formal help will largely be absent from those venues.[139] Even in venues that are not traditionally associated with a strictly LGBTQ or IPV victim clientele (e.g., college classrooms), there will inevitably be key differences between the types of people who do and do not frequent such venues, particularly when the venue is in a neighborhood where certain demographic groups dominate (e.g., in the case of a college classroom, diversity regarding age, race, ethnicity, and social class may suffer).[140] Only in rare instances[141] have researchers purposely selected a variety of venue types to try to diversify their samples.

Another common nonprobability sampling technique is **convenience sampling,** in which the researcher makes the minimum effort to locate potential subjects, and no effort is made to increase the representativeness of the sample.[142] A common form of this in LGBTQ IPV studies occurs when the researcher posts advertisements, most often on social media websites or in LGBTQ magazines, with the advertisements recruiting either LGBTQ people or LGBTQ IPV victims.[143] Although arguably the quickest, lowest-cost, and easiest approach to finding the target population, convenience sampling will result in a very unrepresentative sample. For example, whereas venue-based sampling within an LGBTQ-oriented organization will locate a variety of IPV victims—some who are still with their abusers and some who are not, some who have sought help and likely many who have not, and so on—study advertisements recruiting LGBTQ IPV victims will automatically exclude those victims who do not yet realize they are victims and, by extension, will decrease the proportion of the sample that has not sought help or may still be with the abuser. Moreover, if the advertisement is placed on a social media website, those who are less likely to use social media websites or the Internet generally (e.g., poorer, older, etc.) have a lower chance of selection.

Still another popular nonprobability sampling technique is **snowball sampling,** where a researcher asks a few LGBTQ people to recruit LGBTQ people they know to participate in a study.[144] Although often a lengthy process, snowball sampling can be particularly beneficial if the target population is small and difficult to locate (e.g., lesbian-identified mothers who have been victims of IPV). Some researchers suggest that this is a reasonable alternative to venue-based sampling in rural areas where there may be no LGBTQ-oriented organizations or where such organizations are predominantly White and middle-class in membership.[145] At the same time, if only people who personally know each other are recruited, chances are good that subjects will be fairly similar to one another demographically, attitudinally, and so forth. Those who do not share these characteristics have a lower chance of inclusion.

Other Sampling Issues.   There are clear tradeoffs that researchers must contend with. Where probability sampling excels—drawing a representative sample that can produce results that more accurately portray the population—nonprobability is lacking. Yet, where nonprobability sampling excels—drawing a large LGBTQ sample in a relatively quick and cost-effective manner—probability sampling tends to fall short. Unfortunately, there are still other challenges in successfully sampling for studies on LGBTQ IPV.

One issue is that many LGBTQ people do not wish to identify themselves as LGBTQ to researchers, often out of fear that researchers cannot be trusted to protect the identities of subjects.[146] Perhaps evidencing this problem, researchers Stephen Owen and Tod Burke's study of same-gender IPV involved mailing questionnaires to one thousand people on the list of a marketing company that targets sexual minorities, and only *sixty-six* of these (less than 7%) were returned.[147] Not only does this create far more work for the researcher to locate an adequately sized sample of LGBTQ people, but a low **response rate** (the percentage of people a researcher asks to participate in a study who agree to participate) also places doubts on the accuracy of study results. Specifically, it raises the possibility that the few people who agreed to participate are different in a key way from those who did not agree, such as regarding their degree of outness, experiences with IPV, and so forth. Increasing response rates is therefore incredibly important for researchers who wish to claim their samples are highly representative of the LGBTQ population. Researcher Gary Gates suggests that one way to increase response rates is to convince potential subjects that their identities will be kept secret. This is easiest to do when identities are kept **anonymous,** wherein the identities of subjects are not even known to the researchers, such as in some online questionnaire studies or telephone interview studies that use software to randomly dial phone numbers without telling the researcher what number is being called. Conversely, studies that are **confidential,** wherein the identities of subjects are known to researchers who promise to keep the identities secret—such as in-person interview studies or mailed questionnaire studies—leave greater room for potential subjects to fear that their identities may be made public accidentally.[148] Another sampling issue is that it is often easier for researchers to find a large number of LGBTQ people to sample from urban areas, where population density is highest, but, as a consequence, LGBTQ people living in rural areas are greatly understudied.[149]

Last, just as it is challenging to sample LGBTQ people because they make up only a small portion of the global population, it is similarly challenging to sample demographic subgroups *within* LGBTQ communities (e.g., trans* people,[150] racial-ethnic minorities, immigrants, etc.). Without special efforts made to recruit these subgroups, research on LGBTQ IPV risks representing the experiences of only the largest—and consequently often the most privileged—LGBTQ subgroups. This in turn may widen the already sizeable knowledge gap for these subgroups, hindering construction of targeted IPV services and policies. It is therefore imperative that researchers actively work to increase the diversity of LGBTQ research samples. This can be achieved with many of the same techniques recommended in this chapter, such as oversampling smaller LGBTQ subgroups during probability sampling and identifying venues to recruit from and advertise in that are frequented by subgroups.

IMPLICATIONS FOR POLICY, PRACTICE, AND RESEARCH

There are several important lessons that can be drawn from research on LGBTQ IPV study methodology. First and foremost, for policymakers, one of the best ways to impact the future of LGBTQ IPV research is to fund it. At the risk of sounding like a funding drive for a public radio or television station, any amount you pledge helps! (Sorry, no giveaway T-shirts or CDs.) Unfortunately, research is not free. Between offering small financial incentives to hundreds or thousands of subjects, paying the salaries of full-time researchers and assistants, and other inevitable costs, for better or worse, knowledge about human existence is expensive to uncover. Also unfortunately, often the most accurate research-study designs— with large, probability samples—are already costly for HC IPV research, and they tend to be even more costly for LGBTQ IPV research because the population is smaller and more difficult to locate. While there are some nonprofit LGBTQ organizations that offer small research grants, typically the biggest dollars come from government agencies. Government requests for proposals for LGBTQ IPV studies can drastically improve the current landscape of this research literature, which has for the most part had to rely on less expensive, smaller, nonprobability samples. While many nations do not yet offer such funding, others have made important strides recently that suggest that tides may be shifting. For example, in 2011, the U.S. government's National Institutes of Health (NIH) determined that it was important to annually earmark millions of dollars in grants for research on LGBTQ health and violence issues, including IPV.[151] Additionally, governments can ask that trans*-status and sexual-orientation questions be added to their large, nationwide studies of IPV—a small and free change that can make a major impact on the quality of available data on LGBTQ IPV.

For practitioners and others working to address LGBTQ IPV, bear in mind that research is not just for full-time researchers. Any time a new or unproven prevention, intervention, or treatment protocol is used to help victims or abusers, it is important to determine whether goals are actually being reached. Whether designed in-house or with the help of local researchers, evaluation studies can determine how efforts to address IPV can be adjusted for maximal impact—and publishing findings can help spread the word about best practices. Additionally, many mental and medical health-care service providers rely on screening questions to determine if a client or patient has been victimized, and those questionnaires can similarly be improved by using the tips laid out in this chapter.

For those who conduct survey research on LGBTQ IPV, this chapter offers a number of important lessons regarding measuring IPV, defining the population, and sampling the population. When measuring IPV, researchers should be careful to distinguish different crime types (e.g., child abuse, peer victimization, and IPV), balance specificity and sensitivity (with scholars more and more today leaning toward sensitivity to be inclusive of various types of IPV), differentiate the many umbrella forms of IPV and be inclusive of the many IPV tactics, use clear IPV time frames (preferably past year or lifetime, to make a study more readily comparable to the rest of the literature), measure both victimization and perpetration (and narrow measurement to a specific relationship if the researcher wishes to study directionality of abuse), and use IPV measures that are inclusive of unique LGBTQ IPV tactics and that have been validated on LGBTQ samples.

When defining the population to be studied, researchers may wish to consider studying LGBTQ IPV rather than the more narrowly defined same-gender IPV, measuring multiple aspects of being LGBTQ beyond self-identity, measuring not only current LGBTQ identity but also identity at the time of IPV (particularly if assessing IPV over a lifetime period when identity may very well have shifted), measuring not only the subject's identity but also the partner's identity as reported by the subject, and using clear terminology in both sample recruitment advertisements and subsequent publications (such as by avoiding vague terms like *lesbian relationships* and *lesbian IPV*).

Regarding sampling this population, one of the biggest challenges facing the expansion of this literature is that the LGBTQ population is comparatively small and, in turn, LGBTQ IPV is numerically less common than HC IPV. There are countless examples of IPV researchers who, only in analysis, come to realize that they have only a handful of LGBTQ subjects. To avoid drawing inaccurate conclusions about their few LGBTQ subjects and to enhance the clarity with which the rest of the HC IPV data can be interpreted, many researchers opt for jettisoning the LGBTQ subjects from collected data. In other cases, researchers keep data from LGBTQ subjects in a predominantly heterosexual-cisgender sample, but their publications share analyses conducted only on the full sample rather than also separate analyses on LGBTQ IPV. While many researchers may be genuinely more interested in HC IPV, it seems that often the decision to ignore LGBTQ people just comes down to the numbers: there are often too few LGBTQ subjects in studies to accurately draw conclusions about them. The only way to really change this is for IPV researchers to become more proactive in recruiting LGBTQ people. As this chapter discusses, there are several ways to do this. While convenience sampling (e.g., posting targeted advertisements), snowball sampling (e.g., asking that an advertisement be shared by study subjects with others they know), and venue-based sampling (e.g., recruiting from the lobby of an LGBTQ community organization) are efficient ways to boost LGBTQ subject numbers, due to their nonprobability nature they offer the least accurate data. Instead, researchers should consider either probability sampling from a general population—by acquiring a non-LGBTQ-specific sampling frame like a telephone book, randomly selecting people to recruit, asking a screening question to determine LGBTQ status, selecting as many LGBTQ subjects as needed, and applying sampling weights in analysis to preserve representativeness—or quasi-probability sampling from LGBTQ venues—by compiling a comprehensive list of local LGBTQ venues stratified by venue type, randomly selecting venues of each type, and attempting to recruit all or a random sample of members of each selected venue. These same techniques can be beneficial in sampling not only LGBTQ people generally but also LGBTQ demographic subgroups that may be smaller and more difficult to locate.

As Joseph Catania and Ron Stall learned in conducting the *Urban Men's Health Study*, there is no such thing as the perfect study. As neat as it would be, sadly, researchers *cannot* read minds. Still, we can get pretty darn close by improving research designs in small but significant ways. As the quality of information about LGBTQ IPV becomes more accurate, the hope is that the world will be armed with the tools necessary to one day help victims cope, abusers reform, and IPV slowly fade away.

3

___

WHAT IS LGBTQ INTIMATE PARTNER VIOLENCE (IPV)?

She knew about my transgender status. . . . She was happy when she thought I was more like a transvestite, you know, cross-dressing, but as it carried on, she wasn't happy about it. She started threatening to tell my friends about it if I didn't do what she wanted. . . . I trusted her, but she abused that. . . . After we broke up, she went around my friends and told them I was transgender.[1]

Research has shown that abusers can be creative in their methods to control and manipulate their victims. Unfortunately, the social and legal stigma of being LGBTQ can significantly expand the range of abusive tactics at the disposal of their partners. LGBTQ IPV—abuse within a current or former romantic or sexual relationship involving at least one LGBTQ partner—can come in a variety of underlying forms: psychological, physical, and sexual IPV, as well as intimate-partner homicide. These IPV forms can be expressed through a variety of tactics, not all of which are recognized in the criminal statutes of every nation. Frequencies of these tactics in turn can exhibit both similarities and sharp differences across sexual orientations and trans*-cisgender identities. While a number of studies have provided only a single estimate of how many trans* people in the United States[2] and sexual minorities in Australia,[3] Canada,[4] Japan,[5] Latin America,[6] the Netherlands,[7] and the United States[8] experience at least one IPV form, these studies vary substantially in which forms of IPV are included in their estimates, some of these studies do not describe which forms are included, and none of them provide separate estimates for each IPV form. To provide a more nuanced understanding of LGBTQ IPV, this chapter instead focuses on studies that examine the tactics within and frequencies of each form of LGBTQ IPV (psychological, physical, and sexual IPV, along with intimate-partner homicide), as well as data on the relationship context of LGBTQ IPV (its directionality and where and when it occurs) and outcomes for victims.[†]

† Two brief notes about this chapter. First, as reviewed previously, estimates from nonprobability-sampled studies should be viewed as only rough approximations (particularly studies on trans*

PSYCHOLOGICAL LGBTQ IPV

If she said to me, "Where do you want to eat?" and I'd say, "Why don't we go to this restaurant?" and we would go to this restaurant and what would happen is she would find someone there or, god forbid, we would run into someone I knew, or she knew, someone would say hi to us and she would say, "Oh, you wanted to come here because they were here? Oh, you had plans to meet her? You want to fuck him?" And she'd start going on and on, and so I quit saying where we should go, and her behavior, it never quit. There would be some guy sitting at a table and she'd be like, "Oh, you're looking at that guy. What the fuck are you looking at him for?" And then she'd start on the guy, "Oh, you're looking at her? Oh, you want to fuck her?" When I'm eating there and she would just go on and on, and I'd be like, "Max, you're the one who said let's come here, remember?" And it wouldn't matter whose idea it was; nothing I ever said mattered because everything I was in trouble for was made up, you know what I mean? I didn't go there because I wanted to fuck that guy. It was all her shit, so it didn't matter if I said let's go to this restaurant.[9]

Jealousy is often perceived to be a sign of love—as in, *I want to be with you so badly that I have to make sure you don't cheat on me or do anything to jeopardize this relationship.* While the internal emotion may not be inherently harmful, whenever jealousy is expressed verbally or through external actions like stalking, it has the potential to generate control over the victim. As Ronna, a lesbian in the United States, vividly illustrates in her story above, abusers can use jealousy as a seemingly legitimate excuse to silence their victims, make them feel inadequate, push them to do what the abuser wants, and create a sense of apprehension and fear about everyday acts—even an act as seemingly simple as going out to dinner. Soon after the restaurant incident, Ronna began cutting off ties with male friends.[10] Whether abusers use jealousy or another rationale to try to legitimize their actions, it is clear that abuse does not need to be physical or sexual to severely curtail the freedom and emotional well-being of victims. Toni, a woman who was an IPV victim in a "lesbian relationship" in Australia, recognizes the public perception of physical IPV as *real* abuse, but she knows from personal experience that other forms of abuse can be just as terrifying: "There's specific incidents of physical abuse like that people would identify, I suppose, as violence. To me probably—although they were horrific, they weren't the most difficult. It was the psychological abuse that I

---

populations where subsample sizes can be very small). Second, for ease of interpretation, prevalence rates are categorized by sexual minority men, sexual minority women, and trans* individuals of any sexual orientation. Bear in mind, though, that studies vary extensively in how they define sexual minority populations—by either sexual orientation self-identity, history of sexual activities with a given gender, history of relationships with a given gender, gender of the IPV perpetrator, or sometimes various combinations of these—and in which relationships they assess IPV—relationships with partners either of any gender or of only the same gender. In cases where researchers report rates by sexual orientation rather than the gender of sexual minorities, the same is done here.

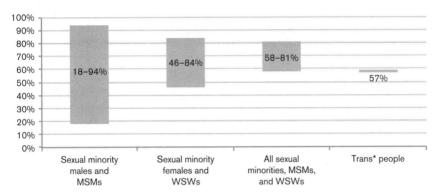

FIGURE 2. Range of adult psychological LGBTQ IPV lifetime victimization prevalence.

found really hard—just the name-calling, and—not just. It's the name-calling and the total indifference towards the situations I was experiencing in my life."[11]

Unfortunately, research spanning Australia, Canada, China, the United Kingdom, and the United States has found psychological LGBTQ IPV—nonphysical, nonsexual abuse, often termed "emotional" abuse—to be incredibly prevalent.

Victimization Prevalence

Research on psychological IPV among trans* people is relatively scarce. According to two studies on U.S. nonprobability samples, 59% of trans* adolescents have experienced psychological IPV in the past year,[12] and 57% of trans* adults experience it in their lifetimes.[13] (See figure 2.)

By comparison, significantly more research has been conducted on psychological IPV among sexual minorities, with results pointing to a high risk for victimization. Among adults, studies not distinguishing findings by gender identity have found that lifetime victimization prevalence estimates range from 58% to 81% among sexual minorities and people who have sex or relationships with those of the same gender.[14] Meanwhile, other studies have found that 18–94% of adult sexual minority men and MSMs[15] as well as 46–84% of adult sexual minority women and WSWs[16] have experienced psychological IPV. (See figure 2.) This range of rates for sexual minority women in particular is comparable to the mean lifetime psychological IPV victimization rate (43%) found in a meta-analysis of fourteen studies.[17] Understandably, victimization rates among adults have typically been found to be lower in the handful of studies examining IPV in the past five years,[18] past year,[19] or current relationship[20] instead of in the subject's lifetime. Several studies, all in the United States, have also examined psychological IPV victimization among sexual minority youths. Findings reveal that psychological IPV is experienced during an unspecified time frame by approximately 16% of college students currently in a same-gender relationship,[21] in the past year by 68% of female sexual minority college students,[22] in the past eighteen months by 21% of middle and high school students who had recently had a same-gender relationship,[23] and in the past year by 17–59% of sexual minority–identified middle and high school students.[24]

While there is a fair amount of variation in victimization rates across these studies, one way to identify a "best guess" of prevalence is to focus on those using probability sampling with a national population, where results should be most accurate. Two such studies exist, one in Canada and the other in the United States. According to analyses of the 2004 Canadian *General Social Survey* (GSS), approximately 27–47% of sexual minorities ever involved in a marital or common-law relationship had experienced psychological IPV in the past five years,[25] and analyses of the aforementioned 2010 NISVS found lifetime victimization rates of 63–76% for sexual minority men and 53–60% for sexual minority women in the United States.[26]

Moving beyond assessing the percentage of people experiencing at least one of a multitude of different psychological IPV tactics, a number of studies have also examined the prevalence for distinct types of psychological IPV tactics, drawing on samples from Australia, Canada, China, Scotland, the United Kingdom, and the United States. While some tactic-specific studies have assessed rates over less common time frames (like the past five years[27]) or only for a sample of all sexual minority IPV victims (where population-based prevalence rates cannot be calculated[28]) or all same-gender stalking victims,[29] most tactic-specific studies have focused on victimization over the life span of subjects. Taken together, these studies paint a clear picture that psychological IPV tactics are highly prevalent among LGBTQ people. (See table 2.) These tactics can include the following:

Closeting: Forcing a victim to hide their trans* or sexual minority status from others by demanding that the victim remain closeted about their status or hide potentially visible indicators of their status. (Only prevalence rates of forcing a sexual minority victim to "act straight" have thus far been empirically assessed.)

Financial abuse: Efforts by an abuser to influence a victim by controlling the victim's financial resources or to pressure a victim into financially supporting the abuser's needs or interests.

Isolation behaviors: Behaviors that have the potential to limit the victim's contact with people like friends (including but not limited to local LGBTQ communities), family, and ex-partners. (This has been measured both as an outcome of any IPV victimization and as a set of specific isolation tactics such as directly asking victims to limit such contact or indirectly implying this through jealous comments and accusations. Not surprisingly, abusers in same-gender relationships appear more likely to try to isolate their victims from same-gender friends than different-gender friends.[30])

Monitoring and stalking behaviors: Following the victim or showing up where the victim is believed to be, asking where and with whom the victim is going, and checking the victim's phone logs, text messages, email messages, web browser history, and social media accounts. (Often researchers collectively label isolation, monitoring, and stalking behaviors as "controlling" IPV tactics, due to their potential to generate direct control over the victim's movements.)

Outing: The opposite of closeting. Outing a victim's trans* or sexual minority status to others, either directly by telling people or indirectly by forcing the victim to show public signs of affection like hand holding or kissing. (Only prevalence rates of forced displays of public affection have thus far been empirically assessed.)

Threats: Threats to out the victim's trans* or sexual minority status, threats against the victim or victim's family, and threats of self-harm or suicide.

Use of children: Making the victim feel guilty about the (victim's or abuser's) children, harming or threatening to harm the children, taking or threatening to take the children, or persuading the victim's "ex-spouse" to try to take the children.

Verbal abuse: Verbal slurs, making the victim feel inferior or inadequate, and embarrassing the victim.

Research has just begun to explore a variety of other psychological IPV tactics that LGBTQ people may experience. For instance, as with HC IPV, studies suggest that LGBTQ IPV abusers may use the marginalized social statuses of victims to control or shame them (sometimes termed "identity abuse"), including regarding victims who have a disability[31] as well as victims who are racial or ethnic minorities,[32] aboriginals,[33] immigrants,[34] elderly,[35] or HIV positive.[36] Additionally, limited evidence exists of LGBTQ people experiencing property damage,[37] emotional neglect,[38] having negative rumors spread about them (including misinformation that the victim is abusive),[39] and being forced to get high or drunk[40] by an intimate partner. One U.S.-based study of middle and high school students examined another greatly understudied set of psychological IPV tactics that involve the use of the Internet: cyber IPV. Cyber IPV might include an abuser sending unwanted sexual photos of the abuser to the victim, an abuser pressuring the victim to send sexual photos of themselves, an abuser sending threatening text messages, or an abuser using the victim's social media account without consent. In this study, it was found that cyber IPV was more likely to be experienced in the previous year by trans* students than cisgender female and male students (56%, 29%, and 23%, respectively), and likewise that it was more likely to be experienced by sexual minority than heterosexual students (37% and 26%).[41]

TABLE 2 Range of adult psychological LGBTQ IPV lifetime victimization prevalence, by tactics

	Sexual minority males and MSMs	Sexual minority females and WSWs	Sexual minorities, MSMs, and WSWs	Trans* people
Closeting				
Forcing to "act straight"	19%[1]	—	—	—
Financial abuse	3–37%[2]	46%[3]	7–18%[4]	57%[5]
Isolation				
Due to any IPV	2–48%[6]	9–54%[8]	12%[10]	43–63%[12]
Due to directly preventing contact	14%[7]	20%[9]	20–31%[11]	15%[13]
Monitoring/stalking	10–49%[14]	8–66%[15]	31%[16]	38–42%[17]
Monitoring/stalking or isolation (i.e., "controlling" IPV)	26–83%[18]	23–56%[19]	—	60%[20]
Outing	—	—	12%[21]	—
Forcing to show affection in public				
Threats				
to out trans* status	—	—		13%[31]
to out LGB status	7–13%[22]	4–29%[25]	4–17%[28]	—
of harm	29%[23]	46–53%[26]	8%[29]	35%[32]
of self-harm/suicide	23%[24]	45–53%[27]	22%[30]	
Use of children (% of parents)	5%[33]	13%[34]	—	28%[35]
Verbal abuse	18–82%[36]	13–89%[37]	45–48%[38]	57–79%[39]

[1] Rowlands, Domestic Abuse among Gay.

[2] Siemieniuk et al., "Prevalence, clinical associations"; Turell, "Descriptive analysis."

[3] Turell, "Descriptive analysis."

[4] Farrell and Cerise, "Fair's fair"; Leonard et al., Coming Forward.

[5] Turell, "Descriptive analysis."

[6] Henderson, "Prevalence of domestic violence"; Pitts et al., Private Lives; Siemieniuk et al., "Prevalence, clinical associations."

[7] Guasp, Gay and Bisexual Men's.

[8] Henderson, "Prevalence of domestic violence"; Pitts et al., Private Lives

[9] Hunt and Fish, "Prescription for change."

[10] Leonard et al., Coming Forward.

11. Farrell and Cerise, "Fair's fair"; Hellemans et al., "Intimate partner violence victimization"; Mak, Chong, and Kwong, "Prevalence in Hong Kong."

12. Pitts et al., *Private Lives*; Roch, Ritchie, and Morton, "Out of sight."

13. Roch, Ritchie, and Morton, "Out of sight."

14. Henderson, "Prevalence of domestic violence"; Pitts et al., Private Lives; Walters, Chen, and Breiding, *National Intimate Partner Survey*; Williams et al., "Relation of childhood sexual."

15. Henderson, "Prevalence of domestic violence"; Pitts et al., Private Lives; Walters, Chen, and Breiding, *National Intimate Partner Survey*.

16. Hellemans et al., "Intimate partner violence victimization."

17. Pitts et al., *Private Lives*.

18. Freedner et al., "Dating violence"; Messinger, "Invisible victims"; Yu, Xiao, and Liu, "Dating violence among gay."

19. Freedner et al., "Dating violence"; Messinger, "Invisible victims."

20. Roch, Ritchie, and Morton, "Out of sight."

21. Mak, Chong, and Kwong, "Prevalence in Hong Kong."

22. Freedner et al., "Dating violence"; Rowlands, Domestic abuse among gay; Turell, "Descriptive analysis"; Yu, Xiao, and Liu, "Dating violence among gay."

23. Walters, Chen, and Breiding, *National Intimate Partner Survey*.

24. Walters, Chen, and Breiding, *National Intimate Partner Survey*.

25. Freedner et al., "Dating violence."

26. Walters, Chen, and Breiding, *National Intimate Partner Survey*.

27. Walters, Chen, and Breiding, *National Intimate Partner Survey*.

28. Farrell and Cerise, "Fair's fair"; Mak, Chong, and Kwong, "Prevalence in Hong Kong."

29. Hellemans et al., "Intimate partner violence victimization."

30. Turell, "Descriptive analysis."

31. Roch, Ritchie, and Morton, "Out of sight."

32. Landers and Gilsanz, "Health of lesbian, gay."

33. Turell, "Descriptive analysis."

34. Turell, "Descriptive analysis."

35. Turell, "Descriptive analysis."

36. Guasp, Gay and bisexual men's; Henderson, "Prevalence of domestic violence"; Messinger, "Invisible victims"; Pitts et al., *Private Lives*; Turell, "Descriptive analysis"; Walters, Chen, and Breiding, *National Intimate Partner Survey*.

37. Henderson, "Prevalence of domestic violence"; Hunt and Fish, "Prescription for change"; Messinger, "Invisible victims"; Pitts et al., *Private Lives*; Turell, "Descriptive analysis"; Walters, Chen, and Breiding, *National Intimate Partner Survey*.

38. Farrell and Cerise, "Fair's fair"; Hellemans et al., "Intimate partner violence victimization."

39. Pitts et al., Private Lives; Turell, "Descriptive analysis."

LGBTQ-Specific IPV Tactics

Despite many similarities with the experiences of heterosexual-cisgender victims, LGBTQ victims often experience psychological IPV in unique ways. Among trans* people, studies suggest that anywhere from 16% to 73% have experienced a form of psychological IPV that takes advantage of the victim's trans* status.[42] Such "anti-trans*" psychological IPV tactics focus on preventing victims from expressing their gender identity. Examples include the following:

- Accusing a trans* victim of not being trans*, male, or female enough, or not being a "real" trans*, male, or female person.[43]
- Outing or threatening to out a victim's trans* status to others.[44]
- Making victims feel ashamed of their trans* status or gender identity (such as by drawing attention to body parts that make the victim feel uncomfortable, not using the victim's preferred name or gendered pronouns, or preventing the victim from telling others about the victim's trans* status or gender identity).[45]
- Stopping victims from maintaining their preferred gendered appearance (such as through demanding that victims present their gendered appearance in a certain way or through destroying clothing and other gendered accessories).[46]
- Stopping victims from taking medication or having medical treatment needed to express their gender identity (such as by withdrawing or withholding financial support for such medical treatment or demanding repayment through illegal work).[47]

Largely anecdotal evidence also suggests that trans* abusers can leverage their trans* status to psychologically abuse their victims, through a variety of tactics:

- Demanding or stealing a substantial portion of the victim's financial resources to pay for gendered clothing and grooming (or by claiming the victim is "not being supportive" when they ask to discuss transition timing or expenses).[48]
- Making cisgender victims feel ashamed of their cisgender status (such as by using *cisgender* as an insult, belittling cisgender people for often self-limiting their gender identities and expression to a male-female binary, or claiming they make a more attractive man or woman than the cisgender victim).[49]
- Threatening suicide while reminding the victim of how many trans* people commit suicide (perhaps either to make the threat appear more credible or to trick victims into believing they are transphobic or at fault in some way for the abuser's suicidality).[50]

This would all suggest that trans* status can be used by and against trans* partners to leverage power in intimate relationships.

Just as trans* status can shape psychological IPV tactics, so too can sexual minority status. Some research finds that upward of 9% of sexual minorities would self-describe themselves as having experienced anti–sexual minority psychological IPV,[51] although these estimates may be artificially low due to researchers' not providing specific tactic examples for subjects to consider. (For instance, other studies focusing on specific tactics found that 19% of sexual minorities had a partner question whether they were a "real" lesbian, gay, or bisexual person,[52] and up to 29% of sexual minority women and 13% of sexual minority men have had a partner threaten to out their sexual minority status to others.[53] This would suggest that far more than 9% of sexual minorities have experienced anti–sexual minority psychological IPV.) Taking many forms, anti–sexual minority psychological IPV tactics can often include the following:

· Accusing a sexual minority victim of not being lesbian, gay, or bisexual enough or not being a "real" sexual minority (e.g., claiming a lesbian victim wants to have sex with men).[54]
· Telling bisexual victims that they should be gay/lesbian instead (e.g., telling a bisexual female partner that all men are oppressive and that they should therefore be lesbian instead).[55]
· Outing or threatening to out a victim's sexual minority status to others.[56]
· Forcing a sexual minority victim to remain closeted or hide potentially visible indicators of their identity.[57]
· Making victims feel ashamed of their sexual minority status (such as by telling a sexual minority victim that they deserve what they get because they are a sexual minority).[58]
· Accusing a sexual minority victim of making the abuser a sexual minority.[59]

Although considerably less research has examined the ways in which abusers can leverage their own sexual minority status to perpetrate psychological IPV, some studies have found that sexual minority abusers who are closeted may tell their same-gender victims to not mention their relationship to anyone or may even tell victims to remain closeted themselves and not interact with sexual minority peers, all with the justification that failing to do so may result in outing the abuser's sexual orientation.[60] Whether intentional or not, silencing victims about their relationship and sexual orientation can have an isolating effect on them if and when they decide to seek help.

Who Is at Greatest Risk?

Because research on psychological IPV among trans* people is limited, it is difficult to determine how risk might differ among this population. According to one Australian study of one hundred trans* people, though, female-identified trans* people (i.e., trans* women) were more likely to experience this than male-identified trans* people (i.e., trans* men). More specifically, trans* women were more likely than trans* men to experience financial abuse (33% and 14%, respectively), isolation behaviors (63% and 43%), monitoring or stalking behaviors (42% and 38%), and verbal abuse (79% and 57%).[61] Additionally, the few IPV studies comparing trans* with cisgender people have found mixed results: one study suggested that trans* people are at a lower risk relative to both male and female cisgender people,[62] two studies found trans* people to be at a higher risk than both male and female cisgender people,[63] and still another study found that trans* women were at a higher risk and trans* men were at a lower risk than both male and female cisgender people.[64] In the absence of additional research, it is not yet possible to discern whether risk of psychological IPV differs among trans* people by age, race, ethnicity, or nationality.

Turning to sexual minorities, while several nonprobability-sampled studies find similar psychological IPV victimization rates for sexual minorities and heterosexuals,[65] it is noteworthy that every probability-sampled study to compare these populations finds sexual minorities to be at a greater risk than heterosexuals.[66] Additionally, rates in probability-sampled studies[67] generally find bisexual people (particularly women) to be at the highest risk of psychological IPV, with gay men and lesbian women at a similar but lower risk. Similarly, two nonprobability-sampled studies found that sexual minority women are at greater risk than sexual minority men.[68] Regarding stalking, one nonprobability-sampled study in Belgium found that, among ex-partners being stalked by their abusers, the specific forms of stalking experienced differed between same- and different-gender victims. In particular, same-gender IPV victims were more likely to receive unwanted messages of affection, receive threatening objects, and have the lives of people close to them intruded upon by the abuser, but they were less likely than different-gender IPV victims to experience "regulatory harassment" (i.e., efforts to complicate the lives of the victim through technological or legal means such as identity theft or calling the police on the victim).[69]

Little research has examined racial and ethnic differences in psychological sexual minority IPV victimization rates, which is particularly problematic given that many studies skew toward a predominantly White sample. The few studies that do touch upon this subject have all emerged from the United States, typically focusing on a single racial or ethnic group. For instance, research in the United States suggests that 33–45% of Latino[70] and 28–41% of Black[71] sexual minority men and MSMs experience this in their lifetimes, 78% of MSMs of Asian or Pacific Islander descent have experienced this within the past five years,[72] and approximately half of Puerto Rican sexual minorities have experienced this during an unspecified time period.[73] Potentially much more telling is the only study to have compared rates of racial and ethnic groups, which found that rates do not differ significantly in the United States among African-Americans, Latinos, and Whites in a nonprobability sample of MSMs in Los Angeles.[74] Whether this finding extends to other sexual minority groups, other cities, rural areas, and other nations remains to be seen.

Even less is known about the influence of aging on psychological IPV among sexual minorities. Due in part to study differences in IPV time frames (e.g., lifetime versus past twelve or eighteen months) between studies on adults and those on youths, it is difficult at this time to determine whether psychological IPV victimization risk changes as sexual minorities age. Moreover, psychological LGBTQ IPV research on the elderly appears to be nonexistent.

Despite seemingly ample data, it is also unclear whether rates among sexual minorities differ between nations. Because there are no multinational studies of psychological IPV available, rates between different studies must be compared. This can be problematic when studies use significantly different methodology (e.g., differences in population type, sampling, IPV tactics, time frames assessed, etc.), making it impossible to know whether rate differences exist in the real world or are artifacts of how the studies were designed. That said, it is possible to identify the most accurate rates available in a given nation, which will come from studies with national probability samples (thus far conducted only in Canada and the United States) and from large, geographically diverse nonprobability-sampled studies in other nations, excluding studies (such as the Canadian GSS) limited to marital or cohabiting relationships. It appears that sexual minority lifetime psychological IPV victimization rates may indeed differ between Australia (34–78%[75]), Belgium (58%[76]), Canada (94%[77]), China (34–81%[78]), and the United States (45–69%[79]). The best available information from the United Kingdom is particularly difficult to compare with that of other nations because of how psychological IPV was defined: the researchers required subjects to meet a certain threshold of IPV frequency and impact to be counted as a victim, undoubtedly contributing to this being the lowest rate out of all assessed nations.[80]

PHYSICAL LGBTQ IPV

She was charm on a stick. And that night we went to a party with fifty people. She'd been lovely all night and from nowhere I just heard her voice go "You fucking cunt, you fucking cocksucker." And the next thing my tea's all over me. Explosion! I left that venue, sneaking in the bushes, getting a taxi.[81]

Physical abuse in the relationships of LGBTQ people is not just physically painful. As the story above of a lesbian victim highlights, when Betty's same-gender abuser threw scalding hot water at her, Betty was simultaneously being blamed and verbally abused by her partner in public. Nonfatal physical IPV—such as a victim having objects thrown at them, being purposely burned, having their hair pulled or arm twisted, being strangled, slapped, punched, scratched, bit, kicked, thrown against walls or objects, held down, or attacked with weapons—generates additional embarrassment, shame, fear, and control, particularly when it occurs in the context of a relationship that is already abusive in other ways. While many victims do fight back, doing so poses risks of further harm to victims, and many victims are too afraid, in shock, or ashamed to resist. When the attacker is a loved one, victims often want to understand and accept the motivations of the abuser, find fault in themselves, and hesitate in fighting back if it means hurting someone they care about. Unfortunately, research spanning Australia, Brazil, Canada, China, South Africa, the United Kingdom, and the United States has found nonfatal physical IPV to be highly prevalent, if to a slightly lesser degree than psychological IPV.

Victimization Prevalence

Research on physical IPV among trans* people is limited. Findings from four studies spanning Australia, Scotland, and the United States indicate that 43–46% of trans* adults experience physical IPV in their lifetimes.[82] (See figure 3.) Rates are also available from a handful of studies using a past-twelve-month time frame,[83] as well as one study distinguishing victimization by primary and casual partners.[84] One of the larger albeit nonprobability studies thus far on trans* populations in the United States found that 33% of trans*-identified people have experienced either physical or sexual IPV in their lifetimes.[85]

Much more research has been conducted on physical IPV among sexual minorities, with studies noting a high victimization risk. Among adults, studies not distinguishing findings by gender identity have found that victimization is experienced in the lifetimes of 7–40% of sexual minorities and people who have sex or relationships with those of the same gender.[86] Other studies have found that 16–48% of adult sexual minority men and MSMs[87] as well as 12–58% of adult sexual minority women and WSWs[88] have experienced this in their lifetimes. (See figure 3.) This range of rates for sexual minority women in particular is somewhat comparable to the mean lifetime physical IPV victimization rate (18%) found in a meta-analysis of fourteen studies.[89] (Rates are also available in a handful of studies with samples of sexual minority victims rather than all sexual minorities,[90] as well as in studies using different IPV time frames, like during the current relationship;[91] the previous four months,[92] twelve months,[93] or five years;[94] lifetime minus any relationships prior to being 16 years of age;[95] or lifetime minus the current relationship.[96]) A substantial number of studies, all using U.S. samples, have also examined physical IPV victimization among sexual minority youths. Among college- and graduate school–aged sexual minority young adults, physical IPV has been experienced in the lifetimes of 14–25%,[97] in the past year of 20–54%,[98] in the past six months of 30%,[99] and during an unspecified time period by 20%.[100] Among middle and high school–aged sexual minority youths, physical IPV has been experienced in the lifetimes of 10–15%,[101] in the past eighteen months of 11%,[102] and in the past year by 12–43% of sexual minority–identified middle and high school students.[103]

Given the broad range of victimization rates across these studies, it may be useful to highlight the results from studies using national probability samples, where

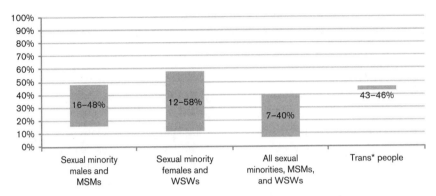

FIGURE 3. Range of adult physical LGBTQ IPV lifetime victimization prevalence.

results should be particularly accurate. Three such studies exist, one in Canada and two in the United States. According to analyses of the 2004 Canadian GSS, at least 16% of sexual minorities had experienced physical IPV in the past five years.[104] Meanwhile, in the United States, physical IPV was found to have been experienced in the lifetimes of 24–55% of self-identified sexual minorities (according to the 2010 NISVS)[105] and in the lifetimes of 31% of people who have had at least one same-gender cohabiting relationship (according to the 1996 *National Violence Against Women Survey,* or NVAWS).[106] Prevalence differences between these Canadian and U.S. studies may be explained in part by the different IPV time frames (past five years for the former study, lifetime for the latter two studies).

LGBTQ-Specific IPV Tactics

To the extent that research has explored it, the types of physical IPV tactics being experienced by LGBTQ people do not appear to leverage their LGBTQ identities (sometimes considered a form of "identity abuse"), with one important exception. Limited research indicates that some abusers of trans* victims have used physical violence against victim body parts that society imbues with gendered meaning, such as genitals and breasts.[107] When viewed in the context of other studies finding that trans* victims have been called "it" by abusers and told not to disclose their trans* status to anyone,[108] physical violence against gendered body parts could be seen as part of a larger mission by some abusers to humiliate and gain power over trans* victims specifically because they are trans*.

Who Is at Greatest Risk?

Due to the limited number of studies on physical IPV among trans* people, it is difficult to determine how risk might differ among this population. That said, according to an Australian study of one hundred trans* people, trans* women and trans* men are almost equally likely to experience physical IPV (46% and 43% in their lifetimes, respectively), although, as one measure of severity, trans* women are far more likely to be physically injured (42% as compared with 29% for trans* men).[109] By comparison, one study using a narrower, past-year time frame found trans* women to be exactly twice as likely as trans* men to experience this.[110] Additionally, of the few IPV studies comparing trans* with cisgender people, results have been mixed: one study indicated that trans* people are at a lower risk relative to both male and female cisgender people,[111] another study instead concluded that trans* people are at a higher risk than both male and female cisgender people[112] (supported by a different study finding that IPV victims are more likely to have experienced physical abuse if trans* than if cisgender[113]), and a final study found that trans* women and men were both at greater risk than cisgender women, while only trans* women were at greater risk than cisgender men.[114] Regarding racial and ethnic differences in victimization risk, only one study has examined this issue among trans* people. According to analyses of a U.S.-based sample of 573 trans* women with a history of sex work, physical IPV rates were highest among White respondents, followed by African-Americans, Latinas, and Asian and Pacific Islanders.[115] Until further research is conducted, it is currently not feasible to discern whether risk might also differ among trans* people by age or nationality.

Regarding sexual minorities, with the exception of analyses on one probability-sampled study that found similar physical IPV victimization rates for sexual minorities and heterosexuals,[116] every other study (both those with nonprobability[117] and probability samples[118]) concludes that sexual minorities are at an elevated risk of physical IPV victimization relative to heterosexuals. Among sexual minorities, with the exception of one large but nonprobability study from the United Kingdom,[119] several national probability studies[120] and nonprobability studies[121] from the United States and one nonprobability study from Australia[122] concur that sexual minority women are at greater risk than sexual minority men. Rates broken down by sexual-orientation identity are largely unavailable outside of studies with U.S.-based samples. In the United States, several studies have consistently found bisexual women to be at the greatest risk of any sexual orientation–gender group, including other sexual minority men and women and heterosexual men and women.[123] Regarding bisexual men in the United States, despite some mixed findings[124] (such as those from the 1996 NVAWS showing behaviorally bisexual men to be at greater risk than behaviorally heterosexual men but not behaviorally gay men[125]), the most accurate studies available—two recent nationally representative probability-sampled studies, one on adults[126] and the other on young adults[127]—conclude that self-identified bisexual men are at higher risk of physical IPV victimization than self-identified gay and heterosexual men.[128] Additionally, the only non-U.S. study to assess rates among bisexuals (albeit behaviorally defined rather than self-identified bisexuals) confirms that bisexual men are at an elevated risk, finding that behaviorally bisexual men (i.e., MSMW) are more likely than behaviorally heterosexual men (i.e., MSW) to experience physical IPV in South Africa.[129] In sum, sexual minorities are at a higher risk than heterosexuals, and, among sexual minorities, women and most especially bisexuals are at the greatest risk of experiencing physical IPV.

While many LGBTQ IPV studies rely on racially and ethnically homogenous samples, some studies (all in the United States) have drawn on a sample of a single racial or ethnic minority group. Findings include physical IPV being experienced in the United States by 33–35% of Latino[130] and 27–28% of Black[131] MSMs in their lifetimes, 63% of Asian American MSMs in the past five years,[132] and 26% of Puerto Rican sexual minority males[133] and 7–13% of all sexual minority Puerto Ricans[134] during an unspecified time period. Outside the United States, estimates on racial-ethnic subgroups are largely nonexistent. Just as important, since methodological differences can sometimes explain why rates differ between studies, it is unfortunate that there are few studies that have directly compared prevalence rates among racial and ethnic groups. Among the only such studies, one on MSMs in the United States found no statistically significant difference in physical IPV prevalence between White (26%), Latino (22%), and African-American subjects (21%), whereas a study of MSMs in South Africa found that racial-ethnic minorities were more likely to experience physical IPV.[135] Whether these distinct findings are due to actual national differences or are artifacts of methodological differences is unclear, just as it remains to be seen whether racial-ethnic minorities are at lesser or greater risk than, or at the same risk as, dominant groups among other sexual-orientation groups and in other nations.

The only multinational study of physical LGBTQ IPV focused on a nonprobability sample of over two thousand sexual minority–identified MSMs residing in six nations. Past-year physical IPV victimization rates were relatively consistent (6–12%), with the highest rates found in South Africa (12%), Australia (9%), and the United Kingdom (9%) and the lowest rates found in the United States (6%), Brazil (7%), and Canada (7%).[136] The utility of these findings is tempered of course by the use of nonprobability sampling and an all-male sample. Unfortunately, beyond this study, all other nation-specific prevalence rates come from separate studies (most using nonprobability sampling), thereby generating doubt as to whether rate differences are real or are artifacts of different study methodologies. That said, based on the most accurate information available on sexual minorities in each nation, lifetime physical IPV victimization rates appear to vary slightly between Australia (17–48%[137]), Belgium (15%[138]), Canada (16%[139]), China (24–40%[140]), South Africa (26%[141]), the United Kingdom (12–20%[142]), and the United States (25–57%[143]).

SEXUAL LGBTQ IPV

She was very controlling as far as sexually. She had to always be the one to initiate and it was when she wanted. That's when we would have sex. After the physical abuse started happening she wouldn't take no for an answer. And typically it was after there had been—like after she had hit me. At first she would just bitch and bitch and bitch until I finally was like okay, whatever, and I'd just lay there and whatever. But towards the end of our relationship, which it was five years, towards the end of the relationship there—she would physically force me to have sex. She would rape me. And I think that happened probably two or three times towards the end of our relationship.[144]

Susan, a lesbian woman who had been abused by a female partner, describes here what she sees as the dividing line between "rape" and all other nonconsensual sex: *the use of physical force.* In addition to experiencing forced sex (or what she terms "rape"), Susan had also experienced sexual intercourse without giving consent (i.e., verbal or clear nonverbal agreement to proceed). For instance, there were times when her abuser would verbally harass her into sex (e.g., "She wouldn't take no for an answer," "She would just bitch and bitch and bitch until I finally was like okay, whatever"), and there were times she would physically abuse her immediately prior to but not during sex, possibly as a means to weaken any potential resistance by Susan.[145] Susan is of course not alone in assuming that such coerced sex is not rape: many nations and jurisdictions similarly define rape in their criminal laws as only sexual penetration involving either force, threat of force, or the inability to resist (such as being heavily under the influence of alcohol or other drugs, or being so young as to be deemed by society as legally not able to consent to and understand the ramifications of sex with an adult).[146]

The limitation of such definitions of rape, of course, is that they devalue the seriousness of all other nonconsensual sex. Indeed, studies in some nations have found that many victims do not resist nonconsensual sex (instead freezing up or, as Susan says, "just lay[ing] there"), often out of fear of what is about to happen and a sense that they cannot escape.[147] Despite the absence of force, nonconsensual, coerced intercourse can still have extremely negative effects on victims.[148]

With this in mind, sexual LGBTQ IPV can be viewed as a broad spectrum of sexual acts that a victim is asked to engage in under heavy influence of substances, is forced into, or is coerced into. Although researchers typically focus only on attempted and completed forced sexual penetration (whether with a penis or other object), a host of other, less commonly researched sexual acts can similarly become sexual IPV when attempted through coercion, heavy substance use, or force, such as sexual touching,[149] sending or receiving nude photos of either partner,[150] controlling the use of condoms or dental dams,[151] or purposely giving a partner a sexually transmitted infection. While less common than both psychological and physical LGBTQ IPV, sexual LGBTQ IPV, research tells us, nonetheless happens at an alarming rate.

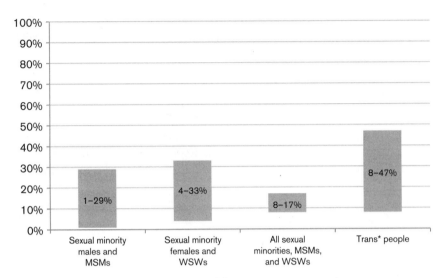

FIGURE 4. Range of adult sexual LGBTQ IPV lifetime victimization prevalence.

Victimization Prevalence

For better or worse, in comparison to the dearth of studies addressing sexual coercion, the relative wealth of data on sexual penetration through force or through substance-based incapacitation provides the clearest picture of how often sexual LGBTQ IPV occurs. It is therefore these forms of sexual LGBTQ IPV—forced and substance-facilitated—that this section refers to.

Only a handful of studies have examined sexual IPV among trans* people. Four studies spanning Australia, Scotland, and the United States find that 8–47% of trans* adults experience sexual IPV in their lifetimes.[152] (See figure 4.) (An additional study of lifetime rates is less directly comparable due to distinguishing victimization by primary and casual partners.[153]) Notably higher rates were found in a U.S. study, which concluded that 61% of trans* adolescents have experienced sexual IPV in just the past year.[154] One possible explanation for this discrepancy is the relatively small number of trans* subjects (n = 18) in that particular study. One of the larger albeit nonprobability studies thus far on trans* populations in the United States found that 33% of trans*-identified people have experienced either sexual or physical IPV in their lifetimes.[155]

The considerably deeper research literature on sexual minorities highlights a similarly high victimization risk. Among adults, while two studies both have suggested that only 8% of all sexual minorities and people who have sex with those of the same gender have experienced sexual IPV in their lifetimes,[156] a third found that 17% experienced this in their lifetimes.[157] Higher estimates have also been found in a large number of studies that examine men and women separately. Specifically, 1–29% of adult sexual minority men and MSMs[158] as well as 4–33% of adult sexual minority women and WSWs[159] have experienced sexual IPV in their lifetimes. (See figure 4.) This range of rates for sexual minority women in particular is comparable to the mean lifetime physical IPV victimization rate (14%) found in a meta-analysis of fourteen studies.[160] (Rates are also available from several studies with samples of sexual minority IPV victims[161] and sexual minority sexual-assault victims[162] rather than all sexual minorities, studies with samples of sexual assault victims regardless of perpetrator type,[163] and studies using time frames other than lifetime [such as in the most recent relationship],[164] all but the most recent relationship,[165] the previous twelve months[166] or five years,[167] or lifetime minus any relationships prior to being 16 years of age.[168]) A number of studies, all from the United States, have estimated sexual IPV victimization prevalence among sexual minority youths. Among college- and graduate school–aged sexual minority young adults, sexual IPV has been experienced in the lifetimes of 6–43%,[169] in the past year by 13–35%,[170] and during an unspecified time period by 14%.[171] Among middle and high school–aged sexual minority youths, sexual IPV has been experienced in the lifetimes of 14–22%[172] and in the past year of 20–23% of sexual minority–identified middle and high school students.[173]

One way of sifting through these broad ranges to identify what may be the most accurate estimates is to examine national probability samples. Unfortunately, all such studies to date have been in the United States. According to the 2010 NISVS, sexual IPV is experienced in the lifetimes of 22% of bisexual women, but prevalence was too low to be accurately estimated for all other sexual minority groups.[174] When considerably narrowing the definition of a sexual minority person to one who has had cohabiting relationships with a person of the same gender, analysis of the 1996 NVAWS found that approximately 8% of these behavioral sexual minorities experience sexual IPV in their lifetimes.[175] Each of these estimates is limited in its own ways, and they provide little insight on rates in other nations.

LGBTQ-Specific IPV Tactics

Research on unique forms of sexual IPV has been largely absent with regards to sexual minority victims, although limited evidence indicates that some sexual minority IPV abusers may use a victim's bisexual identity (and its link with a stereotype of hypersexuality) as a justification for rape.[176] Additionally, scholars indicate that trans* victims often do experience sexual IPV in unique ways. One study in Scotland suggests that 6% of trans* people experience "transphobic sexual abuse" in an intimate relationship,[177] what some might label as subform of "identity abuse." What this actually looks like is not made clear by this particular study, but other studies have suggested that anti-trans* sexual IPV can manifest itself in a variety of ways:

- Nonconsensually touching a trans* victim's body parts that have or had a gendered meaning (e.g., genitals, chest, etc.).[178]
- Arguing that "real" men and women prefer rough sex as a justification for coerced (or forced) sex with a trans* victim.[179]
- Claiming there is no safe way to have sex with trans* bodies as a justification for coercing a trans* victim into unprotected sex.[180]
- Not allowing the victim to ever initiate sex as a way to prove that the perpetrator is a "real" man.[181]

These sexual IPV tactics—of which to date we largely have only anecdotal evidence—hint that some abusers of trans* victims draw upon traditional gender norms as a means to justify their sexually abusive behaviors.

Who Is at Greatest Risk?

It is difficult to determine how risk might differ among trans* people and between trans* and cisgender people, largely because research on this topic is still in its infancy. Still, one study from Australia indicated that trans* men may be slightly more likely than trans* women to experience sexual IPV (14% and 8%, respectively).[182] Research is mixed on whether trans* or cisgender people are more likely to experience this, with two studies finding that trans* people are at greater risk[183] and one study finding the opposite to be the case.[184] Only one study has examined racial and ethnic differences in victimization risk, finding that risk did not differ significantly by race or ethnicity among 573 trans* women in the United States with a history of sex work.[185] Given the small number of studies on this subject, it is not yet possible to determine whether risk among trans* people varies by age or nationality.

Regarding sexual minorities, with the exception of two studies[186] (which found either similar sexual IPV victimization rates for sexual minorities and heterosexuals or slightly higher rates for sexual minorities among men but not women), all other studies (both those with nonprobability[187] and probability samples[188]) find that sexual minorities are more likely than heterosexuals to experience sexual IPV victimization. Among sexual minorities, with the exception of three studies finding that sexual IPV risk is either higher[189] or equally as high for men[190] as compared to women, several studies from Australia[191] and the United States[192] concur that sexual minority women are at greater risk than sexual minority men. This is not surprising, unfortunately, given that sexual minority women are more likely than sexual minority men to experience sexual violence outside of intimate relationships as well.[193] In addition to one South African study,[194] studies providing rates by specific sexual orientations predominantly draw on samples from the United States. With the exception of one study,[195] most studies have found bisexuals to either be at the same[196] or higher risk[197] of sexual IPV victimization as compared with gay and lesbian people—although two U.S. probability studies[198] suggest that only bisexual women and not bisexual men are at an elevated risk.

Several studies (all in the United States) have sampled a single racial or ethnic group, with findings suggesting that sexual IPV is experienced in the United States by 10–12% of Latino MSMs in their lifetimes[199] and 3% in their most recent relationship,[200] 15–22% of Black MSMs in their lifetimes,[201] 41% of Asian-American MSMs in the past five years,[202] and 25% of sexual minority male Puerto Ricans[203] and 10–16% of all sexual minority Puerto Ricans[204] during an unspecified time period. Only two studies—one from South Africa and the other from the United States— have compared racial-ethnic groups among sexual minorities, with the former finding that racial-ethnic minorities are more likely to experience sexual IPV[205] and the latter finding no significant difference in rates between minorities and Whites.[206]

The only multinational study of sexual IPV among sexual minorities drew on a nonprobability sample of over two thousand sexual minority–identified MSMs from Australia, Brazil, Canada, South Africa, the United Kingdom, and the United States. Past-year sexual IPV victimization rates were nearly identical across these nations (3–5%).[207] Obviously, this finding must be understood in the context of this being a nonprobability, all-male sample that may not speak to what is happening in other sexual minority groups or other nations. Beyond this study, all nation-specific prevalence rates come from different, typically nonprobability studies, making cross-study comparisons relatively imprecise. Given that caveat, when the most accurate information available on sexual minorities in each nation is examined, lifetime sexual IPV victimization rates appear to vary slightly between Australia (8–25%[208]), Canada (4–10%[209]), China (23–29%[210]), Germany (3%[211]), South Africa (23%[212]), the United Kingdom (4–15%[213]), and the United States (22%[214]). Additionally, in the Netherlands, in a study of twenty-one sexual minorities with a "mild intellectual disability," 29% had experienced intimate partner sexual abuse.[215]

LGBTQ INTIMATE-PARTNER HOMICIDE

Maria reported controlling and jealous behavior, with continuous incidents of physical violence and stalking by Cynthia. She reported that police were called repeatedly, and they did not take these incidents seriously. Cynthia had threatened to kill herself, Maria, and Maria's children if Maria ended the relationship. Furthermore, Cynthia had been violent outside the home and had been arrested in the year prior to the attempted femicide. After Maria restated that the relationship was over, Cynthia set Maria's house on fire while the family was home.[216]

Thankfully, Maria and her children were able to escape by jumping out of a window.[217] Unfortunately, many attempts on the lives of LGBTQ partners are successful. Considering the ultimate toll it takes on victims, **intimate partner homicide**

(IPH) is extremely understudied in the LGBTQ IPV literature, with only a handful of studies on same-gender IPH across just three nations (Australia, Canada, and the United States), just one annual study on IPH by or against those who are known to identify as sexual minorities, and no studies on IPH by or against trans* individuals. This may be due in part to a lack of awareness of the problem by some researchers. For instance, in a study of all 230 articles mentioning IPH across every newspaper during 1998 in Washington State, a grand total of zero mentioned same-gender IPH. Though occurring, LGBTQ IPH remains nearly invisible in the media and to many in society, which may in turn lead some researchers to not consider studying it. That said, IPH research is especially important, since it may be able to unlock clues about how to literally save lives. In a quest to study this issue, researchers have stumbled on unique methodological barriers, along the way finding hints that LGBTQ IPH is both very real and prevalent.

Unique Methodological Problems and Solutions

For the sake of clarity, chapter 2 focused on the methodological issues inherent in research on *most* forms of LGBTQ IPV: psychological, physical, and sexual abuse. The rules are different, though, when it comes to researching LGBTQ IPH. Simply put, there is extremely limited access to quality data.

Unlike in traditional IPV survey studies that directly contact perpetrators and victims, IPH perpetrators may be difficult to contact if arrested or incarcerated, and IPH victims are of course quite literally impossible to gather data from. Perpetrators of IPH not caught or convicted not only are difficult to identify but pose serious ethical and safety concerns for researchers. LGBTQ people's interest in potentially committing IPH in the future may be understudied for the same ethical and safety reasons, with only one study examining homicidality by IPV perpetrators. (In that study, of 288 same-gender IPV perpetrators referred for counseling in an unspecified nation over two decades ago, the researcher found that an astounding 20% of men and 19% of women felt homicidal.[218]) Taking a different tack, some researchers have asked IPV victims whether they believe their abuser is capable of IPH, with one study of a nonprobability sample of eighty-four female same-gender physical or sexual IPV victims finding that 51% believed their abuser to be capable of killing them.[219] A small number of studies have found that 4% of sexual minority men[220] and 4% of sexual minority women[221] may experience death threats by a partner, especially bisexual victims.[222] Only one study[223] has examined attempted (but not completed) IPH, perhaps because such data is rarely aggregated at the national level and made publicly available.

However, instead of assessing the potential for future IPH, researchers are far more likely to focus on completed IPH that has come to the attention of a nation's criminal-justice system. While a convenient way to learn about a large number of incidents, this research strategy presents its own pitfalls. Such law-enforcement data is often filtered by a federal government into a national database of the most basic information on IPH incidents, which can lack detail at both the individual and relationship levels. For example, it appears that no attempt has been made by law enforcement or governments of any nation to assess the sexual-orientation identity or trans* status of IPH perpetrators or victims (although one organization in the United States[224] has provided some very limited information on trans* IPH victims). In some instances, same-gender IPH may be recorded by law enforcement, but this may never make it into national data repositories and government reports, either because same-gender IPH is omitted entirely or because only IPH in marital relationships is included. (For instance, in the Canadian government's annual efforts to collect IPH data from all law-enforcement agencies in the nation, nonspousal IPH was not required to be reported for data collection until 1991,[225] same-gender spousal IPH data was not collected until 1997,[226] and, despite now having same-gender IPH annual data, as recently as 2012 the annual report by the government on family violence prevalence mentioned IPH only generally, but not specifically same-gender IPH.[227])

Another potential limitation of government IPH data is that same-gender IPH may not even be recognized as IPH by law enforcement, prosecutors, and government databases on homicide statistics. In some instances, stereotypes of IPV as being solely between men and women may lead some police officers to automatically assume that same-gender homicide must be between friends or roommates, and not intimate partners.[228] In other situations, prosecutors may purposely not treat an IPH as between intimate partners. Consider the case of Angie Zapata, a trans* woman in the United States who went on a date with Allen Andrade, a cisgender male. Upon learning that Ms. Zapata was trans*, Mr. Andrade bludgeoned her to death with his fists and a fire extinguisher, later telling investigators that he had "killed it."[229] In 2009, he was tried and convicted of first-degree murder and a hate crime.[230] Certainly this appears to be a crime motivated by a hate bias, and, in the U.S. criminal-justice system, the prosecution's treatment of this as a hate crime had the effect of enhancing the incarceration sentence. At the same time, this was also clearly a case of IPH—yet discussion of the IPV context was largely left out of the court case and media coverage, overshadowed by the hate bias. Finally, in some nations—such as with the U.S. government's homicide data-collection program (the *Uniform Crime Report*'s "Supplementary Homicide Reports")—homicide between former intimate partners who were never in a spousal relationship is not reported as IPH, instead typically being reclassified as homicide between "acquaintances."[231] This is a strange data-collection decision. Research suggests that same-gender IPV victims who escape abusers (i.e., "ex"-partners) are at risk of being murdered.[232] Ex-*spouse* classifications are always included in homicide reporting, yet same-gender couples typically could not become ex-spouses in the United States until 2015 (since same-gender marriage was not legal throughout the

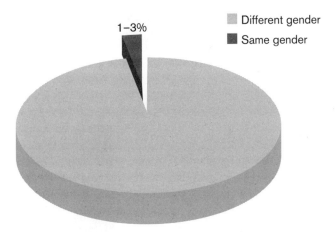

FIGURE 5. Percentage of IPH occurring between different- and same-gender partners.

nation until then). When IPH is not labeled as IPH by the criminal-justice system and in subsequently collected homicide data, there is strong potential for analyses and policy decisions to be incomplete.

Victimization Prevalence

Working within these notable data constraints, researchers have attempted to assess what proportion of IPH is between partners of the same gender. These proportions are lowest when looking at IPH perpetrated only by current or past spousal (and common-law) partners. For instance, of spousal IPH in Canada, only approximately 0.2% between 1974 and 2010 was between partners of the same gender.[233] This percentage is five to thirty times greater when adding in current and past nonspousal intimate partners: of both spousal and dating IPH incidents throughout Canada, 1% during 1991–2000[234] and 3% during 2003–2013[235] were between same-gender partners. A similar percentage of all IPH was found to be between same-gender partners in Australia (2% of IPH throughout the nation during 1989–2010[236]) and, when omitting former dating relationships, in the United States (approximately 2–3% of IPH throughout the nation during 1976–2001[237]). (See figure 5.)

Unfortunately, because national-level efforts throughout the world have not yet been undertaken to assess how many people experience same-gender relationships, it is impossible at this time to accurately estimate what proportion of these individuals will experience IPH. However, as an extremely imprecise same-gender IPH prevalence estimate, one could compare existing data on the estimated

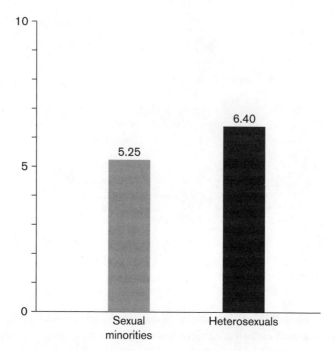

FIGURE 6. Annual IPH rate among sexual minorities and heterosexuals (per 1,000,000).

number of sexual minority–identified adults in a nation with the number of same-gender IPH cases in a given year. In the United States, for instance, it was recently estimated that over eight million adults identify as lesbian, gay, or bisexual.[238] Although reports on same-gender IPH in the United States are outdated, the most recent report found 1,092 same-gender IPH incidents from 1976 to 2001, for a mean average of 42 incidents per year.[239] If all sexual minorities and only sexual minorities experienced same-gender relationships (which is of course not the case, thereby making this an imperfect estimate), approximately 0.0005% of sexual minorities would have been murdered by a same-gender intimate partner in any given year. As a base of comparison, there were approximately 308 million adults in the United States in 2010.[240] If we assume approximately 8 million identified as a sexual minority,[241] 300 million might have identified as heterosexual. It was found that 49,915 different-gender IPH incidents occurred from 1976 to 2001, for a mean average of 1,920 incidents per year.[242] If all heterosexual-identified adults and only heterosexual adults experienced different-gender relationships (again, not the case all the time), approximately 0.0006% of all heterosexuals would have been murdered by a different-gender intimate partner in any given year. (See figure 6.)

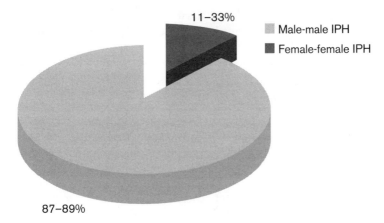

11–33%

■ Male-male IPH
■ Female-female IPH

87–89%

FIGURE 7. Percentage of same-gender IPH in male–male and female–female relationships.

This would indicate that sexual minorities are almost as likely to be murdered by a same-gender intimate partner as heterosexuals are to be murdered by a different-gender intimate partner in the United States. Again, this is a very crude, inaccurate estimate, making false assumptions that only sexual minorities have same-gender relationships, only heterosexuals have different-gender relationships, and every adult has one and only one relationship every year. It is also specific to the United States. However, this does provide at least tentative evidence that sexual minorities and heterosexuals are at a similar risk of experiencing IPH, which would thus appear to be the only form of IPV for which this is the case.

IPH risk, of course, may not be the same for men and women. Indeed, research suggests that, as with different-gender IPH, same-gender IPH is predominantly perpetrated by men. This was found to be the case in Australia (88% of same-gender IPH from across the nation during 1989–2010 was perpetrated by a man[243]) and the United States (approximately 87–89% of same-gender IPH during 1976–2001 from across the nation was perpetrated by a man,[244] and a comparable 89% of IPH in "long-term" same-gender relationships in the city of Chicago during 1965–93 was perpetrated by a man[245]). (See figure 7.) Notably, the proportion of IPH perpetrated by men appears to be even greater in same-gender IPH (87–89%) than different-gender IPH (62–77%).[246] Same-gender IPH rates are not broken down by sexual-orientation identity in any nation. The only study to assess IPH victim sexual orientation sampled from a predominantly LGBTQ population and therefore cannot provide accurate sexual minority IPH prevalence estimates; however, it can provide preliminary evidence of IPH prevalence among male versus female sexual minorities. According to this study of IPV-related reports to any of the NCAVP centers throughout Canada and the United States in 2014, approximately 80% of the twenty reported IPH incidents involving a sexual minority–identified victim were perpetrated against gay male victims and 20% against lesbian female victims (although not necessarily in a same-gender relationship).[247] It is perhaps not surprising that this study found that most sexual minority IPH victims are gay-identified, given that most same-gender IPH victims are men.

Means, Motives, and Context

Although additional information on same-gender IPH is scarce, research from Australia and the United States strongly suggests that same-gender IPH occurs in the context of other forms of IPV victimization, particularly physical and controlling abuse.[248] As compared with different-gender IPH, the means of murder in same-gender IPH incidents appear less likely to be a gun and more likely to be a knife or physical force, both in Australia[249] and the United States,[250] which one study suggested meant that same-gender IPH methods were more brutal and painful for victims.[251] Some research in the United States has also suggested that same-gender IPH perpetrators are more likely to use a gun if they are female rather than male.[252] Finally, one study in Australia and another in the United States provide some insights into what motives and contexts might precipitate same-gender IPH. In arguably one of the most comprehensive studies of same-gender IPH to date, in Australia, researchers Alexandra Gannoni and Tracy Cussen analyzed 1989–2010 data from the nationally representative *National Homicide Monitoring Program*—which provided police and toxicology reports—and supplemented this with perpetrator mental health records along with reports from perpetrator court cases. They found a broad spectrum of perceived motivations behind same-gender IPH incidents, from "domestic arguments" (25%) and "other argument" (13%) to money (9%) and jealousy (9%). While ending the relationship was less often the precipitating motive (6%), by comparison it was the second most common motive for different-gender IPH (19%). According to victim toxicology reports and perpetrator police reports, alcohol or drugs were used around the time of the homicide and in the systems of both victims (same-gender IPH, 61%; different-gender IPH, 41%) and perpetrators (same-gender IPH, 45%; different-gender IPH, 43%) more often for same-gender IPH than different-gender IPH. Based on police reports, coronial records, and court records, only 13% of same-gender and 8% of different-gender IPH perpetrators had a mental disorder at the time of the homicide.[253] A similarly innovative study was led in the United States by Nancy Glass and colleagues on female same-gender IPH spanning eleven cities from 1994 to 2000. Interviews were conducted with people close to the victim or perpetrator (e.g., family) from five cases of completed female same-gender IPH (supplemented with police and medical examiner records), and interviews were also conducted with four survivors of attempted female same-gender IPH (whose partners had a clear intent to kill and had a method that had the potential to achieve this goal, according to background information collected from a variety of government and local agencies). They found that physical IPV increased in severity and frequency over time in these relationships, extremely controlling IPV was common, and often the perpetrator had previously attempted or threatened suicide. In seven of the nine incidents, the victim had tried to end the relationship or was estranged from the perpetrator in the year leading up to the homicide. Of the five completed femicides, in three of those relationships the perpetrator had previously threatened to kill the victim—and in all three cases, the victim did not believe that the perpetrator was capable of killing them.[254]

REGARDING BISEXUAL IPV VICTIMS

Regarding bisexual-identified people and those who have had relationships with both men and women, as previously discussed, it appears that bisexuals (and MSMWs and WSWMs) are at greater risk of all forms of IPV than any other sexual-orientation group.[255] Why this might be is unclear. Research is mixed on whether they are more likely to experience IPV in a same- or different-gender relationship. While some research indicates that bisexual men are more likely to be abused by a woman and bisexual women are more likely to be abused by a man,[256] other research suggests that both bisexual men and women are most likely to be victims of a male abuser,[257] and still other research finds that bisexual men and women are both equally likely to have male and female abusers.[258]

DYNAMICS OF LGBTQ IPV

In addition to research on the prevalence of LGBTQ IPV, a number of studies have begun to examine the context of abuse. In particular, we are just beginning to get a better understanding of the directionality of LGBTQ IPV, where it occurs, and when.

Directionality

To illustrate our point further, we take a fictitious case involving a mother with three children. Her husband works for an accounting firm, and she is a homemaker. She has twice been hospitalized as a result of his abuse. One night he comes home late and drunk. She begins to raise her voice and call him names. He starts to walk toward her; she tells him not to touch her. He smiles and continues toward her. She throws a vase at him, and it hits him in the arm. He grabs her by the hair and tells her that if she doesn't shut up, he will smash her face. So far, it's 1:2 on the CTS [Conflict Tactics Scale]. She then kicks him hard in the shins. It's now 2:2. He pounds her head into the wall several times, and she reaches out and scratches his face. He lets go, and she runs out of the house and goes to her sister's house for the next three days. It's 3:3 on the CTS.[259]

Arguably the greatest limitation of IPV-prevalence research is that it almost always entails asking about IPV tactics used and received without providing any context on why partners used IPV tactics. As the fake story above highlights, IPV measures like the Conflict Tactics Scale (CTS)[260] fail to account for the possibility that some IPV tactics might be used in self-defense, to ward off an abuser. That is, without additional information, it is highly likely that some abusers are mislabeled by researchers as "victims," some victims are mislabeled as "abusers," and some people may even be simultaneously abusers and victims. Particularly given the penchant for people to speculate without evidence as to whether LGBTQ IPV is[261] or is not[262] typically "mutual battering," data on this subject is needed now more than ever. Efforts to help victims, rehabilitate perpetrators, and prevent LGBTQ IPV might benefit from a clearer understanding of who is actually perpetrating abuse, and how many "abusers" are in a typical relationship.

A good starting point in better understanding the directionality of abuse in LGBTQ IPV is to determine the prevalence of **bidirectional IPV** (IPV involving two users of IPV tactics) and **unidirectional IPV** (IPV involving one user of IPV tactics) by asking subjects if they have ever only used, only received, or both used and received IPV tactics. Research among LGBTQ people is unfortunately very limited on this very basic question. It appears that no directionality research has been conducted on trans* populations anywhere or on sexual minorities outside Canada and the United States. Additionally, with the exception of one study focusing on psychological IPV,[263] all existing directionality studies on sexual minorities have either focused only on physical IPV or merged all (nonfatal) forms of IPV in analysis, leaving a substantial gap in knowledge about the directionality of psychological and sexual LGBTQ IPV.

Even more problematic, though, is the fact that nearly all "directionality" research on LGBTQ IPV has not really assessed directionality. With the exception of one study—a study of a quasi-random sample of sixty-nine Canadian men, which found that, in a same-gender "focal relationship," half of the relationships involving physical IPV had two physical IPV perpetrators[264]—all other studies on this topic have assessed the proportion of sexual minorities who have used, received, or both used and received IPV at some point during a specified time period, including in the past thirty days,[265] past year,[266] past five years,[267] past six years,[268] or the subject's lifetime.[269] These studies indicate that, among sexual minorities who have ever been in an IPV relationship (whether as a victim, perpetrator, or both), 31–78% have both used and received some form of IPV in their lifetimes.[270] (Other studies have provided estimates among all sexual minorities rather than only those sexual minorities in IPV relationships,[271] or they have provided more detail about just bidirectional IPV relationships.[272]) What that literally means is that some LGBTQ people have both used and received IPV tactics—but we have no idea of whether that happened in the *same* relationship or if, instead, they used IPV in one relationship and received it in another. To label this as "mutual battering" or even "bidirectional IPV" may be misleading, as it incorrectly implies that reciprocity of abuse is occurring at the relationship level, when the data so far does not support that conclusion.

Limited research has examined motivations within relationships involving two IPV users. One study of lesbian women reported that 56% of female subjects in same-gender and 30% of female subjects in different-gender IPV relationships had used IPV only in self-defense (along with another 42% and 30%, respectively, who had used IPV both in self-defense and due to "mutual aggression").[273] Another study of lesbian women who had been involved in same-gender IPV found that 34% had fought back with the intention of hurting or injuring their attacker.[274] Still another study found that 23% of LGBTQ IPV perpetrators were motivated by self-defense, and 28% used IPV in retaliation.[275] These studies provide only half of the picture, of course, since they do not tell us what percentage of subjects in a bidirectional IPV relationship had a partner who was motivated solely by self-defense. Additionally, some scholars have questioned whether quantitative studies can accurately estimate the prevalence of self-defense, since victims may have been blamed by their abusers and encouraged to mislabel their self-defensive actions as "fighting back" or "mutual aggression,"[276] and some abusers may perceive themselves as lacking control in their relationships and may be more likely to blame others for their own abusive actions.[277] Researchers have only just begun to examine how bidirectional sexual minority IPV might differ from unidirectional sexual minority IPV (such as regarding Michael P. Johnson's typology categorizing IPV relationships by the various combinations of unidirectional and bidirectional controlling behaviors and physical violence), which may provide further insights into the context of self-defense.[278]

It is conceivable that bidirectional IPV does not always involve partners with clear roles (like abuser, victim acting in self-defense, or mutual batterer). Instead, some scholars believe that bidirectional LGBTQ IPV can sometimes involve the roles of victim and abuser shifting back and forth throughout the course of a relationship.[279] At the moment, this is almost entirely speculation. One researcher wrote in 1996 that she had heard secondhand from advocates that shifts in abuser-victim roles in same-gender IPV relationships are "rare";[280] she was then cited in 2000 as proof of this phenomenon[281] (although the "rare" qualifier was removed and the secondhand nature of the information was also omitted); this citation in turn was cited in 2006[282] (although by this point the original secondhand information had become "research," and what was originally described as a "rare" occurrence became something that occurred "often"). The only evidence of shifting power dynamics in LGBTQ IPV relationships comes from a 2002 study of 102 women who had experienced same-gender IPV across multiple cities in Canada, of whom 3 described themselves as victims initially but who also became perpetrators as the relationship progressed.[283] It is unclear from this study whether roles actually shifted for substantial periods of time or if, instead, this study is simply showing that certain partners may be more responsible for certain IPV incidents than others. This is not to say that roles cannot shift in bidirectional IPV relationships, but there is little to no supporting evidence of this thus far.

Where and When

Locations of LGBTQ IPV are incredibly understudied, which is unfortunate given the value of this information for prevention and intervention. That said, research from North America suggests that 76% of LGBTQ IPV incidents occur in the home,[284] although trans* victims are approximately two and a half times more likely than cisgender sexual minorities to experience an incident in a public space.[285] Research is mixed on whether risk differs between rural and urban areas, with one study of sexual minority adolescents from Canada finding girls to be at greater risk in rural areas and boys to be at greater risk in urban areas.[286]

Research from the United Kingdom suggests that abuse (not necessarily during the entire relationship period) lasts on average twenty-eight to twenty-nine months for sexual minority men and women,[287] while a study from Australia found the entire abusive relationship to last closer to thirty-six months.[288] Some research suggests that longer relationships are more likely to encounter IPV. For instance, in a U.S. study of HIV-positive, predominantly sexual minority men, it was found that both physical and sexual IPV were over twice as likely to occur in more-committed than casual relationships.[289] Some evidence suggests that physical IPV among sexual minorities does not emerge right away in a relationship (for 79%, not until the third month of dating)[290] but that once it does, the frequency of abuse usually increases over the course of the relationship.[291] Some researchers[292] have found empirical evidence of what Lenore Walker termed a "cycle of violence,"[293] a recurring cycle of tension building, a violent incident, and a honeymoon period of apologies and promises for change by the abuser. It is less clear what is happening in relationships where the cycle does not occur[294]—a topic in need of further exploration. Little is also known about which forms of IPV emerge first and in what sequence throughout the course of an abusive LGBTQ relationship.

After a sexual minority victim leaves an abuser, research suggests that approximately 6% of men[295] and 9% of women[296] in the United Kingdom continue to experience abuse by the same abuser. Some research from Belgium indicates that same- and different-gender IPV victims are typically stalked by a former abuser for a similar length of time, experiencing on average five or six stalking incidents postbreakup.[297] The risk of victims experiencing a future abusive relationship with a different abuser also appears to be considerable. For instance, research from the United Kingdom finds that both male and female sexual minority victims who experience at least two IPV incidents have been in relationships on average with

1.5 different abusers—indicating that many victims escape abusers only to be re-victimized in subsequent relationships.[298] A nationally representative study from the United States finds that bisexual women and men are more likely to have multiple abusers (40% and 46%, respectively), as compared with lesbian and gay men (21% and 11%).[299]

OUTCOMES FOR VICTIMS

Weapons such as knives and brooms had been used to threaten or assault me with during her violent rages but she had never been sexually violent. This soon changed. During one fight in which she had me pinned to the floor, she threatened to rape me with the broom handle she held. I almost laughed because it sounded so absurd. I quickly learned how serious she was.[300]

IPV is in and of itself a harrowing experience. Unfortunately, the nightmare often does not stop there, with consequences for victims continuing long after the relationship ends. Outcomes often include the following: fear for safety, injury, mental health issues, substance use, economic-related outcomes, and sexual risk-taking.[†] Understanding these may vastly improve the accuracy with which service providers determine the LGBTQ IPV outcomes to screen for and to treat among victims.

1. *Fear:* An unfortunately common outcome of LGBTQ IPV is fear for safety. Research suggests that 10–13% of trans* people,[301] 13–39% of sexual minority men,[302] and 14–48% of sexual minority women[303] have experienced fear in an intimate relationship.

2. *Injury:* An astounding 16–42%[304] of trans* people, 3–42% of sexual minority men,[305] and 4–37% of sexual minority women[306] have been physically injured in an intimate relationship.

3. *Mental health issues:* Another common LGBTQ IPV outcome is experiencing negative mental health issues, like feeling stress and anxiety,[307] feeling sad[308]

---

† Unfortunately, research is often hampered by a limitation that is at once obvious and difficult to overcome: "outcomes" can sometimes actually precede and even help precipitate abuse. For example, if researchers find that LGBTQ people who are depressed are also more likely to experience IPV, what are the cause and effect? Quite likely, many victims come to feel a deep sense of shame and helplessness because of IPV, and in turn depression becomes an outcome of IPV. At the same time, it is possible that some abusers seek out potential mates whom they feel superior to or can have power over. A person struggling with mental health issues—or substance-abuse problems, suicidality, school dropout, HIV-positive status, and so on—may therefore appear to be a prime target for an abuser, and in those particular cases IPV may be an indirect outcome. To be clear, this is not to say that the victim is to blame for IPV—only a criminal is responsible for a crime—but it is important to distinguish IPV outcomes (which will be important for service providers to treat) from preexisting conditions (which may additionally serve as warning signs to be addressed in prevention programming and IPV screening). With the exception of a handful of outcomes (e.g., injury, fear for safety), "outcomes" reviewed in this chapter should be understood as likely not only outcomes but also, at least in some instances, risk factors.

or depressed,[309] or having posttraumatic stress disorder symptoms.[310] Research suggests that 76% of trans* people,[311] 3–42% of sexual minority men,[312] and 20–46% of sexual minority women[313] have experienced mental health problems in an intimate relationship. Additionally, with one exception,[314] several studies have found that IPV is associated with suicide attempts or suicidal ideation among sexual minorities.[315]

4. *Substance use:* Substance use has been repeatedly found to be associated with IPV among sexual minorities.[316] With a handful of exceptions,[317] research has found IPV among sexual minorities to be associated with cigarette use,[318] alcohol use,[319] and illicit drug use[320]—including cocaine, downers, ecstasy, GHB, heroin, methamphetamines, LSD, and opium.[321]

5. *Economic-related outcomes:* A small number of studies suggest that LGBTQ IPV may have a current or future impact on the economic viability of victims. For example, research suggests that 17% of sexual minority women[322] and 27% of trans* people[323] have had to miss work or school because of IPV victimization. Additionally, among sexual minority male youths, it has been found that IPV victimization is more common among those who had run away from home or were living in a shelter, a group home, or on the street.[324]

6. *Sexual risk-taking:* Among sexual minorities, with few exceptions,[325] experiencing IPV is associated with sexual risk-taking behaviors, including engaging in unprotected sex,[326] transactional sex,[327] and other sexual behaviors that may negatively impact quality of life.[328] With two exceptions,[329] research on sexual minority men and MSMs overwhelmingly finds that IPV victims are more likely to be HIV-positive.[330] Among HIV-positive victims, one study suggests that IPV is associated with degraded health related to HIV. Specifically, according to a longitudinal study of 687 HIV-positive sexual minority male patients at an HIV clinic in Canada, it was found that IPV victims are more likely to not visit their clinic for over a year (and consequently have their viral load significantly increase) and more likely to be diagnosed with AIDS.[331]

IMPLICATIONS FOR POLICY, PRACTICE, AND RESEARCH

This chapter offers several key lessons on how societies can better address LGBTQ IPV. First, policymakers need to sweep away myths that LGBTQ IPV is rare and inconsequential. They need to be made aware that psychological,[332] physical,[333] and sexual IPV[334] has generally been found to be *more* prevalent among sexual minorities than heterosexuals. Additionally, while results are mixed as to whether trans* or cisgender people are more likely to experience IPV, IPV rates for trans* people[335] are comparable to those found among sexual minorities. Likewise, research has shown LGBTQ IPV to have several negative effects, ranging from fear for safety to injury, mental health issues, substance use, economic-related outcomes, and sexual risk-taking. The high prevalence and costs of LGBTQ IPV should provide ample justification for policymakers to revise government responses to IPV to become more inclusive of LGBTQ IPV—not only by making existing responses accessible to LGBTQ people but also by editing these responses to reflect the unique ways in which LGBTQ IPV can manifest itself (e.g., IPV tactics considered when determining whether to grant an order of protection). Additionally, while much is known about the prevalence of LGBTQ IPV in some nations, in many nations research is thin, particularly on trans* IPV. One simple way to rectify this is with the annual data collection many governments often do to ascertain arrest rates and victimization rates for IPV: by adding in a requirement of assessing the gender of abusers or the sexual orientation or trans* status of victims, this data could greatly expand our understanding of how LGBTQ IPV rates differ internationally. This is particularly the case with IPH because knowledge about it almost exclusively comes from government-mandated data reporting from law-enforcement agencies. While the limited information on same-gender IPH suggests it is rare, data on same-gender IPH has been limited thus far to just two nations (Australia and the United States), and no data exists anywhere on trans* IPH.

Second, for practitioners and others directly working with those involved in LGBTQ IPV, there are several important lessons from the research literature. To begin, while there is considerable overlap in the abusive tactics used in HC IPV and LGBTQ IPV, there is also ample divergence. Knowing the tactics unique to LGBTQ IPV may be helpful in IPV screening and treatment, and it can also be helpful in practitioner trainings. As this chapter has documented, there are many unique forms of psychological, physical, and sexual IPV that leverage the victim's LGBTQ status: accusing the victim of not being a true LGBTQ person, making a victim feel ashamed of being LGBTQ (or deserving of abuse because they are LGBTQ), preventing a trans* victim from maintaining their gender performance (such as by limiting access to their clothing or hormone medications), nonconsensually touching or physically assaulting parts of a trans* victim's body that have gendered meaning, outing or threatening to out a victim's LGBTQ identity, forcing a victim to remain closeted about their LGBTQ identity and the existence of their relationship with the abuser, using gender norms to justify sexual violence with a trans* victim (e.g., by saying "real" men like rough sex), and so forth. Although considerably less examined, scholars speculate that some LGBTQ abusers may use their LGBTQ status to justify their abuse with victims, such as by presenting themselves as being a target of discrimination and therefore incapable of having power in a relationship. In addition to IPV tactics, it is helpful for mental health-care providers and other practitioners to be aware of the possible aforementioned outcomes of LGBTQ IPV, which should be kept in mind for IPV screening, treatment, and referrals. Research also indicates that LGBTQ IPV most often occurs in the home, emerges slowly, and escalates over time. Just as important as what is known is what is not known. Contrary to speculation that LGBTQ IPV is[336] or is not[337] typically "mutual battering," almost no data on the use and receipt of IPV in the *same* relationship exists. Even though the one study to actually examine this found bidirectional physical IPV to occur in half of same-gender IPV relationships,[338] another study finds that the majority of these relationships involve a victim fighting back solely in self-defense,[339] suggesting that even bidirectional LGBTQ IPV may not usually be "mutual battering" (i.e., involving two "abusers"). Additionally, contrary to speculation by some scholars,[340] there is little to no supporting evidence of victim-abuser roles switching back and forth in LGBTQ IPV relationships. This is not to say that true "mutual battering" does not exist or that victim-abuser roles cannot switch over the course of LGBTQ IPV relationships, but there is currently so little research on these topics that it is impossible to know what is actually happening. The thus-far-unfounded myth that LGBTQ IPV is always mutual, if unchallenged in practitioner trainings, can very negatively impact how victims are responded to and treated.

Third, for researchers, there are several gaps or near gaps in this literature that should be explored in the future. The topics that appear to have the least available information include IPV prevalence among trans* people, how LGBTQ IPV prevalence and outcomes differ among subpopulations (e.g., by race-ethnicity, age, etc.), whether LGBTQ IPV typically involves one or two IPV users in the *same* relationship rather than just in the same time period (including when IPV is defined by its many forms rather than just solely physical IPV), the context of bidirectional LGBTQ IPV such as regarding the motivation of self-defense, and the sequence of events in LGBTQ IPV relationships (particularly which IPV forms emerge when in relation to one another, as well as the immediate triggers and justifications used for specific incidents). Additionally, research has thus far found that for the most part bisexuals are at greater risk of psychological,[341] physical,[342] and sexual IPV[343] victimization than any other sexual-orientation group. With research mixed on whether bisexuals tend to have male or female abusers, clearly more research is needed to ascertain whom bisexuals are typically abused by and why bisexuals are at an elevated risk.

Understanding the basics of IPV—who did what, where, when, and to what effect—is an important first step in raising awareness about LGBTQ IPV and improving societal responses. Perhaps equally as important, though, is the *why*. This is the big question that we shall turn to in the next chapter.

4

WHY DOES LGBTQ IPV HAPPEN?

My father screamed at me and cut me down and was contemptuous or ridi-
culing of me my whole life. He was full of rage. My mother was unable to
stand up to him. I felt like most of my life I protected her. I have a contempt
for passivity in any form. . . . I was furious and contemptuous of all people
at all times, so the woman I was with [in my first adult same-gender relation-
ship] was insecure, not the sharpest tack in the box and I have no doubt
I picked her for exactly those reasons, so that I could feel superior to her
and so our relationship was more or less constantly me pointing out her
stupidity. I was both in subtle ways and in quite overt ways cutting her
down, denigrating her brains or ability, anything pretty much. That was
also the relationship where I had my first and only attempt at physical
violence.[1]

Margaret describes above an all-too-common experience of abusers. Having been psychologically abused as a child by her father and witnessing her mother's helplessness, Margaret grew up with a desire for greater control over her life. Unfortunately, that need for control extended to her first same-gender relationship, in which she would go on to abuse her partner.[2] This linear storytelling—abuse as a child leading to being abusive in adulthood—can be helpful in many ways. For Margaret and any subsequent mental health treatment she might partake in, recognizing a key reason for her abusiveness may be vital in rehabilitation. Likewise, identifying reasons LGBTQ IPV happens can facilitate the creation of prevention programs and guide future research.

At the same time, human behavior is infinitely more complex than Margaret's story might imply. For instance, psychological research has demonstrated that our lives can often consist of a series of unrelated experiences, and it is only later on that we revise our memories by assuming they were part of a single, cohesive life story. The ability to create meaning and purpose out of our past can be comforting and help us learn valuable lessons. Still, in our attempts to repeatedly make sense of our lives, we risk overemphasizing certain explanations of behavior while deemphasizing or completely ignoring others.[3] Michele Bograd, an IPV researcher and

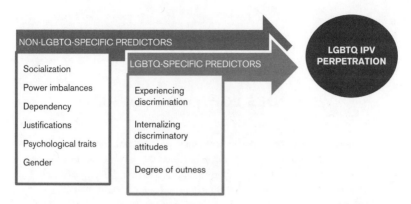

FIGURE 8. Forces predicting LGBTQ IPV perpetration.

theorist, suggests that researchers may also have a tendency to oversimplify explanations of IPV. More specifically, in a quest to boil IPV down to the "most common" explanations, researchers may risk ignoring factors linked to socially
marginalized and demographically smaller groups. Bograd explains: "Yet do our
theories, most often written in neutral universal language, illuminate the experiences of all touched by domestic violence, or do they unintentionally force those
whose experiences differ from the mainstream to the margins?"[4]

Ultimately this speaks to an important ongoing debate: whether there are one
primary or multiple explanations of IPV.[5]

To examine the underpinnings of this debate, this chapter explores perpetration theories that may apply to both HC IPV and LGBTQ IPV (including socialization, power imbalances, dependency, self-justifications, and psychological
traits), the contested role of gender in understanding HC IPV and LGBTQ IPV,
and unique catalysts for LGBTQ IPV (including experiencing discrimination,
internalizing discriminatory attitudes, and degree of outness). (See figure 8.)
Relatedly, this chapter also examines the ways in which barriers to escape for
victims can help maintain an LGBTQ IPV relationship (including not recognizing IPV, dependency, fear, and hurdles in reaching out for help). (See figure 9.)
Finally, this chapter exposes barriers that are making it more difficult to see the
big picture of why LGBTQ IPV happens (including fears of excusing abusers
and blaming victims, challenges in distinguishing causes from outcomes, and
doubts over whether there are one or multiple explanations of IPV). In the face
of mounting evidence that IPV has a myriad of causes, Bograd challenges us to
ask ourselves a simple question: Who exactly benefits from a one-size-fits-all IPV
theory?

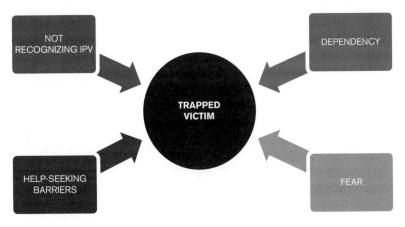

FIGURE 9. Forces deterring LGBTQ IPV victims from seeking help or leaving.

NON-LGBTQ-SPECIFIC PREDICTORS

Researcher and theorist Donald Dutton lauds "the advantage of being parsimonious" in IPV perpetration theories; that is, he prefers a theory that "applies to both heterosexual and lesbian battering without needing recourse to separate models of explanation."[6] A number of scholars concur, arguing that any IPV perpetration theory that applies only to HC IPV is (due to its exclusionary nature) offensive and "heterosexist."[7] These scholars often steer clear of factors that might be difficult to apply broadly to all IPV (especially gender and sexual orientation) and instead focus on non-LGBTQ-specific predictors. These include predictors pertaining to socialization, power imbalances, dependency, abuse justifications, and psychological factors. In some instances, these predictors encourage or enable abusers to perpetrate abuse. In other instances, these predictors may make victims appear to be more ideal targets—such as by becoming more self-blaming, less likely to question abuse, and less likely to attempt to escape—which in turn may encourage abusers to initiate and escalate IPV. (See figure 8.)

Socialization

One prominent set of theories of LGBTQ IPV suggests that people are often socialized into (or informally taught) attitudes that condone and encourage IPV. For abusers, this socialization may increase the likelihood they perpetrate IPV. For victims, this socialization may unfortunately draw in abusers looking for compliant targets, and it may make it more likely that abusers feel comfortable initiating abuse. Socialization sources can include childhood exposure to violence, peers, prior IPV relationships, non-IPV victimization experiences, the media, and age-specific sources.

A considerable amount of research has indicated that childhood exposure to violence can increase the likelihood of both IPV perpetration and victimization among sexual minorities. Beginning with perpetration, among sexual minorities, IPV perpetration has been found to be predicted by the perpetrator's witnessing child abuse of siblings (studied and confirmed thus far only among women),[8] experiencing incest with siblings (also studied and confirmed only among women thus far),[9] experiencing child abuse (for both[10] men[11] and women,[12] with the exception of one study[13] finding no relationship), having parents who have experienced child abuse,[14] and witnessing IPV between their parents (for both men[15] and women,[16] although three studies[17] have found, to the contrary, that witnessing interparental IPV is not associated with IPV perpetration). A qualitative study of female same-gender IPV relationships in which the abusers had experienced child abuse provides two valuable insights into why childhood exposure to trauma may encourage adult IPV perpetration: first, such experiences may be believed to elicit sympathy from victims that can keep them from leaving their abusers; and second, some abusers may learn from their victimization experiences that abuse is a legitimate expression of love or response to conflict.[18] Interestingly, two studies suggest that, among sexual minority men, their adult IPV perpetration is predicted only by their having experienced child abuse[19] and having witnessed interparental IPV[20] perpetrated by their mothers and not by their fathers—raising important but as yet unanswered questions about the role of the gender identity of the adult modeling abusive behaviors.

Among sexual minorities, childhood exposure to violence has also been found to be associated with adult IPV victimization, suggesting that socialization into violence-condoning attitudes may transform them as adults into more ideal targets for abusers. Specifically, among sexual minorities, IPV victimization has been found to be predicted by victims' witnessing child abuse of siblings (studied and confirmed thus far only among women),[21] experiencing incest with siblings (also studied and confirmed only among women thus far),[22] experiencing child abuse (for both men[23] and women[24]), and witnessing IPV between their parents (for both men[25] and women,[26] although some research[27] has found no association with witnessing interparental IPV). Interviews with female same-gender IPV victims indicated several reasons why childhood exposure to trauma may have increased their risk for adult IPV victimization: childhood trauma may lead some to rely heavily on partners for emotional support (with such dependency increasing vulnerability for abuse), may lead some to justify and excuse abuse (which may enable and facilitate their future victimization), and may lead some to be emotionally hardened or numb to abuse (which may encourage them to ignore or not actively resist IPV victimization).[28] As with research on perpetration, two studies have found that, among sexual minority men, their adult IPV victimization is predicted only by their having experienced child abuse[29] and having witnessed interparental IPV[30] perpetrated by their mothers and not by their fathers. Because IPV victimization and perpetration can often co-occur (such as when a victim fights back in self-defense), it is important to keep in mind that childhood exposure to abuse could be linked to adult IPV victimization primarily because these victims may often be perpetrators, or such exposure could be conversely linked to adult IPV perpetration primarily because these perpetrators may often be victims. Scholars have yet to adequately untangle causes from covariates, and future research is recommended.

All of the aforementioned research has focused on sexual minorities who were exposed to violence as children by presumably heterosexual parents. Very few studies have examined the impact of childhood exposure to violence perpetrated by sexual minority or same-gender parents. This is a considerable oversight, given both that IPV is highly prevalent among sexual minorities and that many sexual minority families have children. For example, in the United States, it has been estimated among adults ages 22 to 55 that 34% of female same-gender cohabiting couples and 22% of male same-gender cohabiting couples are raising children.[31] Initial research in this area has found that, of sexual minority women in same-gender relationships with children, 14–30% report that either they or their partner has abused the children, and 26% indicate that their children have witnessed them being abused by a partner.[32] (Scholars speculate that the immediate impact of exposure to parental IPV—including psychological, psychosomatic, and physical effects—is likely similar for children of LGBTQ and heterosexual-cisgender parents, although children of LGBTQ parents may face additional pressures to remain silent due to fears of outing their parents to those who might subsequently wish to discriminate against either the parents or their children.[33]) Whether this exposure to violence in childhood by sexual minority parents then predicts adult IPV perpetration or victimization is still unclear. Researchers have also not yet examined among trans* people the influence of exposure to violence in their childhoods on their IPV victimization or perpetration in adulthood, nor has research explored the outcomes for children who witness IPV between trans* parents or who are abused by a trans* parent.

In addition to childhood exposure to violence, other sources of IPV-condoning socialization for LGBTQ people might include peers, prior IPV relationships, non-IPV victimization experiences, and the media. The only study to date to examine the impact of peers on LGBTQ IPV unfortunately did not distinguish between the impact of peers and family. Specifically, it found that female undergraduate students who had experienced same-gender relationships were more likely to have perpetrated or been a victim of IPV if they had either a friend or family member perpetrate IPV as well.[34] Prior IPV relationships may also socialize LGBTQ people. For instance, one study suggests that lesbian women are more likely to be involved in an IPV relationship (as a victim, perpetrator, or both) if they had been involved in such a relationship in the past (as a victim, perpetrator, or both).[35] Exactly why this is the case is not yet clear. It may indeed be that prior IPV experiences teach LGBTQ people that abusive behaviors are acceptable responses to conflict and cannot be prevented, but it could also be that people experience multiple IPV relationships for the same underlying causes (e.g., childhood exposure to violence, etc.) unrelated to socialization in a prior IPV relationship. Additionally, research indicates that experiencing non-IPV victimization (whether psychological, physical, or sexual) by a peer or stranger predicts IPV victimization among sexual minority men.[36] Again, this could be explained by socialization processes (i.e., coming to believe that victimization of any type is normal or even justified, including IPV), but it also may be that there is a single underlying predictor of both general victimization and IPV victimization for these individuals (e.g., high degree of outness). A largely untapped area in LGBTQ IPV research is the role of the media in socializing abusers into abuse-condoning attitudes. It has been speculated that the absence of healthy LGBTQ relationships in the entertainment media has left a gap in culturally available knowledge about these relationships, thereby increasing the chance that abusers and victims alike assume that abuse is normal.[37] One study also noted that, of popular online pornographic films depicting sex acts between two men, 10% displayed coerced sex and 20% rape, in addition to an unspecified number that depicted IPV.[38] That said, no study has yet to attempt to directly link the consumption of media—be it news, entertainment, pornography, or any other type—to LGBTQ IPV, a topic ripe for future research-based inquiry.

Finally, it is possible that there are age-specific sources of socialization that, in conjunction with biological maturation, help explain IPV risk. Beyond the few exceptions finding no association with age,[39] research suggests that sexual minorities are more likely to be victims of IPV if they are younger,[40] with some variation by IPV form (e.g., IPV tactics involving use of children are more likely to be used in middle or older age,[41] whereas psychological IPV is more likely to be used in adolescence[42]). Some evidence suggests that sexual minorities are most likely to experience IPV in their twenties and thirties.[43] It is possible that young adults are socialized into attitudes that encourage jealousy and IPV generally, although it is also conceivable that sexual minorities have fewer sources of socialization at this age, with fewer available models of long-term, healthy sexual minority relationships among peers and in the media.

Power Imbalances

As just one indicator of power imbalances in relationships, research suggests that over a third of sexual minority relationships are not egalitarian in decision-making,[44] and this in turn is associated with IPV.[45] Imbalances of power between partners may increase the likelihood of IPV for two key reasons: having *greater* power than one's partner may encourage IPV perpetration (i.e., creating a sense of superiority as well as access to resources that make it harder for victims to leave),[46] but it also may be that having *less* power than one's partner may encourage IPV perpetration (i.e., creating a desire to overcome a sense of "disempowerment" by dominating one's partner[47]). For researchers, discerning which partner has "greater" power is complex because there are multiple sources of power. This means that people can simultaneously receive power and privileges on one axis of inequality and disadvantages and discrimination on another axis of inequality.[48] Likewise, simply because there are differentials in societal privileges between partners does not inherently mean that this will result in IPV.[49] That said, research has begun to examine various sources of power imbalances between LGBTQ partners, with a particular focus on age, class, race and ethnicity, immigrant status, and medical and mental health.

Power imbalances in intimate LGBTQ relationships may potentially be derived from age-based factors. One study has found that substantial age differences between sexual minority partners (i.e., ten or more years) predict greater IPV frequency,[50] while another study reported that 45% of recent sexual minority male IPV victims felt that age differences were a trigger for IPV incidents.[51] Interviews with sexual minority IPV victims in Japan suggest that some cultures may normalize and legitimize relationships in which older partners have considerably greater power and control than their younger partners, which may in turn discourage younger victims from questioning older abusers.[52] Preliminary evidence also suggests that younger victims are less likely to be believed when seeking help regarding an older or elderly abuser.[53] Beyond explicit age differences, research also has found that gaps in relationship experience (likely impacted by age) also facilitate IPV. Specifically, sexual minorities are at increased risk of IPV if it occurs in their first relationship,[54] where victims may not be aware of what healthy relationships look like and may feel less qualified to challenge the behavior of abusers. Relatedly, one qualitative study suggests that sexual minorities who have been out for a shorter period of time than their partners may hold less power in their relationships and could be at greater risk of IPV victimization[55]—a possibility that has not yet been studied with more-representative samples.

Power imbalances emerging from class-related factors may also facilitate LGBTQ IPV. There are a range of as yet largely unexamined reasons economic class may be linked to IPV: poor victims may feel more dependent on wealthier abusers,[56] poorer abusers may feel disempowered by their low income and seek a greater sense of power by abusing their partners,[57] and finances and work may become sources of stress that trigger conflicts and in turn abuse.[58] Evidence is fairly mixed on the importance of class in LGBTQ IPV. Competing studies have found that both higher income[59] and lower income[60] are associated with sexual minority IPV victimization, while other research finds income to be entirely unassociated with victimization.[61]

One study has found lower income to be linked with IPV perpetration.[62] Additionally, sexual minorities who are employed full-time are at greater risk of IPV victimization than those who are unemployed or employed part-time.[63] Education, which is typically positively associated with income and class status, has also been examined. In particular, less education has been found among sexual minorities to be associated[64] (and not associated[65]) with risk of IPV victimization, just as less education is associated with IPV perpetration.[66] The relatively small batch of studies on income and IPV lend credence to the findings of the considerably more robust (if still modestly sized) literature on education and IPV, which tentatively indicates that less education (and likely therefore lower income) increases risk for both sexual minority IPV victimization and perpetration. As with age differentials, it is possible that income, employment, and educational differentials between partners predict LGBTQ IPV. To date, only partner differentials in employment have been studied, with findings indicating, unexpectedly, that sexual minorities whose partners have different educational terminal degrees (specifically a college or graduate degree for one partner and a high school or lower degree for the other partner) are *less* likely to encounter IPV.[67] Another study asked recent sexual minority male IPV victims about what they perceived to be IPV triggers generally, although not necessarily in their own relationships. While examining general perceptions rather than personal experiences, this study found that many believed age differences (45% of the sample), income differences (44%), and education differences (39%) are triggers for IPV.[68] Significantly more research is needed to illuminate the connections between class-based factors and LGBTQ IPV.

Power imbalances may also emerge from racial and ethnic factors, which may in turn also be linked to LGBTQ IPV. Scholars have speculated that racial-ethnic minority victims are ideal targets in part because abusers can play upon some victims' internalized racist (i.e., self-blaming) attitudes and fear of racist responses by anyone from whom victims are considering seeking help. Likewise, a racial-ethnic minority abuser may elicit sympathy from a victim, who may fear that the abuser will encounter racism (such as from the police) should the victim report the abuser.[69] While these IPV pathways do not require that abuser and victim be of different racial-ethnic backgrounds, one can imagine that power imbalances would be exacerbated when this is the case. Notably, research has found that IPV is more likely to occur among sexual minority partners who are of different races or ethnicities.[70] Regarding the race and ethnicity of individual sexual minorities, IPV perpetration in the United States has been found to be associated with being non-White[71] as well as being unassociated with race-ethnicity generally.[72] Conversely, IPV victimization appears to be associated with being non-White (in Brazil,[73] South Africa,[74] and the United States[75]), White (for certain IPV forms in the United States[76]), non-White or White (with similar risk in one study in the United States),[77] or an ethnic native (in Canada[78] and the United States[79])—although research has also found race and ethnicity to be entirely unassociated with IPV victimization among sexual minorities (in Australia, Canada, the United Kingdom,[80] and the United States[81]). Taken together, with one exception,[82] the existing body of research on sexual minorities indicates that racial-ethnic minorities are either just as likely as or more likely than Whites to perpetrate and experience IPV, and interracial couples may be at particular risk of IPV.

Research also indicates that, although comparatively understudied, power imbalances pertaining to immigrant status can contribute to LGBTQ IPV.[83] In one of the few studies on this issue, interviews were conducted with Asian-American sexual minority women who had been involved in same-gender IPV relationships. A key finding was that being "undocumented" (i.e., living in a nation but not having legal resident or citizen status) generates understandable fear of being deported, which in turn can influence both victims and abusers. For undocumented victims, fear of deportation may make them more malleable targets of abusers, facilitating their initial abuse and its escalation. For undocumented abusers, fear of deportation can generate a desire to control an intimate partner, one of the few people who may be aware of their undocumented status and with the potential power to alert authorities. For more recent immigrants (including those who are documented), abusers may fear that native-born people will be alluring and attractive to victims, motivating abusers to generate greater control over their victims.[84] It is possible that immigrant LGBTQ IPV victims experience unique IPV tactics (such as threats of deportation, being told that abuse is normal in their culture, and so on). Although not yet examined in depth, one study of predominantly LGBTQ IPV victims found that approximately 0.2% experienced "anti-immigrant bias" in a relationship (although this bias was not defined by the authors).[85] Additionally, no study in any nation appears to have estimated whether immigrant status (and undocumented status) increases risk for LGBTQ IPV.

Last, power imbalances in LGBTQ relationships may emerge from health disparities, and this may facilitate leverage and stated justifications for IPV. Very little research has examined the role of disabilities, with two studies finding that IPV is more likely to be experienced by sexual minorities with a "physical or mental limitation"[86] or who are either deaf or hard of hearing.[87] It is possible that there are unique tactics used by abusers of victims with disabilities, as one study hinted at when it found that 0.2% of LGBTQ IPV victims experience "anti-disability bias" in an abusive relationship (although this bias was not defined by the authors).[88] Most research on health disparities and LGBTQ IPV has addressed instead the *human immunodeficiency virus* and acquired immunodeficiency syndrome (i.e., HIV and AIDS), with scholars focusing almost exclusively on MSMs. MSMs are at a greater risk of contracting HIV and AIDS than other men and women, although of course these conditions are not exclusive to MSM populations.[89] With two exceptions,[90] research fairly conclusively has found that MSMs and sexual minority men are more likely to experience

IPV if they have been diagnosed with HIV[91] or another sexually transmitted infection (STI).[92] The only research in this area on trans* people found trans* women to similarly be at an elevated risk of IPV victimization if they are HIV positive.[93] Research is more mixed on whether HIV is linked to IPV perpetration, with findings indicating that they are associated among MSMs in Australia[94] and the United States[95] but not other nations.[96] Limited evidence suggests that HIV-positive sexual minorities experience shame, fear of not being loved, fear of their serostatus being outed, reliance on medication and financial resources for treatment that can be stolen by abusers, and fear of negative responses by those who they might turn to for support—all of which may make these individuals considerably more appealing targets for abusers looking for emotionally dependent and socially isolated victims. On the other hand, HIV-positive abusers may threaten to or actually infect their victims or not use condoms, just as they may elicit sympathy to keep victims from leaving.[97] A study of recent sexual minority male IPV victims found that 57% believed that IPV incidents could be triggered by partners having differing HIV statuses (one being HIV positive and the other HIV negative), 39% felt that IPV could be triggered by just talking about HIV statuses, and 26% believed that discussions of safe sex could trigger IPV.[98] One study suggests that 2% of LGBTQ IPV victims experience "HIV/AIDS-related bias" (which the study's authors do not define).[99]

Dependency

Some evidence suggests that dependency on partners is associated with sexual minority IPV (with no research in this area yet on trans* IPV). Dependency in sexual minority IPV relationships has been examined primarily from two angles: codependency, and also dependency by abusers on victims. Regarding codependency, scholars speculate that "fusion" within some sexual minority relationships (i.e., extreme codependence and isolation from society) can be both an understandable coping mechanism in the face of a homophobic society and, at the same time, a potential source of stress and conflict.[100] Indeed, research has found that codependent fusion (e.g., feeling emotionally codependent, extensively sharing time and resources together, etc.) predicts female sexual minority IPV.[101] It is possible that some "open relationships"—in which there is an agreement between partners to not be monogamous—exhibit lower codependency, which may explain why one study found MSMs in such relationships to be less likely to experience physical IPV.[102]

At the same time, some have theorized that dependence by abusers on victims is the key predictor, with IPV being precipitated by an abuser perceiving that the victim desires greater independence.[103] Certainly, research suggests that attempts by a victim to gain greater independence can become a source of conflict (far more often than an abuser's attempts to gain independence).[104] Still, even when an abuser's fear of abandonment is unfounded, the mere possibility that a victim *might* one day lose interest in them is enough for some abusers to want to isolate the victim from friends, family, and potential romantic competition.[105] A female same-gender abuser explains how this paranoia can morph into IPV: "I used to be way more jealous, but I really work on that. I was feeling insecure that someone was better than me and I would lose my girlfriend and when you think you're losing someone you love, you try to control them . . . such as where are you going, with who, when are you coming back, and I don't like you going with so and so."[106]

Indeed, research on sexual minorities finds that IPV perpetration is predicted by the abuser's "insecure attachment" (feeling more dependent and fearing abandonment), both with people generally[107] and with one's victim.[108] Additionally, constant expressions of jealousy—which can arise from extreme reliance or dependence on one's partner—have been found to be triggers for conflict[109] and to predict longer periods of abuse.[110] One study of recent sexual minority male IPV victims noted that 93% believed jealousy to be a trigger for IPV, while another 94% cited dishonesty and 86% lack of trust as additional triggers for abuse.[111]

Of course, it may be that both codependence *and* an abuser's dependence are important predictors of sexual minority IPV. An interesting possibility, though, is that the reason codependence predicts sexual minority IPV is that, by definition, codependent relationships include an abuser who feels dependent on the victim. In other words, perhaps only the abuser's dependence matters, and codependence is irrelevant. Some evidence supports this possibility, with research finding that conflict in IPV relationships is more likely to arise as a result of the abuser's dependence on the victim rather than the reverse.[112] At the same time, one study found that sexual minorities who are more dependent (or, more specifically, who are insecurely attached and feel subsequent anxiety) are more likely to experience *victimization*,[113] suggesting that perhaps dependence by both partners might indeed predict IPV. This is a logical possibility, given that research has found that sexual minorities are at an increased risk of victimization if they are dependent on abusers for specific, compelling reasons—such as being financially dependent[114] or being emotionally dependent due to a need to cope with HIV.[115] Dependence by victims on abusers may make it easier for abusers to initiate and escalate abuse, safe in the knowledge that victims will find it very difficult to leave them.

Justifications

In the broader criminology literature, scholars theorize that criminals often try to find ways to justify their actions to themselves. These justifications, termed "techniques of neutralization," help neutralize their potential guilt, making it easier for them to break the law and hurt people.[116] Anecdotal evidence suggests that LGBTQ abusers similarly justify their actions, convincing themselves that they actually lack power in their relationships[117] and that the victims are to blame for motivating them to be abusive.[118] Due in part to myths surrounding IPV (e.g., that women do not have the capacity to hurt partners, that men always have the capacity to defend themselves, that IPV occurs only in different-gender relationships, etc.), some LGBTQ abusers may not even recognize that their actions are abusive.[119]

One important area of research on IPV justifications addresses the role of substance use. With one notable exception,[120] studies find alcohol[121] and drug use[122] to be associated with sexual minority IPV perpetration. Two studies suggest that anywhere from 25% to 64% of sexual minority IPV abusers may be under the influence of substances around the time of at least one abuse incident,[123] and a case study of an alcoholic sexual minority abuser found that participation in an alcoholism treatment program coincided with a reduction in her IPV perpetration.[124] Interestingly, one study found that lesbian women in a same-gender relationship are more likely to experience physical and psychological IPV victimization if on average the abuser consumes more alcohol than the victim.[125] Reasons for this link between substance use and IPV perpetration are still largely unexplored, but several possibilities have been speculated on. Certainly, alcohol and other psychoactive substances have been shown to increase the likelihood of aggression.[126] This appears to be information widely accepted among sexual minorities, with one study finding that 91% of sexual minority male IPV victims and 91% of sexual minority male nonvictims perceive alcohol and drugs to be triggers for IPV.[127] At the same time, because the potentially negative effects of substance use are widely known, it has been theorized that some abusers may rationalize their actions to themselves and their victims by claiming they have no control over themselves when high.[128] Some small-scale studies interviewing LGBTQ IPV abusers provide tentative support for this conclusion.[129] One MSM abuser describes this process of abdicating responsibility and laying full blame on alcohol: "Um, I beat the crap out of him. . . . And I, I feel sorry that I did that to him, but it was the alcohol, I know, I know it was. Because I don't, I would not have done that, if not."[130] Although not well documented, research also indicates that abusers may use the victim's substance use to justify being abusive.[131] One MSM IPV victim even implied that his abuser *intentionally* upset him so as to get him to use substances, which in turn the abuser could then draw on to excuse subsequent abuse: "They made you get pissed, so you went out and got high. Now you go back home and they're already calmed down, and now they're going to get mad because you went out and got all blasted."[132] While the existence of a connection between substance use and sexual minority IPV perpetration has been verified, research has yet to clarify the exact reasons for this—particularly as to whether the pharmacological effects of alcohol and other drugs are being used by abusers as prepackaged justifications for hurting their partners.

Psychological Factors

It has long been speculated that abusers have a unique perspective on what are reasonable responses to conflict and fears of abandonment. When taken to the extreme, these psychological views and impulses may increase the likelihood of IPV perpetration.[133] Little research has examined the role of psychological traits and disorders in IPV perpetration among sexual minorities, and it appears that no research at all has been done yet on trans* populations. The few studies on sexual minority IPV suggest that there may indeed be a link between perpetration and psychological disorders. These psychological predictors include symptoms of the following: adjustment disorders (i.e., having difficulty coping with something stressful, which might manifest itself in a variety of ways including becoming isolated and aggressive),[134] antisocial personality disorder (i.e., having repeated disregard for the feelings and well-being of others, which may be associated with aggression and crime),[135] borderline personality disorder (i.e., having unstable relationships and views of self, which might be caused in part by extreme fear of abandonment),[136] depression,[137] impulsivity disorder (i.e., having an inability to stop oneself from committing acts that harm oneself or others, sometimes feeling tension before and satisfaction after the action),[138] paranoia personality disorder (i.e., paranoia and mistrust of people),[139] and posttraumatic stress disorder.[140]

THE ROLE OF GENDER

A major source of debate among IPV scholars is whether gender norms and gender inequality—long theorized to encourage and enable male-to-female HC IPV—also explain LGBTQ IPV.[141] The answer hinges on not only competing interpretations of IPV data but also competing definitions of gender.

One possibility is that gender-based IPV theories are entirely wrong. This position typically draws on evidence of "gender symmetry" in different-gender physical IPV: research finds that women are as likely as men to use physical violence in a different-gender relationship,[142] that they are as likely to initiate violence at least once in a relationship,[143] and that self-defense does not explain all or even most of this violence by women.[144] A substantial number of scholars have specifically pointed to the existence of same-gender IPV as further evidence that gender must be irrelevant, not only in same-gender IPV but also in different-gender IPV.[145] So the argument goes: if men can be victims in same-gender relationships, if women can be perpetrators in same-gender relationships, and if men and women are equally likely to use physical violence in different-gender relationships, how could gender matter in IPV at all? As researcher Claire Renzetti aptly puts it, the existence of same-gender IPV is being used ultimately "to bolster the claim that 'women do it too.'"[146] Whether out of a genuine sense of outrage or to quiet detractors, a subset of these researchers have even gone as far as to subtly imply that some researchers who advocate in favor of gender-based IPV theories are really political operatives, lying (whether consciously or not) to serve political goals. For example, gender-based IPV theories have been called "*radical* feminist sociopolitical *ideology,*"[147] "the feminist *political view,*"[148] "feminist *dogma,*"[149] the "feminist *agenda,*"[150] "feminist *propaganda,*"[151] and "feminist *disinformation*"[152] (emphasis added).

Another possibility is that gender-based IPV theories do explain different-gender IPV but not same-gender IPV. Certainly there is some reason to suspect that gender is a key factor in at least different-gender IPV. Despite considerable evidence of "gender symmetry" in the perpetration of physical violence in different-gender relationships, when examining the broader IPV context, different-gender IPV appears to be more often perpetrated by men. Men initiate physical violence in a greater percentage of conflicts in their relationships,[153] women are more likely than men to use violence in self-defense,[154] and women are more likely than men to be injured by a partner.[155] Moreover, women are far more likely than men to be victims of sexual IPV, intimate-partner stalking, and intimate-partner homicide.[156] Men have also been found to be far more likely to perpetrate most crime generally, adding to speculation that there is something about being male that increases the likelihood of aggression.[157] In light of the seeming predominance of HC IPV being perpetrated by men, a number of IPV scholars have argued that this may be explainable in part by masculinity norms and gender inequity.[158] Indeed, some research suggests that men who perpetrate different-gender IPV are more likely to perform stereotypical (heterosexual) masculinity norms,[159] men are more likely to leverage their on-average-greater economic power into control over different-gender partners,[160] and unemployed men may be particularly likely to assault employed female partners as a way to reassert what they perceive to be their rightful position as male head of household.[161] Even female HC IPV perpetration is influenced by gender norms and inequity. For instance, research indicates that many men do not take seriously physical HC IPV perpetrated against them by female partners because of gendered assumptions that women are weak, allowing some men an opportunity to show their power by being dismissive of female violence, whereas for other male victims the inability to label female-perpetrated abuse as abuse hinders them from seeking needed help.[162] That said, several researchers believe that gender-based IPV theories do not apply to same-gender IPV because both partners have the same gender identity (and therefore presumably the same gender-norm performances and gendered power).[163] They contend that gender is a key explanatory factor only for different-gender IPV, whereas very different factors help explain same-gender IPV. To some, it is acceptable and perhaps even preferable to have one set of theories explain HC IPV (i.e., gender-based theories) and a completely different set of theories explain LGBTQ IPV.[164] To others, this means that gender-based IPV theories need to be discarded entirely under the assumption that IPV theories that apply to only some IPV relationships (i.e., HC IPV) but not others (i.e., LGBTQ IPV) must be invalid,[165] with some going a step further by noting that they find HC IPV-focused theories to be offensive and "heterosexist."[166]

A final possibility is that gender-based IPV theories actually apply to both HC IPV and LGBTQ IPV. At the crux of this perspective is the argument that critics of gender-based IPV theories have misinterpreted these theories. For the most part, the aforementioned critics of these theories have relied on gender identities of perpetrators and victims to make their case. (That is, these critics have argued that gender is irrelevant to IPV specifically because physical IPV perpetration rates are similar for male-identified and female-identified people.) In response to this critique, a number of scholars point out that gender-based IPV theories have never claimed that simply identifying as male will make men perpetrate IPV. Instead, these theories contend that IPV is encouraged and enabled by two factors: the performance of certain gender norms, and interpersonal power inequities. That scholars have most readily recognized these two factors in different-gender IPV does not preclude the possibility that they might play a role in same-gender IPV.[167]

Scholars have begun to examine the roles of both gender norms and interpersonal inequality in same-gender IPV. Early theorizing on gender norms in same-gender IPV relationships took the position that most abusers—regardless of their gender identity or sexual orientation—perform "hegemonic masculinity" norms (i.e., the most societally accepted set of unwritten rules associated with how male-identified people are supposed to think and act).[168] This is a logical possibility to consider, not only because feminist scholars have long theorized that women can perform masculinities (and men femininities)[169] but also because hegemonic masculinity norms include abuser-like qualities, such as encouraging one to act in control, be emotionally closed off, and be willing to use aggression when needed.[170] Studies have found that many in the general public already assume that same-gender IPV abusers are more masculine than their victims,[171] while many sexual minority men believe that male same-gender IPV can be triggered by both partners playing "alpha male" roles.[172] That said, research is very mixed on this question, with different studies finding that the performance of hegemonic masculinity norms is[173] and is not[174] predictive of same-gender IPV perpetration. Indeed, research on gender performance in same-gender relationships more generally finds that sexual minorities tend to perform a broad range of gender norms that often do not conform to heterosexual gender stereotypes.[175] Nancy Baker and her colleagues raise an interesting possibility: What if IPV perpetration is not linked to every aspect of hegemonic masculinity but only to certain components within it (e.g., being emotionally closed off, willingness and ability to fight, etc.)?[176] If that is the case, it might mean that IPV researchers should be assessing the performance of individual gender norms rather than treating certain norms as always co-occurring in a cohesive set. This may also account for the mixed results on the role of gender norms in the majority of same-gender IPV relationships. For instance, research suggests that some same-gender IPV victims perform more traditionally feminine emotional roles (e.g., are more emotionally communicative and nurturing) than their partners, which in some cases they are pressured into doing by their abusers and in other cases may make them more vulnerable to being abused.[177]

According to limited empirical research on predominantly small samples, it is also possible that gender norms do not play out the same way in each LGBTQ IPV relationship, instead having a broad range of influences that vary across relationships. For example, in same-gender IPV relationships with one partner who is more masculine and another who is more feminine, some research suggests that sexually insertive men (i.e., "tops") often see their active role in intercourse as emblematic of and reinforcing their power over a more submissive, sexually receptive male partner (i.e., a "bottom").[178] Other research suggests that masculine-acting female victims sometimes feel their gender performance requires them to be protective of their feminine-acting female abuser even when that means not hitting back in self-defense,[179] which in some cases might actually trigger conflicts when a feminine-acting female abuser negatively perceives these protective instincts as her victim treating her as weak.[180] Some studies have found that male same-gender IPV victims view their abusers' abuse[181] and their own retaliation[182] as caused and justified in part by hegemonic masculinity-norm performance. Still other studies suggest that IPV conflict could be triggered by the gender performance of a partner shifting over the course of a relationship, such as changing from more stereotypically feminine to more stereotypically masculine.[183] Largely anecdotal evidence hints that gender-norm performance may also be important in trans* IPV: this might be the case when trans* male IPV perpetrators and trans* female IPV victims view IPV as an affirmation of their gender identity (e.g., as one trans* female victim noted, "Being beaten made me feel more like a woman")[184] or when abuse of trans* victims is rationalized by using the victim's gender identity (e.g., claiming that "real" women or men like "rough sex," or physically assaulting a trans* man to make him more "manly").[185] Also, as will be discussed more extensively later in this chapter, sexual minority victims might not realize they are being abused and abusers might not realize they are being abusive,[186] specifically because they do not conform to the HC IPV gendered stereotype of a masculine cisgender male abuser and feminine cisgender female victim (e.g., myths that male victims should be able to take it "like a man"[187] and that women are too kind and weak to ever be abusive[188]). As will be discussed in the next chapter, potential supporters of LGBTQ IPV victims may not take the abuse as seriously for the same reason.[189]

In addition to linking IPV to the performance of gender norms, gender-based IPV theories also implicate interpersonal power inequities, and here it has similarly been suggested that LGBTQ IPV can fit within these models. While gender inequality still clearly impacts LGBTQ IPV relationships (for the reasons described above), scholars suggest that at their core, gender-based IPV theories are pointing out that a partner who has access to greater societal power of any kind (e.g., on average greater economic wealth, greater protection by the law, greater levels of prestige, lower likelihoods of being discriminated against, etc.) may also feel entitled to power over a demographically marginalized intimate partner and will have greater resources to achieve that power. Beyond gender identity and gender performance, sources of interpersonal inequity that might influence IPV could draw on differences between partners in regards to their age, race and ethnicity, immigrant status, trans*-cisgender status, sexual orientation, degree of outness, health and (dis)ability, and so forth.[190] In particular, as the next section of this book will highlight, the cloud of discrimination against trans* and sexual minority people can both encourage stress-related abuse[191] and mask the seriousness of LGBTQ IPV.[192] Ellyn Kaschak, author of *Intimate Betrayal: Domestic Violence in Lesbian Relationships,* emphasizes the importance of not limiting our understanding of LGBTQ IPV power inequities to gender:

> Yet while neither partner in a lesbian relationship enjoys male privilege and power, we all live in a society that promotes hierarchy, power differential, inequality and, yes, violence. These are endemic to patriarchy and why should they not find their way into relationships lived in this cultural milieu? Additionally, lesbian relationships are directly influenced by other societal power inequities that impact all citizens, including sexism, and those based in class, race, ethnic, and economic inequality, as well as interpersonal differences in power.[193]

If indeed we are willing to broaden our understanding of gender (from simply gender identity to also gender performance) and interpersonal inequity (from just sexism to also racism, classism, heterosexism, cissexism, ageism, ableism, and so on), it becomes clear that both gender and in turn gender-based IPV theories are relevant to LGBTQ IPV.

THE ROLE OF SEXUAL ORIENTATION AND TRANS* STATUS

Calls for a one-size-fits-all theory of IPV causation tend to lose traction when we consider that IPV can have different causes for different populations. For LGBTQ people, the risk of IPV is uniquely elevated specifically because of how societies often negatively treat LGBTQ people. Perceived and experienced discrimination have been theorized to predict LGBTQ IPV for a number of reasons.

Theories of LGBTQ-Specific IPV Predictors

Even in discriminatory societies, simply being LGBTQ does not necessarily result in a lowered quality of life or negative attitudes about oneself and other LGBTQ people. Indeed, research suggests that many LGBTQ people form tight communities and positive self-identities in part to insulate themselves from homophobia and transphobia, thereby improving well-being.[194] At the same time, discrimination has the potential to negatively impact the lives of many LGBTQ people, and, among those strongly affected, it is possible that risk of IPV increases.

One posited theory is that extensive discrimination shapes some LGBTQ people into ideal targets, who are then particularly vulnerable to abusers looking for a controllable victim. LGBTQ people who are most negatively impacted by discrimination (e.g., strongly fear and have experienced homophobia or transphobia, are not "out" to most people they know, etc.) may be targeted by abusers because such victims would be least likely to seek help (out of fear of a discriminatory response by help givers), could be most influenced by threats of outing, and would be the most likely to feel deserving of abuse (which, according to limited research,[195] may be especially an issue for those whose religious faith stigmatizes LGBTQ people).[196]

Drawing on the concept of socialization, a different theory suggests that some abusers hurt LGBTQ victims because the abusers think the victims are deserving of abuse. LGBTQ people who internalize extremely homophobic and transphobic attitudes may have a low opinion not only of themselves but also of other LGBTQ people. This in turn may result in some LGBTQ abusers having a lower regard for their LGBTQ victims, which may help them justify becoming abusive.[197]

Disempowerment theory instead suggests that some LGBTQ people feel societal discrimination so intensely that they experience a feeling of powerlessness. In turn, to regain a sense of control in their lives, some may attempt to control their partners.[198]

Last, drawing on the criminological concept of strain, minority stress theory posits that societal discrimination can generate extreme stress for some LGBTQ people. More specifically, one possible response to that stress is to cope through aggression, such as IPV perpetration.[199]

In each case, research is fairly limited in directly proving these theories. For example, LGBTQ IPV research[200] that claims to assess "minority stress" often assesses only potential sources of stress (e.g., a subject's degree of outness) without actually measuring whether subjects felt stress from those sources (e.g., how much stress a subject experiences as a result of their degree of outness). Instead, most research on LGBTQ-specific causes of IPV has focused on discovering whether there is a link between discrimination and LGBTQ IPV perpetration and victimization, rather than going a step further to assess why that link might exist. In particular, research has examined associations between LGBTQ IPV and five discrimination-based factors: (1) perceiving that society is homophobic or transphobic, (2) experiencing discrimination, (3) experiencing non-IPV violence victimization motivated by an anti-LGBTQ bias, (4) believing in homophobic or transphobic attitudes (i.e., "internalized homophobia/transphobia"), and (5) having a low degree of outness (i.e., purposely not sharing your sexual orientation or trans* status with certain people, often out of fear of discriminatory responses). For some factors, research is just beginning to explore these connections with

LGBTQ IPV, and in many cases studies have drawn opposite conclusions. For at least certain subpopulations, though, it appears that homophobia and transphobia may uniquely impact the causal pathways into LGBTQ IPV perpetration.

Perceiving Society as Discriminatory

Of the only two studies to examine this factor, no link has been found between the degree to which one perceives society as discriminatory against LGBTQ people and the likelihood that one perpetrates or experiences LGBTQ IPV.[201]

Experiencing Discrimination

Research tends to find that experiencing LGBTQ-related discrimination does predict LGBTQ IPV perpetration,[202] although, somewhat counterintuitively, one study found that experiencing *less* LGBTQ-related discrimination was predictive of LGBTQ IPV perpetration.[203] Research is more mixed on whether experiencing discrimination also predicts LGBTQ IPV victimization, with several studies finding that there is[204] and is not[205] an association.

Experiencing a "Hate Crime"

Only one study to date has assessed whether experiencing an anti-LGBTQ-motivated crime (i.e., a "hate crime") is associated with LGBTQ IPV. It found that it predicted neither perpetration nor victimization.[206]

Internalizing Homophobic or Transphobic Attitudes

Research is also mixed on whether the degree to which one accepts homophobic or transphobic attitudes is linked with LGBTQ IPV, with research finding that it does[207] and does not[208] predict perpetration and does[209] and does not[210] predict victimization. One study found that IPV perpetration is particularly linked with the internalization of attitudes morally or religiously condemning sexual minorities as sinful.[211]

Low Degree of Outness

IPV research is limited on the degree to which LGBTQ victims and perpetrators are "out" about their sexual orientation or trans* status. Specifically, research has found that a low degree of outness is[212] and is not[213] associated with LGBTQ IPV perpetration. Perhaps even more confounding, different studies suggest that LGBTQ IPV victimization is associated both with lower[214] *and* higher[215] degrees of outness. Adding to the confusion, some studies have also found victimization to be entirely unrelated to outness.[216] One qualitative study suggests that partner differentials in length of outness—specifically for sexual minorities who have been out for shorter periods of time than their partners—may predict IPV victimization,[217] and another study of recent sexual minority male IPV victims found that

64% felt that one partner being closeted was a trigger for IPV incidents and 52% felt that both partners being closeted was a trigger.[218] One study in the southwestern African nation of Namibia found that closeted abusers can be verbally abusive in public with same-gender victims as a means of maintaining a facade of heterosexuality, while other closeted abusers may try to maintain their heterosexuality facade by reinterpreting previous consensual same-gender intercourse as their having been raped.[219]

WHY DO VICTIMS STAY?

> It seems to me that if Bill lives with Joe and Joe makes a practice of pummeling Bill, then Bill would have the good sense to just pack a suitcase and get the heck out of there. . . . But if his love or dependency is so intense that he chooses to stick around, whose problem is his fat lip or bloody nose? Not mine, not society's, and surely not the cops or a judge. In such matters, it is the choice of the individual.[220]

While abuse is always and only the fault of abusers, understanding the forces that maintain IPV relationships also requires learning why victims stay. To the outside world, two things often seem crystal clear: IPV is wrong, and victims should leave their abusers. That many victims do not immediately leave can cause some—like the author of the above *Chicago Tribune* article—to (incorrectly) assume that victims either must enjoy being abused or do not care if they are abused. Indeed, for many victims, one of the first questions they will be asked by friends and family is "Why don't you just leave?" While limited evidence suggests that sexual minority victims are more likely than heterosexual victims to seek help,[221] studies indicate that anywhere from 22% to 82% of LGBTQ IPV victims tell no one of the abuse.[222] Unfortunately, a network of hidden barriers is often incredibly effective in trapping many LGBTQ IPV victims: these barriers can include not recognizing IPV, dependency, fear, and hurdles in reaching out for help. (See figure 9.) As this chapter will explore, leaving is never as simple—or as safe—as it sounds.

Not Recognizing IPV

Research indicates that a key reason that many LGBTQ IPV victims do not seek help or leave their abusers is that they do not recognize their abusers' behaviors as abusive.[223] Indeed, one small study of U.S. college and university LGBTQ students who were experiencing ongoing physical IPV found that by far the most common reason victims did not report IPV was that they viewed it as "no big deal."[224] For example, approximately 49% of MSMs[225] and 25% of trans* people[226] who have experienced IPV do *not* self-label as victims of IPV. As one female same-gender IPV victim explains, "I didn't know it was domestic violence. And so, you know, there was no way for me to try to reach out, if I didn't know what it was."[227] Recognition of abuse appears to be directly tied to the type of IPV experienced. According to a study of same-gender IPV, psychological IPV victims are least likely to self-label as victims, sexual IPV victims are slightly more likely, and physical IPV victims are most likely to self-label as victims, with victims of multiple IPV types also more likely to recognize the abuse.[228] A study of bisexual IPV victims reveals similar difficulties with recognizing that psychological IPV is real abuse.[229] No study has assessed whether inability to recognize abuse differs substantially among LGBTQ people by sexual orientation, trans* status, or gender. That said, one study found that same-gender IPV victimization decreases relationship satisfaction among women but has no impact on relationship satisfaction among men, raising the possibility that men may find it particularly difficult to recognize IPV.[230]

Research suggests that there are a variety of reasons LGBTQ IPV victims may have difficulty recognizing IPV in their relationships. In some cases, LGBTQ IPV victims may not recognize abuse if it does not appear to conform to the popular stereotype of an abuser attacking a victim for no reason. When abusers can successfully deflect responsibility for their actions, victims may be less likely to view them as abusers and themselves as victims. For instance, LGBTQ IPV abusers are noted to often be very effective in convincing victims that the abuse is the victim's fault because they upset the abuser.[231] Additionally, victims often are encouraged to empathize with abusers who belong to marginalized groups (such as abusers who are LGBTQ,[232] HIV positive,[233] or have a disability[234]), being led to believe that abusers are simply acting out discrimination-induced stress and that these abusers are too emotionally fragile to have their harmful behaviors challenged. As one employee of The Northwest Network, a U.S. LGBTQ community organization, noted, "Frequently we hear batterers say, 'I have a disability so I can't batter,' 'I'm genderqueer so I can't batter,' 'I'm a person of color so I can't batter.' There is no identity that inherently bars people from being batterers."[235] Evidencing this strategy, when one cisgender female victim of a trans* male abuser attempted to confront her abuser, she says he deflected attention by claiming, "This is not about you, it's about me. *I'm* transitioning, not you."[236] This effectively silenced her and was used to excuse his behavior. Likewise, some evidence suggests that LGBTQ IPV organizations may be willing to print materials for visitors on IPV tactics used *against* trans* people but not on IPV tactics used *by* them, perhaps once again informed by a myth that members of marginalized groups cannot be abusive.[237] In other cases, abusers from marginalized demographic groups may elicit empathy without directly demanding it. Laura, a victim of same-gender IPV, expresses this desire to protect her abuser from a society that discriminates against them: "I'm all Eileen has in this world. I would never do anything to make people think badly of her."[238] Likewise, another female same-gender IPV victim indicates that she felt responsible for taking care of her abuser: "The person who could be big and angry could just as easily be intensely vulnerable and incredibly loving. For all her suffering, I thought I could love her pain away—that I just had to love her bigger, better."[239] When abusers are not out about their sexual orientation, they may tell victims to not disclose the existence of their relationship (and of course the IPV) to anyone because doing so would out them.[240] (As a possible indication of this dynamic, one study found that IPV abusers are even more likely to try to prevent victims from seeking medical help if the victim has experienced same-gender relationships, perhaps due to a fear that doctors may screen not only for IPV but also for sexual orientation.[241]) Thus, when victims are encouraged to blame themselves and empathize with abusers, it becomes significantly more difficult to recognize IPV.

Gendered myths of IPV being predominantly male-to-female have also been found to be a key reason LGBTQ IPV victims do not recognize IPV and seek help or leave.[242] Research finds that LGBTQ IPV victims who consider the severity of their victimization to be minor are less likely to seek help,[243] and perceptions of severity are undoubtedly impacted by assumptions of who can be a "real" abuser and a "real" victim. As one female same-gender IPV victim notes, "I wouldn't have known. Because domestic violence was something that happened between men and women, you know? It didn't even dawn on me."[244] For example, one study of gay IPV victims found that 44% reported that a reason they stayed with their abuser was that they did not realize that same-gender IPV existed.[245] A number of studies have similarly found that the notion of "lesbian utopia"—the belief that female same-gender relationships are ideal and inherently peaceful—hindered sexual minority women's ability to recognize and seek help for IPV in their relationships.[246] Jane, who had been raped by a female partner, explains how expectations of who can and cannot perpetrate rape made it difficult for her to label this experience as rape: "I thought that rape was only if some guy beat you up in an alley and, you know, ripped your clothes off, fucks you, and then leaves."[247] In some cases, when partners in a same-gender IPV relationship do not conform to the stereotypes of a masculine abuser and feminine victim, victims may find it particularly challenging to recognize IPV,[248] especially for masculine victims who feel their gender performance conflicts with the notion of needing help.[249] It is possible that the impact of these IPV stereotypes on recognizing abuse might be magnified for certain generations, such as for generations that grew up during the 1970s in a nation experiencing the emergence of the male-to-female-focused battered women's movement.[250] IPV stereotypes also undoubtedly vary by nation. For instance, a study of sexual minority men in Japan indicated that many of these men believed the United States to be significantly more violent and homophobic than Japan. As a result, they (incorrectly) assumed that LGBTQ IPV occurs only in the United States and is largely nonexistent in Japan—a belief that likely hinders recognition of LGBTQ IPV when it does occur in Japan.[251]

Finally, some LGBTQ IPV victims may not recognize IPV and therefore may not seek help or leave because it is their first relationship. Research suggests that many LGBTQ IPV victims do not leave because they do not know what a healthy LGBTQ relationship should look like.[252] This problem appears to be particularly common in first relationships, where there is little personal experience to draw on and often few LGBTQ peers who are out and in healthy, long-term relationships.[253] As one female sexual minority IPV victim puts it, "I had never been in a relationship with another woman before, and since she was more experienced, I just thought *this is how lesbian relationships were supposed to be.*"[254] Ellen, a female same-gender IPV victim, explains how she longed for that first romantic interest. When it finally arrived, she felt unsure how to proceed when her partner began abusing her:

> It was my first relationship. First long-term relationship. But you know I was—I was head over heels madly in love and I thought this was the relationship for life. And it started out really good. This woman was nine years older than myself. It was verbally abusive to start off with and then physically. I was, quite often had black eyes and she tried—she almost killed me once. Strangled me and then this went on for three years. . . . I was too young and insecure about the whole relationship—gay relationships, whatever. Anybody could have walked all over me.[255]

Thus, not only misinformation but also lack of information about LGBTQ relationships can make it difficult for some LGBTQ people to recognize abuse in their relationships and, in turn, to seek help.

Dependence

Another key reason that many LGBTQ IPV victims do not seek help or leave their abusers is that they feel dependent on their abusers, whether financially or emotionally. Regarding financial dependence, one small study of male sexual minority IPV victims found that nearly one in five (19%) stayed with their abusers in part due to financial dependence.[256] Cohabitation has been noted to complicate efforts to escape LGBTQ IPV, when rent and other expenses may be shared with abusers.[257] In focus-group interviews with sexual minority youths ages 18 to 24, one concern mentioned by subjects was the possibility that a partner could out them to their parents, which, beyond creating emotional damage within the family, could also result in the child being kicked out of their home or financially cut off by parents.[258] Among HIV-positive[259] and trans*[260] victims, abusers may withdraw their financial support for needed medications and treatments. Like all barriers to escaping IPV, financial dependence does not completely bar LGBTQ IPV victims from leaving their abusers—but it does make it significantly harder when an abuser's apologies and promises of change must be weighed against leaving and the resulting prospect of potential homelessness and starvation.

Just as powerful is the tug of emotional dependence and love, keeping many LGBTQ victims from seeking help or leaving.[261] Research suggests that LGBTQ people often come to rely on intimate partners to create a safe space in which they can feel accepted and supported, insulating them to a degree from a discriminatory society. Unfortunately, that reliance also makes them less likely to leave if the partner becomes abusive.[262] Yolanda, a young African-American trans* woman unable to afford desired hormone medications, explains how she had low self-esteem due to not having a body that matched her gender identity, and how her dependence on partners for emotional support unfortunately made her an ideal target for abusers:

> For a long, long time I didn't have money and that meant no hormones. I was looking for acceptance in my relationships—but a lot of 'em [partners] just thought they could abuse me because no one else would want to be with me. I allowed it for a minute. A friend told me about this doctor and counselor who could help me get hormones. That changed everything. I was finally looking like I felt I was [in terms of my gender identity]. I didn't have to be afraid anymore. And that made me feel like anything was possible in my life. I got a job and a good relationship. I even went back to school and was a pretty decent student.[263]

For Yolanda, it was only after she gained access to hormone medications, rebuilt her self-esteem, and became less emotionally reliant on her partner that she finally generated the courage to leave her abuser. As one female same-gender IPV victim details, the fact that a partner becomes abusive does not mean your affection and loyalty for the abuser disappear: "From the inside, life is held in powerful contradictions. I loved our profound intimacy that, when good, was quite magical. The person with whom at times I felt the most safe, the most alive, was the same person at times I both dreaded and feared."[264] This would suggest that leaving an abuser also can mean simultaneously leaving a best friend and loved one, thereby making the decision to leave much more complex. When the abuser is also the victim's first partner, the built-up emotional need for a romantic connection can make it particularly difficult to leave.[265] Magnifying this emotional reliance is a concern that the victim may never find another person whom they love and who loves them.[266] Living near a small LGBTQ community, where dating options may be very limited, can exacerbate this problem.[267] When victims hope to find a future partner who is not only LGBTQ but also of a particular race, ethnicity, age, body type, or other demographic group, perceived dating options can shrink dramatically. One victim explains this dilemma of whether to accept abuse when the only alternative appeared to be loneliness:

> I kept going back to this relationship that wasn't working for me in part because of my own internal sense that this was all there was. I believed there would never be another mixed Latino queer who would love a fat, mixed Latina femme. I didn't see a community where I was desired, where fat bodies were loved and celebrated, and I didn't know a community that loved and relished fabulous femmes in all of our beau-

tiful, flashy brilliance. I didn't know there were others who would love me as I am. What I knew was a beautiful community that was loving and open but didn't always know how to make space for everyone in it.[268]

Complicating matters further, it has been reported that abusers who share friends with victims may even spread rumors that it was really the victim who was abusive, which in turn may cut victims off entirely from local LGBTQ communities and dating options.[269]

Many victims very much want the relationship to work out, and stay in the hope that abusers will change soon.[270] Abusers often encourage this hope, such as when they attempt to convince their victims to return to them after the victims leave.[271] Whether it is financial or emotional dependence, many LGBTQ IPV victims have a great deal to lose if they leave their abusers, leading to complicated decisions in situations where no perfect option is available.

Fear

Fear of negative consequences for leaving can lead many LGBTQ IPV victims to remain with abusers. For some victims, when fear of harm and emotional distress reach critical levels, this can tip the scales and make leaving feel safer than staying.[272] Until that tipping point, though, many victims decide to stay because they fear that IPV will escalate should they leave.[273] Many victims specifically stay out of fear of being outed by the abuser, which could have far-reaching consequences that are emotional (e.g., being ostracized by friends and family), financial (e.g., having difficulty finding a new job in a nation without antidiscrimination laws), and legal (e.g., risking incarceration in nations that criminalize being LGBTQ).[274] Some research suggests that being outed not just as LGBTQ but also as an IPV victim can be doubly stigmatizing, and this stigma could be further magnified in pockets of certain racial, ethnic, and immigrant communities that might see LGBTQ IPV as bringing shame to both the victim and the victim's family.[275] As one Asian-American lesbian victim of IPV explains, "Everyone knows each other, and people take sides so you don't talk about it to protect yourself and her."[276]

Beyond the fear of IPV escalating and of being outed, LGBTQ IPV victims may also stay with abusers out of fear of further stigmatizing themselves. Research suggests that many LGBTQ IPV victims remain in abusive relationships in part out of concern that their victimization will stigmatize them in the eyes of those they are already out to.[277] Specifically, LGBTQ IPV victims who are out may have already waged an extensive campaign to gain acceptance for their LGBTQ identity from important people in their lives, and some victims may fear losing that hard-earned acceptance if they disclose their victimization. Ultimately, they may risk being ostracized by currently accepting friends and family if they seek help. Laura, a female same-gender IPV victim, sums up this conundrum: "When I told them about being gay they couldn't accept it. Now Eileen is in my life, and at least my mom has finally come around. How could I give her a reason to reject me again?"[278] This concern is mirrored for trans* people and those who date them, as illustrated by Maria, a sexual minority cisgender woman who was abused by a trans* partner: "I can't tell [my family] the whole truth cause I'm busy convincing them that trans is okay [and that they don't need to be worried about me]. I needed them to understand and believe trans, and that was true of all of my friends, but especially my family because I knew they would think trans people were crazy if they heard that this person was treating me that way."[279]

Ultimately, LGBTQ IPV victims may fear that friends and family will perceive their victimization to be caused by them *being* LGBTQ.

While this fear can be localized (i.e., fearing that disclosing victimization could stigmatize the victim), this fear can also extend beyond the victim. In particular, victims may fear that disclosing victimization could be perceived as confirming negative stereotypes of *all* LGBTQ people and that, therefore, seeking help might result in increasing societal discrimination.[280] It has been speculated that this fear can be potent for those LGBTQ people who have achieved respect in their families and communities, whose relationships might be looked to as a healthy and happy model that furthers the legitimacy of all LGBTQ relationships.[281] One female sexual minority IPV victim in just such a situation discusses the pressures she felt: "I was in this fishbowl, and if I was to tell somebody what was going on, then . . . they'd look at the whole lesbian thing and, 'See, it's not supposed to be that way, because look what happened to you.' And it really added a lot of pressure . . . because I really felt like I had to represent a good relationship. And prove that I made the right choice."[282]

This sense of responsibility to proudly represent your entire demographic group—even when that means masking the abuse in your relationship—is echoed by research on racial and ethnic minority communities,[283] suggesting that this pressure may be magnified for LGBTQ racial-ethnic minorities.[284] In some instances, the pressure on LGBTQ IPV victims to positively represent LGBTQ communities may not just be self-generated pressure but can also be encouraged by friends. Female same-gender IPV victim Adrienne Blenman provides a heartbreaking account of her seeking help from friends, who responded by urging her to keep silent lest she hurt the image of all LGBTQ people:

> The lesbians I did speak to were adamant that I not talk about this too much or go to any type of shelter for help. Their biggest fear (and a very realistic one) was that the lesbian community as a whole would suffer even more abuse and derision from heterosexual society, which already saw us as sick and perverse. Not finding any kind of support from my own community of women hurt almost as much as the betrayal I felt in the relationship.[285]

This concern of representing one's demographic group positively, even if this means hiding IPV, must be understood in the context of discrimination in society. This fear is derived directly from that discrimination and concerns over exacerbating it. LGBTQ IPV victims may also not seek help and remain with abusers because of fears related to their children. Research on sexual minority IPV victims who are mothers finds that having more children and having younger children increases the chances they will seek help,[286] suggesting that victims fear that their children are at risk of being harmed either directly by abusers or indirectly by witnessing IPV.[287] (Not surprisingly, limited research also suggests that pet owners may fear that an LGBTQ IPV abuser will harm their pets should they attempt to leave.[288]) LGBTQ IPV victims may also fear that the abuser will out them to their children, who may not be aware of their LGBTQ status.[289] Lastly, LGBTQ IPV victims may fear a loss of access to their children should they leave.[290] This fear could be based on misperceptions or realities of custody laws, as was the case with Laurie, a same-gender IPV victim and mother who did not tell her health-care provider about the victimization out of concern that "they might take my baby or something."[291] This fear can be particularly potent in nations where same-gender partners cannot legally co-adopt a child or adopt the biological child of a same-gender partner: in such cases, victims may not have any legal connection to their abuser's biological children, and as such they may have no legal route to guarantee they will ever be able to see their children again.[292] Likewise, many same-gender IPV victims have children from previous different-gender relationships, and they may either have full custody or share custody with their former different-gender partner. Should their same-gender IPV victimization become public knowledge, though, in nations whose courts show preference for placing children with different-gender couples, they may have to worry that the courts will cede custody of their children to their ex-partner.[293]

Barriers to Seeking Help

Researcher Joan McClennen notes that LGBTQ IPV victims are "double closeted," silenced not only by fear of their abuser but also by a fear that a discriminatory society will not wish to help them.[294] Indeed, a final key reason that LGBTQ IPV victims may not seek help or leave is that they have concerns about the process of seeking help.[295] These concerns can include perceiving help to be unavailable, as well as perceiving existing help to be unwelcoming. To begin, some LGBTQ IPV victims may believe that there are no services available to them, which may be a particular concern for trans* and male IPV victims in nations where services are most geared toward cisgender women.[296] As the next chapter will illustrate, unfortunately this concern is still valid in many regions, and victims who have been turned away from services specifically because they are LGBTQ may be deterred from seeking other sources of help.[297] For certain types of LGBTQ IPV victims, help-giving resources might seem entirely inaccessible for a variety of other reasons, such as their not speaking the language used by services or fearing deportation if they seek help.[298] In some nations, LGBTQ people may also be less likely to have health insurance, which would in turn hinder their abilities to seek help from health-care providers.[299]

Additionally, many LGBTQ IPV victims remain with their abusers because they perceive potential sources of help to be unwelcoming, likely doing more harm than good. As chapter 3 discussed, a common practice of LGBTQ IPV abusers is to actively isolate victims from their friends and family,[300] which may lead some victims to fear that those who used to be closest to them will feel spurned and will be uninterested in helping. Moreover, for LGBTQ victims, a conscious choice might be made not to discuss their abuse with those who have shown themselves to be homophobic or transphobic in the past.[301] As one lesbian victim of IPV explained, her family had not yet "come to grips with the fact that I am a lesbian [so] how are they going to come to grips with the fact that I'm a lesbian that was abused on top of it."[302] Research finds that this fear of a discriminatory response and not being taken seriously extends to more formal sources of help like IPV victim agencies and law enforcement.[303] Indeed, one longitudinal study found that female same-gender IPV victims who believed that no one would take their victimization seriously were significantly more likely to experience abuse over a greater sustained period of time.[304] Some victims note that, after experiencing trauma, they have no desire or energy to educate often ill-informed and prejudiced service providers on the realities of LGBTQ IPV.[305] Concerns over a discriminatory response may be heightened for victims who are closeted about being LGBTQ,[306] likely in part because closeted people often are already concerned by broader societal discrimination, and likely in part because of a fear that word of their LGBTQ status could reach people important to them like family. For instance, a Canadian study of sexual minority IPV victimization found that outness and help-seeking frequency were directly linked among victims, with people who were more closeted also being likely to seek help a smaller number of times.[307] Likewise, research on female same-gender IPV victims found that they were far more likely to try to resolve their victimization on their own rather than seek help if they were either closeted or ashamed of their sexual orientation.[308] As one trans* IPV victim explains, "[I] didn't want to tell any service providers about the relationship problems as explaining the details would have required me to come out. . . . I was worried service providers would be ignorant of trans identities and potentially even quite prejudiced."[309] In some cases, LGBTQ IPV abusers play into this fear of discriminatory responses by directly telling victims that no one they ask for help from will take LGBTQ IPV seriously[310] or that police may even incorrectly arrest the victim if the victim is not physically smaller than the abuser.[311] As the next chapter will explore, this concern is not entirely invalid, with considerable evidence of

WHY DOES LGBTQ IPV HAPPEN?   **123**

discriminatory attitudes and behaviors existing in pockets of every type of help-giving resource. For particular types of LGBTQ people, additional factors may contribute to perceptions that they will be discriminated against by these supposed sources of help. These additional factors might include fears of racism by law enforcement and service providers,[312] being discriminated against by law enforcement due to the victim's social class (e.g., law enforcement taking IPV less seriously than other crimes in a high-crime-rate neighborhood, law enforcement suggesting that the victim could block an abuser's return home by installing a new door lock that the victim cannot financially afford, etc.),[313] concerns that word will spread if services are sought in a tightly knit immigrant or racial-ethnic community,[314] and misunderstanding what forms of evidence of abuse will be accepted by a criminal justice system (such as believing in the myth that forensic evidence is unobtainable for female same-gender sexual assault[315]).

SEEING THE BIG PICTURE

Seeing the big picture of why IPV happens is complicated by several issues. These include moving past fears of excusing abusers and blaming victims, distinguishing causes from outcomes, and, ultimately, considering whether there are one or multiple explanations of IPV.

To begin, a number of scholars have noted their concern that discussion of LGBTQ IPV causes may lead some to excuse the actions of abusers and blame victims.[316] Patrick Letellier, one of the founding researchers of LGBTQ IPV, sums up this perspective: "To attribute a perpetrator's violence to any outside cause or force is to excuse the violence or blur the responsibility for its occurrence."[317] According to a Canadian study of counselors who address sexual minority IPV in their work, this fear extends to some service providers. One counselor explains her inner tension in both wanting to place blame squarely on the shoulders of abusers and yet at the same time wanting to understand why IPV happens: "So if there is a propensity to handle problems in a physical way, it [stress] may help to release, to disinhibit that kind of response. (Pause) And I hate myself when I talk like this because I feel really strongly when I talk about perpetrators being held responsible for their behaviors."[318] While it is important to remember that IPV perpetration is a choice and that abusers are responsible for their actions, research does strongly suggest that these choices are influenced by certain factors. The more we know about what encourages abuse, the better prepared society will be to create prevention-education programs, rehabilitative batterer-intervention programs, victim mental health service provision, and government policy. Likewise, considering reasons why victims remain with abusers (and directing policy to make victim services more available to LGBTQ IPV victims) might be perceived as placing responsibility for IPV on the shoulders of victims. Again, while it is vital that victims not be made to feel responsible for ending or even escaping IPV—ultimately we must remember that the responsibility for crimes rest with criminals alone—if studying and decreasing barriers to escape helps save even one victim from continuing to endure abuse, the effort would be well worth it.

Another important question is whether "causes" are actually "outcomes," whether vice versa is sometimes the case, and whether perhaps they might even be "covariates" that co-occur but are neither cause nor effect. This is often difficult to untangle because most research on IPV is cross-sectional (collecting data once) rather than longitudinal (collecting data over a longer period of time), making it challenging to determine whether a factor emerged prior to, during, or after IPV occurred. For example, as chapter 3 highlighted, many LGBTQ people who use violence in relationships also receive violence,[319] and, among these IPV user-receivers, many of them use violence only in self-defense.[320] This suggests that, at least in some cases, subjects identified in survey research as "perpetrators" may actually be victims who fought back in self-defense. In other cases, perpetrators may have been victims in previous relationships. This all raises the possibility that a factor like substance use that co-occurs with LGBTQ IPV perpetration in a cross-sectional survey study could have multiple conflicting meanings: this may mean we are looking at abusers who became abusive in part because of their substance use, abusers who used substances to cope with and justify their abusive behavior, victims who fought back in self-defense and are coping with substance use, victims who are coping with substance use and were perpetrators in previous relationships, and abusers and victims who happen to use substances for reasons only indirectly related to IPV (such as drinkers perhaps being more likely to frequent social venues where abusers tend to look for future partners). Additionally, because human behavior often has not only immediate causes but also long-developing causes, it is possible that the theorized "causes" of LGBTQ IPV perpetration discussed in this chapter may be "mediated" by additional factors—that is, A causes B, and in turn B causes IPV perpetration. For instance, research finds that internalized homophobia is linked with relationship fusion as well as decreased satisfaction with one's life and intimate relationship, each of which then in turn increases the likelihood of (i.e., mediates) IPV perpetration.[321] This raises the complex question not only of whether LGBTQ IPV has multiple causes but also of whether those causes are actually multiple-step processes. Longitudinal research is needed in the future to more clearly illuminate the common pathways to perpetration.

In the end, making sense of competing causes of LGBTQ IPV requires more than just accounting for the free will in choices made by abusers and the complexity of discerning cause from effect. In particular, there are so many potential causes that it becomes challenging to ascertain which theorized causes are most important. In some cases, scholars have argued that IPV must have only one set of causes that apply equally well to all relationship types, and factors that appear to apply to only one type of relationship (such as those involving sexual minorities) must not be very significant causes if they do not transcend gender and sexual-orientation boundaries.[322] Others have argued that we should not ignore IPV causal factors just because they do not apply equally well to all relationship types because, ultimately, reflecting the complexities of reality should be the goal of IPV theories, not creating oversimplified versions of realities.[323] Certainly there is evidence that LGBTQ IPV has multiple catalysts that do not appear to all have the same root cause and that gender may impact LGBTQ IPV in different ways than it does with HC IPV; and an emerging area of research suggests that there may be causes unique to LGBTQ IPV. Simply uncovering the range of LGBTQ IPV causes is a worthy goal for research, but a good next step will be to determine how these causes interact within individual abusers. One possibility posited by some researchers is to view IPV causes as additive. In this "syndemic model," the odds of a particular outcome steadily increase for each "cause" or risk factor that applies to them. Often same-gender or LGBTQ IPV has been used in a syndemic model as a causal factor, along with health-care costs and utilization,[324] of HIV transmission and sexual risk-taking.[325] Applied to predicting IPV perpetration, this model posits that a person who has experienced childhood exposure to violence *and* uses substances is at greater risk of perpetrating IPV than a person who has only one of these risk factors. This assumption, though, might mask further complexities, such as the possibility that some IPV risk factors are themselves associated with one another (e.g., substance use as a coping mechanism for childhood exposure to trauma), and therefore their co-occurrence may not actually greatly increase risk of IPV perpetration. It is also distinctly possible that the clusters of causes that are most potent in explaining HC IPV may not be the same as those for LGBTQ IPV, and primary causes may likewise differ among subgroups in LGBTQ populations.

IMPLICATIONS FOR POLICY, PRACTICE, AND RESEARCH

Looking at the landscape of research on the causes of LGBTQ IPV, there are several clear lessons that can be drawn for policy, practice, and research. For policymakers, one of the easiest ways to decrease the risk of LGBTQ IPV occurring is by raising awareness of its existence. Research consistently finds that many LGBTQ IPV victims do not leave their abusers because they do not recognize they are being abused.[326] Scholars speculate that a key reason for this is that models of healthy and unhealthy LGBTQ relationships are largely absent from public discourse and the media.[327] Particularly in first relationships, research repeatedly concludes that LGBTQ IPV can go unrecognized because victims and abusers do not know whether their experiences are normal for LGBTQ relationships.[328] In some instances, governments can contribute to this problem by creating public media campaigns (e.g., government websites, informational radio and television spots, etc.) that discuss only HC IPV, as was found to be the case in the 2000s in Australia.[329] By including discussions of healthy and abusive LGBTQ relationships in these public media campaigns, governments can help prevent LGBTQ IPV (by decreasing the chances an LGBTQ person believes their abusive behaviors are "normal") and can help victims escape (by ensuring they recognize the warning signs of LGBTQ IPV). In addition to raising awareness about LGBTQ IPV, the harder but likely more impactful contribution that policymakers can make is to decrease discrimination in society. As reviewed in this chapter, LGBTQ people are more likely to perpetrate IPV for a whole host of reasons that share discrimination as their origin: internalizing the homophobic and transphobic attitudes of society has been shown in many studies to predict LGBTQ IPV perpetration[330] and victimization;[331] experiencing discrimination has also predicted perpetration[332] and victimization.[333] Being closeted—which is often caused by fearing discriminatory responses—may also predict perpetration[334] and victimization.[335] Policymakers play a direct role in fostering or dispelling homophobic and transphobic cultures, not only through public media campaigns but by leading through action: governments that protect LGBTQ human rights through antidiscrimination laws and through inclusion in law-based rights (such as the rights to be LGBTQ, to marry, and to adopt children) send a message to their societies that LGBTQ people are equal human beings and that discrimination will not be tolerated. (See chapter 6 for a discussion of how governments can work to improve access to LGBTQ human rights.)

For practitioners and others working to address LGBTQ IPV, it is important to screen for, and address with abusers, the multitude of potential causes of perpetration so as to decrease the risk of recidivism. This will be particularly the case for agencies and practitioners focused on helping abusers rehabilitate, such as certain mental health counselors and batterer-intervention programs. These potential causes include the aforementioned factors: socialization into violence-condoning attitudes, abuser–victim power imbalances, dependency between abusers and victims, justifications abusers tell themselves and their victims, psychological traits, gender performance, discrimination-induced stress and feelings of disempowerment, discrimination-induced internalization of homophobic or transphobic attitudes, and discrimination-induced low degrees of outness. Likewise, mental health-care providers and IPV victim organizations should be aware of reasons victims do not leave abusers: not recognizing IPV, financial and emotional dependency, fear (of IPV escalating, being outed, further stigmatizing themselves, further stigmatizing all LGBTQ people, and having children taken away), and perceptions that victim resources are either nonexistent or discriminatory. Many victims seek help before they are prepared to leave their abusers for good, and being able to systematically address the many factors tying victims to their abusers may decrease the chances that victims return to abusers or enter into future abusive relationships. Prevention-education programming can also benefit from an understanding of the justifications abusers tell themselves and their victims, as well as an understanding of the barriers to help-seeking that first responders and bystanders should be cognizant of.

Last, for researchers, there is still a great deal of information that needs to be uncovered about why LGBTQ IPV happens. To begin, consider the primary causal theories espoused by scholars: abusers target LGBTQ victims who feel most discriminated against and stigmatized because such victims may be less likely to resist or seek help; abusers target their LGBTQ victims because they are acting on internalized discriminatory attitudes learned from society; abusers are releasing stress caused by discrimination; and abusers are regaining a sense of power they felt was taken from them by discrimination. In each case, beyond anecdotal evidence and small-scale qualitative interview studies, there is actually very little quantitative research that has systematically tested whether these theories represent reality for most LGBTQ IPV abusers. For instance, when researchers have studied minority stress theory, they have studied only the factors that might induce stress (e.g., low degree of outness, internalized homophobic attitudes, etc.) rather than whether they actually have induced stress. We cannot assume, for instance, that all closeted LGBTQ people are equally stressed by being closeted. Research is needed to test the currently dominant theories in a more direct way. Additionally, while scholars have done an excellent job of finding a variety of potential causes of LGBTQ IPV, it is still unclear which are the most common—an important distinction that could greatly improve the effectiveness of services. Moreover, it is also unclear why some perpetrators desist from abuse after their first LGBTQ IPV relationship while others continue abusive patterns in future relationships. Nonprobability studies of female same-gender IPV suggest that 4% of victims have at some point been abused by the same person,[336] and having perpetrated abuse in past relationships is linked with perpetrating IPV with greater frequency in a later relationship.[337] With these exceptions, serial LGBTQ IPV perpetration—what predicts it and, in turn, how it might be best prevented and intervened in—has largely not yet been studied. Finally, most research on causes of IPV and barriers to help-seeking have thus far excluded trans* abusers and trans* victims—a major knowledge gap that researchers can help fill.

5

HOW CAN WE IMPROVE
NONGOVERNMENTAL RESPONSES?

I actually was one who called the hotline and was told in a completely inap-
propriate way, "Well, we'll have someone try to call you." And I'm in a situa-
tion where I'm in a restaurant and my partner's outside and I can't go out
there because she is going to hit me, and they are like, "Well, we'll have the
lesbian director call you back."[1]

One day you wake up and realize that your partner is the source of immense pain
in your life, but leaving—and deciding even if you should leave—brings with it
many questions and risks. Could someone you trust really be capable of abuse?
Will your partner try to stalk and hurt you if you leave? Are you risking being
outed and losing family, friends, employment, or housing? Significantly, do the
risks of leaving outweigh the risks of staying? In their darkest hours, when so
much is at stake—possibly their very lives—many realize they cannot stop an
abuser on their own. LGBTQ IPV victims turn to a variety of **help-giving resources
(HGRs)** for assistance in coping with and escaping abuse: friends, family, acquaintances, support groups, mental health-care providers, medical health-care providers, LGBTQ community agencies, IPV victim agencies and hotlines, IPV victim
shelters, and (as will be discussed in the next chapter) the criminal justice system.
The potential clearly exists for HGRs to make a meaningful, positive impact in the
lives of LGBTQ IPV victims. Despite the reality that "recovery" from LGBTQ IPV
victimization is a complex and often never completed process,[2] research[3] provides
inspiring examples of HGRs being respectful and supportive of LGBTQ identities
while offering both valuable advice and needed assistance.

   Still, victims face a conundrum when considering seeking help: HGRs have the
capacity for both empathy and oppression—and victims may not know which they
are getting until after they ask for help. Unfortunately, if an LGBTQ IPV victim
happens to turn first to a homophobic, transphobic, or dismissive HGR, that can
deter the victim from seeking further help. Explains one female sexual minority
IPV victim, "How can I take something so serious as to get help for me, if the people around me are not, by me being a lesbian? It's like—I called the police just

exactly once. And I'll never do that again. Because usually, it's a big old macho guy, and they won't take it serious."[4] A common response to this problem is to train one individual at a given HGR agency to be the go-to person for either all LGBTQ IPV victims or all LGBTQ people generally. The use of such specialists or LGBTQ community liaisons is problematic on a number of levels—such as multiplying the liaison's workload, or making the victim feel like a "special" case isolated from the remainder of an agency's services and clients.[5] That said, by far the clearest danger in this overreliance on one trained employee is that the liaison may not be available at the particular moment when a victim seeks help. As Dana, an IPV victim agency service provider, notes, untrained employees can be put in a challenging position: "You may have a situation where you're the only person here and the client comes to the door. What are you gonna do? You can't turn her away."[6] When this happens, results can be disastrous. In some instances, untrained HGRs may just turn the victim away or tell them to come back later when the liaison is there. As Megan explains in the statement at the top of this chapter, when she contacted an IPV victim hotline because she was being stalked by her abuser and feared she was in imminent physical danger, she was told that they could not help her at the moment because the liaison was not available. A former LGBTQ IPV victim agency director notes that a lack of agency-wide training ultimately means that the quality of responses a victim receives—ranging from helpful and respectful to dismissive and outright discriminatory—ultimately comes down to the luck of the draw: "A lot of survivors I dealt with talked about the 'advocate from hell,' you know, if you get a good advocate and you happen to call on the right night at the shelter, you're in good shape, if you call on the wrong night you're in very bad shape. . . . it's not a pretty picture."[7]

While HGRs often operate as separate fiefdoms that rarely communicate and collaborate, from a victim's perspective they may appear to form a single armored shield that can save them. With one chink in that armor, the facade of a shield fades, leaving many LGBTQ IPV victims feeling even more trapped than they did before they sought help.[8]

This chapter explores the challenges and opportunities that nongovernmental HGRs face in assisting LGBTQ IPV victims. Ultimately, armed with the knowledge of how and why LGBTQ IPV happens, societies can work toward a day in which no victim must fight IPV alone.

FROM WHOM DO VICTIMS SEEK HELP?

LGBTQ IPV victims seek help from a wide range of HGRs, including what might be termed "informal" HGRs—individuals who do not work for a service-providing organization, such as family, friends, neighbors, and religious advisors—and "formal" HGRs—those who do work for a service-providing organization, including those employed with support groups and mental health-care organizations, medical health-care organizations, LGBTQ agencies not primarily focused on IPV, IPV victim agencies and hotlines, IPV victim shelters, and the criminal justice system. (See figure 10.) Research consistently finds that victims are most likely to seek help from friends. More specifically, while estimates vary by study, somewhere between 34% and 69% of LGBTQ IPV victims seek help from friends.[9] While these can be the abuser's friends or mutual friends, most often these are solely friends of the victim,[10] and some research suggests that LGBTQ and HC friends are equally likely to be sought out.[11] After this, research consistently finds that mental health-care providers (sought out by 6–58% of LGBTQ IPV victims) and family (12–35%) are the second and third most often utilized HGRs, with most studies[12] (with two exceptions[13]) finding the former to be more commonly sought out than the latter. Beyond the top three HGR types, no more than one-fifth of victims seek help from law enforcement (0–20%),[14] support groups (9–19%),[15] or medical health-care providers (1–19%).[16] After this, help-seeking tapers off considerably, with somewhere between only 0% and 15% seeking assistance from (in order of most- to least-often-sought-out HGRs, based on the highest available estimates) religious advisors,[17] IPV hotlines,[18] IPV shelters,[19] neighbors,[20] attorneys,[21] LGBTQ agencies not primarily focused on IPV,[22] mainstream IPV agencies,[23] and, last—and ironically—IPV agencies focused primarily on LGBTQ IPV.[24]

It is important to note that five studies were excluded from the aforementioned estimates and accompanying table, either because the researchers recruited portions of their samples directly from HGRs[25] or because the researchers asked help-seeking questions only of victims who viewed their relationships as problematic.[26] In both cases, it is likely that these subsets of victims—those who are motivated to seek or already are seeking help—may exhibit greater HGR utilization than the typical LGBTQ IPV victim. Indeed, this particular subset of studies did find higher help-seeking prevalence rates across nearly all types of HGRs. For example, 60–85% sought help from friends,[27] 51–75% from mental health-care providers,[28] 20–60% from family,[29] 4–65% from law enforcement,[30] 42% from support groups,[31] and 27–63% from medical health-care providers.[32] As compared with the previously detailed studies,[33] estimates from these five studies may be upwardly biased and therefore may not provide the most accurate picture of HGR utilization patterns.

In sum, when focusing on what are likely more representative and accurate estimates,[34] LGBTQ IPV victims appear to be most likely to seek help from informal HGRs—namely, friends and family—as well as certain types of formal HGRs—primarily mental and medical health-care providers and law enforcement. Unfortunately, those organizations specifically designed with the sole purpose of addressing IPV—IPV victim agencies, hotlines, and shelters—have among the lowest utilization rates. Most of these studies sampled only one LGBTQ sub-population (such as sexual minority women), and the rare exceptions typically did

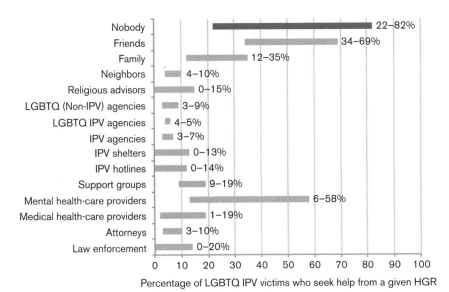

FIGURE 10. From whom do LGBTQ IPV victims seek help?

not break results down by sexual orientation or gender. That said, limited research on samples including both male and female sexual minority IPV victims suggests that female sexual minority IPV victims are more likely than male sexual minority IPV victims to seek help from nearly all types of HGRs,[35] with the starkest gap being in seeking help from mental health-care providers.[36] The main exception appears to be with law enforcement, to whom male sexual minority IPV victims are more likely to report IPV victimization.[37] Among LGBTQ IPV victims, one study suggests that trans* victims are the least likely to report to police.[38]

EXACTLY HOW HELPFUL ARE HELP-GIVING RESOURCES?

Estimating the helpfulness of HGR types can be quite challenging. This is because HGR helpfulness likely varies *within* a specific HGR type, like IPV shelters: helpfulness depends on which shelter is visited, which of the several services from the same shelter is being assessed (such as the quality of intake interviews versus a shelter-based support group), and which of several shelter employees is being focused on. Like most social science research, studies providing HGR helpfulness ratings tap into only broad differences in the experiences of subjects. Simply put, these ratings are neither praise for nor an indictment of all who belong to a particular HGR type. That said, what low helpfulness ratings *do* indicate is an underlying problem that, if

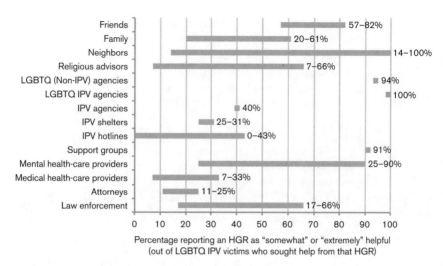

FIGURE 11. Among LGBTQ IPV victims who sought help from a particular resource, what percentage found it helpful?

not identified and fixed, could on average set back the recovery process of LGBTQ IPV victims and may deter them from seeking further assistance.

A number of studies have asked LGBTQ IPV victims how helpful the HGR types they have used are. Typically, these studies have assessed degree of helpfulness on a four-point scale, from "extremely" and "somewhat" helpful to "a little bit" and "not at all" helpful.[39] Following the common practice of the authors of these study reports, "a little bit" and "not at all" helpful are being treated in this section as inadequate responses to a situation as serious as an IPV victim seeking help, and, as such, only "somewhat" and "extremely" helpful are being treated as truly helpful.[40] One additional study[41] provided a more clear-cut if less detailed assessment of perceived HGR helpfulness, permitting subjects to rate an HGR only as either helpful or not. (See figure 11.)

According to one study, the highest-rated HGRs are agencies whose primary focus is on LGBTQ IPV (100% of victims reported such agencies as either "extremely" or "somewhat" helpful) and LGBTQ agencies whose primary focus is not on IPV (94%), along with support groups (91%).[42] It is difficult to know if these results are accurate since they draw upon only one study, but it is telling that the highest-rated HGRs in that study (and any study) are those whose overarching mission is to serve LGBTQ people. While other non-LGBTQ-specific HGRs have been found in some studies to be highly rated, different studies find those same HGRs to be infrequently rated as helpful: these include neighbors (14–100%),[43] mental health-care providers (25–90%),[44] law enforcement (17–66%),[45] religious advisors (7–66%),[46] family (20–61%),[47] and IPV hotlines (0–43%).[48] For nearly all other HGR types, only a small percentage of LGBTQ IPV victims find them to be helpful, including (in order of most to least likely to be rated as helpful, based on the highest available estimates) mainstream IPV victim agencies (40%),[49] medical health-care providers (7–33%),[50] IPV victim shelters (25–31%),[51] and attorneys (11– 25%).[52] In fact, when examining HGRs assessed by more than one study (and thus based on corroborated estimates), the only HGR that consistently ranks as helpful by at least half of all LGBTQ IPV victims is friends (57–82%).[53] This is reflected in most studies, which find friends to be either the most[54] or the second-most[55] likely to be rated as helpful as compared with all other HGRs. Not surprisingly, research suggests that the victim's friends are more likely to be found helpful than the abuser's friends or mutual friends.[56] Although there appears to be little consistency across studies in HGR helpfulness rankings beyond friends, three studies found mental health-care providers to be either the most[57] or the second-most[58] likely to be rated as helpful, and no study found them to be ranked in the bottom half of HGRs. As for the type of mental health services being received, one study indicates individual mental health counseling is nearly twice as likely to be perceived as helpful as couples counseling.[59] This is perhaps not surprising given that scholars find that the dialogue in couples counseling can be manipulated by abusers and may also serve as a catalyst for an abuser to inflict further harm on their victims.[60]

Overall, it appears that the HGRs that are most likely to be perceived as helpful by LGBTQ IPV victims are also among those they are most likely to seek help from—specifically, friends and mental health-care providers—along with LGBTQ-focused agencies, which they are unfortunately unlikely to seek help from. The remaining HGRs provide a mixed bag, with studies suggesting that their likelihood of being helpful to a particular LGBTQ IPV victim ranges from mediocre to poor. Studies have generally not attempted to assess whether perceived HGR helpfulness varies by the gender and sexual orientation of LGBTQ IPV victims, with one exception. One study of LGBTQ IPV victims found that the likeliness of rating an HGR as helpful does not significantly differ by gender, for every HGR type.[61] This would suggest that HGR types that tend to be less likely to be rated as helpful are found on average to be problematic by all types of LGBTQ IPV victims.

RESPECT AND TRAINING

Many of the problems with some HGRs that will be discussed in this chapter come down to two issues: respect and training. To begin, the distinction between informal HGRs (those not affiliated with service-providing organizations, like friends and family) and formal HGRs (those affiliated with service-providing organizations, such as mental health providers and shelter staff) is an important one because their ultimate purposes differ. Informal HGRs should provide emotional support, validation to victims that they are experiencing IPV and do not deserve it, and, if desired, advice and assistance on utilizing formal HGRs (all of which have generally been found by LGBTQ IPV victims to be helpful approaches[62]). While formal HGRs also have a duty to provide emotional support and validation, they must be prepared to provide effective services as well. The success of these missions hinges upon informal and formal HGRs having a basic level of *respect* for LGBTQ IPV victims—accepting and taking seriously both their LGBTQ identities and their IPV experiences. A lack of respect may signal to victims that they are not truly victims, do not deserve help, and may be further emotionally abused by the HGR itself—all of which may push victims back into their abusive relationships. In addition to respect, formal HGRs in particular must also receive *training* on the uniqueness of LGBTQ IPV so that they can provide tailored services that will maximize positive effects for LGBTQ IPV victims. A lack of training on the nature of LGBTQ IPV—and in turn a reliance on knowledge of HC IPV to make often inaccurate assumptions about LGBTQ IPV—may result in less effective services and, furthermore, may signal to victims that they are not truly welcome.

As will be examined in this chapter, the degree to which HGRs are achieving these goals—respect and training—varies considerably by HGR type: again, these can include friends and family, health-care systems (including mental and medical health-care providers as well as support groups), and mainstream and LGBTQ-focused IPV organizations (including IPV victim agencies, hotlines, and shelters).

FRIENDS AND FAMILY

Friends

Friends and family are the most commonly utilized informal HGRs. Friends in particular—primarily the victim's friends rather than the abuser's or mutual friends[63]—play a key role in helping LGBTQ IPV victims, primarily because research consistently finds them to be by far the most likely resource to which victims will turn for help.[64] (Some research suggests that victims are equally likely to reach out to LGBTQ and HC friends.[65]) As one indication of the degree to which friends are relied upon, a study of gay men found that 66% knew a male same-gender IPV victim.[66] According to research, friends are so heavily relied upon at least in part due to a mistrust of the alternatives, which can be perceived to be less respectful and ultimately not welcoming to LGBTQ people.[67] One trans* IPV victim explains: "I don't talk to organisations. I talk to individuals who I know. There isn't organisations out there to help. To be honest, see, if you get a crisis like that, it's an immediate thing. It's immediate, you need help. . . . where do you seek help immediately? It's not there, it just isn't there."[68]

By comparison to formal HGRs and family, friends may be perceived as providing a safe space, particularly those friends who have responded positively when the victim came out to them about their sexual minority or trans* status.[69] Additionally, some friends may reach out to victims rather than always vice versa, as friends may be in a unique position as bystanders to recognize when IPV is emerging in a victim's relationship.[70]

As for how effectively friends assist LGBTQ IPV victims, the capacity for a positive impact is clearly there. Friends can and should show respect for the victim—respect for their LGBTQ identity as well as the seriousness of the IPV they have experienced—so as to encourage victims to recognize that they do not deserve to be abused. Friends can and should provide emotional support. Friends can and should provide advice and assistance on reaching out to more formal HGRs. Research does indeed suggest that friends consistently rank as one of the only above-average HGRs in terms of perceived helpfulness, with somewhere between 57% and 82% of LGBTQ IPV victims reporting friends to be helpful.[71] These statistics could be viewed through an optimistic lens: clearly victims feel that their friends are doing a better job of helping them than nearly anyone else in their lives. However, a more critical assessment of these statistics suggests that somewhere between one-fifth and one-half of victims do not feel that their friends are adequately helpful. Moreover, these broad statistics fail to capture the nuanced ways in which responses by friends can be further improved.

First, it is possible that some friends hold discriminatory views about LGBTQ people and may believe in inaccurate stereotypes about LGBTQ IPV. No study to date has systematically assessed these negative views among friends who have provided help to LGBTQ IPV victims. That said, studies of college and university students—who, like most friends, are not required to received antidiscrimination or LGBTQ IPV knowledge training—consistently find that same-gender IPV is viewed as less serious[72] and even legal.[73] Perhaps as a consequence of views that are dismissive of LGBTQ IPV, one study of one hundred lesbian victims of IPV found that common responses by friends included denying the problem, blaming the victim, and cooperating with the abuser.[74] One victim describes the response by her friends: "My friends brushed it off, didn't believe [my partner] was abusive, said it was a two-way street. One said a good fist fight might clear the air."[75] The researcher reported this to be, unfortunately, a typical response in the study.

Second, friends may tell victims to remain silent. In homophobic and transphobic societies, LGBTQ people may in some cases view their intimate relationships as a way to validate the healthiness and normalcy of being LGBTQ. IPV may be perceived by some LGBTQ people as setting back a movement to reduce discriminatory attitudes in society. As such, researchers have found a number of cases in which LGBTQ IPV victims have been told by their LGBTQ friends to keep quiet about the abuse, to not seek further help from friends or any other HGR, out of fear that doing so will further stigmatize an already stigmatized population.[76] As one LGBTQ IPV victim put it bluntly, LGBTQ people "just don't want to hear [about the abuse]. They want me to shut up as soon as possible."[77] In other instances where LGBTQ friends are closeted, they may fear being outed simply by publicly associating with other LGBTQ people, and, as a result, they may be less willing to help an LGBTQ IPV victim.[78] Unfortunately, while perhaps well intentioned, drastic efforts to deter victims from seeking further help may leave them trapped in their abusive relationships.

Third, the often small size of LGBTQ social groups can also mean that victims are more likely to share friends with their abusers. In such environments, when victims seek help, it can backfire. Interviews with female sexual minority IPV victims find that friends often feel the need to take sides, sometimes siding with the abuser simply because they are closer friends.[79] Another study found that abusers can be particularly adept at convincing friends that the victim is crazy and, perhaps, that the victim is actually the abuser, ultimately turning a victim's friends against the victim.[80]

Fourth and last, even when friends do empathize with the victim, they may be ill equipped to provide more than emotional support. Perhaps understandably, LGBTQ friends may themselves be mistrusting of formal HGRs, perceiving them to be discriminatory and not welcoming to LGBTQ IPV victims. As a consequence, research suggests that they are often willing to tell victims to leave their abusers but unwilling to provide any concrete advice or assistance regarding utilizing formal HGRs.[81]

Clearly, research suggests that friends of victims are positioned to have the highest possible impact of all HGRs: they are by far the most likely to be sought for help, and, of all the HGRs that LGBTQ IPV victims contact, they consistently rate their friends as being the most helpful. At the same time, research indicates that friends can be dismissive of IPV, do not always provide the best possible advice, and may be hesitant to guide victims to HGRs that have the potential to be discriminatory. This is by no means surprising, since friends are not trained professionals. If there is, then, one fairly obvious solution to improving the helpfulness of friends (however challenging it may be to execute), it is that friends *should* be trained, through either school-based or community-based IPV-prevention education programs. (See chapter 6 for further discussion of IPV-prevention education programs.)

Family

Family ranks in the top three HGRs most likely to be sought for help by LGBTQ IPV victims.[82] Like friends, family, too, can play a valuable role in helping victims—from validating the suspicions of victims that they do not deserve this treatment, to emotional support, to advice and assistance in contacting formal HGRs. As one possible indication of the importance of family, a study of female sexual minority IPV victims found that the degree to which families are helpful significantly predicts victims terminating their relationships earlier.[83] (This result of course should be viewed with some caution. Early relationship termination may not in and of itself be an ideal outcome if it is done unsafely, without the assistance of formal HGRs. Additionally, it is possible that the type of victim to seek help from family is particularly motivated to seek help from other HGR types and that it is the help from other HGRs, not family, that contributes to early relationship termination. That said, taken at face value, this study does provide tentative support for the position that victims take the advice of their families seriously, that family can become a critically important HGR for LGBTQ IPV victims.)

While the potential is there for family to become a valuable HGR, this is unfortunately often not the case, with somewhere between two-fifths and four-fifths of victims reporting that their families did not provide adequate help.[84] Indeed, qualitative interviews have documented cases in which families have been dismissive of the seriousness of the abuse when an LGBTQ IPV victim comes to them for help.[85] It is specifically out of fear that family will be discriminatory that some LGBTQ IPV victims opt to seek help from friends instead of family.[86] Lynn, a female same-gender IPV victim, experienced this concern: "I mean, no matter who she was, they weren't gonna like her, but they—I felt like I didn't want them to say 'Oh look. See? You know it's because you're a lesbian. If you weren't a lesbian, this wouldn't happen.'"[87] It is unfortunate that families are at once highly likely to be sought out for help and, at the same time, often unprepared to offer that assistance. In a way, there seems to be a disconnect between victim perceptions of family as helpful and the actual, more limited nature of family capacities for help. One study of sexual minority women appears to reinforce this point. In it, researchers asked sexual minority women to imagine a hypothetical scenario in which they were IPV victims and sought help from their families. They were also asked if they had actually experienced IPV in their lives. The researchers found that, as compared with IPV victims, nonvictims were more likely to assume that their families would be helpful to an IPV victim.[88] Although there are other possible explanations for this finding, it does suggest that, once victims actually seek help from family, their perceptions of family as a safe and helpful resource begin to degrade.

As with friends, families have the potential to be an invaluable HGR because they are among the most sought out HGRs by LGBTQ IPV victims, and victims who trust their families may be particularly likely to heed their advice. The trouble is that, just as with friends, families are rarely trained to deal with LGBTQ IPV. This is a point that becomes particularly evident when their low helpfulness ratings are examined. Still, it is hard to entirely blame those families who inadequately respond to LGBTQ IPV when they are not equipped with the information needed to combat myths and discriminatory societal messages. Arming them with antidiscrimination and LGBTQ IPV knowledge training could make the difference. It is possible that, as school-based prevention education programs and media awareness campaigns come to be more inclusive of LGBTQ IPV issues, future generations of parents will be better prepared to handle such horrific news from a loved one. At the same time, for a more immediate impact, prevention education programs could be developed for adult communities.

Other Informal HGRs

Beyond friends and family, little research has been done on other types of informal HGRs. Two exceptions include neighbors and religious advisors. Studies have provided wildly different pictures of whether LGBTQ IPV victims find neighbors helpful in addressing their situations (somewhere between 14% and 100% of victims do find them helpful), and the same can be said for religious advisors (7–66% find them helpful). Marvin Ellison, a Christian theological scholar, suggests that religious advisors and clergy often play a valuable role in assisting their communities with HC IPV. At the same time, he argues, discriminatory beliefs—suffused throughout society and often ingrained in religious texts and practices—have held religion back from making a more meaningful contribution to helping LGBTQ IPV victims. Addressing discrimination, Ellison concludes, is the first step toward religious communities becoming a more inviting and effective HGR.[89] Interviews with several Black lesbian victims of IPV lead to a similar conclusion: the perception of homophobia reigning in the victims' local churches deterred them from seeking help from clergy who may have otherwise been viewed as a key source of comfort and guidance.[90] In any event, for the time being, neither religious advisors nor neighbors are likely to be sought out by LGBTQ IPV victims.[91] Friends and family appear to be the dominant informal HGRs most likely to assist victims.

HEALTH-CARE SYSTEMS

Medical and mental health-care systems are often run by nongovernment employees within agencies that may receive some government funding, although in other instances they may be directly run by a government agency. In either case, LGBTQ IPV victims consistently report that mental health-care providers (e.g., clinical psychologists, psychiatrists, etc.) represent the HGR that is either the second[92] or third most likely[93] to be sought out for help with victimization (being sought by somewhere between 6% and 58% of victims depending on the study examined). Support groups—a more informal, group-based source of mental health treatment—and medical health-care providers (e.g., physicians, nurses, etc.) are sought out less often, by up to one-fifth of victims (9–19% seek help from support groups,[94] while 1–19% seek help from medical health-care providers[95]). In each case, health-care systems can play invaluable roles in helping LGBTQ IPV victims. Just as with informal HGRs, formal HGRs like health-care systems can show respect for victims by believing them (enough to screen them for IPV rather than dismissing warning signs) and by treating their LGBTQ identity positively, can (if clinically appropriate) provide emotional support, and can refer victims to other types of appropriate HGRs such as IPV victim agencies and shelters. In addition, as formal HGRs, health-care systems should also be able to provide needed mental and medical health-care services that are tailored for LGBTQ IPV victims.

While health-care systems often can and do play valuable roles in helping LGBTQ IPV victims, research suggests that there is a lack of consistency in the quality of these responses. Support groups were found in one study to be rated as ("somewhat" or "extremely") helpful by nearly all subjects (91%),[96] and evidence from three additional studies provides tentative support that group formats are indeed very popular.[97] That said, the record is less sparkling for other health-care systems. In particular, depending on which study is examined, anywhere from as high as 90% to as low as 25% of LGBTQ IPV victims rate mental health-care providers as helpful,[98] and only 7–33% of LGBTQ IPV victims rate medical health-care providers as helpful.[99] Researchers have documented numerous instances in which responses by health-care systems have been less than ideal. In some cases, mental health-care providers have been found to question the legitimacy of the victim's LGBTQ identity—such as when a therapist told an LGBTQ IPV victim client that the client was not really gay but "just confused,"[100] or when another therapist of an LGBTQ IPV victim client "started quizzing me on why I thought I was bisexual!"[101] Such responses express the provider's homophobic attitudes and, in turn, may deter victims from seeking further help from that and perhaps any other HGR. In other cases, qualitative interviews with female sexual minority IPV victims find that mental health providers can be dismissive of the seriousness of LGBTQ IPV,[102] attitudes that have also been found to be pervasive among graduate school students training to be counselors.[103] Equally as detrimental are cases where LGBTQ IPV victims report that their medical[104] or mental health providers[105] blamed them for their own victimization—a tendency that also has been found to be common among counseling graduate school students.[106]

These examples of discrimination highlight the need for a more respectful and tailored approach to LGBTQ IPV victim service provision, one that is more systematically employed than it is today. Scholars and practitioners emphasize several positive steps that can help health-care systems become more effective HGRs for LGBTQ IPV victims: tailored training, tailored IPV screenings and danger assessments, tailored mental and medical health-care services, tailored safety planning, and tailored HGR referrals.

Training

While not all health-care practitioners will be trained in IPV, many do receive such training and education during graduate school and, afterward, through brief "continuing education" seminars. However, with few exceptions,[107] research suggests that rarely does this training for mental[108] and medical health-care providers[109] move beyond the topic of HC IPV into LGBTQ IPV. Medical health-care providers in particular often rely on online medical resources to update themselves on research and recommended practices regarding issues impacting a current patient, and as such they generate ad hoc, self-guided training that can have an immediate impact on patient care. Unfortunately, often these resources also lack information on LGBTQ IPV—as was found back in 2010[110] and remained the case in 2015[111] regarding UpToDate, one of the most widely utilized[112] online medical resources by physicians in the United States. (For instance, while UpToDate provides physicians with detailed information on such topics as the nature of HC IPV, HC IPV screening protocols, and HC IPV covariates to be screened for and treated, none of this information is tailored to LGBTQ IPV. It only briefly mentions that same-gender IPV—notably not trans* IPV—*exists* and that a special referral may be needed.) The absence of LGBTQ IPV knowledge training in health-care systems could be due to a variety of factors, such as a lack of awareness[113] that LGBTQ IPV is prevalent, serious, and unique. In some cases, providers may inaccurately assume that they have never treated an LGBTQ IPV victim patient (and therefore do not need training), a perception that can be fueled by failure to adequately screen patients for sexual orientation, trans* status, or IPV victimization.[114] Whatever the reason, mental and medical health-care providers often appear to assume that training on just HC IPV is adequate, as was found to be the case in a small study suggesting that 40% of mental health-care providers do not think that sexual orientation should be considered in IPV victim treatment.[115]

That said, several scholars[116]—and indeed the LGBTQ IPV research literature detailed in this book—highlight that the causes, nature, and outcomes of LGBTQ IPV as well as barriers to help-seeking for LGBTQ IPV victims differ enough from those of and for HC IPV to warrant a tailored approach to service provision. Scholar Leanne Tigert warns of the dangers of a one-size-fits-all treatment for lesbian IPV victims, although this point could be just as well applied to any LGBTQ IPV victim: "Simply to transpose the same regimen of treatment from straight couples and individuals to lesbian couples and individuals is not only counterproductive, but could add to the problem, reinforcing abusive patterns."[117] In some cases, scholars have implied that it is sufficient for a small number of providers or agencies to be trained as LGBTQ IPV experts, recommending that health-care providers keep a list of such expert referrals should they encounter an LGBTQ IPV victim.[118] While specialist referrals are a good first step, an overreliance on them can have two key drawbacks: in many regions LGBTQ IPV-focused HGRs simply do not exist,[119] and, just as important, the initial encounter between an untrained HGR and an LGBTQ IPV victim can be so negative and discriminatory (such as in any of the aforementioned examples among health-care providers) that it deters LGBTQ IPV victims from seeking further help, driving them back toward their abusers.

It is for these reasons that it is imperative that training become more systematic and widespread throughout health-care systems, ingrained in medical and psychology graduate school courses, clinical training, ongoing-education seminars, and regularly used online practitioner resources. Training can be broken into two interrelated components: antidiscrimination training, and LGBTQ IPV knowledge training.

Several scholars indicate that antidiscrimination training is necessary and should be required throughout health-care systems.[120] In societies where homophobia and transphobia are widespread, it is safe to assume that some mental and medical health-care practitioners may hold discriminatory attitudes that can encourage them to belittle victims for being LGBTQ,[121] blame IPV on the victim being LGBTQ,[122] or perhaps even deter LGBTQ IPV victims from disclosing IPV or visiting their office.[123] Antidiscrimination training teaches providers how to project an image of respect for LGBTQ clients and patients, which can be achieved through a variety of measures: having nondiscrimination policies in visible locations like an agency's website and intake forms;[124] using LGBTQ symbols, images, terminology, testimonials, and facts in service advertisements, agency websites, agency facility posters, and brochures;[125] and using gender-neutral and patient-preferred terminology during intake, screening, and treatment.[126] Importantly, antidiscrimination training goes beyond projecting the image of respect to actually generating greater respect for LGBTQ people among health-care providers. Although such a policy is not a formal part of antidiscrimination training, health-care providers may also become more accepting of LGBTQ people if more LGBTQ people are hired in the health-care setting; being able to relate to LGBTQ coworkers can be a good first step toward relating better to LGBTQ clients and patients.[127] As health-care providers become more respectful of LGBTQ people, this in turn reduces the chances that health-care systems retraumatize LGBTQ IPV victims and deter them from further help-seeking.

In addition to antidiscrimination training, it is critically important that health-care systems require widespread training on LGBTQ IPV, a position advocated for by scholars[128] and victims[129] alike. LGBTQ IPV knowledge training should include basic information on the causes, nature, and outcomes of LGBTQ IPV, and barriers to help-seeking regarding LGBTQ IPV—including how these dynamics can differ among lesbian, gay, bisexual, and heterosexual people as well as between trans* and cisgender people. If an organization feels ill equipped to provide this training for its members, it has been suggested that specialists and organizations that do have expertise in addressing LGBTQ IPV—such as any of the many North American member organizations in the National Coalition of Anti-Violence Programs (NCAVP)—could be recruited to offer such training or provide instructions on how to do so.[130] Moreover, LGBTQ IPV knowledge training should provide specific recommendations for practitioners on how to tailor their services for

LGBTQ IPV victims. These recommendations should at minimum govern: (1) IPV screening, (2) the provision of core medical or mental health services, and (3) safety planning and HGR referrals. Research and recommendations pertaining to each of these topics are addressed below.

Screening

Screening, or determining whether a patient or client is experiencing IPV, is a common practice among mental and medical health-care service providers. For counseling centers that focus primarily on serving IPV victims, screening can be automatically built into the intake procedures for all new clients. More commonly, in general-practice counseling centers, hospitals, and medical clinics, IPV screening is often conducted only when warning signs of IPV are present (e.g., bruising that is inconsistent with the explanation provided by a patient). The number and type of questions may vary significantly by environment but typically include items on feeling unsafe or experiencing physical violence in a current or past relationship, with psychological and sexual IPV (unfortunately) often inquired about only in longer screening protocols. Screening can also include what are sometimes referred to as "danger assessment" or "risk assessment" questions, which help determine the victim's risk of being revictimized by the abuser or engaging in self-harm and suicidal behaviors.[131] For those clients and patients who screen positive either for past IPV victimization or for risk of future IPV-related harm, providers can adjust treatment to be more effective, screen for known IPV covariates that may warrant additional treatment (such as substance abuse, depression, and any of the other potential IPV outcomes discussed in chapter 3), and offer referrals to other relevant HGRs.[132]

Screening is of course effective in generating assistance for victims only if the screening actually occurs. According to one study, a majority of sexual minority men are in favor of being screened for IPV at every health-care visit, with 92% concurring that being screened helps ensure that victims get needed help. Moreover, while some providers may fear that asking about LGBTQ status or IPV could be perceived as offensive or invasive,[133] 96% of sexual minority men report that being screened would be viewed as a sign that the health-care provider took interest in their lives and concerns.[134] While health-care practitioners often are trained on IPV warning signs that should trigger them to ask IPV screening questions, research suggests that some mental[135] and medical health-care providers[136] ignore those indicators specifically for LGBTQ clients and patients because they may not believe that LGBTQ IPV is prevalent or serious. In such cases, screening may fail to occur despite indications that it is warranted. Clinical psychologist Christopher Alexander explains how he was startled to learn that he had long-standing clients who had experienced IPV but had not previously disclosed this, in large part because Alexander had not thought to screen them for it:

Only recently, for example, have I started asking my gay male clients about aggression and violence in their lives. One man with whom I work told me of a relationship he was in many years ago where he was beaten regularly. I remember being horrified at the details of the abuse, and I wanted to ask him why he waited almost two years before disclosing this information to me. I realized that he wasn't withholding information about his life. Rather, I simply had failed to ask the right questions. As I start asking questions about abuse, I am startled at how common this phenomenon is.[137]

Thus, a critical first step in increasing the use of IPV screening with LGBTQ clients and patients is to train mental and medical health-care providers about the existence of LGBTQ IPV as a prevalent and serious phenomenon. Moreover, concerns for patient or client safety should trump any discomfort the provider might experience in asking screening questions.

When health-care providers do screen for IPV victimization, three barriers may limit IPV disclosure by LGBTQ victims: the abuser being present during screening, the provider using inappropriate gender terminology, and sexual orientation and trans* status not being inquired about. First, many scholars emphasize the importance of screening an IPV victim separate from an abuser, particularly because the victim may choose to not disclose IPV so as to avoid violent retribution by the abuser.[138] Unfortunately, when an abuser accompanies a same-gender IPV victim during the IPV screening process, providers may not ask the abuser to leave if it is assumed that the abuser is just a friend, an assumption encouraged by the stereotype that IPV occurs only between different-gender partners.[139] In some instances a health-care provider may wish to encourage a victim to have a friend accompany them to service appointments for emotional support,[140] although it should be kept in mind that the victim may feel pressure to ask the abuser to be the accompanying "friend." Second, IPV screening questions may use gendered terms that incorrectly assume that the victim's abuser is of a different gender, such as by asking a female same-gender IPV victim, "What is his name?"[141] Beyond being inaccurate, inappropriately gendered terminology may signal to LGBTQ IPV victims that the health-care provider assumes that all people are or should be heterosexual. In turn, victims may perceive this as an indicator that the provider may be homophobic and cannot be trusted.[142] As one female same-gender IPV victim explains, when a provider incorrectly presumed that her abuser was male, this raised concerns that her provider might be homophobic, which in turn led her to pretend she was heterosexual: "It would be helpful if healthcare providers wouldn't just automatically assume that it's a man. Because I would play along with it, if they automatically assumed, I'd play along with that, so I could stay safe with them."[143]

As a consequence of this risk, many scholars and health-care providers now recommend using gender-neutral terminology in IPV screening questions, such as using *someone* or *partner* instead of more-gendered language like *man, he,* *boyfriend,* or *husband.*[144] Third, whether because of an assumption that all people are heterosexual and cisgender or because of a fear of making clients and patients feel uncomfortable, health-care providers may fail to directly ask clients and patients about their LGBTQ status.[145] Drawing on an epidemiological model that emphasizes the importance of sexual behaviors in the spread of sexually transmitted infections, some scholars encourage physicians to ask whether a patient "has sex with women, men, or both" as a proxy for sexual orientation,[146] making the false assumption that sexual-intercourse history always perfectly aligns with one's relationship history and sexual-orientation self-identity. Inquiring more directly about gender, sexual orientation, and trans* status is valuable in two ways: knowing LGBTQ status will largely lead to avoiding the two aforementioned disclosure barriers during IPV screening (i.e., providers would be much more likely to recognize a potential abuser accompanying the victim and much less likely to use gender-inappropriate terminology if they know the victim's LGBTQ status), and it will also enable providers to offer treatment and HGR referrals that are tailored to the unique experience of LGBTQ IPV instead of HC IPV. Some scholars[147] have speculated that screening for LGBTQ status prior to screening for IPV victimization (rather than reversing the screening order) may create an opportunity for providers to show that they are respectful—which, in turn, may increase willingness to disclose IPV victimization, although that claim has not yet been evaluated.

An additional concerning trend should be considered when screening for LGBTQ IPV: it is often assumed without evidence that LGBTQ IPV and HC IPV tactics can be effectively screened for by using identical questions. Many scholars advocate for gender-neutral IPV screening questions because they are more respectful of LGBTQ clients and patients.[148] Although never explicitly stated, the other benefit of any one-size-fits-all response to IPV—like gender-neutral screening questions—is that it limits the amount of work for providers, who for now need to keep track of only one set of questions. There are two potential problems with this approach: excluding unique LGBTQ IPV tactics, and evaluating screening tools with only HC IPV victims. First, screening originally designed for HC IPV victims may exclude common LGBTQ IPV tactics—a problem evident among screening questions that scholars and organizations[149] have suggested for use with LGBTQ IPV victims. While these provide fine templates from which to develop screening questions, when providers excluded tactics unique to LGBTQ IPV like outing, some victims may be misidentified as nonvictims. Only one IPV screening tool[150] and one danger assessment[151] have been tailored to at least some degree to the unique tactics of LGBTQ IPV, with only the latter being evaluated. Second, the other problem with relying on gender-neutral, one-size-fits-all screening questions is the assumption that all IPV victims are the same and that, therefore, it must be acceptable to evaluate IPV screening questions only with HC IPV victims. With only two exceptions,[152] IPV screening and danger-assessment questions are almost never evaluated for their effectiveness in correctly identifying LGBTQ IPV victims, instead either going unevaluated entirely or being evaluated only with HC IPV victims. Although it is possible that screening tools can be equally effective in identifying HC and LGBTQ IPV victims among patients and clients, it is troubling that little research has been conducted to support this assumption. Ultimately, many mental and medical health providers rely on screening tools designed for HC IPV victims, adapt them to use gender-neutral terminology, and hope—without evidence—that they will be equally effective in positively identifying LGBTQ IPV victims. The potential cost of such a gamble is that some LGBTQ IPV victims may be slipping between the cracks.

A final major problem that can arise during and after screening is that health-care providers may have difficulty distinguishing abusers from victims. Stereotypes as well as abusers encourage the belief that same-gender IPV is usually "mutual battering," where both partners are abusers.[153] Indeed, when researchers provided therapists with a fake story of an IPV relationship, the therapists were more likely to assume they were reading about mutual battering if the names of the story characters were of the same gender rather than different genders.[154] Some scholars have argued that mental health providers should indeed be prepared for the possibility that most of their clients may be mutual batterers rather than solely victims,[155] while others have urged providers to assume that LGBTQ IPV mutual battering is largely nonexistent.[156] Unfortunately, as previously discussed, very little research has been conducted on the directionality of abuse within LGBTQ relationships. One study did find that half of same-gender physical IPV victims also perpetrated physical IPV in the same relationship,[157] but this is not very useful information on its own without also knowing the reason that bidirectional physical IPV occurred. For instance, research suggests that self-defense is a major motivator of physical violence in sexual minority IPV relationships,[158] and a partner who fights back only in self-defense is generally not thought of as an abuser. (All other LGBTQ IPV directionality studies examined use and receipt of violence in a time period but not in a specific relationship,[159] which means they do not provide any information on relationship-specific "mutual battering" as it is typically conceived.) The dearth of research on LGBTQ IPV mutual battering is not proof that it never occurs, but neither is there conclusive evidence that most LGBTQ IPV is bidirectional. Compounding the lack of knowledge on LGBTQ IPV mutual battering, even those in clearly unidirectional IPV relationships can be difficult to assign "victim" and "abuser" labels to during screening and treatment. Research suggests that many LGBTQ IPV abusers maintain "definitional hegemony," an ability to control how the public views the direction and nature of abuse in a relationship. Abusers may blame victims and downplay the seriousness of abuse by drawing on stereotypes of LGBTQ IPV as being less severe,[160] and they may even view themselves as lacking power in the relationship and as being discriminated against by society.[161] Conversely, victims may be encouraged by abusers to blame themselves for motivating the abuser and for fighting back in self-defense, and they may be more ashamed and reluctant to discuss the abuse.[162] For now, there is no screening tool or strategy that will always accurately distinguish abusers from victims; this is instead a skill that clinicians learn through extensive experience and training.[163] Like any instinct, though, assumptions of who can be a "real" abuser or victim may be subconsciously influenced by biases like homophobia and transphobia—a possibility that can be guarded against in part through antidiscrimination and LGBTQ IPV informational training.

Core Services

Once an LGBTQ patient or client has screened positive for IPV victimization, health-care providers may then need to alter their core medical or mental health services. Beyond the other tools discussed in this chapter section—screening, safety planning, and referrals—little has been written about how LGBTQ IPV disclosure impacts the core services of medical health-care providers. One of the only articles on the topic suggests that, just as with HC IPV, physicians should be sure to document all violent incidents as described to them by an LGBTQ IPV victim, as well as note any physical signs of IPV victimization—all of which may be important should the victim choose to proceed with filing charges through the criminal justice system. Additionally, physicians can arrange follow-up calls and visits to check in on the victim.[164]

Considerably more has been written about how to provide mental health-care treatment tailored to LGBTQ IPV victims, including a number of summary articles over the past several decades.[165] As some scholars have pointed out, being abused does not necessarily mean an LGBTQ IPV victim needs mental health-care treatment, which means that it is of course important that providers screen for mental health issues among victims.[166] When counseling is warranted, with rare exceptions,[167] scholars generally recommend using individual counseling with victims, rather than couples counseling with a victim and abuser simultaneously, where victims may fear retribution for discussing their abusers.[168] Unfortunately, research finds that both psychology counseling graduate school students[169] and clinical and counseling clinicians[170] are more likely to recommend couples counseling instead of individual counseling for same-gender IPV victims than for different-gender victims. This may be due to the fact that, as one study notes, graduate students training to be mental health-care providers view same-gender IPV as less severe than different-gender IPV,[171] suggesting that perhaps some providers incorrectly think that the likelihood of victimization is so low already for same-gender IPV victims that couples counseling will not pose any additional risk.

Undoubtedly, there are many viable modes of counseling. The fact that one has not been discussed yet in the context of LGBTQ IPV does not mean that it will be ineffective. Likewise, the fact that a particular counseling mode has been discussed in research on LGBTQ IPV does not mean that it is widely practiced. That said, one mode of counseling that has been proposed as ideal for LGBTQ IPV victims is person-centered or Gestalt therapy, which places the pace and direction of counseling in the hands of the client. In this mode, through open-ended questions and with victims receiving help in honing their answers, victims may begin to trust providers more, disclose more information, and ultimately come to a realization on their own that they are being abused and that this is unacceptable. Waiting for the victim to psychologically make it to this point can take time and patience on the part of mental health-care providers, a particular challenge when in the meantime many victims will discontinue services and return to their abusers for such reasons as love and fear of the abuser.[172] However, this risk in not entirely avoidable, and the payoff of having patience in counseling can be worthwhile. Specifically, because the motivation to accept help—whether help in coping with ongoing abuse or help in leaving an abuser—comes from within, the shift in the victim's view of abuse is believed to be longer lasting and empowering. It also is believed to help the victim feel more independent and capable of change rather than feeling reliant on the counselor to save them.[173] Some scholars have suggested that labeling one's own victimization as IPV is impossible if one does not know the definition of IPV. Thus, some have suggested that mental health-care providers should educate their clients about LGBTQ IPV.[174]

Regarding topics to be covered during counseling, scholars and practitioners recommend touching upon at least the following: what forms of IPV the victim experienced,[175] the strength of their social support networks (e.g., whom is the victim out to and from whom do they feel comfortable seeking help)[176] and ongoing barriers to seeking help (e.g., receiving discriminatory responses by HGRs, being negatively impacted by laws like same-gender marriage bans, and so on),[177] the degree to which victims have internalized homophobic or transphobic beliefs and any other justifications an abuser uses for their abuse,[178] and the degree to which victims have experienced discrimination due to any aspect of their identity.[179]

Additionally, scholars and practitioners believe it is important for mental health-care providers to create an unintimidating environment in which victims feel believed and accepted.[180] For instance, interviews with ten mental health-care providers who had worked with sexual minority IPV victims emphasized that providers should show complete support and acceptance of the victim, be sensitive to the emotional needs of victims, be open to new viewpoints other than the providers' own, avoid expressing discriminatory attitudes, and avoid pathologizing being LGBTQ.[181] It has also been recommended that service providers move beyond gender-neutral terminology during screening into more tailored terminology during treatment, by both mirroring the client's use of gender, sexual orientation, and trans* terminology and (particularly when clients refer to themselves with potentially derogatory terms like *dyke, fag,* and *homosexual*) asking what gender and sexual-orientation terminology the client prefers.[182] Such a welcoming environment may encourage further disclosures and communication with victims, assist victims in rebuilding a sense of self-worth and independence, and facilitate other treatment goals.

Safety Planning and HGR Referrals

Last, health-care providers can help LGBTQ IPV victims plan for the future through safety planning and HGR referrals. Safety planning—creating a detailed strategy for how to either leave an abuser or remain with an abuser in a way that minimizes the risks of further harm to the victim—is strongly encouraged for both mental[183] and medical health-care providers[184] working with LGBTQ IPV victims. Many victims are not prepared to leave their abuser, for any number of possible reasons discussed in chapter 4. In such cases, a health-care provider may create a safety plan with the victim with strategies for how to remain with the abuser while decreasing risk of further victimization. When victims are prepared to leave, safety planning is equally as important, as leaving can trigger some abusers to stalk, assault, and even murder their victims. Several excellent safety-plan templates exist,[185] with many of the most common elements offered in table 3. For the most part, safety-planning protocols are identical for HC and LGBTQ IPV victims, with perhaps the exception of emergency-bag items needed by trans* victims for their gender identity, such as identity documents, hormone medications, and so on. The most significant difference, though, comes not in the safety-plan template but in its execution: many of the help-seeking strategies built into most plans (e.g., staying at a shelter, calling police in case of danger) may be viable for HC IPV victims but less so for LGBTQ IPV victims, such as when an HGR has demonstrated discriminatory attitudes in the past or may categorically refuse to help LGBTQ IPV victims.[186] Given this possibility, it is important for health-care providers to suggest specific alternatives for LGBTQ IPV victims who may not be able to follow through with more traditional, HGR-reliant safety plans.

Related to safety planning, health-care providers can assist LGBTQ IPV victims with preparing for the future by referring them to relevant HGRs. Screening and intake protocols can help identify the types of HGRs a victim may benefit from. For victims, identifying local HGRs specializing in LGBTQ IPV is not only a difficult and time-consuming task but also a task that exposes them to unnecessary risks, should the abuser, for example, notice the web browser history of the victim and realize the victim is trying to leave. It is therefore strongly recommended that mental[187] and medical health-care providers[188] alike keep updated lists of HGRs in their local communities that specialize in helping LGBTQ IPV victims. Sometimes these lists can be difficult to construct when HGR organizations dedicated to LGBTQ IPV victims do not exist or are rare in an area. As is often the case, instead

TABLE 3 Suggested safety-planning items

Safety planning for remaining with abuser	Safety planning for leaving abuser
Identify safer places at home (e.g., rooms with several exits and a lack of potential weapons or sharp objects).	All of the items in a safety plan for remaining with an abuser (see list to the left) and the following items.
Be aware of the forms of communication that can be monitored by abusers (e.g., phone calls, texts, emails, social media account messages, web browser histories).	Recognize that victimization risk may temporarily increase when leaving. Begin varying your daily schedule in the weeks and days leading up to your leaving (to decrease abuser's suspicion when your schedule changes on the day you leave).
Develop a support system of trusted people (e.g., family, friends, coworkers).	Plan the following in advance:
Call the police when there is danger.	— what shelter to stay at
Pack an emergency bag in case a quick escape is needed (e.g., change of clothing, keys, money, identity documents, medication such as hormone therapies, information for a local shelter).	— the exact route you will take to the shelter — any legal representation you may need (e.g., for custody or criminal hearings) — any other needed services

only certain people within a mainstream HGR agency may specialize in LGBTQ IPV, and typically no central list of such individuals exists. Facing just such a problem, the Battered Lesbian Task Force of the New Jersey Coalition for Battered Women arrived at an underutilized yet surprisingly effective solution: they asked therapists (primarily those who came recommended by others, those who requested to be added to the list of LGBTQ IPV provider specialists, and those already on such a list) to complete a questionnaire assessing their knowledge of LGBTQ IPV and LGBTQ general issues, and they offered training to anyone who appeared in need of it based on the questionnaire. This information was then used to generate a relatively extensive list of specific mental health-care providers with expertise in LGBTQ IPV.[189] Beyond identifying appropriate HGRs for a referral list, health-care providers should become aware of any legal barriers that LGBTQ IPV victims may face in their local area that would inhibit their ability to access these HGRs.[190] (E.g., as will be discussed in chapter 6, some local or national governments may bar same-gender IPV victims from accessing restraining orders, and some may even criminalize being LGBTQ.) In such regions, HGR referrals would need to be adjusted to reflect the resources actually available to victims.

IPV VICTIM ORGANIZATIONS

Many types of organizations are designed with the sole purpose of providing services to IPV victims. In some cases, these organizations may provide one service, as might be the case with an IPV victim telephone hotline or emergency shelter. Often, though, a variety of services are integrated into a single agency, such as when an agency runs a victim hotline and shelter while also offering legal and mental health services, all designed for IPV victims. These agencies tend to be run by nongovernment employees but partially receive funding from the government. Many local, regional, and federal governments also have entire departments dedicated to acting as pseudo–IPV victim agencies, referring victims to the numerous IPV victim agencies in their communities while sometimes also operating their own IPV victim telephone hotline. Perhaps more than any other HGR, IPV victim organizations have the greatest potential to help IPV victims with both their immediate challenges—through shelter services, referrals to legal services, and so on—and longer-term challenges—through often providing in-house counseling, support groups, and an extensive listing of HGR referrals. Unfortunately, utilization of these services can be quite low, and quality of services regarding specificity and discrimination also often leaves room for improvement.

Extensive Barriers to Admission

Ironically, despite the agencies' dedicated mission of serving victims, only a small percentage of LGBTQ IPV victims actually seek help from IPV hotlines (which are sought out by only 0–14% of LGBTQ IPV victims[191]), IPV shelters (0–13%[192]), mainstream IPV agencies (3–7%[193]), and agencies primarily focused on LGBTQ IPV (4–5%[194]). In many cases this is due to exclusionary practices by IPV organizations, which, through formal policies and informal practices, turn LGBTQ IPV victims away. For instance, one study found that in China, India, and Japan, despite there being thousands of governmental and nongovernmental IPV agencies available to female victims, zero such agencies are accessible to male victims of any sexual orientation. The researchers also found only a handful of agencies accessible to men in Canada, the United Kingdom, and the United States.[195] In the United States, according to a recent survey of 213 IPV victim agencies randomly sampled from a comprehensive list of nearly two thousand agencies across forty-seven states, most victim services like shelter and support groups are offered to sexual minority women, but only one-half to two-thirds of agencies offered similar services to sexual minority men. This situation is unlikely to change soon, with only 2% of surveyed agencies reporting an intention to expand services to LGBTQ IPV victims and male victims more generally.[196] According to a study of nearly four thousand predominantly LGBTQ IPV victims, over *three-fifths* of LGBTQ IPV victims seeking admission to IPV victim shelters are denied.[197] Some LGBTQ

IPV victims report being told by IPV agencies to hide their gender identity or sexual orientation in order to be admitted for victim services,[198] and some victims indeed have hidden their identities out of fear of being evicted.[199]

Reasons vary for this disparity in utilization patterns with IPV organizations, but one explanation is legal protection for exclusionary policies. IPV agency policies that bar admission to all cisgender male, trans* male, and trans* female IPV victims may be legally sanctioned, as has been reported to be the case in parts of Canada[200] and the United States.[201] For instance, until recently in the United States, IPV agencies that denied access to LGBTQ IPV victims were still eligible for federal funding. With the passage of the 2013 Violence Against Women Act (VAWA) Reauthorization—a law that faced heated opposition by many conservatives in Congress[202]—outright exclusion is no longer permitted ... but large loopholes remain. According to the 2013 VAWA Reauthorization, any IPV agency receiving federal funding still has the right to exclude victims because of "an individual's sex"—such as when a victim is male or trans*—if "sex segregation or sex-specific programming is necessary to the essential operation of a program."[203] The Office for Civil Rights within the U.S. Department of Justice has clarified that trans* victims should be placed in agencies based only on their gender identity, not sex, and that agencies cannot ask about their "anatomy or medical history"—but agencies *are* legally permitted to deny admission to trans* IPV victims if the agency argues that doing so is intended to "ensure the victim's health and safety."[204] In other words, as long as agencies do not say they are excluding victims because they or their clients feel uncomfortable around male and trans* IPV victims (i.e., discriminatory attitudes), federal law appears to generally protect exclusionary policies. Moreover, VAWA—and similar laws in other nations—generally cover only designated IPV agencies. IPV agencies that rely more heavily on private funding rather than government funding may feel pressure to follow the exclusionary preferences of their private donors—a pressure that has been expressed in interviews with IPV agency staff in Canada[205] and the United States.[206] Other non-IPV agencies—such as the many homeless shelters that LGBTQ IPV victims turn to when they get denied access to IPV victim shelters—are not governed by similar federal law and may be permitted to arbitrarily exclude LGBTQ IPV victims.

Another reason for low utilization rates of IPV victim organizations by LGBTQ IPV victims is that, even with organizations that purportedly accept such victims, staff and providers can be influenced by stereotypes of LGBTQ IPV being rare and not serious. Some IPV agency staff suggest that vague admission policies often mean that victims are admitted on a case-by-case basis, where staff conducting screening interviews over the phone and follow-up screening in person have considerable discretion over whether a person is a "real" victim deserving of the limited resources at the agency.[207] Even when a shelter is technically full, shelter staff may also allocate a sofa for a victim perceived to be in grave danger.[208] Interviews with three staff members at U.S. IPV victim shelters reveal that these difficult admission decisions are ultimately governed by stereotypes of a "real" IPV victim, stereotypes that unintentionally may result in the exclusion of sexual minority female IPV victims. For instance, shelter staff described "real" victims as escaping actual abuse rather than simply being homeless and lying about abuse in order to find a free place to stay. Given the small number of beds and resources at shelters, staff reported great concern over "shelter hoppers" who are essentially "fake" victims. As a consequence, after doing "a lot of intakes," staff attempt to develop "instincts" about "who's lying and who's telling the truth."[209] When pressed for details about these instincts, shelter workers provided several indicators of "real" victims: Is the victim willing to share the name of the abuser, regularly attend a support group, report to the police, request an order of protection from a court, and work to secure more permanent housing elsewhere? Likewise, after records kept by some social workers and shelters have been checked into: Is this the first time the victim has been to a shelter? Failure to fit these stereotypes greatly increases the chances that a shelter worker will label a victim as a nonabused homeless person and deny them admission. As the researcher Michelle VanNatta points out, though, these presumed indicators of real victims may disproportionately exclude legitimate IPV victims who are sexual minorities—and, one could add, trans* victims. For instance, LGBTQ victims who are not out or who fear discrimination may understandably be hesitant to reveal the name of their abusers or attend support groups, lest their LGBTQ status become known. Likewise, fear of discrimination by law enforcement along with the omission of LGBTQ IPV from criminal statutes may greatly decrease the likelihood that LGBTQ victims report to law enforcement and seek an order of protection. Discrimination by landlords—and the absence of laws banning such discrimination—may also make it more difficult for some LGBTQ IPV victims to acquire housing and can lead them to seek admission to another shelter after their time limit ends at a previous shelter. Finally, VanNatta points out the most obvious problem with screening out victims who appear to the shelter worker to be homeless: many IPV victims are actually homeless, whether because they are chronically poor or have had to evacuate a home shared with the abuser. VanNatta explains: "Many women experience extreme violence when living on the street or in homeless shelters. Much of this violence, although it involves brutality from intimates and includes chronic coercion and tactics of power and control, is not included in the discourse of 'domestic violence,' a term that insists that a victim have a domestic situation." [210]

Thus, excluding those who appear to be homeless from admission to shelters and other IPV victim agencies likely discriminates against not only LGBTQ IPV victims but also lower-income and homeless IPV victims of all genders and sexual orientations.

Decisions about who is a "real" victim and deserving of services can also rest upon the stereotype that IPV victims must be cisgender women. Not only can this be a primary rationale by female-serving IPV agencies and shelters for excluding cisgender men, but the reasoning is often extended irrationally to trans* IPV victims. Interview data finds that trans* men have been barred from entering IPV victim organization spaces even in cases where the victim identified as female at the time of victimization.[211] Even trans* women, who do identify as female as required by many female-only victim spaces, can be excluded because they were not born biologically as female or do not present as feminine enough: admission can hinge upon irrelevant factors like their physical appearance, pitch of their voice, whether they opted to have medical interventions, or discordance in the name and gender identity currently embodied and those still written on difficult-to-change official documents like birth certificates and driver's licenses.[212] This process of exclusion for trans* IPV victims can be particularly humiliating because it often involves attempts to disrespect and undermine the legitimacy of the victim's gender identity, such as when one U.S. shelter worker asked a trans* victim, "What is between your legs?"[213]

In other cases, IPV victim organizations may exclude cisgender men and trans* people because they believe that their proximity to female different-gender IPV victims could trigger traumatic memories of male abusers. As Mary-Elizabeth Quinn of The Network/La Red argues—and with which the 2013 VAWA Reauthorization in the United States concurs[214]—this is an imperfect rationale for exclusion. Not only does this place the needs of some IPV victims above the needs of other victims, but it also incorrectly assumes that victims can and should be protected from all potential triggers. For example, Quinn points out that shelters never ban all White victims just because some of the victims at the shelter had White abusers, nor do they ban certain smells or clothing colors that might also trigger memories of abusers. Instead, exposure to such potential triggers can be part of the healing process through which victims come to distinguish symbols of their abusers from the actual abuser—a process that helps prepare victims for one day leaving a shelter.[215]

In other cases, IPV victim organizations may bar LGBTQ IPV victims from admission but will refer them onto organizations they believe will be more accepting.[216] This of course assumes that the referrer understands the needs of LGBTQ IPV victims and the available local resources, which may not be the case when the referrer has not received training on LGBTQ IPV.[217] Even when an agency's referral list is comprehensive or an LGBTQ IPV victim creates such a list, organizations specializing in addressing LGBTQ IPV may simply not exist in a region.[218] Even when such organizations exist, if there are too few, victims and service providers may perceive there to be no LGBTQ IPV victim organizations, in turn short-circuiting their search for such organizations. Take, for example, a study of 280 Canadian sexual minority people, which found that only 21% believed that a "gay men's/lesbian's domestic violence program" was accessible in their area, only 17% believed there to be a "crisis help line for GLBT victims of partner abuse" nearby, and 0% and 4%, respectively, believed that a shelter for "battered gay men" or "battered lesbians" was available locally.[219] One reason there may be fewer LGBTQ IPV victim organizations is that general LGBTQ organizations rarely offer services for IPV victims.[220] For instance, one study found that only 16% of "lesbian sexual health" websites mention IPV, with the issues of HIV/AIDS and safe-sex practices being considerably more present on such websites.[221] Interviews with 81 people in four U.S. LGBTQ communities provide one possible explanation for this trend: some LGBTQ organizations may suffer from "activism fatigue," expending so much energy combatting social and legal discrimination (like same-gender marriage bans and inadequate safe-sex education in schools) that IPV victimization can become a low priority.[222] Even when LGBTQ organizations do offer IPV victim services, waiting lists may be common. This may be due to the organization simultaneously pursuing several other time-consuming and resource-draining goals unrelated to IPV, leaving only small amounts of funding to assist victims.[223] Such waiting lists may be strained further when there are too few organizations in a region servicing LGBTQ IPV victims. For instance, in 2011, the Los Angeles Gay and Lesbian Center noted that it was the sole organization in L.A. County providing tailored services to an estimated 261,829 LGBTQ IPV victims.[224] Although not necessarily an issue in all regions, one study found that LGBTQ IPV victim services may be located in wealthier, predominantly White neighborhoods with a more out LGBTQ community, leaving some racial-ethnic minority, lower-income, and closeted victims feeling deterred from traveling to receive victim assistance in locales where they feel like social outcasts.[225] When left with the choice of IPV victim organizations inaccessible due to waiting lists, heterosexual-cisgender admission requirements, or the organizations being located far away, some victims may feel they have no choice but to reach out to an accessible LGBTQ organization with no expertise in IPV.[226]

It should go without saying that the consequences of LGBTQ IPV victims being turned away from IPV victim organizations can be disastrous. While some return to their abusers, others may resort to staying at homeless shelters. Unfortunately, homeless shelters are very poorly equipped for LGBTQ IPV victims, with staff, policies, and services addressing neither IPV effects nor the discrimination LGBTQ people can face in such places.[227] When referrals to organizations specializing in LGBTQ IPV victim services is impractical because these organizations are either nonexistent in an area or have long waiting lists, it becomes that much more important for "mainstream" IPV organizations to accept LGBTQ IPV victims into their doors. Otherwise, these victims may have no one else to turn to for help.

The One-Size-Fits-All Approach

When LGBTQ IPV victims are asked how helpful they found IPV victim organizations, results are less than stellar: less than half of victims who seek assistance from IPV hotlines find them to be helpful (0–43% report them to be "extremely" or "somewhat" helpful),[228] as is also the case with those who seek help from main-stream IPV victim agencies (40%)[229] and shelters (25–31%).[230] By comparison, according to the only study on this HGR type, 100% of LGBTQ IPV victims who seek help from an LGBTQ IPV-focused victim agency report these agencies to be helpful.[231] It is likely that this discrepancy is influenced at least in part by some mainstream IPV victim agencies turning cisgender male and trans* victims away, thereby artificially deflating helpfulness ratings. At the same time, many IPV victim agencies will accept cisgender women, even if they are sexual minority women. For instance, upward of 90–96% of IPV victim organizations in the United States report being willing to accept female sexual minority IPV victims,[232] and 64% report actually providing services to such victims.[233] In the instances where LGBTQ IPV victims do receive services from an IPV victim organization, why would the help be deemed less than optimal?

At the heart of the difference between mainstream and LGBTQ IPV victim agencies is the decision of whether to treat HC IPV and LGBTQ IPV as unique or identical phenomena. Unlike LGBTQ IPV victim agencies, mainstream IPV victim agencies often opt to view these two as identical, and, as such, they opt for services and training that are one-size-fits-all. Comments by staff like "Everyone is treated the same,"[234] "We won't turn them away,"[235] and "We work with anybody"[236] are commonplace in such organizations. The main benefit of such an approach is that it may initially signal to LGBTQ IPV victims that they are welcome. IPV victim agencies may choose to treat all IPV as the same for a variety of other reasons as well. Obviously, some staff members may incorrectly assume that HC IPV and LGBTQ IPV are identical,[237] which may be particularly the case for those trained only in HC IPV and then left to speculate about LGBTQ IPV. Additionally, some staff have indicated that they want all female IPV victims to symbolically stand against IPV in solidarity, and dividing victims into separate groups based on sexual orientation may politically set back broader community movements to combat IPV.[238] Still other staff have shared concerns over the appearance of accepting and respecting LGBTQ people—that doing so may open them and their organizations up to a homophobic and transphobic backlash, including making heterosexual, cisgender female victims at the organization uncomfortable.[239]

Unfortunately, beyond the superficial appearance of accepting all IPV victims into the same organizations, substantive changes to actual training, services, practices, and policies rarely follow. Now-outdated research from the 1990s found that only 10% of IPV victim organizations in the United States provided services tailored for female sexual minority IPV victims. Studies old and new consistently find that many IPV victim agencies do not train their staff on the uniqueness of LGBTQ IPV,[240] which almost certainly also means that agency services and staff interactions with victims will not reflect the uniqueness of LGBTQ IPV. For example, in a paper documenting the efforts of a mainstream IPV victim organization in the United

States to become more inviting to same-gender IPV victims, the author emphasizes that the language of the agency (in materials for and discussions with victims) was changed to be gender-neutral—but there is no mention of efforts to actually tailor the way the organization interacts with LGBTQ IPV victims.[241]

The primary downsides of one-size-fits-all programming are twofold: the absence of tailored services, and the fostering of discriminatory beliefs. First and foremost, because HC IPV and LGBTQ IPV are *not* identical, an agency that treats them as such can touch only upon their commonalities, not their differences. As several scholars point out, this generally means that one-size-fits-all organizations use HC IPV victimization as the base model for all interactions with victims, regardless of whether the victim is HC or LGBTQ.[242] Moreover, when agencies acknowledge and address only IPV experiences shared by all types of victims, this also assumes that justifications used by abusers, IPV tactics, reasons victims stay, and barriers to help-seeking are identical for all victims, such that no victimization experience is assumed to ever be altered by racism, poverty, undocumented-immigrant status, or disability. In other words, one-size-fits-all programs often assume all IPV victims are not only cisgender, female, and heterosexual but also White, middle-class, documented, and able-bodied.[243] As a consequence, hotline-operator HGR referrals, IPV agency screening and safety planning, mental health service provision and support groups, and informal interactions between staff and victims may not reflect the unique experiences and needs of all IPV victim organization clients.

Second, one-size-fits-all programs may discourage the belief that additional antidiscrimination and LGBTQ IPV knowledge training are warranted, which may help discrimination flourish in these organizations. Indeed, a number of studies suggest that IPV victim organization staff can hold deeply homophobic and transphobic beliefs.[244] For instance, one U.S. study reported that, of nineteen trans* victims of "family violence" (which is undefined in the report and may include more than IPV), 21% were harassed or disrespected while at a "domestic violence shelter/program."[245] As interviews with mental health-care providers at IPV victim organizations suggest, staff can often get away with making disparaging remarks to LGBTQ IPV victims (e.g., "that's unnatural"[246]), both because it is difficult for victims to prove that the remarks were made and because victims may fear outing their LGBTQ status. Additionally, because mental health-care providers and their supervisors often have some discretion in choosing which victim is seen by which provider, supervisors may purposely avoid assigning LGBTQ IPV victims to certain providers who have expressed discomfort being in a room with an LGBTQ person. This in turn enables homophobic and transphobic attitudes by staff to go unchallenged.[247] In many instances, staff may simply not take LGBTQ IPV seriously, which can result in equally disturbing staff encounters with victims. Grace Giorgio recalls calling an IPV victim hotline after being raped: "I call the hotline. She just raped me, but I am not sure what to feel, to think. She left, zipping up her zipper and telling me I liked it and to be good. A woman answers the phone. I tell her my story. She balks. She tells me I'm taking up the hotline's precious time."[248]

Often this dismissive attitude stems from not only a stereotype of LGBTQ IPV being less serious but also a general disregard for the well-being of LGBTQ people. For example, when Michelle Fine, the direct services coordinator of a Massachusetts-based IPV agency, emailed service providers and others working to address IPV about an upcoming government hearing to discuss LGBTQ IPV, responses were often very negative, including one person who wrote back, "How dare you compare a woman being beaten by her husband to fags and lesbos."[249] This fusion of dismissiveness with homophobia among IPV victim organization staff unfortunately can result in incredibly negative experiences for LGBTQ IPV victims that may lead them back to their abusers. Moreover, at organizations that fail to challenge homophobia and transphobia among staff, the same discriminatory attitudes can thrive among fellow HC IPV victims, who research finds can be quite hostile to LGBTQ IPV victims located at the same IPV victim organization.[250] For instance, one sexual minority victim recalls being asked "not to be gay in front of one woman's child,"[251] while a trans* victim overheard another victim saying she did not know what to tell her children regarding "*what* she [the trans* victim] was" (emphasis added).[252] Service providers also report that some female HC IPV victims express concerns over being around female sexual minority IPV victims because, drawing on inaccurate negative stereotypes, they assume that all sexual minorities will be sexually attracted to and try to romantically seduce everyone of the same gender, even the children of fellow victims.[253] In some cases, homophobic victims may even leave a shelter specifically to avoid being around sexual minorities, sending a clear message to sexual minority victims that they are not welcome.[254]

In such a hostile environment, LGBTQ IPV victims who choose to stay may continue to face discrimination and harassment. The alternative—attempting to educate IPV victim organization staff and fellow clients about LGBTQ IPV and being LGBTQ—is a lot to place on the shoulders of victims, especially when the reason they come to such organizations is to receive help from supposedly trained experts. Researcher Jeanne Alhusen and colleagues succinctly sum up the impracticality of expecting victims to shoulder this responsibility instead of the IPV victim organization they are receiving services from: "Having to be one's own advocate in an environment in which few people validate the IPV is emotionally exhausting."[255] Likewise, lesbian victims of IPV have voiced their frustration with untrained IPV victim organization staff and service providers, explaining, "We're tired of educating service providers; they don't know what it means to be lesbian"; "It's hard to talk about lesbian abuse when they [service providers] haven't dealt with lesbianism."[256] The decision by some IPV victim organizations to not provide antidiscrimination and LGBTQ IPV knowledge training to staff—a decision often derived from an assumption that IPV is a one-size-fits-all phenomenon—certainly lowers the burden on staff and decreases risks of upsetting discriminatory clients and staff. At the same time, as we can see, there are many major costs to using one-size-fits-all approaches, costs almost entirely shouldered by LGBTQ IPV victims.

Tailored IPV Victim Organizations

Many organizations show that tailoring IPV victim services to the needs of LGBTQ IPV victims is both possible and effective.[257] As several excellent review articles note,[258] there are a number of positive steps that one-size-fits-all IPV victim organizations can take to offer more-tailored services when they encounter LGBTQ IPV victims: (1) preparing the organization for changes, (2) making training mandatory, (3) tailoring services, (4) tailoring advertising and informational materials, and (5) adjusting organization policies.

First and foremost, an organization that has relied on a one-size-fits-all model needs to first be prepared to accept change. Mary-Elizabeth Quinn of The Network/La Red offers detailed suggestions on how to build institutional buy-in to the idea of offering more-tailored services, including recruiting support from fellow staff and service providers, management, and, eventually, the board of directors.[259] Once a substantial portion of an organization exhibits a willingness to make changes, the next step is to conduct a needs assessment by surveying staff and management on what resources are already in place and which need to be created, which Quinn also provides excellent, detailed examples of for reference.[260] Regarding new organizations, researcher and activist Lori Girshick recalls her own experiences in trying to develop a same-gender IPV victim organization. She emphasizes perhaps above all else that, for brand-new organizations typically faced with a lack of not only experience but also resources, gaining support from governmental departments and most especially existing IPV victim organizations can be critical.[261] Reflecting her understandable frustrations over efforts to make progress without active support from others, she notes, "It is unrealistic for an individual (or small group) outside of an agency to attempt to create services without the necessary allies within a variety of agencies in the community."[262] It is ultimately important that an organization preparing to make the leap to offering tailored services have institutional buy-in, an understanding of what specific changes are needed, and the resources needed from within and without the organization to make these changes possible.

Second, training on the nature of LGBTQ IPV and on antidiscrimination should be made mandatory for all staff and volunteers. As previously discussed, a reliance on a single trained liaison can be effective only if the liaison is present, which obviously will not always be the case at the exact moment when an LGBTQ IPV victim seeks help.[263] It should also not be assumed that certain staff members do not require training simply because they are LGBTQ.[264] Training should be provided to all existing and new staff and volunteers, and continuing education workshops should be provided periodically.[265] Where needed, partnerships can be made with LGBTQ IPV victim organizations and more general LGBTQ organizations to offer trainings.[266] Often times, trainings on LGBTQ IPV knowledge are conducted as a separate module added onto main IPV training programs. Some scholars and practitioners have voiced concerns that this approach may encourage the false assumption that HC IPV is most important to know about (because it is addressed in multiple core IPV training sessions) and that LGBTQ IPV is a rare case that does not need to be taken seriously (because it is addressed often in a single, separate session).[267] Interviews with service providers confirm that this problem can indeed arise.[268] As one service provider describes, when having a separate training session on just LGBTQ IPV, the reaction by other providers is often "It's like ok, we gotta do this training. Let's just do it. It's like taking medicine that you don't wanna take."[269] One solution to this problem would of course be to integrate information about LGBTQ IPV and HC IPV into a single training program, where both are touched upon as each subtopic is discussed.

Third, services—indeed, any interaction that staff and service providers have with LGBTQ IPV victim clients—should be tailored to be appropriate for those clients. This begins with modifying screening protocols. Just as with screenings for IPV and danger assessments conducted by mental health-care providers in general-practice settings, screenings conducted by staff and providers at IPV victim organizations should include the following: asking about the victim's gender identity, trans* status, and sexual orientation rather than presuming to know the answers;[270] adjusting the screening items to include unique LGBTQ IPV tactics (e.g., threats of outing), as well as relevant covariates that may warrant additional types of treatment;[271] when preferred gender pronouns are not already known, using gender-neutral terminology (often not the case,[272] such as when IPV victim hotline operators are trained to ask "Is *he* in the house right now?"[273]); and ensuring that no third parties are present during screening who may potentially be abusers masquerading as friends.[274] Particularly challenging for single-gender shelters is that same-gender IPV abusers may present themselves as victims—for reasons ranging from a desire to stalk their victims to truly desiring services—and staff trained only on HC IPV may incorrectly assume that women can only be victims.[275] One female same-gender IPV victim recalls being contacted by an IPV victim organization, inquiring whether she was sure she wanted to leave the organization's services. The problem, though, was that she had never asked to be unenrolled from services. Her abuser had . . . by pretending to be the victim:

> One morning I get this phone call from WI (a service agency). One of the facilitators is calling to ask if I really don't want to be in the group. I'm like, "Of course I do! I can't wait." But she tells me that, according to the secretary, I came in yesterday and told them I wanted to be dropped from the group. That was not me. I realized then

that she had gone in and posed as me and they bought it. I hadn't even told her about the group.[276]

Specifically because organization staff may not be trained to consider that a woman can be an abuser, some female same-gender IPV victims avoid seeking help from female IPV victim shelters.[277] Ultimately, as Mary-Elizabeth Quinn of The Network/La Red aptly points out, failure to accurately differentiate victims from abusers has major implications:

> What would happen if we offered the wrong services to the wrong person? We could place the survivor in danger or in jail and potentially send the message that it was their fault the abuse happened. We could also place the abuser in support services that validate the abuser and tell them they are not to blame for the abuse. We might place the abuser in a confidential shelter or help the abuser get a restraining order against a survivor. This could help the abuser find the survivor or turn a survivor away from services that they need. If we give the wrong services to the wrong person because we are not screening, people get hurt.[278]

As previously discussed, successful screening achieves multiple goals, each of which benefits from tailoring questions to LGBTQ IPV victims: signaling acceptance of LGBTQ people (through either preferred or gender-neutral terminology) and in turn encouraging IPV disclosure and a willingness to receive help; identifying victims eligible for services (and differentiating them from abusers); identifying risk of revictimization and self-harm (in the case of danger assessment); and identifying the forms of IPV victimization and covariates experienced that can be used to guide treatment and referrals to services.

Beyond screening, core services can also be adjusted, such as in-house mental health-care services and support groups (as previously described[279]), as well as shelter accommodations (which may entail offering separate rooms if desired by the victim).[280] One of the pitfalls shelters should be wary of when offering separate housing is that separate HC IPV victim and LGBTQ IPV victim accommodations may not necessarily be equal in quality. For example, according to findings from a 2005 legislative government session in Massachusetts, unlike HC IPV victims—who could reside for up to ninety days in twenty-four-hour supervised emergency shelters—LGBTQ IPV victims were more likely to be placed for much shorter terms in off-site locations (like cheap hotels) where security for screening out abusers was laxer or entirely nonexistent, safety of the venue was questionable (such as being in geographical proximity to frequent criminal activity), and access to ancillary services (like support groups) was sharply limited or impossible. The absence of on-site staff and support services was found to be particularly problematic. Specifically, because victims often still doubt the decision to leave their abusers, with little to no encouragement by absent staff to reinforce the decision to leave, many LGBTQ IPV victims opt to return to their abusers.[281]

Providers and staff at IPV victim organizations can also adjust services in regard to safety planning and HGR referrals. Safety planning is a valuable tool for helping LGBTQ IPV victims develop a detailed strategy for how to minimize risk of the abuser harming them—a tool that can be modified according to whether victims choose to leave or stay with abusers. Safety planning is often conducted at IPV victim organizations, including by IPV victim hotline operators, IPV victim shelter staff and in-house mental health-care service providers, and multiservice IPV victim agencies.[282] (See table 3 as well as any number of excellent published templates[283] for suggestions on safety-planning items.) As discussed previously in the context of mental health-care providers, safety planning can be adjusted for LGBTQ IPV victims by suggesting particularly relevant emergency-bag items (such as gender-identity documents and hormone medications) and by working with victims to identify alternate HGRs to include in the safety plan that may be less likely to be discriminatory or entirely inaccessible.[284] Relatedly, it is key that IPV victim organizations develop a robust referral list of local HGRs specializing in victim services regarding not only HC IPV but also LGBTQ IPV.[285] It cannot be assumed that more-mainstream, one-size-fits-all IPV victim programs will be trusted by victims (as they typically are not according to utilization studies[286]) or that they will offer the most tailored, effective care.

Fourth, service advertising and informational materials can be tailored to LGBTQ IPV victims. Even if an IPV victim organization offers services open to LGBTQ IPV victims, if such victims are unaware that they are welcome, they will not come. Some evidence suggests that this is indeed a major problem across HGR types. According to a 2009 study of 648 staff members at HGRs addressing IPV victimization in the United States—including employees of IPV victim organizations, sexual-assault centers, prosecutor offices, law-enforcement agencies, and offices servicing child victims—most indicated that that there was little to no service advertising targeting LGBTQ IPV victims.[287] Similarly, a study of service providers in Australia found that organizations that do accept LGBTQ IPV victims for services often fail to openly state this anywhere.[288] To ensure that LGBTQ IPV victims know that they can access services, IPV victim organizations are encouraged to clearly state that LGBTQ people are welcome (rather than simply using gender-neutral terminology and hoping this is interpreted correctly) in service advertisements, in addition to in the organization's website and mission statement.[289] Service advertisements should be posted in places most likely to be seen by LGBTQ communities, such as in LGBTQ-centric media publications and websites.[290] Recognizing that not all LGBTQ people share the same language, race and ethnicity, social class, and immigrant status, organizations should advertise services in a broad range of LGBTQ communities as well as in non-LGBTQ-centric neighborhoods (e.g., placing advertisements in media targeting different language communities).[291] While terms like *intimate partner violence, domestic violence,* and *dating violence* may gain instant recognition for those viewing service advertisements, many victims do not yet self-label as victims and may not respond to these terms. Instead, some scholars suggest replacing these terms with their behavioral definitions, such as through the use of specific examples of LGBTQ IPV tactics that victims will more readily be able to identify in their own relationships.[292] Likewise, outreach materials that indirectly advertise an organization's presence— organization brochures, fact sheets, posters, and websites—can include images of same-gender couples and trans* people, testimonials from LGBTQ IPV victims, and information specifically about LGBTQ IPV.[293]

Fifth and last, IPV victim organizations can adjust organization policies to foster an environment that is more welcoming to LGBTQ clients and staff alike. Such policies can govern hiring practices, staff benefits, restrooms, discrimination, and confidentiality. Those conducting hiring of new IPV victim organization staff (and volunteers and service providers) should consider, among other factors, whether potential staff will be prepared to serve LGBTQ IPV victims. As previously discussed, some IPV victim organization staff may hold very homophobic and transphobic beliefs, and they can express these attitudes both indirectly and directly with LGBTQ IPV victims.[294] The presence of such staff jeopardizes the missions of these organizations, potentially through their actions retraumatizing LGBTQ IPV victims and pushing them back to their abusers. Organizations that wish to be serious about serving not just HC but also LGBTQ IPV victims should ask all potential new hires whether they feel comfortable working with and serving LGBTQ people, and only those that answer affirmatively should be considered for employment.[295] Additionally, hiring LGBTQ staff who are out about their LGBTQ identity (and mentioning in employment advertisements placed in LGBTQ-centric media that LGBTQ people are encouraged to apply) can be beneficial on a number of levels, from offering a diversity of opinions on the future direction of the organization, to making LGBTQ IPV victims feel more welcome, to encouraging greater acceptance of LGBTQ people by fellow staff and clients.[296] Beyond hiring practices, the environment for LGBTQ staff can be made more accepting in two key ways: extending staff benefits (like paid sick leave and health insurance) to all staff including those who are LGBTQ as well as their intimate partners, and opening a gender-neutral restroom (which may be preferred by some trans* and genderqueer staff and clients, among others).[297] Given the prevalence of discrimination and harassment against LGBTQ staff and victims at IPV victim organizations,[298] it is strongly recommended that IPV victim organizations establish antidiscrimination policies governing oppressive language and actions by both staff and victims.[299] Confidentiality policies can also play an important role in protecting private and potentially stigmatizing information about victims at an organization. For example, such policies can include stipulations that a victim's LGBTQ identity will not be made known to anyone—even fellow staff—beyond the victim's advocate and the organization supervisor, unless permission is granted by the victim.[300] Antidiscrimination and confidentiality policies should be made known to all new and current staff and victims at an IPV victim organization, and specific protocols should be in place for how to quickly and effectively address breaches of these policies.[301] Clear understanding of these policies is key, not only because it may help deter policy violations but also because the implications of these policies—often written in dense, legal language—may not be obvious. For example, one study found that some staff may hesitate to screen IPV victims for LGBTQ status—an obviously beneficial first step in offering tailored, respectful services—because of an unfounded fear that doing so would violate their organization's antidiscrimination policy.[302] Excellent templates for antidiscrimination and confidentiality policies can be found in, among other places, The Network/La Red's 2010 manual "Open Minds Open Doors."[303]

IMPLICATIONS FOR POLICY, PRACTICE, AND RESEARCH

By examining data on nongovernmental responses to LGBTQ IPV, we can draw a number of lessons for future policy, practice, and research. To begin, for policymakers, although by definition nongovernmental formal HGRs are not directly employed by governments, they often receive government funding contingent upon following certain requirements. For example, as reviewed in this chapter, the 2013 VAWA Reauthorization required that LGBTQ IPV be addressed by IPV victim shelters in order to receive federal funding . . . but then it added a variety of loopholes and exemptions that effectively permit shelters to ban all cisgender men and trans* people.[304] Likewise, hospitals receiving federal funding may be required to offer certain resources to victims. In this sense, policymakers often have leverage in expanding formal HGR access to include LGBTQ IPV victims, and they may likewise have some influence over basic HGR protocols for screening and responding to LGBTQ IPV victims. If indeed policymakers in a given nation offer government funding to formal HGRs contingent upon certain requirements, governments should consider mandating the following: that LGBTQ IPV victims be granted access to an HGR's services or those of an equivalent local organization; that LGBTQ IPV victim services be equal in quality (although not necessarily quantity) to HC IPV victim services (which, as mentioned previously, was found not to be the case in 2005 regarding Massachusetts's emergency victim shelters[305]); and that any preexisting IPV training requirements be expanded to include LGBTQ IPV knowledge training and antidiscrimination training.

Regarding nongovernmental informal HGRs, the good news is that LGBTQ IPV victims are highly likely to seek help from friends and family, and friends in particular consistently rank among the top HGRs in terms of how helpful victims perceive them to be. The bad news is that responses by friends and family can often be inadequate, such as when responses are dismissive of the seriousness of LGBTQ IPV, express homophobic or transphobic attitudes to victims, encourage the victim to remain silent lest IPV negatively reflect upon all LGBTQ people, or discourage victims from seeking help from formal HGRs. Additionally, in small LGBTQ communities, victims often share friends with abusers, deterring victimization disclosure. Although there is no perfect solution to these problems, an important first step would be to expand IPV prevention education programs in schools and communities to include the topic of LGBTQ IPV. As will be discussed in the next chapter, prevention education programs often have a primary goal of decreasing the likelihood that audience members will perpetrate IPV in the future. However, a common secondary goal is to educate "bystanders" (i.e., friends, family, community members) in recognizing the warning signs that someone they know is experiencing IPV and, subsequently, in knowing how to properly intervene and offer assistance to the victim. If more youths and adults received such training, they might be better equipped to respond to the devastating news that an LGBTQ person they know and care about is being abused.

For nongovernmental formal HGRs (mental health-care systems, medical health-care systems, and IPV victim organizations), research suggests that, beyond those organizations that outright exclude LGBTQ IPV victims, many formal HGRs provide one-size-fits-all responses to IPV victims. That is to say, they assume that LGBTQ IPV is identical to HC IPV, and therefore all services are designed solely with HC IPV in mind but made available to both heterosexual-cisgender and LGBTQ victims (often by using gender-neutral terminology and posting nondiscrimination policies). As this book repeatedly emphasizes, though, HC IPV and LGBTQ IPV are *not* identical. In many ways, LGBTQ IPV does share most of the same qualities of HC IPV—*plus* many unique qualities, ranging from causes of perpetration to types of IPV tactics received and barriers to help-seeking. By focusing only on HC IPV, a one-size-fits-all approach may send a signal to LGBTQ IPV victims that they are not truly welcome, and this approach may potentially be less effective because it fails to address any of the unique aspects of LGBTQ IPV experiences.

Fortunately, research offers a number of suggestions on how nongovernmental formal HGRs can offer high-quality responses to LGBTQ IPV victims. As discussed in this chapter, these suggestions address nearly every aspect of interactions with victims: preparing for organizational change, as well as tailoring service advertisements, training, policies, and services. First, nongovernmental formal HGRs that are considering a move to become more inclusive can take a variety of steps to prepare for this change: gain buy-in from service providers followed by management and boards of directors at the organization, then assess the areas in which the organization needs to improve (using the guidelines previously discussed), and partner with local organizations to gain from their expertise and resources.

Second, it is important to find ways to assist LGBTQ IPV victims in feeling more comfortable seeking help from nongovernmental formal HGRs, given that these HGRs can offer a number of high-impact services. While mental health-care providers consistently rank among the top HGRs most likely to be sought out for help by LGBTQ IPV victims, medical health-care providers and IPV victim organizations (including IPV victim hotlines, shelters, and agencies) have among the lowest utilization rates. When a formal HGR does make its services accessible to LGBTQ IPV victims, it is important to find ways to ensure that LGBTQ IPV victims know the services exist and that they are welcome to use them. Therefore, it is recommended that service advertisements explicitly state that LGBTQ people are welcome, rather than using gender-neutral terminology in advertisements and hoping that this will be interpreted correctly. Advertisements can also use LGBTQ symbols, images, terminology, testimonials, and facts. Service advertisements should be placed in LGBTQ-centric publications and on such websites and email listservs, as well as on the HGR's website and in its mission statement. While on average all LGBTQ IPV victims underutilize these types of HGRs, research suggests that sexual minority men are even less likely to seek help, suggesting that separate advertisements could be designed to increase the degree to which male victims access services. Likewise, the physical space of an HGR can serve as advertising for victims when they initially walk through its doors, which means that it is similarly important to have visible symbols of inclusion in lobbies and office spaces (e.g., LGBTQ IPV information and images in office brochures and posters, posting a nondiscrimination policy by the office entrance, etc.).

Third, staff and service-provider training is critically important to becoming a more inclusive nongovernmental formal HGR. Training on knowledge of LGBTQ IPV will help dispel LGBTQ IPV myths as well as facilitate the offering of more-tailored services. This knowledge could briefly cover many of the core subjects of this book, such as myths, causes, types of tactics, prevalence, outcomes, barriers to help-seeking, and legal issues. Training should also cover antidiscrimination, to help increase acceptance of LGBTQ people and decrease the likelihood of discriminatory responses to victims. This training should be mandatory for all staff and service providers at these HGRs rather than the HGRs relying on one trained specialist or liaison to handle all LGBTQ IPV victim clients, given that liaisons are not always available at the time a victim seeks help. Training might need to be HGR-specific in certain instances, such as regarding how to apply LGBTQ IPV knowledge to screening protocols. However, some emerging models in Australia and Canada suggest that interagency trainings that bring together multiple types of HGRs can significantly broaden access to training information and, moreover, can increase communication between HGRs to better assist victims.[306]

Fourth, nongovernmental formal HGR policies can be adjusted to create an environment that is more welcoming to LGBTQ clients, staff, and providers. These improvements can be made through a variety of policies: hiring practices (e.g., ensuring that job advertisements actively recruit LGBTQ people as well as people who are comfortable working with LGBTQ victims), staff benefits (e.g., extending insurance and retirement benefits to the intimate partners of LGBTQ staff), restrooms (i.e., offering at least one gender-neutral restroom for those who do not feel comfortable in a male-only or female-only bathroom), antidiscrimination initiatives (e.g., creating antiharassment policies disallowing verbally and physically abusive behaviors by clients, staff, and providers, creating antidiscrimination policies guaranteeing that LGBTQ IPV victim clients will receive quality services and will not be turned away because they are LGBTQ, ensuring that all are aware of these policies, and designing protocols for breaches of these policies), and assurance of confidentiality (e.g., creating a policy that will ensure that providers cannot share the LGBTQ status of a victim client with anyone other than a direct supervisor without the expressed or written permission of the client).

Fifth, nongovernmental formal HGRs should consider tailoring their services to be more inclusive of LGBTQ IPV victims, including regarding screening, core services, and safety planning and referrals. Most nongovernmental formal HGRs have protocols for recognizing the warning signs of IPV and screening for it (whether as part of or separate from intake procedures and danger assessments). Scholars suggest that these screening protocols could be adjusted in several ways: so that they do not categorically turn away LGBTQ IPV victims and do not ask *sex*-based questions (e.g., about current genitals or sex-reassignment surgery) when determining what *gender* victims identity with (an issue of particular importance with trans* victims); avoid informal practices that increase the chances of turning LGBTQ IPV victims away (such as assuming that LGBTQ victims cannot be "real" victims, or assuming that victims seeking shelter are really just homeless nonvictims simply because, due to understandable fears of being outed and discriminated against, they refuse to share the names of same-gender abusers, participate in support groups, seek help from law enforcement, or file for an order of protection); do not permit a support person to be present during IPV screening (as research suggests that some providers incorrectly assume that a person who accompanies the victim is a friend rather than an abuser if the person is of the same gender as the victim); use gender-neutral terminology (and, once LGBTQ status is inquired about—which it should be—switch to using the terminology preferred by the victim); and add in questions about tactics experienced that are unique to LGBTQ IPV. Core services can also be tailored to be more inclusive of LGBTQ IPV through the following steps: (1) be accepting both of the victim's LGBTQ identity and of the accuracy with which the victim reports on the victimization experience; (2) avoid myth-based assumptions about the nature of LGBTQ IPV (e.g., the stereotypes that most LGBTQ IPV is mutual battering, that female abusers cannot cause serious harm, that male victims cannot be seriously hurt, etc.); (3) use gender-neutral terminology when in doubt, but, preferably, ask victims what terminology they would like the provider to use; (4) for shelters, offer LGBTQ IPV victims the option of separate but equal quality on-site housing accommodations; and (5), during mental health-care treatment, add in a discussion of factors often unique to LGBTQ IPV, such as any IPV tactics the victim may have experienced, the strength of their support network and whom the victim is out to, barriers the victim is experiencing in receiving help from HGRs, and homophobic and transphobic attitudes the victim may have internalized that in turn could be hindering their recovery process. Finally, nongovernmental formal HGRs should be prepared to adjust safety-planning protocols and HGR referrals. When planning for how victims can increase their safety whether remaining with or leaving an abuser, providers should consider suggesting the inclusion of emergency-bag items that trans* victims may need as part of expressing their gender identity (e.g., hormone medications), and they should likewise consider whether LGBTQ IPV victims feel comfortable following through on safety-plan items that require interacting with formal HGRs that may be perceived as discriminatory or exclusionary (e.g., safety plans often mention being prepared to contact law enforcement in an emergency, knowing the process for getting an order of protection, and writing down the location of an IPV victim shelter—all of which may incorrectly assume that victims have no reason to fear being turned away from or discriminated against by these HGRs). Relatedly, medical and mental health-care providers as well as IPV victim organizations are often trained to offer a list of local and national formal HGRs, so that victims may be able to receive a full range of services that the present HGR does not offer. It is important that such HGR referral lists include organizations and providers that are especially trained for and welcoming of LGBTQ IPV victims.

Last, researchers have played and will continue to play a key role in the improvement of nongovernmental formal HGRs. In particular, there are a number of major gaps in our knowledge about these HGRs and the experiences of LGBTQ IPV victims with them. For example, research has yet to systematically assess what aspects of LGBTQ IPV—if any—staff and service providers have received training on, whether during graduate school training, new employee training, or continuing education training seminars. Additionally, although research has provided a bird's-eye view of which types of HGRs are most likely to be utilized by LGBTQ IPV victims, future studies could provide a much finer grain of detail, such as by assessing the utilization of more-specific types of HGRs (e.g., distinguishing one-stop-shop agencies with integrated services from single-service organizations, distinguishing the receipt of information and referrals by IPV victim telephone hotlines from IPV victim informational websites) and by ascertaining the exact triggers that lead LGBTQ IPV victims to seek help in the first place. Research can also more systematically assess how often LGBTQ IPV victims receive discriminatory or dismissive responses from each HGR type. Perhaps most important, though, research largely has yet to illuminate what strategies are working well. Evaluation studies are needed for treatment standards with LGBTQ IPV victims (such as by developing LGBTQ-tailored IPV screening questions and then systematically comparing them with more traditionally used HC IPV screening questions in regard to their relative effectiveness in correctly identifying LGBTQ IPV victims).

6
―――――

HOW CAN WE IMPROVE
GOVERNMENT RESPONSES?

I have the cop's personal cell phone number, and his badge number, and what his first name was even, and he just, he gave me a lot of good stuff. And picked me up to take me to a safe house.[1]

I had called the police . . . just to ask about what would happen if I wanted to have him arrested for hitting, I was almost laughed at. I was told that I needed to "straighten out my lifestyle and then I would be all set." That was it for me. I stayed with him and lived with the abuse, I drank a lot every day and I even started to do some drugs to deal with it, so I wouldn't feel anything. I was also hoping that I would OD and then it would be all over.[2]

The statements above—voices of sexual minorities who experienced relationship abuse—highlight the inherent tension in the power held by governments: in one context governments may provide safety nets for LGBTQ IPV victims and then, in another context, be their oppressors. This has led at least some LGBTQ communities to bypass potentially discriminatory government interventions by turning to a "community accountability" model, in which abusers are expected to apologize and reform with the help of friends, family, and the community. Certainly a non-punitive, rehabilitation-focused approach like community accountability is appealing given that incarceration often has an imperfect effect on limiting future perpetration of IPV.[3] However, as Shannon Perez-Darby of The Northwest Network notes, in the absence of experts trained in the nature of LGBTQ IPV and rehabilitation, community-accountability models can sometimes become vulnerable to abusers who often view themselves as not responsible for their abuse, are practiced at manipulating the truth with others, and are not easily reformed.[4] With considerably more resources and expertise at their disposal, governments have greater potential to address IPV, but more is needed to fully realize that potential. Maximizing a government's ability to make a positive impact on the lives of LGBTQ IPV victims must begin with addressing government policies (including policies governing the right to be LGBTQ, the right to marry, and the right to adopt children), discrimination in criminal-justice systems (including regarding law enforcement and court systems), and inadequacies in current strategies to prevent and intervene in LGBTQ IPV perpetration.

GOVERNMENT POLICIES

When LGBTQ IPV victims turn to HGRs for help in leaving abusers and coping with exposure to trauma, government policies have the potential to greatly assist in this process. Government laws have the power to order the punishment and rehabilitation of abusers, the application of orders of protection that legally bar abusers from contacting and reabusing victims, funding for organizations to provide services to IPV victims, and funding to directly help victims cover legal, housing, and health costs associated with victimization. As of 2013, IPV has been criminalized in eighty-nine nations.[5]

Some policymakers[6] have argued that laws already exist that protect all people from physical and sexual assaults and that IPV laws therefore do not need to be expanded to include LGBTQ IPV victims. However, cobbling together protections from non-IPV assault laws offers considerably fewer comprehensive and swift responses. For instance, in the United States, only when an abuser is being tried under IPV laws can the victim access specialized civil-criminal IPV courts designed to simultaneously and expediently address multiple victim concerns (such as custody of children, divorce from the abuser, civil orders of protection against the abuser, and criminal IPV charges against the abuser). Beyond offering speed and comprehensiveness, specialized IPV courts also may increase the chances of a victim winning on all fronts (because what would otherwise be treated as separate issues are received as a single issue) and decrease the chances that the victim will give up on the legal process (a particular risk if separate trials are needed in the absence of a specialized, one-stop-shop IPV court).[7] Likewise, in the United States, a court can issue an order of protection to deter the abuser from stalking the victim (and to punish any breach of that order). The process of getting that order may be easier (via a lower "burden of proof"), with quicker implementation and more-specific requirements of the abuser (like requiring the abuser to obtain permission to enter the victim's residence to retrieve personal belongings[8]) *if* the order is obtained in civil courts, which are accessible only under IPV law. By comparison, orders of protection obtained in criminal courts, accessible to more general assault victims, may be more difficult to obtain.[9] Moreover, many victims are not prepared to press criminal charges against abusers—particularly out of fear that arrest will trigger retaliation— and prefer instead that the abuser be tried in civil court, which in the United States is generally possible only under IPV laws.[10] In some regions, bail for abusers awaiting trial may be set at a higher amount if the case is being tried under IPV law.[11] Regarding sentencing, in some nations, physical assault may result in a higher prison sentence if it is perpetrated in the context of an intimate relationship.[12] Judges may also be more likely to mandate that guilty parties attend rehabilitative batterer-intervention programs if the abuser is tried under IPV laws rather than more general assault laws.[13] Victims seeking protection under IPV laws may also receive access to free or subsidized HGR services like mental health-care treatment.[14] Going above and beyond protection offered by general assault laws, IPV laws thus are designed to facilitate the process of helping victims receive assistance and justice.

On the surface, in many nations, civil and criminal law governing IPV appears to be accessible to all types of IPV victims, in part because LGBTQ or HC people are rarely mentioned in the legal language. Digging a little deeper, though, it becomes clear that IPV laws often apply only to certain types of people in certain types of relationships, disproportionately excluding LGBTQ victims.[15] To better understand why this is the case, it is important to examine government policies that create these classifications—policies governing the right to be LGBTQ, the right to marry, and the right to adopt children.

The Right to Be LGBTQ

In 2014, the International Lesbian, Gay, Bisexual, Trans, and Intersex Association published a very troubling report. It found that, of the nearly two hundred nations in the world, anal and oral same-gender sexual penetration—often termed "sodomy"—is *illegal* in seventy-eight of them. Additionally, in sixteen nations, the age at which people can legally consent to have sex is higher if the partner is of the same rather than a different gender. Violators may face fines, imprisonment, or, in five nations, the death penalty.[16] There has, thankfully, been considerable progress on this front in the past three decades. For instance, anti-sodomy laws were struck down throughout the United Kingdom in 1982,[17] and they were ruled unconstitutional nationwide in 2003 in the United States[18]—although these unenforceable laws were still on the books in twelve U.S. states as recently as 2014, a symbolic reminder that homophobia is alive and well.[19] Although obviously not the only negative effect of these laws, the devastation wrought for same-gender IPV victims by anti-sodomy laws is magnified because seeking help would entail admitting to a crime of your own: being a sexual minority.

Beyond risking being labeled a criminal, LGBTQ IPV victims who seek help must also contend with the possibility that their economic and social lives may unravel if they are outed when seeking help. As of 2014, only sixty-one nations prohibit discrimination in employment based on sexual orientation,[20] while only forty-seven prohibit discrimination against trans* people.[21] Employment discrimination can even extend to militaries. For instance, one study found that same-gender IPV victims in the U.S. military were afraid to seek help because, until 2011, the official military policy of "Don't Ask, Don't Tell" required soldiers to be discharged if they came out.[22] LGBTQ people can also be legally discriminated against in realms beyond employment. For instance, the Human Rights Campaign reported in 2015 that, in the majority of U.S. states, not only can LGBTQ people be legally fired, not hired, and not promoted because they are LGBTQ (in twenty-eight of fifty states), but LGBTQ people also can be legally evicted and denied housing (twenty-eight states) as well as legally denied service in public accommodations like restaurants, movie theaters, libraries, and stores (twenty-eight states), simply because they are LGBTQ.[23] Thus, seeking help for IPV victimization may risk the victim's LGBTQ status becoming public knowledge, and this in turn can present a whole host of problems, ranging from being banned from stores to being fired and evicted. These concerns in nations like the United States may understandably give some victims pause in seeking help.

For trans* victims in particular, seeking help may be problematic because their very identities may be questioned and deemed insufficient. Many nations like the United States make it challenging for trans* people to change the gender identity on their government-issued documents (e.g., passports, driver's licenses, and birth certificates), some nations requiring sex-reassignment surgery, psychiatric evaluation, or even sterilization.[24] It is therefore unfortunately very common that trans* people have a gender identity that does not match the one listed on their official documents, and, by definition, their sex at birth will also not match their gender identity. When HGRs and IPV laws require a victim to be of a certain "sex" (which often assumes that sex equals gender and that all people are cisgender), trans* victims may be viewed as not "real" men and women and therefore not eligible for assistance.[25]

The Right to Marry

IPV laws often require that the abuser and victim be currently or previously joined by certain kinds of legally recognized relationships, such as marital or different-gender cohabitating relationships.[26] When an intimate relationship is defined so restrictively, these requirements can all but exclude same-gender IPV victims from legal protections. This is because in the vast majority of nations throughout the world, it is illegal to marry someone of the same gender. Until 2000, same-gender marriage was illegal in every nation of the world. By 2015, there had been only marginal gains: just twenty-two nations plus sections of Mexico had fully legalized same-gender marriage.[27] Similar barriers to accessing IPV laws may exist for trans* victims, since IPV laws often limit protection to people of different *sexes,* leaving room for courts to interpret this to mean sex, gender identity, or both. This in turn results in situations where a trans* IPV victim may be denied an order of protection because the victim and abuser were born of the same sex, even though they may have identified with different genders at the time of the abuse.[28]

The intent to discriminate specifically against sexual minorities can be most plainly seen in regions directly excluding same-gender IPV victims from legal protection. For instance, in 1998, seven U.S. states prohibited orders of protection for same-gender couples,[29] all the while in some cases still permitting different-gender *friends* to obtain an order.[30] By 2015, while no such outright ban exists anymore in the United States, one U.S. state (South Carolina) did have higher eligibility standards for same-gender IPV victims (who are eligible for orders of protection only if they are or have been married or have a child in common) than for different-gender IPV victims (who are eligible for orders if they are or have been married, have a child in common, *or have ever cohabitated together*).[31] (Of course, prior to the 2015 U.S. Supreme Court case *Obergefell v. Hodges,* in which same-gender marriage was ruled constitutionally protected nationwide, South Carolina's marriage requirement for obtaining orders of protection would have been legally impossible for a same-gender IPV victim to meet.) Relatedly, prior to 2003, it was reported that rape statutes in the United States often had lesser penalties if the perpetrator and victim were of the same gender rather than different genders.[32]

It has been speculated that there are two primary explanations for overt attempts to exclude same-gender IPV victims from IPV legal protections: either policymakers are honestly unaware of the existence and severity of LGBTQ IPV, or they are aware and nonetheless have a disregard for the well-being of LGBTQ people.[33] Certainly, some policymakers may understandably be unaware of LGBTQ IPV because the global movement to address IPV has focused almost exclusively on HC IPV. For example, in 1992, the United Nations (UN) urged member nations to treat violence against women as a form of discrimination against women. By 2004, the UN was prepared to pass a resolution to promote the "elimination of domestic violence against women," spurring on a substantial wave of new laws criminalizing IPV. Unfortunately, the language of this UN resolution entirely ignores IPV against men and trans* victims, and, owing to its emphasis on violence against "spouses," it appears to overlook same-gender IPV victims in nations where same-gender marriage is banned.[34] In an effort to maintain pressure on nations to criminalize IPV, the UN keeps statistics on different-gender IPV prevalence in all member nations, yet no such statistics are kept on same-gender IPV.[35] This would suggest that some nations might exclude LGBTQ IPV victims from IPV laws because the broader global movement to address IPV has rendered LGBTQ IPV invisible. Of course, it is also possible that some policymakers are aware of LGBTQ IPV victims and simply do not care as much about their well-being. This position appears to be espoused by several policymakers who have argued that including same-gender IPV under IPV laws will create a "slippery slope" leading to the legalization of same-gender marriage—an argument that makes some logical sense only if these policymakers believe that LGBTQ people are generally not deserving of equal rights. This "slippery slope" argument has been expressed by conservative policymakers in the United States seeking to exclude LGBTQ victims from the 2013 VAWA Reauthorization,[36] and it was similarly expressed by conservative policymakers in Hong Kong over a 2009 amendment to its Domestic Violence Ordinance.[37]

Some nations and local governments have attempted to be more inclusive of same-gender IPV victims by making the language of IPV laws not only gender-neutral but also devoid of requirements like having to be in a marital or different-gender relationship. In some such cases, IPV laws may use language such as "living as a spouse,"[38] "spouse-like,"[39] or "members of an unmarried couple"[40] to signify that committed intimate relationships outside of legal marriage should still be protected. As some U.S. scholars point out, there are two problems with such one-size-fits-all IPV laws. First, when preexisting HC IPV laws are rewritten to be gender-neutral, typically only HC IPV tactics are listed as types of IPV protected under the law; other tactics unique to LGBTQ IPV may not get added in. (For example, when Michael Richardson of Washington, D.C., filed for a permanent order of protection because his male same-gender IPV abuser had outed him to his colleagues and family and threatened to ruin his life [among several other IPV tactics], the trial court dismissed the petition for the order on the grounds that D.C.'s IPV law did not list such forms of abuse as IPV.[41]) Second and perhaps even more problematic, when IPV laws neither explicitly include nor explicitly exclude same-gender IPV victims, courts have considerable leeway in interpreting such laws. When these IPV laws exist in the context of a state or nation that has other types of laws restricting the definition of family to different-gender relationships—such as regions with same-gender marriage bans—attorneys have successfully argued that seemingly gender-neutral IPV laws can be assumed to exclude same-gender IPV victims.[42] In other cases, judges have looked to previous, non-gender-neutral versions of local IPV laws to try to interpret the meaning of current gender-neutral IPV laws.[43] When it comes to minors (e.g., those under the age of eighteen), IPV laws can also on the surface appear applicable to LGBTQ victims but nonetheless present barriers to access. For instance, in some regions, IPV laws governing minors may require consent from a parent or legal guardian to seek an order of protection. While such laws may not explicitly ban LGBTQ IPV victims from acquiring orders, LGBTQ IPV victims may be less likely than HC IPV victims to ask family to consent to an order of protection in situations where victims are not yet out to family about their sexual minority or trans* status.[44] As one indication of the extent of this problem in the United States, according to a 2010 report, nine states prohibit minors from petitioning for an order of protection on their own behalf, while another nine states ban minors from ever receiving orders regardless of who petitions.[45] Research has not assessed the degree to which other nations share this problem. The inclusion of minors in IPV victimization laws, as occurred in 2013 in the United Kingdom,[46] may be an important first step in offering the full range of legal protections to minors.

Because IPV laws can directly and indirectly exclude LGBTQ IPV victims, such victims are often left searching for remedies in a second-tier legal system that, as previously discussed, may offer less comprehensive and expedient responses. As this book demonstrates, LGBTQ IPV victims are absolutely deserving of legal protections and should be included in IPV laws. Because attempts to use gender-neutral language have led to confusion and often a loss of protections for LGBTQ IPV victims, it is recommended that LGBTQ people and their relationships be more directly included in the language of IPV laws. Additionally, these changes must be communicated to HGRs and LGBTQ communities. One unfortunate effect of the unclear legal status of LGBTQ IPV victims is that, even in regions where LGBTQ IPV victims are legally protected, research finds that victims may not be aware of this.[47] Just as troubling, law enforcement and other HGRs may not know that their local IPV laws cover LGBTQ IPV victims, resulting in situations where victims are incorrectly told that they are not protected by the law.[48] Scholar Grace Giorgio describes just such a situation with a same-gender IPV victim she had interviewed:

> When Val, a White, college-educated woman in her thirties, sought assistance from a support agency, the advocate told her erroneously that because the two women did not live together and were both women, Val was not eligible for an order of protection, even though the state where Val lives includes same-sex partners in its domestic violence statute. When Val discovered that the advocate's information was false, she decided against seeking further assistance because it would be "more of a hassle, more disappointment."[49]

For Val, being misled about her legal rights resulted in her losing faith in HGRs. This heartbreaking story suggests that, beyond actual changes in IPV laws to make them more inclusive, communication about the extent of legal protections can be clearer between governments, HGRs, and LGBTQ IPV victims.

The Right to Adopt Children

In many regions, IPV laws cover those who have a child in common, regardless of whether other relationship criteria (e.g., married, cohabitating) are met.[50] Additionally, victims of IPV maintain a right to see their legally recognized children even after separating from the abuser, and victims may also have enhanced odds of winning complete custody of children specifically because children may be at risk of negative outcomes if they remain with abusers. More specifically, IPV victims often can get protection by the law and maintain contact with their children *if* the law views the victim as a legal parent or guardian. If a victim helped raise a child with the abuser but has not been designated as a legal parent of the child, the victim may be less likely to be eligible to receive protections under IPV law (e.g., for orders of protection, etc.). Moreover, they will most likely not have any legal right to demand custody of the child, let alone the right to even see the child again. Because while the best interest of the child is typically considered when a child has one nonabusive parent and one abusive parent, that point is often deemed irrelevant if the nonabusive parent is not legally designated as a parent.[51] Legal parenting rights are thus critically important for IPV victims.

In many nations, legal parental rights are automatically conferred on those who biologically help conceive or give birth to a child. In same-gender relationships between cisgender partners, it is not physiologically possible for both partners to become legal parents of the same child in this manner. Instead, for both partners in such relationships to become legal parents of the same child, they have two options: joint adoption (in which both partners become the legal guardians of a child that neither gave birth to), or second-parent adoption (in which a person who holds legal guardianship of a child such as one born in a previous relationship allows a current partner to also gain legal guardianship over that child). Unfortunately, as recently as 2014, joint adoption between same-gender partners was legal in only fifteen nations, and only second-parent adoption by a partner in a same-gender relationship was legal (but joint adoption was not) in just another five nations.[52] As a consequence, same-gender IPV victims are less likely to be eligible for protections under IPV laws, and they may have no right to custody over their children, resulting in children remaining with abusers and being barred by abusers from contacting the victim.[53] Sharon Stapel, the IPV unit director at a legal-services organization, highlights the seeming arbitrariness of IPV laws that protect relationships with coparented children in a region that does not legally permit same-gender couples to have children: "For example, a woman who has a child by a man she met only once at a holiday party would have access to family court to obtain an order of protection because of the impregnation, yet a same-sex survivor of a multi-decade relationship that resulted in no children in common would not. These examples demonstrate the unintentional absurdity in defining intimacy."[54]

The right to adopt children is part of a larger package of rights LGBTQ people are often denied throughout the world, such as the right to marry and the right to even be LGBTQ. The bigger picture is often a story of demeaning LGBTQ people by treating them as subhuman and undeserving of equal, human rights. One of the many unfortunate consequences of this treatment by some governments has been that LGBTQ people are being harassed, beaten, raped, stalked, and killed by partners in a world that—whether due to ignorance or to discriminatory beliefs—places legal roadblocks in their path to reaching safety.

LAW ENFORCEMENT

Our data included one encounter with a same-sex couple. . . . After noticing that one of the men was bleeding, the officer notified the victim that he was "unable to take any official action" and left. Afterward, the officer told the observer that he "left so quickly because [the man] had been bleeding, and he did not want to deal with any 'bleeding fags.'"[55]

The police came out three or four times. It was always a neighbor who called. They would just tell us to behave and that, you know, that we needed to act like ladies. They didn't even ask for an explanation. They just told us to go and you know, whenever they would come they would just say you guys need to be quiet. When she was hitting me outside and they came and I was physically bruised she—she didn't even try and explain it away at all. She just kind of stood there and then the police left. But after the police left it was awful. Because even though it wasn't me that was calling she still blamed me.[56]

Among all HGRs, law enforcement ranks high in its potential to positively impact the lives of LGBTQ IPV victims. Law enforcement is entrusted with enforcing criminal IPV laws, acting as a primary access point for victims looking to seek orders of protection or to press charges against an abuser. Law enforcement often is also empowered to take measures to keep the peace in society, intervening in emergency situations to protect abuse victims regardless of whether they are covered under local IPV laws. Moreover, by labeling LGBTQ IPV victims as legitimate victims in the eyes of the law, law enforcement can serve as a catalyst for victims to receive a whole host of free or subsidized victim services. (For instance, having filed charges with the police against an abuser is a factor considered by some shelter staff in determining which victims to admit.[57]) Thankfully, research does indicate that, in the majority of cases, law enforcement has positive intentions in helping LGBTQ IPV victims. For example, of LGBTQ IPV victims reporting to police in the United States, 79% indicate that officers act in a courteous or emotionally indifferent manner, rather than being outright discriminatory.[58] Lending further weight to these perceptions by victims, when officers in the United States are directly asked about their behavior, about the same percentage report having never acted in a discriminatory manner to LGBTQ people in any context.[59] In spite of numerous real-life exceptions,[60] studies asking about perceptions of a fake IPV story find that law enforcement[61] (and those training to work in the criminal-justice system[62]) view same-gender IPV as seriously as different-gender IPV. Qualitative interviews with victims,[63] as well as policy reforms advocated for by some in law enforcement,[64] offer further evidence that law enforcement is, on average, a force of positive change in the lives of LGBTQ IPV victims.

That said, law enforcement remains an underutilized HGR, with somewhere between 0% and 20% of LGBTQ IPV victims seeking help from law enforcement.[65] Among LGBTQ IPV victims, one study suggests that trans* victims are the least likely to report to police.[66] These low utilization rates may be influenced by perceptions of law enforcement as being discriminatory against LGBTQ people—perceptions that are widely held among LGBTQ people.[67] Of course, beyond perceptions, many do have negative experiences during interactions with law enforcement, with studies finding that anywhere from 34% to 83% of LGBTQ IPV victims feel that law enforcement is only a little or not at all helpful.[68] There may be several reasons for these negative perceptions and experiences: these might include discriminatory attitudes held by some in law enforcement, as well as discriminatory actions taken regarding whether IPV incidents are labeled as IPV by law enforcement, whether an arrest is made, who is arrested, and whether HGR referrals are given to the victim.

Discriminatory Beliefs

Regarding discriminatory beliefs, research indicates that a substantial minority of officers do not offer the same respect and investigative diligence to LGBTQ IPV victims that they do to HC IPV victims. To begin, there is often a general lack of respect for LGBTQ people among many in law enforcement. One eye-opening study in 2002 of 249 U.S. police officers found negative views of sexual minorities to be pervasive. In this study, a substantial minority of officers reported believing that sex between two men or two women is "just plain wrong" (25% felt this regarding male-male sex and 47% regarding female-female sex); the majority of officers felt that sexual minorities should not be allowed to "speak in public," "teach in colleges," or have books about them in libraries (73%, 71%, and 69%, respectively, felt this way); and the majority of officers believed that sexual minorities could not be as good as heterosexuals at being law-enforcement officers (85% felt this way regarding hypothetical sexual minority male officers and 74% regarding hypothetical sexual minority female officers).[69] Relatedly, by comparison with other HGRs, law enforcement is less likely to report understanding the beliefs and concerns of sexual minorities.[70] Additionally, in the United States, 25% of officers admit to having intentionally acted in a discriminatory way toward a sexual minority (although not necessarily an IPV victim),[71] 21% of LGBTQ IPV victims report officers being openly hostile to them,[72] and 10% of LGBTQ IPV victims report that officers have engaged in some type of police misconduct with them, such as verbal or physical abuse.[73] Interviews with victims offer countless examples[74] of officers using hate speech to silence and dismiss the concerns of LGBTQ IPV victims: there are the officers who sling homophobic epithets at sexual minority IPV victims, calling them "a couple of dykes,"[75] "bleeding fags,"[76] or "queer devil"[77]; there are the officers who draw on gender stereotypes to be dismissive of same-gender IPV victims, saying to a male victim, "Quit crying, don't be a sissy,"[78] or to a female victim that "we needed to act like ladies"[79]; there are the transphobic officers who insist on referring to trans* female IPV victims as "mister"[80] or tell them to "shut up, faggot"[81]; and there are the officers who tell victims that they deserve to be abused because they are LGBTQ.[82] As one female same-gender IPV victim explains, law enforcement that expresses these blatantly hateful attitudes can feel like an extension of abusers: "I felt more beaten, more threatened and scared. I mean, here is this big hairy guy holding a gun, and a stick on his side, telling me to shut the f—up, and go sit down. That's just what I needed, after what I had been through."[83]

Obviously, holding discriminatory attitudes does not by default mean that an officer will express those attitudes with victims. Still, when homophobic and transphobic beliefs go unchallenged in a police department, it seems naive to expect that no officers will act on these beliefs.

Discrimination in the Labeling of IPV

It is critically important that law enforcement correctly identify LGBTQ IPV as IPV, rather than as some other crime like physical assault between "friends" or "roommates." This is because if a crime is labeled as a general assault rather than IPV, the likelihood of arrest may decrease,[84] and, in resulting court cases, victims may lose special IPV-related considerations (such as the court requiring an abuser to receive batterer treatment, or a victim being able to utilize battered woman's syndrome as a legal justification for using violence in self-defense).[85] Unfortunately, one study found that police in the United States label two-thirds of all LGBTQ IPV incidents as *not* being IPV.[86] While some police may mislabel IPV as another crime, many will also not report any crime as having occurred. For instance, according to a study of law-enforcement interactions with same-gender IPV victims in Australia, it was found that police do not write a report in 47% of such cases.[87]

Discrimination in Arrests

In cases where a report is taken and the crime is believed to be IPV, research is mixed on whether the likelihood of arrest differs between same-gender and different-gender IPV. According to a study of the nearly twenty-three thousand incidents of noncohabiting, nonmarital IPV reported to police in Canada in 2008, the police arrested and charged someone less often in same-gender IPV cases than in different-gender IPV cases (65% and 81%, respectively). Conversely, in the United States, analyses of the hundreds of thousands of IPV incidents reported to law enforcement in 2000 (both cohabiting and not, marital and not) found that an arrest was just as likely to occur in same-gender IPV cases as in different-gender IPV cases (about half of the time for both), with arrests being slightly more common in male than female same-gender IPV cases (53% and 47%, respectively).[88] (Other studies weighing in on the likelihood of arrest have been imprecise, either because they have estimated the IPV arrest likelihood for all sexual minorities and all heterosexuals rather than just for those with IPV-related police interactions[89] or because they have used the existence of current same- and different-gender cohabiting relationships as a proxy for assuming the genders of partners in past IPV relationships with police involvement.[90]) It is difficult to know if differences between the Canadian and U.S. findings are real national differences (perhaps influenced by differences in mandatory arrest policies) or can be explained by other factors, such as differences in the types of IPV relationships assessed (noncohabiting and nonmarital IPV for the former, all types of IPV relationships for the latter). The only study to specifically examine arrests with sexual IPV incidents

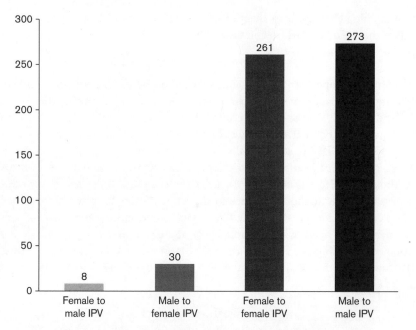

FIGURE 12. Rate of dual arrest among IPV incidents reported to police (per 1,000). (Police are ten to thirty times more likely to arrest *both* partners in same-gender IPV cases than in different-gender cases.)

found that likelihood of arrest in the United States for such crimes did not significantly differ between same-gender and different-gender couples.[91]

While law enforcement may not discriminate in the likelihood of making an arrest, they may in terms of *who* is arrested. When law enforcement incorrectly arrests victims, the message is sent that victims are to blame for their own victimization. Moreover, by being mislabeled as an abuser, a victim may have a much harder time accessing victim-designated resources (e.g., shelters, support groups). Not only may such mislabeled victims be more likely to lose a court case against an abuser, but they may also be more likely themselves to become incarcerated. In instances where both partners are arrested, a mutual restraining order may be issued, which abusers can use to manipulate the victim by threatening to lie to the police, telling them that the victim violated the order. In sum, arresting the victim can set off a sequence of events that may irreparably harm the victim's chances of seeking help and justice.[92]

Research finds that U.S. law enforcement is far more likely to arrest *both* partners (i.e., "dual arrest") than just one if partners are of the same gender. An analysis was conducted of all 577,862 IPV police records gathered in the year 2000 by

2,819 police departments across nineteen U.S. states back in 2000.[†] Findings revealed that *dual arrests were nearly ten times more likely to occur in same-gender IPV incidents as compared with female-to-male IPV cases* and *over thirty times more likely as compared with male-to-female IPV cases.*[93] (See figure 12.)

One certainly plausible explanation of this dual-arrest disparity is that law enforcement is more likely to encounter mutual battering in same-gender than in different-gender IPV police calls. In the absence of direct evidence of the reasons for why dual arrests are being made, it is distinctly possible that this gap represents real differences in the cases reported to law enforcement. Future research would do well to examine the dual-arrest gap in different-gender and same-gender IPV police interactions, both by analyzing the arrest justifications in officer reports and by comparing these to other triangulating data such as the likelihood of a case dismissal and other judicial outcomes.

There are at least some reasons, though, to be skeptical that the dual-arrest gap is entirely based on actual differences in rates of different-gender and same-gender mutual battering. First, only one study thus far provides any evidence that both partners in a same-gender relationship might use and receive IPV tactics.[94] When it does occur, a substantial portion appears to be explained by victims fighting back in self-defense,[95] which hardly could be called "mutual battering." Second, research finds considerable evidence that men and women have used and received physical IPV tactics at some point in their lives about as often in different-gender relationships[96] as in same-gender relationships.[97] These studies do not offer any indication of the prevalence of mutual battering, both because they tend to examine violence used and received in a time period rather than in the same relationship and because they ignore nonabusive motivations like self-defense. Still, what these studies do suggest is that, if some in law enforcement are arresting simply based on the use of violence irrespective of whether it was motivated by self-defense, it appears that dual arrests should be happening at similar rates in different-gender and same-gender IPV police calls. Third, as previously mentioned, according to LGBTQ IPV victims, in about two-thirds of cases coming to the attention of law enforcement, IPV is not labeled as IPV at all,[98] calling into question whether law enforcement is always able to accurately read who is doing what to whom in same-gender IPV relationships. Fourth and last, many victims state that they were incorrectly arrested. A study of 510 LGBTQ IPV victims who reported to the police found that 9% of the *victims* were arrested by the police.[99]

---

† Note that the U.S. government at the time required police to indicate a primary perpetrator even in cases where police perceived that both partners might be perpetrators and should both be arrested. The researchers of this study thus distinguished dual arrests in different-gender IPV relationships when the primary perpetrator was male (which they labeled as "male-to-female" IPV) versus female (which they labeled as "female-to-male" IPV).

Thus, a substantial portion of those experiencing arrest in a same-gender IPV relationship view themselves as victims being misidentified by police as abusers.

If indeed at least some portion of the dual-arrest gap is explained by misreading same-gender IPV incidents, what possible reason for this could there be? Pooja Gehi, then an attorney with a trans* legal-advocacy organization called the Sylvia Rivera Law Project, offers one reason police may be inclined to arrest both partners in an LGBTQ IPV relationship: confusion. Gehi explains: "[W]hen my clients who are survivors of domestic violence call the police for assistance, they often end up getting arrested either instead of, or along with, their abuser. . . . Rather than investigate the situation, police officers tend to arrest based on assumptions and often explain that since they were 'confused,' they just arrested everyone."[100]

Gehi is alluding to the possibility that many officers hold stereotypes of the "typical" IPV relationship, which they may assume to be male-to-female unidirectional abuse. When presented with same-gender or trans* IPV, without stereotypes to easily draw on, law enforcement may try to arrest either the more masculine partner or both partners.[101] Several instances have also been documented in which law enforcement has threatened dual arrest if the same-gender victim and abuser cannot work out their conflicts on their own,[102] further suggesting that some in law enforcement view dual arrest as a convenient solution to what they view as a confusing situation. That said, until further research is collected, this is for the most part just speculation: for now, it is difficult to know for certain why this substantial dual-arrest gap exists, just as it is difficult to know whether the gap exists at all outside the United States.

Discrimination in HGR Referrals

In instances where law enforcement does recognize that an LGBTQ IPV victim is indeed a victim, one of the responsibilities often given to law enforcement is to provide information about IPV and referrals to HGRs. Unfortunately, this rarely happens. For instance, in one study, researchers contacted local law-enforcement agencies in over seven hundred cities across all fifty U.S. states, and they requested the documents that law-enforcement officers give to IPV victims at the scene of an emergency 911 call. Of the 1,793 documents received (most of which notably were published by IPV victim organizations), document topics ranged from the nature of IPV to developing a safety plan, working with police and the criminal-justice system, long-term victim services, and ancillary services related to employment, housing, substance use, and so forth. While providing ample information about male-to-female IPV and relevant HGR referrals, only 15% of the documents mentioned same-gender or female-to-male IPV. Of the 501 documents created by law-enforcement agencies themselves, 7% stated that police can refer same-gender or female-to-male IPV victims to HGRs, 4% made brief mention of the existence of same-gender or female-to-male IPV, and 0% stated that police will respond to same-gender IPV.[103]

Similarly, in a study of same-gender IPV victims in Australia who interacted with police, in only 12% of cases did the police provide the victim with a copy of the government's *Victim's Guide to Support Services and the Criminal Justice System.*[104] One rather disturbing story documented by researchers entails an LGBTQ IPV victim who was not offered HGR referrals by police but instead was told that they could sleep on the floor by the heating grate to keep warm for the night.[105] The officers involved clearly recognized that the victim was in need of some kind of IPV-related assistance, yet they failed to care enough to provide that help or refer the victim to HGRs.

Training and Protocols

While the majority of LGBTQ IPV victims do not interact with law enforcement, the vast majority of law-enforcement officers who work with IPV cases will encounter LGBTQ IPV victims at some point in their careers.[106] When victims have a negative experience with an officer—whether because the officer expresses homophobic or transphobic beliefs, fails to label IPV as IPV, incorrectly arrests the victim, or fails to offer HGR referrals—anecdotal evidence indicates that some LGBTQ IPV victims are less likely to contact the police or any other HGR for help in the future.[107] Taken together, this suggests that all law-enforcement personnel who might potentially deal with IPV cases should be trained to deal with LGBTQ IPV. Training should cover the nature of LGBTQ IPV and how law enforcement can positively interact with victims.[108] This education should also encompass anti-discrimination training to reduce homophobic and transphobic attitudes and increase the respect given by officers during interactions with LGBTQ IPV victims, such as by requiring the use of gender-neutral and inclusive language.[109]

The number of trained officers matters a great deal in how well law enforcement can respond to victims. Some police departments may train only a single liaison officer on LGBTQ IPV, who then can have LGBTQ IPV victims referred to them by fellow officers and by IPV victim organizations.[110] As with the use of liaisons in other types of HGRs, the flaw in this organizational structure is that liaisons may not always be available when an LGBTQ IPV victim needs them. More to the point, liaisons cannot be used when the responding officer at the scene does not yet know if the victim is LGBTQ, and it will therefore often be a nontrained officer who forms the victim's initial impression of law enforcement. Training all officers who could potentially ever encounter IPV victims would be preferable as a way to avoid this inevitable problem. Research is mixed on the degree to which training on LGBTQ IPV is provided to law enforcement. One study found that 84% of twenty-nine surveyed U.S. police departments did offer some training on same-gender IPV,[111] whereas another study conversely found that only 30% of ninety-one U.S. police officers with IPV case experience had ever received same-gender IPV training,[112] and no study has yet assessed the degree to which officers are trained on trans* IPV or the degree to which officer training occurs outside the United States

Beyond training, law enforcement should design protocols that strictly govern interactions between law enforcement and LGBTQ IPV victims, covering at minimum investigative techniques, arrest decisions, and HGR victim referrals. Unfortunately, research suggests that formal LGBTQ IPV police protocols are rare, with less than one-fifth of U.S. police departments having specific policies regarding same-gender IPV.[113] No study has yet examined the extent to which departments outside the United States use protocols addressing same-gender IPV, nor the extent to which departments in any nation use protocols addressing trans* IPV.

COURTS

The clerk was friendly when she gave Robin the paperwork and began giving her instructions. When Robin said the person she wanted a restraining order against was her ex-girlfriend, . . . the clerk wasn't so nice anymore. She sort of rolled her eyes. . . . She began repeating everything Robin said, not for clarity I thought, but out of some kind of disbelief. . . . She said . . . "Well, you can fill out the form anyway, but if she doesn't have any weapons, you don't have a very good case, do you?" . . . [Robin] cried. She was frustrated and started doubting that she would be granted a restraining order. . . . We ended up leaving.[114]

In the relatively rare instances in which an LGBTQ IPV relationship comes to the attention of attorneys or courts, judicial systems have the greatest authority of any HGR to create an immediate and potentially lasting change in the lives of victims and abusers. When the powers of civil and criminal courts are considered collectively, courts can issue orders of protection, fine and incarcerate abusers, order abusers to attend rehabilitative batterer-intervention programs, ensure that victims have access to HGRs, and provide financial support to victims in dealing with the legal, health, and housing costs created by victimization. That said, LGBTQ IPV victims are less likely to seek help from an attorney than from nearly any other HGR (with attorneys being sought out by only 3–10% of LGBTQ IPV victims[115]). This low utilization rate may be explained by a variety of factors, but one of these factors is undoubtedly a perception of judicial systems as discriminatory and ineffective in regard to helping LGBTQ IPV victims. For instance, when looking at even the most positive estimates, attorneys are rated as either somewhat or very helpful less often than every other HGR type (by 11–25% of LGBTQ IPV victims[116]). Why are courts so often viewed as hostile to LGBTQ IPV victims, and what can be done to change this?

There is very little direct evidence that court personnel—attorneys, court staff, and judges—hold discriminatory beliefs regarding LGBTQ people. Anecdotal stories do highlight the existence of such discriminatory beliefs in courts, just not the extent to which they exist. For instance, scholars have documented instances in which judges and court staff have expressed transphobic attitudes, such as by appearing visibly unnerved in the presence of trans* people and by calling trans* people "it" or "he-she" in open court.[117] Attorneys like Sandra Lundy have reported that discriminatory beliefs are subtly being infused into the LGBTQ IPV court cases that their firms are involved in. Lundy explains:

> As a lawyer, I know from experience that litigating openly queer cases in civil court is never easy. You can be sure that somehow, somewhere, when you least expect it, homophobia will rear its ugly head in the courtroom. . . . Even where state law covers same-sex as well as heterosexual domestic violence, the chances are that the laws are not enforced equally and that same-sex litigants are treated with less dignity, sympathy, and respect than their straight counterparts.[118]

Certainly, as with other HGRs, court personnel could benefit from antidiscrimination training, antidiscrimination policies, and protocols for breaches of these polices.[119] Additionally, although legal barriers often prevent research on jurors, one study of 171 U.S. college students examined attitudes about hypothetical IPV court cases. According to this study, college students feel that same-gender IPV victims are less believable than different-gender IPV victims, and believability was directly tied to their recommendations for abuser sentencing.[120] (Concerns over these types of attitudes among actual jurors deciding LGBTQ IPV court cases have led some scholars to recommend that during voir dire, the juror-selection process, attorneys should screen out potential jurors based on their homophobic and transphobic beliefs.[121]) Generally, though, researchers have not systematically studied what percentage of court personnel and jurors hold discriminatory beliefs about LGBTQ people and LGBTQ IPV.

That said, while direct evidence of discriminatory beliefs is thin, indirect evidence of these beliefs is ample when looking at the actions taken by court personnel. Specifically, discrimination against some LGBTQ IPV victims has been found in several phases of the IPV judicial process: determining whether a case will reach trial, reliance on inaccurate stereotypes during trials, and rulings by courts.

Barriers to Reaching Court

One way in which judicial systems may discriminate against some LGBTQ IPV victims is by deterring them from continuing with a case. Anecdotal evidence suggests that some court clerks do just this, telling LGBTQ IPV victims that their odds of winning a case are so low that it is not worth continuing the process.[122] In other instances, attorneys may refuse to take LGBTQ IPV victims as clients specifically because they are LGBTQ,[123] such as when a same-gender IPV victim was told outright by an attorney, "Oh, we don't prosecute same-sex domestic violence."[124] Attorneys may be so dismissive that they imply that the victim is better off looking elsewhere for help, like when a same-gender IPV victim found her attorney to be less interested in learning about the IPV experience than in "what two women did in bed."[125] Attorneys can also decide to try an LGBTQ IPV case in court but not label it as LGBTQ IPV. This might entail attorneys reframing LGBTQ IPV as abuse between friends,[126] or LGBTQ IPV may be tried as a completely different offense like a hate crime.[127] Although not systematically studied, it has been suggested that some attorneys may not screen for LGBTQ status and instead just assume all victims are heterosexual and cisgender,[128] which may be one reason why LGBTQ IPV is not always labeled as LGBTQ IPV in courts. Of course, many LGBTQ IPV victims may not wish to disclose their LGBTQ status to attorneys or courts because of a fear of discriminatory outcomes both inside and outside of judicial systems.[129] While it is impossible to try an LGBTQ IPV case as IPV if the victim is unwilling to admit to the existence of an intimate relationship, the choice to come out should preferably be made by the victim, which is why it has been suggested that attorneys screen victims not only for being LGBTQ but for the degree to which they are out. In addition, because the LGBTQ status of victims may inevitably become public record in certain situations—as can often be the case in regions requiring trans* victims to be referred to in court only by the name and gender listed on their legal documents—it is important for attorneys to inform closeted LGBTQ people of the risk of being outed before they decide whether to proceed.[130] One bright spot in the process of trying to access courts may rest with judges. Specifically, one study found that courts in Trinidad are not any more or less likely to dismiss a same-gender IPV case than a different-gender IPV case before it reaches trial.[131]

Reliance on Discriminatory Stereotypes in Court

A number of scholars contend that court personnel draw heavily on the stereotype of IPV being predominantly perpetrated by a masculine man against a feminine woman, both of whom are cisgender and heterosexual. When an IPV case fits this stereotype, it is believed that jurors and judges are already socialized by society to sympathize with the female victim and to rule in her favor.[132] Unfortunately, LGBTQ IPV can never perfectly fit this stereotype, automatically putting many victims at a disadvantage in winning cases. To combat this problem, some attorneys may feel pressured to present to the court an image of LGBTQ IPV relationships that mirrors male-to-female HC IPV as closely as possible. For instance, female sexual minority victims may be encouraged by attorneys to dress in a far more stereotypically feminine manner than they are accustomed to, so as to better fit the stereotype of a feminine female victim.[133] Similarly, anecdotal evidence indicates that trans* female victims may find it easier to conform to an HC IPV stereotype and to win cases when they physically appear to be a cisgender female.[134] However, when judges and attorneys are aware of a victim's trans* status, they may come to view victims by their birth sex rather than gender identity. Beyond being disrespectful of the victim's gender identity, viewing trans* victims myopically by birth sex can result in additional negative stereotypes being applied in court. For instance, a trans* female victim of a cisgender male abuser may be treated as a male victim in a same-sex relationship, leading some to draw on negative stereotypes of men as always being able to defend themselves and of IPV in same-sex relationships as always being mutual battering.[135] One additional negative stereotype relevant to IPV cases is that trans* people are deceptive; this erroneous assumption stems from the belief that no one can legitimately *want* to have a gender identity that does not "match" their biological sex, and therefore it is presumed that trans* people are actually lying about their gender identity to achieve certain nefarious goals. Although researchers have not yet studied the use of this stereotype in IPV cases, it has been used by attorneys to discredit trans* people in non-IPV court cases. Take the case of Monica James, a trans* woman, being tried for attempted murder. During her trial, the prosecutor drew on the trans* deceiver stereotype by saying to the jury, "How can you trust this person? He tells you he is a woman; he is clearly a man."[136] Anecdotal evidence also suggests that some attorneys purposely use incorrect gender pronouns to refer to a trans* person in IPV cases as a strategy to both upset them and to hurt their credibility, indirectly conjuring this image of trans* people as deceptive and untrustworthy.[137]

The stereotype of all IPV as male-to-female HC IPV also influences LGBTQ IPV cases in which the victim kills the abuser to prevent being killed by the abuser. Many nations like the United States will not punish victims for killing in self-defense, a situation in which victims feel that killing is the only way to prevent themselves from being killed. The case for self-defense often rests on proving that the abuser was either in the act of trying to kill the victim or threatened to do so imminently. When victims kill abusers under other circumstances, such as when the abuser is sleeping, it becomes legally harder to prove that the IPV victim was acting in self-defense. To address this issue, defense attorneys in such cases can ask an IPV expert to testify in court that IPV victims often experience "battered woman's syndrome" (BWS). Not an official mental disorder but rather a mind-set, BWS occurs when victims feel it is impossible to escape severe (and often cyclical and escalating) abuse because the abuser has shown the capacity to threaten, stalk, and harm the victim. In such a circumstance, attorneys and testifying experts may argue that victims reasonably felt that killing the abuser was the only way to escape, and they may further argue that victims have gained an intricate understanding of the warning signs of future abuse and the credibility of threats, such that a victim may have good reason to believe an abuser who threatens to kill them one day. The concept of BWS is ultimately used to help IPV victims not be punished for having killed abusers in an attempt to escape them.[138] As the name "battered *woman's* syndrome" would suggest, BWS expert testimony often revolves around research on male-to-female HC IPV.[139] Thus, although the conditions that give rise to BWS are by no means unique to male-to-female HC IPV, stereotypes often make it less obvious for jurors and judges to associate BWS with LGBTQ IPV. In turn, although it has worked before in some instances,[140] it has been speculated that BWS may prove to be a largely unsuccessful legal defense in LGBTQ IPV cases.[141] Systematic evidence of this bias is still absent in research, and existing findings are mixed. Anecdotal evidence suggests that courts may be less likely to even permit BWS expert testimony in same-gender IPV cases, and that when it is permitted, jurors may be more likely to outright reject the argument that BWS is applicable.[142] At the same time, when a recent study presented 442 U.S. college students with a fake story of a person being attacked by and then killing a same-gender intimate partner, students were less likely to rate the shooter as guilty if the story included BWS testimony than if it did not have such testimony.[143] Although this study lacks the real-world context of actual court cases, results tentatively suggest that BWS testimony may help same-gender IPV victims in proving self-defense cases.

Discriminatory Court Outcomes

Research has yet to systematically assess whether convictions, fines, orders of protection, and most other court outcomes differ between LGBTQ IPV and HC IPV cases. For this reason, some scholars have called for a court-watch program to track sentencing practices in LGBTQ IPV court cases.[144] However, scholars have long speculated that mutual restraining orders are more likely to be given by courts for same-gender IPV cases[145]—a logical if unproven assumption, given that research shows law enforcement to be far more likely to arrest both partners in incidents involving same-gender IPV than in those involving different-gender IPV.[146] Mutual restraining orders are clearly problematic if misapplied in cases of unidirectional IPV. Beyond making victims feel guilty for abuse they have not committed, mutual restraining orders hinder victims from accessing victim HGRs, and they provide abusers with leverage over victims when abusers threaten to pretend the victim violated the protection order.[147] Interviews with victims suggest that mutual orders are erroneously given in some cases, although they do not indicate how common this is. For instance, consider the situation of Ronna, who went to the police immediately after her same-gender abuser, Kate, tried to strangle her. Although the police included photographs in their records and noted that there was bruising on Ronna and not on Kate, the judge ordered mutual orders of protection and told the women, according to Ronna's recollection, to "try to get along."[148] There is also some evidence that judges water down requirements in orders for same-gender offenses. According to a 2003 study of 227,941 active orders of protection in California—including but not limited to IPV cases—it was found that orders involving people of the same gender were less likely to have firearm restrictions written directly into the order.[149] Finally, although not systematically studied, now-outdated anecdotal evidence from the 1990s suggests that some judges may fail to require that convicted same-gender IPV abusers go through a rehabilitative batterer-intervention program.[150]

PREVENTION AND INTERVENTION

While HGRs and governments understandably devote a great deal of attention to helping victims, preventing IPV before it happens (i.e., "prevention") and preventing it from happening again (i.e., "intervention") are vital to limiting the number of people who become victims in the future. Regarding prevention, while some community-based programs exist, most IPV prevention programs are geared toward middle schools, high schools, and colleges. In many of these school-based programs, a trained educator meets weekly with students to discuss such interrelated topics as the nature of healthy relationships, myths about IPV, IPV warning signs, forms of and dynamics within IPV, IPV outcomes, how to intervene as a "bystander" (i.e., what to do if you believe that someone you know is an abuser or victim), and where to seek help. In addition to providing potential future victims with information to recognize and respond to abuse in their relationships, these programs are intended to prevent people from perpetrating IPV by undercutting the validity of IPV myths often used to justify IPV and by creating empathy for victims. A substantial number of IPV prevention programs have been systematically evaluated to confirm their effectiveness in reshaping attitudes and, in some cases, decreasing the number of students perpetrating and experiencing IPV at the program site.[151] Unfortunately, none of the evaluated programs have yet to incorporate information about LGBTQ IPV,[152] instead using either a one-size-fits-all IPV model (i.e., ignoring all unique aspects of LGBTQ IPV while using gender-neutral language) or an HC IPV model (which is often most apparent when these programs review the role of gender norms with a strictly heterosexual perspective). Among nonevaluated programs, while several incorporate LGBTQ IPV as a special case not fully integrated into the programs,[153] a small number of programs have been designed to focus exclusively on LGBTQ IPV.[154] Unfortunately, without being evaluated, these programs have not yet been proven to be effective in reshaping attitudes and preventing LGBTQ IPV. Scholars have rightly called for the creation of LGBTQ IPV prevention programs,[155] whether that means editing existing HC IPV programs to be truly inclusive (such as by using the excellent suggestions in "Voices Unheard," by LGBT Youth Scotland[156]) or creating entirely separate programs just for LGBTQ audiences. Given the clear and extensive role of homophobia and transphobia in LGBTQ IPV perpetration, victimization, and responses to victims, it would also be beneficial for prevention programs to include antidiscrimination training.[157] Additionally, because many prevention programs are run in conjunction with the distribution of IPV fact sheets and brochures, it would be valuable to ensure that the provided information about IPV and local victim HGRs is relevant to not just HC IPV but also LGBTQ IPV.[158]

Once IPV has occurred, it is important that steps are taken to decrease the likelihood of the abuser perpetrating IPV again. This is because recidivism (i.e., committing IPV again after being previously arrested or convicted) is typically quite common. For instance, one study found that, of 519 randomly sampled cases on IPV (but not necessarily LGBTQ IPV) from a U.S. municipal court, 33% of the abusers were arrested on IPV charges again within a year.[159] Although nongovernmental, counseling-based programs[160] and counseling activities[161] exist that focus on LGBTQ IPV abuser rehabilitation, only one such program has been evaluated (in a small, now two-decade-old study),[162] and none have been widely implemented. Lack of interest in nongovernmental rehabilitative programs may in part stem from such programs requiring abusers to voluntarily participate. When left up to the abuser, nonparticipation may be appealing because some abusers do not view themselves as abusers, do not wish to risk their LGBTQ identity being outed, or do not wish to risk drawing the attention of law enforcement. This is of course especially problematic in light of the fact that very few abusers end up being convicted by a court, and as a result there may be little to encourage them to receive help.

That said, one of the few times societies can require abusers to attend a rehabilitative program, often termed a "batterer-intervention program" (BIP) or a "perpetrator-intervention program," is when a judge mandates it as part of sentencing. While BIPs have generally been found to be limited in their effectiveness to reduce recidivism, they may help some abusers.[163] As discussed in chapter 1, BIPs are traditionally multisession discussion- and lecture-based education programs that often follow one of two models: cognitive behavioral therapy (CBT), or the Duluth model. Whereas CBT focuses on unlearning abusive tendencies and rebuilding positive conflict-resolution skills, the Duluth model emphasizes unlearning patriarchal beliefs that encourage some men to desire and feel entitled to control over women.[164] While aspects of both BIP models—CBT and Duluth—will be relevant to some degree to LGBTQ IPV abusers, neither is designed to include any of the many unique LGBTQ IPV myths, motivations, or tactics. The Duluth model is particularly problematic for LGBTQ IPV abusers because, with its focus on patriarchal ideology, it assumes that all IPV is HC IPV.[165] Unfortunately, research suggests that in the United States the Duluth model (whether on its own or in combination with CBT) dominates in BIPs.[166] According to a study of thirty-seven BIP guidelines used by state coalitions and state government departments in the United States in 1997, patriarchy was listed as the key cause of IPV in 70% of the guidelines.[167] Fast-forward to 2009, and another study found that, of fifty-three BIP guidelines spanning forty-two U.S. states, 78% used the Duluth model, indicating that little has changed. Not surprisingly, according to this same study, 51% of U.S. BIP guidelines focused solely on male perpetrators in their stated purpose or in their use of gendered pronouns. Only one BIP guideline directly mentioned women as abusers.[168] This does not mean that courts will permit LGBTQ IPV abusers to skip BIPs; it just means that they will often be placed in a BIP that is not designed to actually reduce the recidivism of the crime they committed. Indeed, according to a study of 276 people who operate BIPs in the United States, 78% of BIPs would welcome same-gender IPV abusers.[169] In the rare cases where a U.S. court places an LGBTQ IPV abuser in a BIP that offers a separate LGBTQ IPV abuser group, these groups tend to follow the same program as HC IPV groups. More often, though, LGBTQ IPV abusers are typically assigned to the same group as HC IPV abusers, again receiving identical content tailored to reducing HC IPV perpetration.[170] A similar story may be playing out in the United Kingdom, where research indicates that only 8% of BIPs overtly indicate in publicly available materials that they are inclusive of same-gender IPV abusers.[171]

Scholars call for the development of BIPs that better target the rehabilitative needs of LGBTQ IPV abusers.[172] If we follow the logic of the Duluth model to undermine the myths and justifications that often encourage and enable HC IPV perpetration, it stands to reason that a BIP tailored to LGBTQ IPV could decrease recidivism by tackling the myths and justifications unique to LGBTQ IPV. An important question to consider is whether program authors should create completely separate BIPs for LGBTQ IPV abusers or if, instead, they should attempt to integrate LGBTQ IPV information into HC IPV BIPs to make them truly appropriate for a mixed audience. Some evidence might suggest that the latter is a more feasible approach. According to a study of 276 U.S. BIP operators, only 1% of abusers in BIPs are same-gender IPV abusers. This would suggest that, in most regions, there might not be enough LGBTQ IPV abusers to financially warrant a separate LGBTQ IPV BIP. Instead, governments may wish to infuse an HC IPV BIP with information and myths regarding LGBTQ IPV. A small number of North American BIPs tailored primarily to LGBTQ IPV have been reported on[173]—in addition to likely several more-tailored BIPs that have not been reported on—which may potentially serve as a template for other governments, although, importantly, no evaluation testing their effectiveness has been published. Indeed, it would appear that no evaluations have been done to date on BIPs designed to be inclusive of LGBTQ IPV issues.[174] In sum, BIPs addressing LGBTQ IPV should be developed—whether as separate programs or, perhaps more realistically, as highly edited versions of HC IPV programs—and to establish their effectiveness, evaluation programs are sorely needed.

IMPLICATIONS FOR POLICY, PRACTICE, AND RESEARCH

The literature on government responses to LGBTQ IPV raises a number of suggestions for future policy, practice, and research. For policymakers, the first step to addressing IPV is criminalizing it. While many nations choose to incarcerate abusers, attempt to rehabilitate them, or use some combination of these, a government that instead legalizes abuse provides tacit approval and leaves victims with few options for escape. This nightmare scenario, unfortunately, is reality through-out most of the world. As of 2013, IPV was *legal* in over half of all nations.[175] This simply must change. The short- and long-term harmful effects of IPV to victims and their children—be it HC IPV or LGBTQ IPV—represent a crystal-clear public health threat.

In nations that have criminalized IPV, governments already have a major posi-tive impact on the lives of IPV victims, often offering a streamlined process through which to obtain court-granted benefits (e.g., orders of protection, custody of chil-dren, financial assistance in paying victimization-related costs such as attorney fees, etc.). Many governments also already have a substantial impact on abusers, who, by being tried and convicted under IPV laws, may have higher bail, longer incarcera-tion sentences, and mandatory rehabilitative treatment. While non-IPV sexual- and physical-assault laws offer many of the same protections, IPV laws typically go a step further, simplifying the process of receiving assistance, enhancing abuser penalties, and authorizing batterer treatment. Unfortunately, these protections are not extended to all IPV victims. Specifically, LGBTQ IPV victims often remain unprotected by IPV laws because such laws may narrow coverage to only certain relationship types: these might include different-gender relationships (problematic not only for same-gender IPV victims but, in many cases, for different-gender IPV trans* victims because of their birth sex), marital relationships (problematic in the vast majority of nations that ban same-gender marriage), and relationships with a child in common (problematic in the vast majority of nations that ban same-gender joint and second-parent adoption). In some nations like the United States, gender-neutral language has been applied to IPV laws to help expand their coverage to include LGBTQ IPV victims. As discussed previously, court cases in the United States demonstrate that this approach does not guarantee that LGBTQ victims will be covered under these laws. Scholars suggest that the clearest way to ensure that LGBTQ IPV victims receive protection under IPV law involves a two-step process: explicitly including LGBTQ IPV victims in the language of IPV laws, and ensuring that LGBTQ people legally have access to all the rights that might qualify a person for protection under IPV laws (such as access to the rights to be LGBTQ, marry, and adopt children).

For those formal HGRs that execute IPV law on behalf of governments—including law enforcement, courts, and BIPs—research offers a number of sugges-tions regarding improving the impartiality and effectiveness of responses to LGBTQ IPV. For law enforcement, discrimination should have no place in the language used with victims or abusers, nor should it impact whether an arrest is made at all, whether a dual arrest is made, or whether HGR referrals are given. For courts, discrimination should play no role in which cases reach trial, the accept-ance of inaccurate stereotypes during trial, or the severity and extensiveness of sentencing. Beyond largely anecdotal and indirect evidence, it is unclear how pervasive discrimination is in the criminal-justice system. Still, law-enforcement departments and courts can be proactive by offering mandatory antidiscrimination and LGBTQ IPV knowledge training to any personnel who may one day interact with LGBTQ IPV victims—training that some research suggests is currently lacking. For court-mandated BIPs, what is clear from research thus far limited to the United States is that the dominant model for rehabilitating IPV abusers, the Duluth model, assumes that IPV is always male-to-female HC IPV. What is less clear is whether this is an effective treatment for LGBTQ IPV abusers, but it is a question that governments should be considering. To be proactive, BIPs could be redesigned to address LGBTQ IPV, most especially the myths and justifications that often facilitate abuse.

Last, for researchers, arguably the area with the least amount of research-based knowledge is government responses to LGBTQ IPV. Not only is existing research on this topic largely limited to the United States, but even in the United States there are significant gaps. This is particularly unfortunate given the massive role governments play in deterring and punishing IPV perpetration, requiring rehabilitative treatment of abusers, and offering certain (albeit imperfect) protections to victims. The list of blind spots in research is long, but here are some of the big ones. There has yet to be systematic research on any of the following issues: how many nations have IPV laws that cover LGBTQ IPV victims (and what if any are the legal limitations to access, such as requiring marriage in a nation that bans same-gender marriage); how extensively has law enforcement received training on LGBTQ IPV outside the United States (although existing research on this topic in the United States could be expanded) and antidiscrimination training anywhere in the world; how extensively have court personnel (such as judges, court clerks, etc.) received antidiscrimination training anywhere in the world; to what extent are discriminatory verbal harassment and other abuses perpetrated by law enforcement and court personnel against LGBTQ IPV victims anywhere in the world; to what degree do court outcomes differ in same-gender versus different-gender IPV cases anywhere in the world (including but not limited to rates of dismissal, conviction, issuing single and mutual orders of protection, and mandating that abusers attend rehabilitative BIPs, controlling for all other relevant variables like crime severity); to what degree do law-enforcement processes differ in same-gender versus different-gender IPV cases anywhere in the world (including but not limited to differences in chances that a police report is written, indications in reports of the degree to which officers suspect one or both partners of perpetration, reasons that officers in the United States are more likely to conduct dual arrests than to arrest a single partner, whether dual arrests are more common for same-gender IPV police calls in other nations beyond the United States, and whether partners are arrested and charged with IPV or different crimes); the degree to which different models of treatment are used in BIPs outside the United States (although this could be looked at again in the United States since existing U.S. data is quickly becoming outdated) and exact differences between these models (e.g., topics covered, whether LGBTQ abusers are placed in separate groups or the same groups as HC abusers); and the effectiveness of different BIP models on LGBTQ versus HC IPV abusers anywhere in the world (including not only the models most commonly used with abusers already but also newly created models that are designed either solely for LGBTQ abusers or for both LGBTQ and HC IPV abusers). There is still a great deal to know about what strategies governments are using to address LGBTQ IPV and how effective those have been. Researchers can be at the forefront of uncovering what if anything governments can do to improve their responses and, ultimately, better serve LGBTQ IPV victims.

7

CONCLUSIONS

Where Do We Go from Here?

Not being out leads to a secret relationship, which can easily lead to secret abuse. I think about the power of language. Naming a relationship—acknowledging an existence—helps to identify real violence in a real relationship.[1]

JAI DULANI

Take a moment to close your eyes, and imagine an IPV victim. Whom do you see? What do they look like?

Many of us may picture a woman with a black eye or bruises. A Google Image search of the term *domestic violence* returns almost exclusively this image, often with her male abuser looming in the background. This type of image is displayed on countless websites and brochures of community organizations and government agencies that address IPV. There is an obvious logic to this choice: the majority of HC IPV victims are women. Women are more likely than men to become victims of different-gender sexual IPV, injurious physical IPV, partner stalking, and partner homicide.[2] On a more visceral level, though, popular gender stereotypes of heterosexual-cisgender women (e.g., weak, passive, to be cared for) and men (e.g., strong, assertive, being responsible for others) add weight to the image of male-to-female HC IPV. It is an image we understand on a gut level because it tells a familiar, gendered story of those with power dominating those who lack it.

Of course, IPV happens in other types of relationships, too. With few exceptions, research consistently finds that sexual minorities (and MSMs and WSWs) are *more likely* than heterosexuals (and MSWs [men who have sex with women] and WSMs [women who have sex with men]) to experience psychological,[3] physical,[4] and sexual IPV.[5] While results are less conclusive about whether trans* or cisgender people are at greater risk, victimization rates for trans* people[6] are on a par with those found among sexual minorities. Moreover, outcomes for LGBTQ IPV can be quite severe, ranging from mental health issues and substance abuse to sexual risk-taking, economic problems, fear for safety, and physical injury.

All that said, we have to point out the elephant in the room: because there are fewer LGBTQ people in the world, there are numerically far fewer LGBTQ IPV victims than HC IPV victims. The question then becomes, *What should the world do with LGBTQ IPV victims?*

To some, silence is the best path. For instance, a number of LGBTQ IPV victims report seeking help from LGBTQ friends and being told to remain quiet, lest IPV further stigmatize an already stigmatized population.[7] Several scholars have also advocated for silence, but for a different reason. They have argued that, if antifeminist researchers and activists become aware of LGBTQ IPV, they could use this as a rationale to try to steer funding and public discourse away from addressing male-to-female HC IPV.[8] Indeed, many[9] have already tried to argue that the existence of LGBTQ IPV is proof that female-to-male HC IPV must be prevalent. For others, silence is less a political strategy and more a result of buying into myths. Consider the numerous studies that find that college students,[10] counseling graduate school students,[11] and IPV victim organization staff[12] tend to believe that same-gender IPV is less severe than different-gender IPV. Countless instances have been documented in which certain informal[13] and formal[14] HGRs were dismissive of LGBTQ IPV victims, believing their experiences to not be "real" abuse. For victims, silence may also be the preferred option, whether because they fear violent retribution by abusers,[15] fear discriminatory responses by homophobic and transphobic HGRs,[16] are emotionally or financially dependent on the abuser,[17] or perhaps do not recognize they are being abused.[18]

Moreover, as Jai Dulani notes in the opening remarks of this chapter, many LGBTQ people choose to remain closeted about their identities and relationships because they live in a society that does not accept them for who they are. When this happens, not only is the abuse invisible, but so, too, is the relationship it exists in, making seeking help that much more challenging.[19] Unfortunately, homophobia and transphobia are fixtures in many nations throughout the world: sodomy is illegal in seventy-eight nations, just twenty-two nations have legalized same-gender marriage,[20] just fifteen nations have legalized same-gender joint adoption,[21] and employment discrimination against sexual minorities has been prohibited in only sixty-one nations and for trans* people in just forty-seven nations.[22] In reflecting on the limited legal protections for LGBTQ IPV victims in the United States, scholars Debora Ortega and Noël Busch-Armendariz consider the selective amnesia many seem to have regarding past human rights battles: "Undoubtedly in twenty years, future generations will ask, 'Did that really happen? What was America thinking? Was there really a time when equal rights were not afforded to LGBT people?' They will ask with the same disbelief with which current generations question the policies of separate drinking fountains and entrances for African-Americans during segregation, for example."[23]

Legally enshrined discrimination against LGBTQ people creates very real barriers to accessing protections under IPV law, as discussed in chapter 6. More broadly, though, when LGBTQ people are denied equal human rights, it sends a message that their well-being and safety are not high priorities in society, and it erodes victim trust in potential sources of help. It helps maintain silence around LGBTQ IPV.

There is just one problem with silence: in the vacuum, LGBTQ IPV flourishes. When we remain silent about LGBTQ IPV, abusers and victims alike struggle to recognize IPV in their relationships. When we remain silent, researchers and policymakers gear their efforts to addressing HC IPV and often leave LGBTQ IPV untouched. When we remain silent, HGRs use one-size-fits-all approaches that ignore the unique aspects of LGBTQ IPV, or they outright exclude LGBTQ victims. When we remain silent, abusers are emboldened, and LGBTQ IPV victims remain trapped. As one female same-gender IPV victim notes, seeking help becomes nearly impossible when no one has even heard of LGBTQ IPV: "[E]very time I say, 'I was almost killed by a woman,' people just say, 'By a woman? You've got to be kidding me.'"[24] How does a victim ask for help with a crime that is invisible?

If silence is not the answer, then the way forward must be through awareness. This must infuse all aspects of our collective response to LGBTQ IPV—from creating inclusive IPV laws and expanding related LGBTQ human rights protections to making trainings mandatory for HGRs on LGBTQ IPV knowledge and antidiscrimination, tailoring HC IPV–oriented services to address LGBTQ IPV, and generating more-targeted service advertising and educational media to signal that HGRs are welcoming to LGBTQ IPV victims. This does not necessarily mean that there should be an exactly equal number of formal HGR organizations and related funding to address HC IPV and LGBTQ IPV; the disparity in number of victims simply does not warrant that. Still, small changes do need to be made across the board in all formal HGRs so that no victim is left relying on the availability of one trained liaison or access to one LGBTQ-specific HGR with waiting lists. These changes should be substantive (such as by reflecting the realities of LGBTQ IPV in screening, core services, safety planning, and HGR referrals) rather than solely cosmetic (such as by just switching to gender-neutral terminology during intake procedures). There are ample resources to go around to permit existing formal HGRs to make a more concerted effort to help LGBTQ IPV victims, whether by offering certain separate LGBTQ-only services or by integrating LGBTQ IPV information into existing HC IPV-oriented services.

Ultimately, while research tells us that there is much work still to be done, it is important that we recognize that we *can* make it happen. The learning process will be arduous at first, but many HGRs have already successfully made this leap through collaborations with experienced LGBTQ IPV HGRs and LGBTQ community organizations.[25] While policymakers likewise can continue helping expand access to protections under IPV laws and LGBTQ human rights legislation, much has already changed in access to these protections and rights in just the past two decades. In her reflections on the continuing movement to address same-gender IPV—and, we could add, all LGBTQ IPV—scholar Lori Girshick emphasizes that change is hard but by no means impossible: "Those of us willing and able to keep on pushing must do so. It is not impossible to change ways of thinking, ways of behaving, even laws and power structures. History is filled with examples of social change—and the changes we try to make and *will* make around same-sex domestic violence will make history."[26]

Change *is* possible. Moreover, by reflecting on the immense treasure trove of research reviewed in this book, we can find a road map that offers detailed routes to improving future policy, practice, and research. Together, we can help make the invisible visible.

APPENDIX

BOOK METHODOLOGY

To identify journal articles, books, and book chapters on LGBTQ IPV, several databases were exhaustively searched for mention of a synonym for IPV in the abstract (e.g., *relationship violence, couple violence, spousal violence, partner violence, family violence, interpersonal violence, dating violence, domestic violence, physical violence, emotional violence, psychological violence, sexual violence,* etc.—with the word *violence* replaced with alternate terms like *violent, conflict, aggression, abuse, victimization, perpetration, assault, battering,* etc., and with variations in suffixes, such as *sexually, psychologically,* etc.—in addition to other standalone terms like versions of the words *rape, stalking, coercive,* etc.) in conjunction with a term appearing anywhere in the publication that relates to LGBTQ people (e.g., *lesbian, gay, bisexual, trans, transgender, transsexual, queer, sexual minority, GLB, GLBT, GLBTQ, LGB, LGBT, LGBTQ, homosexual, homosexuality, sexual orientation, genderqueer, same sex, same gender, minority stress, minority stressors, non-heterosexual, non-heterosexuality, intersex, sexual identity, non-conforming, WSW, women who have sex with women, MSM, men who have sex with men, MSMW, men who have sex with men and women,* etc.—with care to use alternate suffixes such as plural versions of terms).

The following databases were searched using an integrated search box: Applied Social Sciences Index and Abstracts, ERIC, Ethnic NewsWatch, GenderWatch, International Bibliography of the Social Sciences, Linguistics and Language Behavior Abstracts, PAIS International, Published International Literature on Traumatic Stress, ProQuest Criminal Justice, ProQuest Education Journals, ProQuest Political Science, ProQuest Social Science Journals, ProQuest Sociology, Social Services Abstracts, Sociological Abstracts, and Worldwide Political Science Abstracts. All told, this integrated search screened 2,190 journals and book citations, and a total of 3,704 journal articles and books met the initial search criteria. In addition, the same search terms were screened for in several other databases not available for this integrated search, including EbscoHost, Google Scholar, PubMed, and

PsychInfo. With rare exceptions, master's theses and dissertations were excluded, as were newspaper articles. Most of the journal articles and books found were duplicates of the prior integrated search, but several additional publications were identified. Finally, a regular Google web search for many of the same terms was used to identify LGBTQ IPV reports published online by major LGBTQ organizations and research institutes. All searches were conducted in English, although any article referenced by another selected article in another language was, wherever possible, translated into English using the website language translator function in the Google Chrome web browser.

Once the initial batch of articles and books were found, article and book abstracts were screened for eligibility by conducting a word search for several keywords to determine whether the terms were used because the publication actually offered information about LGBTQ IPV or were being mentioned offhand. There were many reasons a search term might appear in a publication that was not actually about LGBTQ IPV: for example, numerous articles mention in the opening page that IPV happens in all types of relationships regardless of gender, sexual orientation, and so forth, and then the rest of the article would proceed to be entirely about HC IPV; other times a study may have actually included sexual orientation or trans* identity as variables in a survey, but, beyond stating how many respondents reported each identity type, the authors did not discuss any analyses involving those variables; still other times the search terms brought up countless articles not about IPV at all, which often occurred with such terms as "sexual assault" and "coercion" (particularly when the victim–perpetrator relationship was never inquired about by the researcher); and last, the search terms may appear in the references only and nowhere in the main text (such as the term *interpersonal violence* appearing in references from the *Journal of Interpersonal Violence*). Only publications that included either discussion of or data on LGBTQ IPV were utilized for this book.

All told, 609 journal articles, book chapters, books, and reports on LGBTQ IPV are drawn upon for this book, covering nearly all of the published English-language research literature since its inception in 1977 up through early 2016. This forty-year-old research literature is accompanied in this book by information from over a hundred additional publications from outside the LGBTQ IPV literature that provide context for the literature (e.g., research on LGBTQ discrimination, etc.).

As with all research, there are limitations to this book's comprehensiveness. This book is inclusive of all published journal articles (peer-reviewed and non-peer-reviewed), book chapters, and books identified through an extensive keyword search using the various databases previously described, in addition to reports on the subject published by key LGBTQ organizations and research institutes. That said, there are unfortunately gaps in the search that likely resulted in some publications being omitted. For example, with rare exceptions, this book does not include the following: master's theses or dissertations, newspaper articles, information published solely on websites, downloadable website files that are either not in a report format (such as partial reports[1] lacking basic information on sampling or data-collection procedures and as such proving challenging to interpret) or not from known reputable organizations or institutes, any publication that did not get netted by the keyword searches or were not available in the databases searched, any publication that was identified as part of the literature but unobtainable through the state academic library sharing program of the author's state of residence (which happened only rarely), and, importantly, any publications not available in English. The latter exclusion criterion likely helps explain why the vast majority of identified publications on LGBTQ IPV originate from English-language-centric nations such as Australia, Canada, the United Kingdom, and the United States. This suggests that findings and implications discussed in this book may not be fully applicable to nations with a dearth of English-language publications on this subject. It is therefore encouraged that endeavors similar to this book be undertaken in other nations, which can then be translated and reprinted internationally to facilitate further improvements to how the world addresses LGBTQ IPV.

NOTES

PREFACE

1. Gundlach, "Sexual molestation and rape."

INTRODUCTION

1. Dulani, "Revolution Starts at Home."
2. Messinger, "Marking 35 Years."
3. M. J. Brown and Groscup, "Perceptions."
4. Carlson, "Student Judgments"; Sorenson and Thomas, "Views of Intimate Violence"; Younglove, Kerr, and Vitello, "Law Enforcement Officers' Perceptions."
5. Ahmed, Aldén, and Hammarstedt, "Perceptions"; Basow and Thompson, "Service Providers' Reactions"; Poorman, Seelau, and Seelau, "Perceptions of Domestic Abuse"; Russell, Chapleau, and Kraus, "When is it abuse?"; Seelau and Seelau, "Gender-Role Stereotypes"; Seelau, Seelau, and Poorman, "Gender and Role-Based Perceptions"; Wise and Bowman, "Comparison of Beginning Counselors."
6. Walters, "Straighten Up."
7. Jackson, "Same-Sex Domestic Violence."
8. Gates, *How Many People.*
9. Gates, *How Many People.*
10. Statistiska centralbyran, "Befolkningsstatistik."
11. Ball, "Gay men."
12. Harned, "Multivariate analysis of risk markers," 1179–1197; Turell, "Descriptive analysis."

13. Ansara, "Exploring the patterns"; Barrett and St. Pierre, "Intimate partner violence"; Porter and Williams, "Intimate violence among underrepresented"; Walters, Chen, and Breiding, *National Intimate Partner Survey*.

14. Ansara, "Exploring the patterns"; Messinger, "Invisible victims"; K. A. McLaughlin et al., "Disproportionate exposure to early-life"; Porter and Williams, "Intimate violence among underrepresented"; Walters, Chen, and Breiding, *National Intimate Partner Survey*.

15. Messinger, "Invisible victims"; K. A. McLaughlin et al., "Disproportionate exposure to early-life"; Porter and Williams, "Intimate violence among underrepresented"; Walters, Chen, and Breiding, *National Intimate Partner Survey*.

16. Walters, Chen, and Breiding, *National Intimate Partner Survey*.

17. Leonard et al., *Coming Forward;* Pitts et al., *Private Lives*.

18. Mak, Chong, and Kwong, "Prevalence in Hong Kong"; Yu, Xiao, and Liu, "Dating violence among gay."

19. L. A. Eaton et al., "Men who report."

20. Guasp, *Gay and Bisexual Men's;* Henderson, "Prevalence of domestic violence"; Hunt and Fish, "Prescription for change."

21. Finneran et al., "Intimate partner violence."

22. Dank et al., "Dating violence experiences"; Landers and Gilsanz, "Health of lesbian, gay"; Pitts et al., *Private Lives;* Turell, "Descriptive analysis"; Zweig et al., *Technology, Teen Dating Violence.*

23. Turell, "Descriptive analysis."

24. Nemoto, Bödeker, and Iwamoto, "Social support, exposure"; Pitts et al., *Private Lives;* Turell, "Descriptive analysis"; Roch, Ritchie, and Morton, "Out of sight."

25. Nemoto, Bödeker, and Iwamoto, "Social support, exposure"; Pitts et al., *Private Lives;* Turell, "Descriptive analysis"; Roch, Ritchie, and Morton, "Out of sight."

26. Alhusen, Lucea, and Glass, "Perceptions of and Experience"; Barnes, "'I Still'"; Barnes, "'Suffering'"; Donovan and Hester, "'I Hate the Word'"; Donovan and Hester, "Seeking help"; Duke and Davidson, "Same-sex intimate partner violence"; Elliott, "Shattering illusions"; Hassouneh and Glass, "Influence of Gender-Role Stereotyping"; Merlis and Linville, "Exploring a community's response"; E. M. McLaughlin and Rozee, "Knowledge about heterosexual versus."

27. Barnes, "'Suffering,'" 236.

28. Hassouneh and Glass, "Influence of Gender-Role Stereotyping," 317.

29. Merrill and Wolfe, "Battered Gay Men."

30. Jackson, "Same-Sex Domestic Violence"; Walters, "Straighten Up."

31. N. Brown, "Stories from Outside"; N. Brown, "Holding tensions."

32. N. Brown, "Stories from Outside," 377.

33. Wallace, *Family Violence.*

34. Elliott, "Shattering illusions"; Jackson, "Same-Sex Domestic Violence."

35. Sylaska and Walters, "Testing the extent."

36. Poorman, Seelau, and Seelau, "Perceptions of Domestic Abuse"; Seelau and Seelau, "Gender-Role Stereotypes."

37. Sorenson and Thomas, "Views of Intimate Violence."

38. Blasko, Winek, and Bieschke, "Therapists' Prototypical Assessment."

39. Kaplan and Colbs, "Shattered Pride"; Jackson, "Same-Sex Domestic Violence."

40. da Luz, "Legal and Social Comparison."

41. Walters, Chen, and Breiding, *National Intimate Partner Survey*.

42. Ackerman and Field, "Gender Asymmetric Effect"; Blosnich and Bossarte, "Comparisons."

43. National Coalition of Anti-Violence Programs, *Lesbian, Gay, in 2013*.

44. Pitts et al., *Private Lives*.

45. Freedner et al., "Dating violence"; Henderson, "Prevalence of domestic violence"; Pitts et al., *Private Lives;* Walters, Chen, and Breiding, *National Intimate Partner Survey;* Yu, Xiao, and Liu, "Dating violence among gay."

46. Roch, Ritchie, and Morton, "Out of sight."

47. Henderson, "Prevalence of domestic violence"; K. A. McLaughlin et al., "Disproportionate exposure to early-life"; Pitts et al., *Private Lives;* Walters, Chen, and Breiding, *National Intimate Partner Survey*.

48. Pitts et al., *Private Lives;* Roch, Ritchie, and Morton, "Out of sight."

49. Brand and Kidd, "Frequency of physical aggression"; Henderson, "Prevalence of domestic violence"; K. A. McLaughlin et al., "Disproportionate exposure to early-life"; Pitts et al., *Private Lives;* Walters, Chen, and Breiding, *National Intimate Partner Survey*.

50. Jackson, "Same-Sex Domestic Violence."

51. DeKeseredy, "Future directions"; Kimmel, "'Gender Symmetry'"; Straus, "Future research."

52. Harway and O'Neil, *What Causes Men's Violence?*

53. B. Little and Terrance, "Perceptions of domestic violence."

54. Hill et al., "Intimate partner abuse."

55. Hassouneh and Glass, "Influence of Gender-Role Stereotyping," 317.

56. National Coalition of Anti-Violence Programs, *Lesbian, Gay, 2011*.

57. Aulivola, "Outing Domestic Violence," 162–77.

58. Tesch et al., "Same-sex domestic violence."

59. Hamby and Jackson, "Size does matter"; Kay and Jeffries, "Homophobia, heteronormativism"; Santos, "'Between two women.'"

60. Balsam and Szymanski, "Relationship quality"; C. Kelly and Warshafsky, "Partner abuse"; McKenry et al., "Perpetration of gay"; Oringher and Samuelson, "Intimate partner violence."

61. Peplau, Veniegas, and Campbell, "Gay and lesbian relationships."

62. Baker et al., "Lessons from examining."

63. Bimbi, Palmadessa, and Parsons, "Substance use, domestic violence"; Blosnich and Bossarte, "Comparisons"; Farrell and Cerise, "Fair's fair"; Jacobson, Daire, and Abel, "Intimate Partner Violence"; Mena, Rodríguez, and Malavé, "Manifestaciones de la violencia"; Messinger, "Invisible victims"; Pitts et al., *Private Lives;* Turell, "Descriptive analysis"; Walters, Chen, and Breiding, *National Intimate Partner Survey;* Waterman, Dawson, and Bologna, "Sexual coercion."

64. Messinger, "Invisible victims."

65. Renzetti, "Poverty of services."

66. Cheung, Leung, and Tsui, "Asian male domestic violence"; Hines and Douglas, "Reported availability."

67. Babcock, Green, and Robie, "Does batterers' treatment work?"

68. Austin and Dankwort, "Standards for batterer programs."

69. Cannon and Buttell, "Illusion of inclusion"; K. Davis and Glass, "Reframing the Heteronormative Constructions."

70. Austin and Dankwort, "Standards for batterer programs."

71. Babcock et al., "Does batterers' treatment work?"

72. Crenshaw, "Mapping the Margins," 1261.

73. Alhusen, Lucea, and Glass, "Perceptions of and Experience," 8.

74. Blenman, "Hand That Hits," 60–62.

75. Balsam, "Nowhere to Hide."

76. Alhusen, Lucea, and Glass, "Perceptions of and Experience," 8; Duffy, "There's no pride."

77. Sprigg, "Questions and Answers."

78. Baker et al., "Lessons from examining"; Htun and Weldon, "Civic origins"; Jablow, "Victims of abuse."

79. Baker et al., "Lessons from examining"; Jablow, "Victims of abuse."

80. Weldon, *Protest, Policy.*

81. United Nations, "UNiTE to End Violence."

82. World Health Organization, "Prevention of intimate partner."

83. Erbaugh, "Queering approaches"; J.M. Goldberg and White, "Reflections on approaches"; Howe, *Sex, Violence and Crime.*

84. Ristock, "Decentering heterosexuality," 66.

85. Donnelly, Cook, and Wilson, "Provision and Exclusion"; Renzetti, "Poverty of services."

86. Anderson, "Theorizing gender"; Dobash and Dobash, *Women, Violence.*

87. DeKeseredy, "Future directions"; Kimmel, "'Gender Symmetry.'"

88. Archer, "Sex differences in aggression"; Straus, "Dominance and symmetry."

89. DeKeseredy, "Future directions"; Kimmel, "'Gender Symmetry.'"

90. Holtzworth-Munroe, "Female perpetration"; Lupri, "Institutional resistance"; McNeely, Cook, and Torres, "Is domestic violence"; Straus, "Future research."

91. Cook, *Abused Men;* Dutton, "Patriarchy and wife assault"; Dutton, Nicholls, and Spidel, "Female perpetrators"; Hamel, "Toward a gender-inclusive conception."

92. Dutton, Nicholls, and Spidel, "Female perpetrators," 10.

93. Hamel, "Toward a gender-inclusive conception," 40.

94. Bouchard, *Abused Men;* Christensen, "Balancing the Approach"; Easton, "Family Violence"; Feitz, "Demonizing men"; T. Martin, "What about Violence"; Westover, "Include All Forms."

95. Coleman, "Lesbian battering"; Coleman, "Treating the Lesbian Batterer"; Island and Letellier, *Men Who Beat Men.*

96. Worcester, "Women's Use of Force."

97. Dragiewicz and DeKeseredy, "Claims about Women's Use."

98. Chalabi and Burn-Murdoch, "McDonald's 34,492 Restaurants."

99. Yu, Xiao, and Liu, "Dating violence among gay."

100. Cheung, Leung, and Tsui, "Asian male domestic violence."

101. Hines and Douglas, "Reported availability."

102. Colm, "Freedom and Strategy," 178.

103. Cheung, Leung, and Tsui, "Asian male domestic violence"; Renzetti, "Poverty of services"; Hines and Douglas, "Reported availability."

104. Aulivola, "Outing Domestic Violence"; Bornstein et al., "Understanding the experiences."

105. Alhusen, Lucea, and Glass, "Perceptions of and Experience."

106. Ahmed, Aldén, and Hammarstedt, "Perceptions"; Basow and Thompson, "Service Providers' Reactions"; Bernstein and Kostelac, "Lavender and Blue"; Dolan-Soto, "Lesbian, gay, transgender"; Poorman, Seelau, and Seelau, "Perceptions of Domestic Abuse"; Russell, Chapleau, and Kraus, "When is it abuse?"; Seelau and Seelau, "Gender-Role Stereotypes"; Seelau, Seelau, and Poorman, "Gender and Role-Based Perceptions"; Wise and Bowman, "Comparison of Beginning Counselors."

107. Itaborahy and Zhu, *State-Sponsored Homophobia.*

108. Masci, Sciupac, and Lipka, "Gay Marriage around the World."

109. Itaborahy and Zhu, *State-Sponsored Homophobia.*

110. McCarthy, "Nearly 3 in 10."

111. P. Taylor, "Survey of LGBT Americans."

112. Durso and Gates, "Serving Our Youth."

113. Itaborahy and Zhu, *State-Sponsored Homophobia.*

114. Trans Respect versus Transphobia Worldwide, "Legal and Social Mapping."

115. Global Action for Trans Equality, "Gender Identity."

116. Katz-Wise and Hyde, "Victimization Experiences."

117. Grant, Mottet, and Tanis, "Injustice at Every Turn."

118. Itaborahy and Zhu, *State-Sponsored Homophobia.*

119. Pascoe, "'Dude, you're a fag,'" 336.

120. Pascoe, "'Dude, you're a fag,'" 336.

121. Nicolas and Skinner, "'That's so gay.'"

122. Livia and Hall, *Queerly Phrased.*

123. Fisher, "Social desirability bias."

124. Diamond and Wilsnack, "Alcohol abuse among lesbians"; Gundlach, "Sexual molestation and rape."

125. Island and Letellier, *Men Who Beat Men;* Leventhal and Lundy, *Same-Sex Domestic Violence;* Lobel, *Naming the Violence;* McClennen and Gunther, *Professional's Guide to Understanding;* Renzetti, *Violent Betrayal;* Renzetti and Miley, *Violence in Gay, Lesbian.*

126. Kaschak, *Intimate betrayal;* Ristock, *Intimate Violence, LGBTQ Lives.*

127. Girshick, *Woman-to-Woman Sexual Violence.*

128. Ristock, *Intimate Violence, LGBTQ Lives.*

129. Donovan and Hester, *Domestic Violence and Sexuality;* Rowlands, *Domestic Abuse among Gay.*

130. Ristock, *Intimate Violence, LGBTQ Lives.*

131. Merrill, "Understanding domestic violence"; Messinger, "Marking 35 Years"; Nowinski and Bowen, "Partner violence against heterosexual"; Patzel, "Lesbian partner abuse"; Poorman, "Forging community links"; Randle and Graham, "Review of the evidence"; Renzetti, "Violence in lesbian relationships"; Renzetti, "Violence and abuse"; Richards, Noret, and Rivers, "Violence and abuse"; Ricks, Vaughn, and Dziegielewski, "Domestic violence"; Ristock, "Beyond ideologies"; Ristock and Timbang, "Relationship violence";

J. A. Roberts, "Integrative review"; Robson, "Lavender Bruises"; Rohrbaugh, "Domestic violence, same-gender relationships"; Russo, "Lesbian and bisexual battering"; Stiles-Shields and Carroll, "Same-sex domestic violence"; Talicska, "Out of One Closet"; Tully, *Lesbians, Gays, Empowerment Perspective;* Tully, "Domestic violence"; C. M. West, "Leaving a second closet"; Worcester, "Women's Use of Force."

132. T. N. T. Brown and Herman, "Intimate Partner Violence"; Calton, Cattaneo, and Gebhard, "Barriers to help seeking"; Ristock and Timbang, "Relationship violence"; Russell, "Bridging the Gap"; Smollin, "Lesbian, gay, bisexual, transgender"; J. K. Walker, "Investigating trans people's vulnerabilities"; C. M. West, "Partner abuse"; Woodin, Sotskova, and O'Leary, "Intimate partner violence assessment."

2. HOW DO WE KNOW WHAT WE KNOW?

1. Gates, *Sexual Minorities.*
2. Dillman et al., "Response rate."
3. Meyer and Wilson, "Sampling lesbian, gay."
4. Burke and Follingstad, "Violence."
5. Blair, "A probability sample"; Greenwood et al., "Battering victimization"; Relf et al., "Gay identity, interpersonal violence."
6. Greenwood et al., "Battering victimization."
7. Relf et al., "Gay identity, interpersonal violence."
8. Straus, "Measuring intrafamily conflict, violence."
9. Burke and Follingstad, "Violence"; Mason et al., "Psychological aggression"; Murray and Mobley, "Empirical research about same-sex."
10. Adapted from Hoffman, *Old Jews Telling Jokes,* 213; JokeIndexcom, *Driving the Wrong Way.*
11. Burke and Follingstad, "Violence"; Murray and Mobley, "Empirical research about same-sex."
12. Neilson, "Clinical Success, Political Failure?"
13. K. Davis and Glass, "Reframing the Heteronormative Constructions"; Hiebert-Murphy, Ristock, and Brownridge, "Meaning of 'risk'"; M. K. Poon, "Beyond good and evil."
14. McClennen, "Researching gay and lesbian."
15. Peralta and Ross, "Understanding the complexity."
16. Wolfe et al., "Child maltreatment, bullying."
17. Freedner et al., "Dating violence."
18. Barter, "In the name."
19. Straus, "Measuring intrafamily conflict, violence."
20. Straus et al., "Revised conflict tactics scales."
21. Gruber and Fineran, "Comparing the impact."
22. Wolfe et al., "Child maltreatment, bullying."
23. Brand and Kidd, "Frequency of physical aggression."
24. Bernhard, "Physical and sexual violence."
25. American College Health Association, *National College Health Assessment.*
26. Fisher, "Social desirability bias."
27. Sugarman and Hotaling, "Intimate violence, social desirability."

28. Girshick, *Woman-to-Woman Sexual Violence;* Ofreneo and Montiel, "Positioning theory"; Perez-Darby, "Secret joy of accountability."

29. Donovan et al., "Comparing domestic abuse"; Valentine and Pantalone, "Correlates of perceptual."

30. Schwartz, "Methodological issues."

31. Straus, "Measuring intrafamily conflict, violence."

32. Straus et al., "Revised conflict tactics scales."

33. Wolfe et al., "Development and validation."

34. Straus et al., "Revised conflict tactics scales."

35. Wolfe et al., "Development and validation," 291.

36. DeKeseredy and Schwartz, "Measuring the extent."

37. Freedner et al., "Dating violence."

38. Rhodes et al., "Behavioral risk disparities."

39. J. Miller and White, "Gender and adolescent relationship."

40. Olson and Lloyd, "'It depends.'"

41. Hester and Donovan, "Researching domestic violence"; Hester, Donovan, and Fahmy, "Feminist epistemology"; McCarry, Hester, and Donovan, "Researching same sex violence."

42. Coker et al., "Physical health consequences"; Tjaden and Thoennes, *Extent, Nature, and Consequences.*

43. Carvalho et al., "Internalized sexual minority stressors."

44. Gillum and DiFulvio, "Examining dating violence"; Renzetti, "Violence, Preliminary Analysis."

45. Burke and Follingstad, "Violence."

46. Mason et al., "Psychological aggression."

47. Walters, Chen, and Breiding, *National Intimate Partner Survey.*

48. Houston and McKirnan, "Intimate partner abuse."

49. Merrill and Wolfe, "Battered Gay Men."

50. Lie et al., "Lesbians in currently aggressive."

51. Gates, *Sexual Minorities.*

52. Bradford, Ryan, and Rothblum, "National Lesbian Health Care."

53. Andrasik, Valentine, and Pantalone, "'Sometimes You Just Have.'"

54. Henderson, "Prevalence of domestic violence."

55. Renner and Whitney, "Examining symmetry."

56. Bimbi, Palmadessa, and Parsons, "Substance use, domestic violence."

57. S. H. Friedman et al., "Intimate partner violence victimization."

58. Halpern et al., "Prevalence of partner violence."

59. Galvan et al., "Abuse in close relationships."

60. Ramachandran et al., "Intimate partner violence."

61. L. A. Eaton et al., "Men who report."

62. Gillum and DiFulvio, "Examining dating violence."

63. Glass et al., "Female-Perpetrated Femicide."

64. Bartholomew et al., "Patterns of abuse."

65. Follingstad and Edmundson, "Is psychological abuse reciprocal."

66. Kuehnle and Sullivan, "Gay and Lesbian Victimization."

67. American College Health Association, *National College Health Assessment.*

68. Andrasik, Valentine, and Pantalone, "'Sometimes You Just Have.'"

69. Elze, "Against all odds."

70. Burke and Follingstad, "Violence."

71. Renner and Whitney, "Examining symmetry."

72. B. C. Kelly et al. "Intersection of mutual violence."

73. Hellmuth et al., "Reduction"; Landolt and Dutton, "Power and personality."

74. Ellsberg and Heise, *Researching Violence against Women.*

75. Margolies and Leeder, "Violence at the Door."

76. Straus, "Measuring intrafamily conflict, violence."

77. Straus et al., "Revised conflict tactics scales."

78. Follingstad and Rogers, "Validity concerns."

79. Lewis et al., "Minority stress, substance use."

80. Moradi et al., "Counseling psychology research."

81. Finneran and Stephenson, "Intimate partner violence among"; Moradi et al., "Counseling psychology research."

82. Donovan and Hester, *Domestic Violence and Sexuality.*

83. Stephenson and Finneran, "IPV-GBM scale"; Stephenson et al., "Towards the development"; Madera and Toro-Alfonso, "Description of domestic violence."

84. Regan et al., "Measuring Physical Violence."

85. McClennen, Summers, and Daley, "Lesbian partner abuse scale."

86. Matte and Lafontaine, "Validation of a measure."

87. Balsam and Szymanski, "Relationship quality"; N. Brown, "Stories from Outside"; L. A. Eaton et al., "Examining factors"; Freedner et al., "Dating violence"; McClennen, Summers, and Vaughan, "Gay men's domestic violence"; Owen and Burke, "An exploration of prevalence"; Turell, "Descriptive analysis."

88. Baker et al., "Lessons from examining."

89. Alhusen, Lucea, and Glass, "Perceptions of and Experience," 2.

90. Carvalho et al., "Internalized sexual minority stressors"; Freedner et al., "Dating violence."

91. Carvalho et al., "Internalized sexual minority stressors."

92. Walters, Chen, and Breiding, *National Intimate Partner Survey.*

93. Turell et al., "Lesbian, gay, bisexual."

94. Boehmer, "Twenty years"; Head and Milton, "Filling the Silence."

95. Archer, "Sex differences in aggression"; Alexander, "Violence"; Aulivola, "Outing Domestic Violence"; Balsam and Szymanski, "Relationship quality"; Burke and Follingstad, "Violence"; Causby et al., "Fusion and conflict resolution"; Fortunata and Kohn, "Demographic, psychosocial"; Goodman, "Relationship between intimate violence"; Hardesty et al., "Lesbian mothering"; Kulkin et al., "Review of research"; McKenry et al., "Perpetration of gay"; Seelau, Seelau, and Poorman, "Gender and Role-Based Perceptions"; Stevens, Korchmaros, and Miller, "Comparison of victimization"; Waldner-Haugrud, Gratch, and Magruder, "Victimization and perpetration rates"; C. M. West, "Lesbian intimate partner violence."

96. Barrett and St. Pierre, "Intimate partner violence."

97. Barrett and St. Pierre, "Intimate partner violence"; L. A. Eaton et al., "Men who report"; K. A. McLaughlin et al., "Disproportionate exposure to early-life"; Messinger,

"Invisible victims"; C. D. Moore and Waterman, "Predicting self-protection"; National Coalition of Anti-Violence Programs, *Lesbian, Gay, in 2013*; Walters, Chen, and Breiding, *National Intimate Partner Survey.*

98. Landolt and Dutton, "Power and personality."
99. Meyer and Wilson, "Sampling lesbian, gay."
100. Moradi et al., "Counseling psychology research."
101. Peralta and Ross, "Understanding the complexity."
102. Meyer and Wilson, "Sampling lesbian, gay."
103. Meyer and Wilson, "Sampling lesbian, gay."
104. Burke and Follingstad, "Violence."
105. Stevens, Korchmaros, and Miller, "Comparison of victimization."
106. Pitts et al., *Private Lives.*
107. Gates, *How Many People.*
108. Hiebert-Murphy, Ristock, and Brownridge, "Meaning of 'risk'"; Meyer and Wilson, "Sampling lesbian, gay"; Moradi et al., "Counseling psychology research."
109. Walters, Chen, and Breiding, *National Intimate Partner Survey.*
110. Gundlach, "Sexual molestation and rape."
111. Hiebert-Murphy, Ristock, and Brownridge, "Meaning of 'risk.'"
112. Baker et al., "Lessons from examining."
113. Baker et al., "Lessons from examining"; Meyer and Wilson, "Sampling lesbian, gay."
114. Moradi et al., "Counseling psychology research."
115. Moradi et al., "Counseling psychology research."
116. Archer, "Sex differences in aggression"; Alexander, "Violence"; Aulivola, "Outing Domestic Violence"; Balsam and Szymanski, "Relationship quality"; Burke and Follingstad, "Violence"; Causby et al., "Fusion and conflict resolution"; Fortunata and Kohn, "Demographic, psychosocial"; Goodman, "Relationship between intimate violence"; Hardesty et al., "Lesbian mothering"; Kulkin et al., "Review of research"; McKenry et al., "Perpetration of gay"; Ristock, *No More Secrets;* Seelau, Seelau, and Poorman, "Gender and Role-Based Perceptions"; Stevens, Korchmaros, and Miller, "Comparison of victimization"; Waldner-Haugrud, Gratch, and Magruder, "Victimization and perpetration rates."
117. Fortunata and Kohn, "Demographic, psychosocial."
118. McKenry et al., "Perpetration of gay."
119. Bernhard, "Physical and sexual violence."
120. Burke and Follingstad, "Violence."
121. Burke and Follingstad, "Violence."
122. Gillum and DiFulvio, "'There's So Much.'"
123. S. L. Miller, "Expanding the boundaries."
124. Greenwood et al., "Battering victimization"; Meyer, Dietrich, and Schwartz, "Lifetime prevalence"; Meyer and Wilson, "Sampling lesbian, gay."
125. Greenwood et al., "Battering victimization."
126. Bledsoe and Sar, "Intimate partner violence"; Cho and Wilke, "Gender differences"; Cornelius, Shorey, and Beebe, "Self-reported communication variables"; Cunradi, Ames, and Duke, "Relationship of Alcohol Problems"; Douglas and Hines, "Helpseeking experiences"; Felson and Paré, "Reporting of domestic violence"; Graham et al., "Does the relationship"; Han et al., "Childhood sexual abuse"; Hirschel, Hutchison, and Shaw, "Interrelationship

between substance abuse"; B. Martin et al., "Intimate partner violence"; Wright, Norton, and Matusek, "Predicting verbal coercion."

127. Dank et al., "Dating violence experiences."

128. Bogart et al., "Association of partner abuse."

129. Hester and Donovan, "Researching domestic violence"; Lockhart et al., "Letting out the secret"; Renzetti, "Building a second closet."

130. Ansara, "Exploring the patterns"; Barrett and St. Pierre, "Intimate partner violence"; K. A. McLaughlin et al., "Disproportionate exposure to early-life"; Messinger, "Invisible victims"; Porter and Williams, "Intimate violence among underrepresented"; Walters, Chen, and Breiding, *National Intimate Partner Survey.*

131. McClennen, "Domestic violence between same-gender."

132. Greenwood et al., "Battering victimization."

133. Meyer and Wilson, "Sampling lesbian, gay."

134. Meyer and Wilson, "Sampling lesbian, gay."

135. Meyer and Wilson, "Sampling lesbian, gay."

136. Burke and Follingstad, "Violence."

137. Feldman et al., "Intimate partner violence"; Meyer, Schwartz, and Frost, "Social patterning of stress."

138. Carvalho et al., "Internalized sexual minority stressors"; Greenwood et al., "Battering victimization."

139. Anderson, "Theorizing gender."

140. Burke and Follingstad, "Violence."

141. Houston and McKirnan, "Intimate partner abuse."

142. Finneran and Stephenson, "Intimate partner violence among."

143. Burke and Follingstad, "Violence."

144. T. W. Burke, Jordan, and Owen, "A cross-national comparison."

145. Peralta and Ross, "Understanding the complexity."

146. Burke and Follingstad, "Violence"; Meyer and Wilson, "Sampling lesbian, gay."

147. Owen and Burke, "An exploration of prevalence."

148. Gates, *How Many People.*

149. Finneran and Stephenson, "Intimate partner violence among."

150. Tesch and Bekerian, "Hidden in the Margins"; J. K. Walker, "Investigating trans people's vulnerabilities."

151. National Institutes of Health, "Research on LGBTI Populations."

3. WHAT IS LGBTQ INTIMATE PARTNER VIOLENCE (IPV)?

1. Roch, Ritchie, and Morton, "Out of sight," 15.

2. Keuroghlian et al., "Substance use and treatment"; Langenderfer-Magruder et al., "Experiences of Intimate Partner."

3. Sarantakos, "Same-sex couples."

4. Mahony, "Police-reported dating violence"; Ristock, "'And Justice for All?'"; Siemieniuk et al., "Domestic violence screening."

5. DiStefano, "Intimate partner violence."

6. Mimiaga et al., "High prevalence multiple syndemic"; Oldenburg et al., "Transactional Sex among Men."

7. Drijber, Reijnders, and Ceelen, "Male victims."

8. Bogart et al., "Association of partner abuse"; Cameron, "Domestic violence"; N. G. Goldberg and Meyer, "Sexual orientation disparities"; Goodenow et al., "Dimensions of sexual orientation"; Grant, Mottet, and Tanis, "Injustice at Every Turn"; Kalokhe et al., "Intimate partner violence"; Lipsky et al., "Impact of sexual orientation"; Martin-Storey, "Prevalence of dating violence"; Massachusetts Department of Education, *2005 Massachusetts Youth Risk;* Mustanski et al., "Psychosocial health problems"; Pathela and Schillinger, "Sexual behaviors, sexual violence"; Reisner et al., "Sexual orientation disparities"; Rennison, "Intimate partner violence"; A. L. Roberts et al., "Pervasive trauma exposure"; Starks et al., "Syndemic factors"; Starks et al., "Linking Syndemic Stress"; Turell and Cornell-Swanson, "Not all alike"; Valentine et al., "Predictive Syndemic Effect"; Welles et al., "Intimate partner violence"; Zahnd et al., "Nearly four million California."

9. Giorgio, "Speaking silence," 1247.

10. Giorgio, "Speaking silence."

11. Irwin, "(Dis) counted Stories," 207.

12. Dank et al., "Dating violence experiences"; Zweig et al., *Technology, Teen Dating Violence.*

13. Turell, "Descriptive analysis."

14. Hellemans et al., "Intimate partner violence victimization"; Leonard et al., *Coming Forward;* Mak, Chong, and Kwong, "Prevalence in Hong Kong"; Toro-Alfonso, "Domestic Violence."

15. Bartholomew et al., "Patterns of abuse"; Bartholomew et al., "Correlates of partner abuse"; Madera and Toro-Alfonso, "Description of domestic violence"; Siemieniuk et al., "Prevalence, clinical associations"; Toro-Alfonso and Rodríguez-Madera, "Sexual coercion, Puerto Rican"; Turell, "Descriptive analysis"; Walters, Chen, and Breiding, *National Intimate Partner Survey;* Williams et al., "Relation of childhood sexual"; Wu et al., "Association between substance use"; Yu, Xiao, and Liu, "Dating violence among gay."

16. Lie and Gentlewarrier, "Intimate violence in lesbian"; Mena, Rodríguez, and Malavé, "Manifestaciones de la violencia"; Turell, "Descriptive analysis"; Walters, Chen, and Breiding, *National Intimate Partner Survey.*

17. Badenes-Ribera et al., "Intimate partner violence."

18. Ansara, "Exploring the patterns"; Greenwood et al., "Battering victimization."

19. Hester, Donovan, and Fahmy, "Feminist epistemology"; Kubicek, McNeeley, and Collins, "Young Men"; Pruitt et al., "Sexual agreements."

20. A. Davis et al., "Intimate Partner Violence."

21. Edwards and Sylaska, "Perpetration of intimate partner."

22. Pepper and Sand, "Internalized Homophobia."

23. Halpern et al., "Prevalence of partner violence."

24. Dank et al., "Dating violence experiences"; Reuter, Sharp, and Temple, "An exploratory study"; Zweig et al., *Technology, Teen Dating Violence.*

25. Barrett and St. Pierre, "Intimate partner violence."

26. Walters, Chen, and Breiding, *National Intimate Partner Survey.*

27. Barrett and St. Pierre, "Intimate partner violence"; Bimbi, Palmadessa, and Parsons, "Substance use, domestic violence"; Dunkle et al., "Male-on-male."

28. Blosnich and Bossarte, "Comparisons"; Pathé, Mullen, and Purcell, "Same-gender stalking"; National Coalition of Anti-Violence Programs, *Lesbian, Gay, in 2013*; Strand and McEwan, "Same-gender stalking"; Thompson, Dennison, and Stewart, "Are female stalkers"; Tjaden and Thoennes, *Extent, Nature, and Consequences*.

29. Sheridan, North, and Scott, "Experiences of stalking."

30. Stevens, Korchmaros, and Miller, "Comparison of victimization."

31. Barrett and St. Pierre, "Intimate partner violence"; Porter and Williams, "Intimate violence among underrepresented."

32. Kanuha, "Compounding the triple jeopardy"; M. K. Poon, "Inter-racial same-sex abuse"; Ristock, "Responding to lesbian relationship violence"; Waldron, "Lesbians of color."

33. Gilberg et al., *Addressing Domestic Violence*; C. Taylor and Ristock, "We are all."

34. García, "'New Kind'"; Kanuha, "Compounding the triple jeopardy."

35. Todd, "Blue Rinse Blues?"

36. Andrasik, Valentine, and Pantalone, "'Sometimes You Just Have'"; Abdale, "HIV-related violence"; Bartholomew et al., "Correlates of partner abuse"; Letellier, "Twin epidemics"; Lyons, Johnson, and Garofalo, "'What Could Have Been'"; Pantalone et al., "I ain't never"; Pantalone et al., "Investigating partner abuse"; Siemieniuk et al., "Prevalence, clinical associations."

37. Barrett and St. Pierre, "Intimate partner violence"; Bimbi, Palmadessa, and Parsons, "Substance use, domestic violence."

38. Siemieniuk et al., "Prevalence, clinical associations."

39. Bornstein et al., "Understanding the experiences"; Reuter, Sharp, and Temple, "An exploratory study."

40. Bimbi, Palmadessa, and Parsons, "Substance use, domestic violence."

41. Dank et al., "Dating violence experiences"; Zweig et al., *Technology, Teen Dating Violence*; Zweig et al., "Correlates of cyber dating."

42. National Coalition of Anti-Violence Programs, *Lesbian, Gay, in 2013*; Roch, Ritchie, and Morton, "Out of sight"; Scottish Transgender Alliance, "Transgender Experiences in Scotland."

43. Bornstein et al., "Understanding the experiences"; Cook-Daniels, "Intimate Partner Violence."

44. Cook-Daniels, "Intimate Partner Violence"; Roch, Ritchie, and Morton, "Out of sight"; Tesch and Bekerian, "Hidden in the Margins."

45. Cook-Daniels, "Intimate Partner Violence"; Goodmark, "Transgender people," 63; Roch, Ritchie, and Morton, "Out of sight"; Tesch and Bekerian, "Hidden in the Margins."

46. Cook-Daniels, "Intimate Partner Violence"; FORGE, "Trans-specific power"; Goodmark, "Transgender people"; Roch, Ritchie, and Morton, "Out of sight."

47. Cook-Daniels, "Intimate Partner Violence"; Goodmark, "Transgender people"; Roch, Ritchie, and Morton, "Out of sight."

48. Cook-Daniels, "Intimate Partner Violence"; FORGE, "Trans-specific power."

49. Cook-Daniels, "Intimate Partner Violence"; FORGE, "Trans-specific power."

50. Cook-Daniels, "Intimate Partner Violence"; FORGE, "Trans-specific power."

51. Hunt and Fish, "Prescription for change"; National Coalition of Anti-Violence Programs, *Lesbian, Gay, in 2013.*

52. Mak, Chong, and Kwong, "Prevalence in Hong Kong."

53. Freedner et al., "Dating violence"; Mak, Chong, and Kwong, "Prevalence in Hong Kong"; Turell, "Descriptive analysis"; Yu, Xiao, and Liu, "Dating violence among gay."

54. Giorgio, "Speaking silence"; Mak, Chong, and Kwong, "Prevalence in Hong Kong"; Rowlands, *Domestic Abuse among Gay;* Turell, "Descriptive analysis."

55. Leeder, *Treating Abuse in Families.*

56. Farrell and Cerise, "Fair's fair"; Freedner et al., "Dating violence"; Mak, Chong, and Kwong, "Prevalence in Hong Kong"; Turell, "Descriptive analysis"; Yu, Xiao, and Liu, "Dating violence among gay."

57. Rowlands, *Domestic Abuse among Gay.*

58. Mak, Chong, and Kwong, "Prevalence in Hong Kong."

59. Mak, Chong, and Kwong, "Prevalence in Hong Kong"; Rowlands, *Domestic Abuse among Gay.*

60. Donovan and Hester, "'Because she was'"; Walters, "Straighten Up."

61. Pitts et al., *Private Lives.*

62. Turell, "Descriptive analysis."

63. Dank et al., "Dating violence experiences"; Landers and Gilsanz, "Health of lesbian, gay"; Zweig et al., *Technology, Teen Dating Violence.*

64. Pitts et al., *Private Lives.*

65. Follingstad and Rogers, "Validity concerns"; Harned, "Abused women"; Turell, "Descriptive analysis."

66. Ansara, "Exploring the patterns"; Barrett and St. Pierre, "Intimate partner violence"; Porter and Williams, "Intimate violence among underrepresented"; Walters, Chen, and Breiding, *National Intimate Partner Survey.*

67. Barrett and St. Pierre, "Intimate partner violence"; Walters, Chen, and Breiding, *National Intimate Partner Survey.*

68. Farrell and Cerise, "Fair's fair"; Jacobson, Daire, and Abel, "Intimate Partner Violence."

69. De Smet et al., "Unwanted pursuit behavior."

70. Feldman et al., "Intimate partner violence"; Nieves-Rosa, Carballo-Dieguez, and Dolezal, "Domestic abuse and HIV-risk."

71. Williams et al., "Relation of childhood sexual"; Wu et al., "Association between substance use."

72. Tran et al., "Prevalence of substance use."

73. Madera and Toro-Alfonso, "Description of domestic violence"; Toro-Alfonso, "Domestic Violence"; Toro-Alfonso and Rodríguez-Madera, "Sexual coercion, Puerto Rican."

74. Wong et al., "Harassment, discrimination, violence."

75. Leonard et al., *Coming Forward;* Farrell and Cerise, "Fair's fair."

76. Hellemans et al., "Intimate partner violence victimization."

77. Bartholomew et al., "Patterns of abuse."

78. Mak, Chong, and Kwong, "Prevalence in Hong Kong"; Yu, Xiao, and Liu, "Dating violence among gay."

79. Walters, Chen, and Breiding, *National Intimate Partner Survey.*

80. Hester and Donovan, "Researching domestic violence"; Hester, Donovan, and Fahmy, "Feminist epistemology"; McCarry, Hester, and Donovan, "Researching same sex violence."

81. Irwin, "(Dis) counted Stories," 207.

82. Nemoto, Bödeker, and Iwamoto, "Social support, exposure"; Pitts et al., *Private Lives;* Turell, "Descriptive analysis"; Roch, Ritchie, and Morton, "Out of sight."

83. Clements, Katz, and Marx, "Transgender community health project"; Dank et al., "Dating violence experiences"; Zweig et al., *Technology, Teen Dating Violence.*

84. Risser, "Sex, drugs, violence."

85. Keuroghlian et al., "Substance use and treatment."

86. Farrell and Cerise, "Fair's fair"; Hellemans et al., "Intimate partner violence victimization"; Leonard et al., *Coming Forward;* Mak, Chong, and Kwong, "Prevalence in Hong Kong"; Toro-Alfonso, "Domestic Violence."

87. Bartholomew et al., "Patterns of abuse"; Bartholomew et al., "Correlates of partner abuse"; Feldman et al., "Intimate partner violence"; Guasp, *Gay and Bisexual Men's;* Henderson, "Prevalence of domestic violence"; Madera and Toro-Alfonso, "Description of domestic violence"; Messinger, "Invisible victims"; Nieves-Rosa, Carballo-Dieguez, and Dolezal, "Domestic abuse and HIV-risk"; Pitts et al., *Private Lives;* Siemieniuk et al., "Prevalence, clinical associations"; Toro-Alfonso and Rodríguez-Madera, "Sexual coercion, Puerto Rican"; Tulloch et al., "Retrospective reports"; Turell, "Descriptive analysis"; Walters, Chen, and Breiding, *National Intimate Partner Survey;* Williams et al., "Relation of childhood sexual"; Wong et al., "Harassment, discrimination, violence"; Wu et al., "Association between substance use"; Yu, Xiao, and Liu, "Dating violence among gay."

88. Henderson, "Prevalence of domestic violence"; Hunt and Fish, "Prescription for change"; Lie and Gentlewarrier, "Intimate violence in lesbian"; Messinger, "Invisible victims"; Pitts et al., *Private Lives;* Turell, "Descriptive analysis"; Walters, Chen, and Breiding, *National Intimate Partner Survey.*

89. Badenes-Ribera et al., "Intimate partner violence."

90. Blosnich and Bossarte, "Comparisons"; National Coalition of Anti-Violence Programs, *Lesbian, Gay, in 2013;* Stoddard, Dibble, and Fineman, "Sexual and physical abuse."

91. Davis et al., "Intimate Partner Violence."

92. L. A. Eaton et al., "Men who report."

93. Dank et al., "Dating violence experiences"; Finneran et al., "Intimate partner violence"; Finneran and Stephenson, "Intimate partner violence, minority"; Hester and Donovan, "Researching domestic violence"; Kubicek, McNeeley, and Collins, "Young Men"; McCarry, Hester, and Donovan, "Researching same sex violence"; Pruitt et al., "Sexual agreements"; Reuter, Sharp, and Temple, "An exploratory study"; Stephenson, de Voux, and Sullivan, "Intimate partner violence"; Stephenson, Khosropour, and Sullivan, "Reporting of intimate violence"; Zweig et al., *Technology, Teen Dating Violence.*

94. Ansara, "Exploring the patterns"; Bimbi, Palmadessa, and Parsons, "Substance use, domestic violence"; Dunkle et al., "Male-on-male"; Greenwood et al., "Battering victimization"; Tran et al., "Prevalence of substance use."

95. Morris and Balsam, "Lesbian and bisexual women's."

96. Farrell and Cerise, "Fair's fair."

97. Langenderfer-Magruder et al., "Partner Violence Victimization"; K. A. McLaughlin et al., "Disproportionate exposure to early-life."

98. Pepper and Sand, "Internalized Homophobia"; Porter and Williams, "Intimate violence among underrepresented."

99. Edwards et al., "Physical Dating Violence."

100. Edwards and Sylaska, "Perpetration of intimate partner."

101. Freedner et al., "Dating violence."

102. Halpern et al., "Prevalence of partner violence."

103. Dank et al., "Dating violence experiences"; Luo, Stone, and Tharp, "Physical dating violence victimization"; Reuter, Sharp, and Temple, "An exploratory study"; Zweig et al., *Technology, Teen Dating Violence.*

104. Barrett and St. Pierre, "Intimate partner violence."

105. Walters, Chen, and Breiding, *National Intimate Partner Survey.*

106. Messinger, "Invisible victims."

107. Goodmark, "Transgender people."

108. Goodmark, "Transgender people," 63; Roch, Ritchie, and Morton, "Out of sight."

109. Pitts et al., *Private Lives.*

110. Clements, Katz, and Marx, "Transgender community health project."

111. Turell, "Descriptive analysis."

112. Dank et al., "Dating violence experiences"; Zweig et al., *Technology, Teen Dating Violence.*

113. National Coalition of Anti-Violence Programs, *Lesbian, Gay, in 2013.*

114. Pitts et al., *Private Lives*

115. Nemoto, Bödeker, and Iwamoto, "Social support, exposure."

116. Harned, "Abused women"; Harned, "Multivariate analysis."

117. Dank et al., "Dating violence experiences"; L. A. Eaton et al., "Men who report"; Turell, "Descriptive analysis"; Zweig et al., *Technology, Teen Dating Violence.*

118. Ansara, "Exploring the patterns"; Luo, Stone, and Tharp, "Physical dating violence victimization"; Messinger, "Invisible victims"; K. A. McLaughlin et al., "Disproportionate exposure to early-life"; Porter and Williams, "Intimate violence among underrepresented"; Walters, Chen, and Breiding, *National Intimate Partner Survey.*

119. Henderson, "Prevalence of domestic violence."

120. Messinger, "Invisible victims"; Walters, Chen, and Breiding, *National Intimate Partner Survey.*

121. Mena, Rodríguez, and Malavé, "Manifestaciones de la violencia"; Turell, "Descriptive analysis."

122. Farrell and Cerise, "Fair's fair."

123. Messinger, "Invisible victims"; Walters, Chen, and Breiding, *National Intimate Partner Survey.*

124. Messinger, "Invisible victims"; Turell, "Descriptive analysis."

125. Messinger, "Invisible victims."

126. Walters, Chen, and Breiding, *National Intimate Partner Survey.*

127. K. A. McLaughlin et al., "Disproportionate exposure to early-life."

128. K. A. McLaughlin et al., "Disproportionate exposure to early-life"; Walters, Chen, and Breiding, *National Intimate Partner Survey.*

129. L. A. Eaton et al., "Men who report."
130. Feldman et al., "Intimate partner violence"; Nieves-Rosa, Carballo-Dieguez, and Dolezal, "Domestic abuse and HIV-risk."
131. Williams et al., "Relation of childhood sexual"; Wu et al., "Association between substance use."
132. Tran et al., "Prevalence of substance use."
133. Madera and Toro-Alfonso, "Description of domestic violence"; Toro-Alfonso and Rodríguez-Madera, "Sexual coercion, Puerto Rican."
134. Toro-Alfonso, "Domestic Violence."
135. Stephenson, de Voux, and Sullivan, "Intimate partner violence."
136. Finneran et al., "Intimate partner violence."
137. Farrell and Cerise, "Fair's fair"; Leonard et al., *Coming Forward;* Pitts et al., *Private Lives*
138. Hellemans et al., "Intimate partner violence victimization."
139. Siemieniuk et al., "Prevalence, clinical associations."
140. Mak, Chong, and Kwong, "Prevalence in Hong Kong."
141. L. A. Eaton et al., "Men who report."
142. Guasp, *Gay and Bisexual Men's;* Henderson, "Prevalence of domestic violence"; Hunt and Fish, "Prescription for change."
143. Walters, Chen, and Breiding, *National Intimate Partner Survey.*
144. Walters, "Straighten Up," 260
145. Walters, "Straighten Up," 260
146. Bennhold, "Is It Rape?"
147. Bucher and Manasse, "When screams"; Tark and Kleck, "Resisting Rape."
148. Tark and Kleck, "Resisting Rape."
149. Waldner-Haugrud and Gratch, "Sexual coercion in gay/lesbian."
150. Dank et al., "Dating violence experiences"; Zweig et al., *Technology, Teen Dating Violence.*
151. Kalichman and Rompa, "Sexually coerced and noncoerced"; Nieves-Rosa, Carballo-Dieguez, and Dolezal, "Domestic abuse and HIV-risk"; Mak, Chong, and Kwong, "Prevalence in Hong Kong"; Toro-Alfonso, "Domestic Violence"; Toro-Alfonso and Rodríguez-Madera, "Sexual coercion, Puerto Rican."
152. Nemoto, Bödeker, and Iwamoto, "Social support, exposure"; Pitts et al., *Private Lives;* Turell, "Descriptive analysis"; Roch, Ritchie, and Morton, "Out of sight."
153. Risser, "Sex, drugs, violence."
154. Dank et al., "Dating violence experiences"; Zweig et al., *Technology, Teen Dating Violence.*
155. Keuroghlian et al., "Substance use and treatment."
156. Leonard et al., *Coming Forward;* Messinger, "Invisible victims."
157. Farrell and Cerise, "Fair's fair."
158. Bartholomew et al., "Patterns of abuse"; Bartholomew et al., "Correlates of partner abuse"; Feldman et al., "Intimate partner violence"; Guasp, *Gay and Bisexual Men's;* Henderson, "Prevalence of domestic violence"; Krahé et al., "Prevalence of sexual aggression"; Madera and Toro-Alfonso, "Description of domestic violence"; Mak, Chong, and Kwong, "Prevalence in Hong Kong"; Messinger, "Invisible victims"; Nieves-Rosa, Carballo-Dieguez,

and Dolezal, "Domestic abuse and HIV-risk"; Pitts et al., *Private Lives;* Sabidó et al., "Sexual Violence Against Men"; Siemieniuk et al., "Prevalence, clinical associations"; Turell, "Descriptive analysis"; Williams et al., "Relation of childhood sexual"; Wu et al., "Association between substance use"; Yu, Xiao, and Liu, "Dating violence among gay."

159. Brand and Kidd, "Frequency of physical aggression"; Henderson, "Prevalence of domestic violence"; Hunt and Fish, "Prescription for change"; Lie and Gentlewarrier, "Intimate violence in lesbian"; Messinger, "Invisible victims"; Pitts et al., *Private Lives;* Turell, "Descriptive analysis"; Walters, Chen, and Breiding, *National Intimate Partner Survey.*

160. Badenes-Ribera et al., "Intimate partner violence."

161. Blosnich and Bossarte, "Comparisons"; National Coalition of Anti-Violence Programs, *Lesbian, Gay, in 2013.*

162. Sigurvinsdottir and Ullman, "Role of sexual orientation."

163. Hickson et al., "Gay men as victims"; Long et al., "Women's experiences of male-perpetrated"; Stoddard, Dibble, and Fineman, "Sexual and physical abuse."

164. Gonzalez-Guarda, De Santis, and Vasquez, "Sexual orientation and demographic"; Waterman, Dawson, and Bologna, "Sexual coercion."

165. Farrell and Cerise, "Fair's fair."

166. Dank et al., "Dating violence experiences"; Finneran et al., "Intimate partner violence"; Finneran and Stephenson, "Antecedents"; Hester, Donovan, and Fahmy, "Feminist epistemology"; Kubicek, McNeeley, and Collins, "Young Men"; Pruitt et al., "Sexual agreements"; Reuter, Sharp, and Temple, "An exploratory study"; Stephenson, de Voux, and Sullivan, "Intimate partner violence"; Stephenson, Khosropour, and Sullivan, "Reporting of intimate violence"; Zweig et al., *Technology, Teen Dating Violence.*

167. Bimbi, Palmadessa, and Parsons, "Substance use, domestic violence"; Dunkle et al., "Male-on-male"; Greenwood et al., "Battering victimization"; Tran et al., "Prevalence of substance use."

168. Morris and Balsam, "Lesbian and bisexual women's."

169. Langenderfer-Magruder et al., "Partner Violence Victimization"; K. A. McLaughlin et al., "Disproportionate exposure to early-life"; C. D. Moore and Waterman, "Predicting self-protection."

170. Pepper and Sand, "Internalized Homophobia"; Porter and Williams, "Intimate violence among underrepresented."

171. Edwards and Sylaska, "Perpetration of intimate partner."

172. Freedner et al., "Dating violence."

173. Dank et al., "Dating violence experiences"; Reuter, Sharp, and Temple, "An exploratory study"; Zweig et al., *Technology, Teen Dating Violence.*

174. Walters, Chen, and Breiding, *National Intimate Partner Survey.*

175. Messinger, "Invisible victims."

176. Girshick, *Woman-to-woman sexual violence.*

177. Scottish Transgender Alliance, "Transgender Experiences in Scotland."

178. Goodmark, "Transgender people," 63.

179. FORGE, "Trans-specific power"; Goodmark, "Transgender people," 63; Tesch and Bekerian, "Hidden in the Margins."

180. FORGE, "Trans-specific power."

181. N. Brown, "Stories from Outside."

182. Pitts et al., *Private Lives*.

183. Dank et al., "Dating violence experiences"; Turell, "Descriptive analysis"; Zweig et al., *Technology, Teen Dating Violence*.

184. Pitts et al., *Private Lives*.

185. Nemoto, Bödeker, and Iwamoto, "Social support, exposure."

186. Harned, "Abused women"; Harned, "Multivariate analysis"; Turell, "Descriptive analysis."

187. Brand and Kidd, "Frequency of physical aggression"; Dank et al., "Dating violence experiences"; L. A. Eaton et al., "Men who report"; Freedner et al., "Dating violence"; Reuter, Sharp, and Temple, "An exploratory study"; Zweig et al., *Technology, Teen Dating Violence*.

188. Messinger, "Invisible victims"; K. A. McLaughlin et al., "Disproportionate exposure to early-life"; Porter and Williams, "Intimate violence among underrepresented"; Walters, Chen, and Breiding, *National Intimate Partner Survey*.

189. Henderson, "Prevalence of domestic violence"; Mena, Rodríguez, and Malavé, "Manifestaciones de la violencia."

190. Turell, "Descriptive analysis."

191. Farrell and Cerise, "Fair's fair"; Pitts et al., *Private Lives*.

192. Bimbi, Palmadessa, and Parsons, "Substance use, domestic violence"; Blosnich and Bossarte, "Comparisons"; Messinger, "Invisible victims"; Waterman, Dawson, and Bologna, "Sexual coercion."

193. Rothman, Exner, and Baughman, "Prevalence of sexual assault."

194. L. A. Eaton et al., "Men who report."

195. Turell, "Descriptive analysis."

196. K. A. McLaughlin et al., "Disproportionate exposure to early-life."

197. L. A. Eaton et al., "Men who report"; C. D. Moore and Waterman, "Predicting self-protection"; National Coalition of Anti-Violence Programs, *Lesbian, Gay, in 2013*.

198. Messinger, "Invisible victims"; Walters, Chen, and Breiding, *National Intimate Partner Survey*.

199. Feldman et al., "Intimate partner violence"; Nieves-Rosa, Carballo-Dieguez, and Dolezal, "Domestic abuse and HIV-risk."

200. Gonzalez-Guarda, De Santis, and Vasquez, "Sexual orientation and demographic."

201. Williams et al., "Relation of childhood sexual"; Wu et al., "Association between substance use."

202. Tran et al., "Prevalence of substance use."

203. Madera and Toro-Alfonso, "Description of domestic violence"; Toro-Alfonso and Rodríguez-Madera, "Sexual coercion, Puerto Rican."

204. Toro-Alfonso, "Domestic Violence."

205. Stephenson, de Voux, and Sullivan, "Intimate partner violence."

206. Wong et al., "Harassment, discrimination, violence."

207. Finneran et al., "Intimate partner violence."

208. Leonard et al., *Coming forward*; Pitts et al., *Private Lives*.

209. Bartholomew et al., "Patterns of abuse"; Bartholomew et al., "Correlates of partner abuse"; Siemieniuk et al., "Prevalence, clinical associations."

210. Mak, Chong, and Kwong, "Prevalence in Hong Kong"; Yu, Xiao, and Liu, "Dating violence among gay."

211. Krahé et al., "Prevalence of sexual aggression."

212. L. A. Eaton et al., "Men who report."

213. Guasp, *Gay and Bisexual Men's;* Henderson, "Prevalence of domestic violence"; Hunt and Fish, "Prescription for change."

214. Walters, Chen, and Breiding, *National Intimate Partner Survey.*

215. Stoffelen et al., "Homosexuality among people."

216. Glass et al., "Female-Perpetrated Femicide," 613.

217. Glass et al., "Female-Perpetrated Femicide."

218. Farley, "Survey of factors."

219. Glass et al., "Risk for reassault."

220. Guasp, *Gay and Bisexual Men's.*

221. Hunt and Fish, "Prescription for change."

222. Pyra et al., "Sexual minority status."

223. Glass et al., "Female-Perpetrated Femicide."

224. National Coalition of Anti-Violence Programs, *Lesbian, Gay, in 2013*

225. Bunge, *National Trends.*

226. Dauvergne, "Homicide in Canada, 2001."

227. Sinha, "Family violence Canada, 2010."

228. Gannoni and Cussen, "Same-sex intimate partner homicide."

229. Frosch, "Death of Transgender Woman."

230. Frosch, "Murder and hate verdict."

231. Paulozzi et al., "Surveillance for homicide."

232. Glass et al., "Female-Perpetrated Femicide."

233. Bunge, *National Trends;* Dauvergne, "Homicide in Canada, 2001"; Perreault, "Homicide in Canada, 2011."

234. Bunge, *National Trends.*

235. Canadian Centre for Justice Statistics, "Family violence in Canada."

236. Gannoni and Cussen, "Same-sex intimate partner homicide."

237. Mize and Shackelford, "Intimate partner homicide methods"; Paulozzi et al., "Surveillance for homicide"; Puzone et al., "National Trends."

238. Gates, *How Many People.*

239. Mize and Shackelford, "Intimate partner homicide methods."

240. U.S. Census Bureau, "Quick Facts."

241. Gates, *How Many People.*

242. Mize and Shackelford, "Intimate partner homicide methods."

243. Gannoni and Cussen, "Same-sex intimate partner homicide."

244. Mize and Shackelford, "Intimate partner homicide methods"; Paulozzi et al., "Surveillance for homicide"; Puzone et al., "National Trends."

245. Block and Christakos, "Intimate partner homicide."

246. Block and Christakos, "Intimate partner homicide"; Gannoni and Cussen, "Same-sex intimate partner homicide"; Mize and Shackelford, "Intimate partner homicide methods"; Paulozzi et al., "Surveillance for homicide"; Puzone et al., "National Trends."

247. National Coalition of Anti-Violence Programs, *Lesbian, Gay, in 2013.*

248. Gannoni and Cussen, "Same-sex intimate partner homicide"; Glass et al., "Female-Perpetrated Femicide."

249. Gannoni and Cussen, "Same-sex intimate partner homicide."

250. Cooper and Smith, "Homicide trends."

251. Mize and Shackelford, "Intimate partner homicide methods."

252. Paulozzi et al., "Surveillance for homicide."

253. Gannoni and Cussen, "Same-sex intimate partner homicide."

254. Glass et al., "Female-Perpetrated Femicide."

255. Barrett and St. Pierre, "Intimate partner violence"; L. A. Eaton et al., "Men who report"; Luo, Stone, and Tharp, "Physical dating violence victimization"; K. A. McLaughlin et al., "Disproportionate exposure to early-life"; Messinger, "Invisible victims"; C. D. Moore and Waterman, "Predicting self-protection"; National Coalition of Anti-Violence Programs, *Lesbian, Gay, in 2013*; Walters, Chen, and Breiding, *National Intimate Partner Survey*.

256. Balsam, Rothblum, and Beauchaine, "Victimization over life span"; Messinger, "Invisible victims."

257. N. G. Goldberg and Meyer, "Sexual orientation disparities"; Walters, Chen, and Breiding, *National Intimate Partner Survey*.

258. Freedner et al., "Dating violence."

259. Lilith, "Reconsidering the abuse," 208–209.

260. Straus, "Measuring intrafamily conflict, violence"; Straus et al., "Revised conflict tactics scales."

261. Frieze, "Female violence"; M. P. Johnson, "Patriarchal terrorism"; Letellier, "Gay and bisexual male."

262. Aulivola, "Outing Domestic Violence"; Giorgio, "Speaking silence"; Jackson, "Same-Sex Domestic Violence."

263. Bartholomew et al., "Correlates of partner abuse."

264. Stanley et al., "Intimate violence."

265. Wu et al., "Association between substance use."

266. Bartholomew et al., "Correlates of partner abuse"; Kubicek, McNeeley, and Collins, "Young Men"; Lewis et al., "Emotional distress, alcohol use."

267. B. C. Kelly et al. "Intersection of mutual violence."

268. Renner and Whitney, "Examining symmetry."

269. Bartholomew et al., "Correlates of partner abuse"; Carvalho et al., "Internalized sexual minority stressors"; Lie and Gentlewarrier, "Intimate violence in lesbian"; Lie et al., "Lesbians in currently aggressive"; Renzetti, *Violent Betrayal*; Wu et al., "Association between substance use."

270. Carvalho et al., "Internalized sexual minority stressors"; Lie and Gentlewarrier, "Intimate violence in lesbian"; Renzetti, *Violent Betrayal*.

271. Lie et al., "Lesbians in currently aggressive."

272. Follingstad and Edmundson, "Is psychological abuse reciprocal"; Landolt and Dutton, "Power and personality."

273. Lie et al., "Lesbians in currently aggressive."

274. Marrujo and Kreger, "Definition of roles."

275. Donovan, Barnes, and Nixon, "Coral Project."

276. Giorgio, "Speaking silence."

277. Margolies and Leeder, "Violence at the Door."

278. Frankland and Brown, "Coercive control"; Hardesty et al., "Lesbian mothering"; Stanley et al., "Intimate violence."

279. Michael J. Brown and Groscup, "Perceptions"; Elliott, "Shattering illusions"; A. J. Miller, Bobner, and Zarski, "Sexual identity development"; M. K. Poon, "Beyond good and evil"; Ristock, "Responding to lesbian relationship violence."

280. Elliott, "Shattering illusions."

281. A. J. Miller, Bobner, and Zarski, "Sexual identity development."

282. Michael J. Brown and Groscup, "Perceptions."

283. Ristock, "Responding to lesbian relationship violence."

284. Dolan-Soto, "Lesbian, gay, transgender."

285. National Coalition of Anti-Violence Programs, *Lesbian, Gay, in 2013.*

286. C. S. Poon and Saewyc, "Out yonder."

287. Henderson, "Prevalence of domestic violence."

288. Farrell and Cerise, "Fair's fair."

289. Shelton et al., "Prevalence of partner violence."

290. Merrill and Wolfe, "Battered Gay Men."

291. Glass et al., "Risk for reassault"; McClennen, Summers, and Vaughan, "Gay men's domestic violence"; Renzetti, "Violence, Preliminary Analysis"; Renzetti, *Violent Betrayal.*

292. Cruz, "'Why Doesn't He'"; J. J. Johnson, "Same-sex domestic violence"; Leeder, *Treating Abuse in Families;* McClennen, Summers, and Vaughan, "Gay men's domestic violence"; Merrill and Wolfe, "Battered Gay Men"; Ristock, "Responding to lesbian relationship violence."

293. L. E. Walker, *Battered Woman.*

294. Kaschak, *Intimate Betrayal.*

295. Guasp, *Gay and Bisexual Men's.*

296. Hunt and Fish, "Prescription for change."

297. De Smet et al., "Unwanted pursuit behavior."

298. Henderson, "Prevalence of domestic violence."

299. Walters, Chen, and Breiding, *National Intimate Partner Survey.*

300. Blenman, "Hand That Hits," 60.

301. Pitts et al., *Private Lives.*

302. Freedner et al., "Dating violence"; Henderson, "Prevalence of domestic violence"; Pitts et al., *Private Lives;* Yu, Xiao, and Liu, "Dating violence among gay."

303. Freedner et al., "Dating violence"; Henderson, "Prevalence of domestic violence"; Pitts et al., *Private Lives;* Walters, Chen, and Breiding, *National Intimate Partner Survey.*

304. Pitts et al., *Private Lives;* Roch, Ritchie, and Morton, "Out of sight."

305. Henderson, "Prevalence of domestic violence"; K. A. McLaughlin et al., "Disproportionate exposure to early-life"; Pitts et al., *Private Lives.*

306. Brand and Kidd, "Frequency of physical aggression"; Henderson, "Prevalence of domestic violence"; K. A. McLaughlin et al., "Disproportionate exposure to early-life"; Pitts et al., *Private Lives;* Walters, Chen, and Breiding, *National Intimate Partner Survey.*

307. Descamps et al., "Mental health impact"; Pantalone et al., "Investigating partner abuse"; Dyer et al., "Application of syndemic theory."

308. Mustanski et al., "Syndemic of psychosocial health."

309. Descamps et al., "Mental health impact"; Gillum and DiFulvio, "Examining dating violence"; Leung, Cheung, and Luu, "Hardships and interpersonal relationships"; Pantalone et al., "Investigating partner abuse"; Pantalone, Hessler, and Simoni, "Mental health pathways"; Stall et al., "Association of co-occurring psychosocial"; Tulloch et al., "Retrospective reports."

310. Pantalone, Hessler, and Simoni, "Mental health pathways."

311. Roch, Ritchie, and Morton, "Out of sight."

312. Henderson, "Prevalence of domestic violence"; K. A. McLaughlin et al., "Disproportionate exposure to early-life"; Pitts et al., *Private Lives.*

313. Walters, Chen, and Breiding, *National Intimate Partner Survey.*

314. Blosnich and Bossarte, "Drivers of disparity."

315. Mustanski et al., "Syndemic of psychosocial health"; Pantalone et al., "Investigating partner abuse"; Pantalone, Hessler, and Simoni, "Mental health pathways."

316. Monique J. Brown, Serovich, and Kimberly, "Depressive symptoms"; Glass et al., "Risk for reassault"; Fortunata and Kohn, "Demographic, psychosocial"; Dyer et al., "Application of syndemic theory"; Keuroghlian et al., "Substance use and treatment"; Reisner et al., "Sexual orientation disparities"; Tulloch et al., "Retrospective reports"; Valentine et al., "Predictive Syndemic Effect"; Wu et al., "Association between substance use."

317. Bimbi, Palmadessa, and Parsons, "Substance use, domestic violence"; Davis et al., "Intimate Partner Violence"; Descamps et al., "Mental health impact"; Finneran et al., "Intimate partner violence"; Parsons, Grov, and Golub, "Sexual compulsivity, co-occurring"; Pyra et al., "Sexual minority status"; Tran et al., "Prevalence of substance use."

318. Siemieniuk et al., "Prevalence, clinical associations"; Yu, Xiao, and Liu, "Dating violence among gay."

319. Descamps et al., "Mental health impact"; Langenderfer-Magruder et al., "Partner Violence Victimization"; Lewis et al., "Emotional distress, alcohol use"; Mustanski et al., "Syndemic of psychosocial health"; Schilit, Lie, and Montagne, "Substance use as correlate"; Wu et al., "Association between substance use."

320. Bimbi, Palmadessa, and Parsons, "Substance use, domestic violence"; Klitzman et al., "MDMA ('ecstasy') use"; Koeppel and Bouffard, "Sexual orientation"; Mustanski et al., "Syndemic of psychosocial health"; Siemieniuk et al., "Prevalence, clinical associations"; Strasser et al., "Feasibility study, Atlanta, Georgia"; Wong et al., "Harassment, discrimination, violence"; Wu et al., "Association between substance use."

321. Pyra et al., "Sexual minority status"; Tran et al., "Prevalence of substance use"; Wu et al., "Association between substance use."

322. Walters, Chen, and Breiding, *National Intimate Partner Survey.*

323. Roch, Ritchie, and Morton, "Out of sight."

324. Koblin et al., "Violence and HIV-related risk"; Langenderfer-Magruder et al., "Partner Violence Victimization."

325. Williams et al., "Relation of childhood sexual."

326. Dunkle et al., "Male-on-male"; Feldman et al., "Intimate partner violence"; Feldman et al., "Role of situational factors"; Finneran and Stephenson, "Intimate partner violence, minority"; Houston and McKirnan, "Intimate partner abuse"; Hipwell et al., "Examining links"; Mustanski et al., "Psychosocial health problems"; Mustanski et al., "Syndemic of psychosocial health"; Siemieniuk et al., "Prevalence, clinical associations"; Stephenson, de Voux, and Sullivan, "Intimate partner violence."

327. Davis et al., "Intimate Partner Violence"; Dunkle et al., "Male-on-male"; Oldenburg et al., "Transactional Sex Among Men"; Pyra et al., "Sexual minority status."

328. Parsons et al., "Syndemic production."

329. Dyer et al., "Application of syndemic theory"; Finneran and Stephenson, "Intimate partner violence, minority."

330. Bartholomew et al., "Correlates of partner abuse"; Davis et al., "Intimate Partner Violence"; Feldman et al., "Intimate partner violence"; Greenwood et al., "Battering victimization"; Li et al., "Association of intimate partner"; Mustanski et al., "Psychosocial health problems"; Stall et al., "Association of co-occurring psychosocial."

331. Siemieniuk et al., "Prevalence, clinical associations."

332. Ansara, "Exploring the patterns"; Barrett and St. Pierre, "Intimate partner violence"; Porter and Williams, "Intimate violence among underrepresented"; Walters, Chen, and Breiding, *National Intimate Partner Survey.*

333. Ansara, "Exploring the patterns"; Messinger, "Invisible victims"; K. A. McLaughlin et al., "Disproportionate exposure to early-life"; Porter and Williams, "Intimate violence among underrepresented"; Walters, Chen, and Breiding, *National Intimate Partner Survey.*

334. Brand and Kidd, "Frequency of physical aggression"; Dank et al., "Dating violence experiences"; L. A. Eaton et al., "Men who report"; Freedner et al., "Dating violence"; Reuter, Sharp, and Temple, "An exploratory study"; Zweig et al., *Technology, Teen Dating Violence.*

335. National Coalition of Anti-Violence Programs, *Lesbian, Gay, in 2013*; Nemoto, Bödeker, and Iwamoto, "Social support, exposure"; Pitts et al., *Private Lives;* Roch, Ritchie, and Morton, "Out of sight"; Scottish Transgender Alliance, "Transgender Experiences in Scotland"; Turell, "Descriptive analysis."

336. Frieze, "Female violence"; M. P. Johnson, "Patriarchal terrorism"; Letellier, "Gay and bisexual male."

337. Aulivola, "Outing Domestic Violence"; Giorgio, "Speaking silence"; Jackson, "Same-Sex Domestic Violence."

338. Stanley et al., "Intimate violence."

339. Lie et al., "Lesbians in currently aggressive."

340. Michael J. Brown and Groscup, "Perceptions"; Elliott, "Shattering illusions"; A. J. Miller, Bobner, and Zarski, "Sexual identity development"; Ristock, "Responding to lesbian relationship violence."

341. Barrett and St. Pierre, "Intimate partner violence"; Walters, Chen, and Breiding, *National Intimate Partner Survey.*

342. K. A. McLaughlin et al., "Disproportionate exposure to early-life"; Messinger, "Invisible victims"; Walters, Chen, and Breiding, *National Intimate Partner Survey.*

343. L. A. Eaton et al., "Men who report"; C. D. Moore and Waterman, "Predicting self-protection"; National Coalition of Anti-Violence Programs, *Lesbian, Gay, in 2013.*

4. WHY DOES LGBTQ IPV HAPPEN?

1. Smith, "Women Who Abuse," 136–138.

2. Smith, "Women Who Abuse."

3. McAdams, "Psychology of life stories."

4. Bograd, "Strengthening domestic violence theories," 279–280.

5. Bograd, "Strengthening domestic violence theories."

6. Dutton, "Patriarchy and wife assault," 175.

7. Coleman, "Treating the Lesbian Batterer"; Collins, "Same-Sex Domestic Violence"; Letellier, "Gay and bisexual male."

8. Schilit et al., "Intergenerational transmission of violence."

9. Schilit et al., "Intergenerational transmission of violence."

10. Farley, "Survey of factors."

11. Craft and Serovich, "Family-of-origin factors."

12. Fortunata and Kohn, "Demographic, psychosocial"; Lie et al., "Lesbians in currently aggressive"; Schilit et al., "Intergenerational transmission of violence."

13. Milletich et al., "Predictors of women's same-sex."

14. Farley, "Survey of factors."

15. Craft and Serovich, "Family-of-origin factors."

16. Lie et al., "Lesbians in currently aggressive"; Schilit et al., "Intergenerational transmission of violence."

17. Bartholomew et al., "Correlates of partner abuse"; Milletich et al., "Predictors of women's same-sex"; Reuter, Sharp, and Temple, "An exploratory study."

18. McDonald, "Social context."

19. Bartholomew et al., "Correlates of partner abuse."

20. Craft and Serovich, "Family-of-origin factors."

21. Schilit et al., "Intergenerational transmission of violence."

22. Schilit et al., "Intergenerational transmission of violence."

23. Bartholomew et al., "Correlates of partner abuse"; Craft and Serovich, "Family-of-origin factors"; M. S. Friedman et al., "Gay-related development"; Herrick et al., "Adversity and syndemic production"; Kalichman et al., "Unwanted sexual experiences"; Kalichman et al., "Trauma symptoms, sexual behaviors"; Koblin et al., "Violence and HIV-related risk"; Pantalone et al., "Traumatic revictimization of men"; Parsons, Grov, and Golub, "Sexual compulsivity, co-occurring"; Paul et al., "Understanding childhood sexual abuse"; Phillips et al. "Childhood sexual abuse"; Relf et al., "Gay identity, interpersonal violence"; Stall et al., "Association of co-occurring psychosocial"; Toro-Alfonso and Rodríguez-Madera, "Sexual coercion, Puerto Rican"; Williams et al., "Relation of childhood sexual."

24. Lie et al., "Lesbians in currently aggressive"; Schilit et al., "Intergenerational transmission of violence"; Valentine et al., "Predictive Syndemic Effect."

25. Bartholomew et al., "Correlates of partner abuse"; Craft and Serovich, "Family-of-origin factors"; Herrick et al., "Adversity and syndemic production"; Paul et al., "Understanding childhood sexual abuse."

26. Lie et al., "Lesbians in currently aggressive"; Schilit et al., "Intergenerational transmission of violence."

27. Reuter, Sharp, and Temple, "An exploratory study."

28. McDonald, "Social context."

29. Bartholomew et al., "Correlates of partner abuse."

30. Craft and Serovich, "Family-of-origin factors."

31. Peplau and Fingerhut, "Close relationships of lesbians."

32. Renzetti, "Violence, Preliminary Analysis"; Scherzer, "Domestic violence, lesbian relationships."

33. Nickel, "Children witnessing abuse."

34. Jones and Raghavan, "Sexual orientation, social support."

35. Lie et al., "Lesbians in currently aggressive."

36. Herrick et al., "Adversity and syndemic production."

37. Bornstein et al., "Understanding the experiences"; Ristock, "Cultural politics of abuse."

38. Cusack and Waranius, "Nonconsensual insemination."

39. Bartholomew et al., "Correlates of partner abuse"; Finneran et al., "Intimate partner violence."

40. Barrett and St. Pierre, "Intimate partner violence"; Greenwood et al., "Battering victimization"; Messinger, "Invisible victims"; Stall et al., "Association of co-occurring psychosocial."

41. Turell, "Descriptive analysis."

42. Gillum and DiFulvio, "Examining dating violence."

43. Finneran et al., "Intimate partner violence"; Koblin et al., "Violence and HIV-related risk."

44. Landolt and Dutton, "Power and personality."

45. L. A. Eaton et al., "Examining factors."

46. Messinger, "Marking 35 Years."

47. McKenry et al., "Perpetration of gay."

48. Choudhury, "Violence that dares not"; Holmes, "Destabilizing homonormativity."

49. Choudhury, "Violence that dares not."

50. Harms, "Domestic violence."

51. Finneran and Stephenson, "Antecedents."

52. DiStefano, "Intimate partner violence."

53. Todd, "Blue Rinse Blues?"

54. Donovan and Hester, "'I Hate the Word'"; Donovan and Hester, *Domestic Violence and Sexuality;* Kanuha, "'Relationships So Loving'"; McDonald, "Social context"; Ristock, "Responding lesbian relationship violence"; Tran et al., "Prevalence of substance use."

55. Ristock, *No More Secrets,* 58.

56. Cruz, "'Why Doesn't He'"; McDonald, "Social context."

57. McKenry et al., "Perpetration of gay"; Perez-Darby, "Secret joy of accountability."

58. Finneran and Stephenson, "Antecedents"; Lockhart et al., "Letting out the secret"; Santaya and Walters, "Intimate partner violence."

59. Turell, "Descriptive analysis."

60. Bartholomew et al., "Correlates of partner abuse."

61. Stall et al., "Association of co-occurring psychosocial."

62. Bartholomew et al., "Correlates of partner abuse."

63. Greenwood et al., "Battering victimization."

64. Barrett and St. Pierre, "Intimate partner violence"; Bartholomew et al., "Correlates of partner abuse"; Greenwood et al., "Battering victimization"; Messinger, "Invisible victims."

65. Balsam and Szymanski, "Relationship quality"; Stall et al., "Association of co-occurring psychosocial."

66. Balsam and Szymanski, "Relationship quality"; Bartholomew et al., "Correlates of partner abuse."

67. Harms, "Domestic violence."

68. Finneran and Stephenson, "Antecedents."

69. Kanuha, "Compounding the triple jeopardy"; M. K. Poon, "Inter-racial same-sex abuse"; Waldron, "Lesbians of color."

70. Harms, "Domestic violence"; Stephenson, Sato, and Finneran, "Dyadic, partner."

71. Finneran et al., "Intimate partner violence"; Strasser et al., "Feasibility study, Atlanta, Georgia."

72. Balsam and Szymanski, "Relationship quality."

73. Finneran et al., "Intimate partner violence."

74. Finneran et al., "Intimate partner violence."

75. Balsam and Szymanski, "Relationship quality"; Strasser et al., "Feasibility study, Atlanta, Georgia."

76. Messinger, "Invisible victims."

77. Turell, "Descriptive analysis."

78. Siemieniuk et al., "Prevalence, clinical associations."

79. Turell, "Descriptive analysis."

80. Finneran et al., "Intimate partner violence."

81. Greenwood et al., "Battering victimization"; Stall et al., "Association of co-occurring psychosocial."

82. Messinger, "Invisible victims."

83. García, "'New Kind.'"

84. Kanuha, "'Relationships So Loving.'"

85. National Coalition of Anti-Violence Programs, *Lesbian, Gay, in 2013*.

86. Barrett and St. Pierre, "Intimate partner violence."

87. Porter and Williams, "Intimate violence among underrepresented."

88. National Coalition of Anti-Violence Programs, *Lesbian, Gay, in 2013*.

89. Centers for Disease Control, "Rates of diagnoses"; Purcell et al., "Estimating the Population Size."

90. Dyer et al., "Application of syndemic theory"; Finneran and Stephenson, "Intimate partner violence, minority."

91. Bartholomew et al., "Correlates of partner abuse"; Davis et al., "Intimate Partner Violence"; Feldman et al., "Intimate partner violence"; Greenwood et al., "Battering victimization"; Li et al., "Association of intimate partner"; Mustanski et al., "Psychosocial health problems"; Stall et al., "Association of co-occurring psychosocial."

92. Houston and McKirnan, "Intimate partner abuse."

93. Brennan et al., "Syndemic theory and HIV-related risk."

94. Finneran et al., "Intimate partner violence."

95. Bartholomew et al., "Correlates of partner abuse."

96. Finneran et al., "Intimate partner violence."

97. Abdale, "HIV-related violence"; Andrasik, Valentine, and Pantalone, "'Sometimes You Just Have'"; Bartholomew et al., "Correlates of partner abuse"; Letellier, "Twin epidemics"; Lyons, Johnson, and Garofalo, "'What Could Have Been'"; Pantalone et al., "Investigating partner abuse"; Siemieniuk et al., "Prevalence, clinical associations."

98. Finneran and Stephenson, "Antecedents."

99. National Coalition of Anti-Violence Programs, *Lesbian, Gay, in 2013*.

100. Krestan and Bepko, "Problem of fusion"; D. H. Miller et al., "Domestic violence in lesbian"; Peplau, Veniegas, and Campbell, "Gay and lesbian relationships."

101. Causby et al., "Fusion and conflict resolution"; McClennen, Summers, and Vaughan, "Gay men's domestic violence"; D. H. Miller et al., "Domestic violence in lesbian"; Milletich et al., "Predictors of women's same-sex."

102. Pruitt et al., "Sexual agreements."

103. McClennen, Summers, and Vaughan, "Gay men's domestic violence."

104. Renzetti, "Violence, Preliminary Analysis."

105. McClennen, Summers, and Vaughan, "Gay men's domestic violence."

106. Kanuha, "'Relationships So Loving,'" 1184.

107. McKenry et al., "Perpetration of gay."

108. Bartholomew et al., "Correlates of partner abuse"; Craft et al., "Stress, attachment style"; McClennen, Summers, and Vaughan, "Gay men's domestic violence."

109. Finneran and Stephenson, "Antecedents"; McClennen, Summers, and Vaughan, "Gay men's domestic violence."

110. Glass et al., "Risk for reassault."

111. Finneran and Stephenson, "Antecedents."

112. McClennen, Summers, and Vaughan, "Gay men's domestic violence"; Renzetti, Violent Betrayal.

113. Bartholomew et al., "Correlates of partner abuse."

114. Cruz, "'Why Doesn't He'"; McDonald, "Social context."

115. Bartholomew et al., "Correlates of partner abuse"; Greenwood et al., "Battering victimization"; Li et al., "Association of intimate partner"; Mustanski et al., "Psychosocial health problems"; Stall et al., "Association of co-occurring psychosocial."

116. Hochstetler, Copes, and Williams, "'That's Not'"; Sykes and Matza, "Techniques of neutralization."

117. Perez-Darby, "Secret joy of accountability."

118. Ofreneo and Montiel, "Positioning theory."

119. Girshick, Woman-to-Woman Sexual Violence.

120. Finneran et al., "Intimate partner violence."

121. Bartholomew et al., "Correlates of partner abuse"; Farley, "Survey of factors"; B. C. Kelly et al. "Intersection of mutual violence"; Kelley, Lewis, and Mason, "Discrepant Alcohol Use"; Kelley et al., "Predictors of Perpetration"; Lewis et al., "Emotional distress, alcohol use"; Reuter, Sharp, and Temple, "An exploratory study"; Wu et al., "Association between substance use."

122. Bartholomew et al., "Correlates of partner abuse"; B. C. Kelly et al. "Intersection of mutual violence"; Strasser et al., "Feasibility study, Atlanta, Georgia"; Wu et al., "Association between substance use."

123. Schilit, Lie, and Montagne, "Substance use as correlate"; Toro-Alfonso, "Domestic Violence."

124. Hellmuth et al., "Reduction."

125. Kelley, Lewis, and Mason, "Discrepant Alcohol Use."

126. B. C. Kelly et al. "Intersection of mutual violence."

127. Finneran and Stephenson, "Antecedents."

128. B. C. Kelly et al. "Intersection of mutual violence."

129. Andrasik, Valentine, and Pantalone, "'Sometimes You Just Have,'" 297; Smith, "Women Who Abuse."

130. Andrasik, Valentine, and Pantalone, "'Sometimes You Just Have,'" 297.

131. Andrasik, Valentine, and Pantalone, "'Sometimes You Just Have'"; Cruz and Peralta, "Family violence."

132. Andrasik, Valentine, and Pantalone, "Sometimes You Just Have,'" 297.

133. Coleman, "Lesbian battering"; Coleman, "Treating the Lesbian Batterer"; Letellier, "Gay and bisexual male."

134. Farley, "Survey of factors."

135. Fortunata and Kohn, "Demographic, psychosocial."

136. Fortunata and Kohn, "Demographic, psychosocial."

137. Gillum and DiFulvio, "Examining dating violence."

138. Farley, "Survey of factors."

139. Fortunata and Kohn, "Demographic, psychosocial."

140. Gillum and DiFulvio, "Examining dating violence."

141. McClennen, "Prevailing theories."

142. Archer, "Sex differences in aggression"; Straus, "Dominance and symmetry."

143. Hamberger, "Toward a gender-sensitive analysis"; Straus, "Controversy over domestic violence."

144. Babcock, Miller, and Siard, "Toward a typology"; Barnett, Lee, and Thelen, "Gender differences"; DeKeseredy et al., "Meanings and motives"; Stuart et al., "Reasons for intimate partner"; Hamberger, "Female offenders"; Swan and Snow, "Behavioral and psychological differences"; Weston, Marshall, and Coker, "Women's motives."

145. Bailey, "Treatment of domestic violence"; Bouchard, "*Abused men*"; Christensen, "Balancing the Approach"; Coleman, "Lesbian battering"; Coleman, "Treating the Lesbian Batterer"; Collins, "Same-Sex Domestic Violence"; Cook, *Abused Men*; Vidas, "Childhood sexual abuse"; Dutton, "Patriarchy and wife assault"; Dutton, Nicholls, and Spidel, "Female perpetrators"; Easton, "Family Violence"; Frieze, "Female violence"; George, "Riding the donkey backwards"; Gillis and Diamond, "Same-sex partner abuse"; Gillis and Diamond, "Dynamics of partner abuse"; Hamberger, "Domestic partner abuse"; Hamel, "Toward a gender-inclusive conception"; Koller, "'Ecological fallacy'"; Letellier, "Gay and bisexual male"; Malinen, "Thinking Woman-to-Woman Rape"; T. Martin, "What about Violence"; Merrill, "Ruling the exceptions"; Migliaccio, "Abused husbands"; Schneider, "Particularity and generality"; Westover, "Include All Forms."

146. Renzetti, "On dancing," 196.

147. Hamel, "Toward a gender-inclusive conception," 36.

148. Letellier, "Gay and bisexual male domestic violence victimization," 95.

149. Koller, "'Ecological fallacy,'" 159.

150. Collins, "Same-Sex Domestic Violence."

151. Feitz, "Demonizing men," 52.

152. Feitz, "Demonizing men," 52.

153. Hamberger, "Female offenders"; Hamberger, "Toward a gender-sensitive analysis"; Hamberger and Guse, "Men's and women's use."

154. Barnett, Lee, and Thelen, "Gender differences"; Cascardi and Vivian, "Context for specific episodes"; Hamberger, Lohr, and Bonge, "Intended function"; Makepeace, "Gender differences in courtship."

155. DeKeseredy, "Future directions"; Kimmel, "'Gender Symmetry'"; Walters, Chen, and Breiding, *National Intimate Partner Survey*.

156. DeKeseredy, "Future directions"; Kimmel, "'Gender Symmetry.'"

157. FBI, *Crime in United States*; Lauritsen, Heimer, and Lynch, "Trends"; Walmsley, "World female imprisonment list."

158. Anderson, "Theorizing gender"; Dobash and Dobash, *Women, violence*; Harway and O'Neil, *What Causes Men's Violence?*; Kurz, "Physical assaults by husbands"; Lloyd, "Darkside of courtship"; T. M. Moore and Stuart, "Review of the Literature."

159. Harway and O'Neil, *What Causes Men's Violence?*; T. M. Moore and Stuart, "Review of the Literature."

160. Graham-Kevan and Archer, "Control tactics."

161. Macmillan and Gartner, "When she brings home."

162. Anderson and Umberson, "Gendering Violence"; J. Miller and White, "Gender and adolescent relationship"; Sears et al., "'If it hurts you.'"

163. Bograd, "Strengthening domestic violence theories"; Burk, "Think Re-think"; Carlson, "Questioning the party line"; Craft and Serovich, "Family-of-origin factors."

164. Cannon and Buttell, "Illusion of inclusion"; M. Eaton, "Abuse by Any Other"; Lilith, "Reconsidering the abuse"; Merrill, "Ruling the exceptions."

165. Dutton, "Patriarchy and wife assault."

166. Coleman, "Treating the Lesbian Batterer"; Collins, "Same-Sex Domestic Violence"; Letellier, "Gay and bisexual male."

167. Anderson, "Theorizing gender"; Baker et al., "Lessons from examining"; Cannon, Lauve-Moon, and Buttell, "Re-Theorizing Intimate Partner Violence"; M. Eaton, "Abuse by Any Other"; L. Kelly, "When does the speaking."

168. Carlson, "Questioning the party line"; Cruz, "Gay male domestic violence"; D. Martin, *Battered Wives*; Morrison, "Queering Domestic Violence."

169. Butler, *Gender Trouble*; Halberstam, *Female Masculinity*; C. West and Zimmerman, "Doing gender."

170. Connell, *Gender and Power*; David and Brannon, *Forty-Nine Percent Majority*

171. B. Little and Terrance, "Perceptions of domestic violence."

172. Finneran and Stephenson, "Antecedents."

173. Cruz and Firestone, "Exploring violence"; Herrick et al., "Adversity and syndemic production"; McKenry et al., "Perpetration of gay"; Oringher and Samuelson, "Intimate partner violence"; Stephenson et al., "Intimate partner, familial."

174. Balsam and Szymanski, "Relationship quality"; C. Kelly and Warshafsky, "Partner abuse."

175. Peplau, Veniegas, and Campbell, "Gay and lesbian relationships."

176. Baker et al., "Lessons from examining."

177. Barnes, "'She Expected Her Women'"; Donovan and Hester, "Exploring emotion work."

178. Kubicek, McNeeley, and Collins, "'Same-Sex Relationship.'"

179. Kanuha, "'Relationships So Loving.'"
180. Gillum and DiFulvio, "'There's So Much.'"
181. Cruz, "'Why Doesn't He'"; Oliffe et al., "Gay men."
182. Oliffe et al., "Gay men."
183. Gillum and DiFulvio, "'There's So Much,'"
184. Goodmark, "Transgender people," 96.
185. Goodmark, "Transgender people."
186. Hassouneh and Glass, "Influence of Gender-Role Stereotyping"; Messinger, "Marking 35 Years"; Smollin, "Lesbian, gay, bisexual, transgender."
187. Oliffe et al., "Gay men."
188. Hassouneh and Glass, "Influence of Gender-Role Stereotyping."
189. Ahmed, Aldén, and Hammarstedt, "Perceptions"; Harris and Cook, "Attributions about spouse abuse"; Poorman, Seelau, and Seelau, "Perceptions of Domestic Abuse"; Russell, Chapleau, and Kraus, "When is it abuse?"; Seelau and Seelau, "Gender-Role Stereotypes"; Seelau, Seelau, and Poorman, "Gender and Role-Based Perceptions."
190. Balsam, "Nowhere to Hide"; Bograd, "Strengthening domestic violence theories"; Gilfus et al., "Gender"; Kaschak, *Intimate Betrayal;* McClennen, "Prevailing theories"; McClennen, "Domestic violence between same-gender"; S. L. Miller, "Expanding the boundaries"; Renzetti, "On dancing."
191. Almeida et al., "Violence in the Lives"; Balsam and Szymanski, "Relationship quality"; Brooks, *Minority Stress;* Cano and Vivian, "Life stressors."
192. Ahmed, Aldén, and Hammarstedt, "Perceptions"; Harris and Cook, "Attributions about spouse abuse"; Poorman, Seelau, and Seelau, "Perceptions of Domestic Abuse"; Russell, Chapleau, and Kraus, "When is it abuse?"; Seelau and Seelau, "Gender-Role Stereotypes"; Seelau, Seelau, and Poorman, "Gender and Role-Based Perceptions."
193. Kaschak, *Intimate Betrayal,* 2.
194. Meyer, "Prejudice, social stress."
195. Blenman, "Hand that Hits"; Nava, "Shadow Within."
196. Ellison, "Setting the captives free"; Kulkin et al., "Review of research."
197. Cruz, "Gay male domestic violence"; Tigert, "Power of shame."
198. McKenry et al., "Perpetration of gay."
199. Almeida et al., "Violence in the Lives"; Balsam and Szymanski, "Relationship quality"; Brooks, *Minority Stress;* Cano and Vivian, "Life stressors"; Coleman, "Lesbian battering."
200. Balsam and Szymanski, "Relationship quality."
201. Edwards and Sylaska, "Perpetration of intimate partner"; Stephenson et al., "Dyadic characteristics."
202. Balsam and Szymanski, "Relationship quality"; Carvalho et al., "Internalized sexual minority stressors"; Finneran and Stephenson, "Intimate partner violence, minority."
203. Mendoza, "Impact of minority stress."
204. Carvalho et al., "Internalized sexual minority stressors"; Finneran et al., "Intimate partner violence"; Finneran and Stephenson, "Intimate partner violence, minority"; Herrick et al., "Adversity and syndemic production."
205. Barrett and St. Pierre, "Intimate partner violence"; Herrick et al., "Adversity and syndemic production."
206. Edwards and Sylaska, "Perpetration of intimate partner."

207. Balsam and Szymanski, "Relationship quality"; Bartholomew et al., "Correlates of partner abuse"; Edwards and Sylaska, "Perpetration of intimate partner"; Finneran et al., "Intimate partner violence"; Finneran and Stephenson, "Intimate partner violence, minority"; Kelley et al., "Predictors of Perpetration"; Mendoza, "Impact of minority stress."

208. Carvalho et al., "Internalized sexual minority stressors"; Chong, Mak, and Kwong, "Risk and protective factors"; Milletich et al., "Predictors of women's same-sex."

209. Herrick et al., "Adversity and syndemic production"; Finneran et al., "Intimate partner violence."

210. Bartholomew et al., "Correlates of partner abuse"; Carvalho et al., "Internalized sexual minority stressors"; Edwards and Sylaska, "Perpetration of intimate partner"; Finneran and Stephenson, "Intimate partner violence, minority."

211. Pepper and Sand, "Internalized Homophobia."

212. Edwards and Sylaska, "Perpetration of intimate partner"; Finneran et al., "Intimate partner violence"; Kelley et al., "Predictors of Perpetration."

213. Balsam and Szymanski, "Relationship quality"; Bartholomew et al., "Correlates of partner abuse."

214. Finneran et al., "Intimate partner violence."

215. Bartholomew et al., "Correlates of partner abuse"; Carvalho et al., "Internalized sexual minority stressors."

216. Balsam and Szymanski, "Relationship quality"; Edwards and Sylaska, "Perpetration of intimate partner."

217. Ristock, *No More Secrets*, 58.

218. Finneran and Stephenson, "Antecedents."

219. Stephenson et al., "Intimate partner, familial."

220. Royko, "500,000 Gay Men."

221. Dank et al., "Dating violence experiences."

222. Dank et al., "Dating violence experiences"; Farrell and Cerise, "Fair's fair"; Guadalupe-Diaz, "An Exploration of Differences"; Leonard et al., *Coming Forward;* Rachel Lanzerotti Consulting, "2005–06 Youth Relationship Violence"; Renzetti, "Building a second closet"; Roch, Ritchie, and Morton, "Out of sight"; Turell, "Seeking help."

223. Bornstein et al., "Understanding the experiences"; Calton, Cattaneo, and Gebhard, "Barriers to help seeking"; Cruz, "'Why Doesn't He'"; Gillum and DiFulvio, "'There's So Much'"; Girshick, *Woman-to-Woman Sexual Violence;* Hassouneh and Glass, "Influence of Gender-Role Stereotyping"; Island and Letellier, *Men Who Beat Men;* Merrill and Wolfe, "Battered Gay Men"; Patzel, "Lesbian partner abuse"; Walters, "Straighten Up."

224. Sylaska and Edwards, "Disclosure experiences."

225. Nieves-Rosa, Carballo-Dieguez, and Dolezal, "Domestic abuse and HIV-risk."

226. Roch, Ritchie, and Morton, "Out of sight."

227. Alhusen, Lucea, and Glass, "Perceptions of and Experience," 7.

228. Hester, Donovan, and Fahmy, "Feminist epistemology."

229. Head and Milton, "Filling the Silence."

230. Ackerman and Field, "Gender Asymmetric Effect."

231. Giorgio, "Speaking silence"; Perez-Darby, "Secret joy of accountability."

232. N. Brown, "Stories from Outside"; Perez-Darby, "Secret joy of accountability"; Walters, "Straighten Up."

233. Letellier, "Twin epidemics"; Merrill and Wolfe, "Battered Gay Men."

234. Perez-Darby, "Secret joy of accountability."

235. Perez-Darby, "Secret joy of accountability," 109.

236. N. Brown, "Stories from Outside," 375.

237. Cook-Daniels, "Intimate Partner Violence."

238. Balsam, "Nowhere to Hide," 31.

239. N, "A sliding stance," 165.

240. Walters, "Straighten Up."

241. Pyra et al., "Sexual minority status."

242. Donovan and Hester, "'I Hate the Word.'"

243. Leonard et al., *Coming Forward.*

244. Alhusen, Lucea, and Glass, "Perceptions of and Experience," 7.

245. Merrill and Wolfe, "Battered Gay Men."

246. Alhusen, Lucea, and Glass, "Perceptions of and Experience"; Barnes, "'I Still'"; Barnes, "'Suffering'"; Donovan and Hester, "'I Hate the Word'"; Donovan and Hester, "Seeking help"; Hassouneh and Glass, "Influence of Gender-Role Stereotyping"; Irwin, "(Dis) counted Stories"; E. M. McLaughlin and Rozee, "Knowledge about heterosexual versus."

247. Giorgio, "Speaking silence," 1249.

248. Kanuha, "'Relationships So Loving.'"

249. Ball, "Gay men"; DiStefano, "Intimate partner violence."

250. Todd, "Blue Rinse Blues?"

251. DiStefano, "Intimate partner violence."

252. Cruz, "'Why Doesn't He'"; Head and Milton, "Filling the Silence."

253. Braun et al., "'Risk' and sexual coercion"; Braun et al. "Sexual coercion"; Donovan and Hester, "'Because she was'"; Gavey et al., "Unsafe, Unwanted Sexual Coercion"; Kanuha, "'Relationships So Loving'"; Irwin, "(Dis) counted Stories"; Ristock, "Responding lesbian relationship violence."

254. Kanuha, "'Relationships So Loving,'" 1183.

255. Ristock, "Responding lesbian relationship violence," 102.

256. Cruz, "'Why Doesn't He.'"

257. McDonald, "Social context."

258. Gillum and DiFulvio, "'There's So Much.'"

259. Craft and Serovich, "Family-of-origin factors"; Letellier, "Twin epidemics."

260. Goodmark, "Transgender people."

261. Donovan, "Tackling Inequality."

262. Goodmark, "Transgender people"; McDonald, "Social context."

263. Singh and McKleroy, "'Just getting out,'" 39.

264. N, "A sliding stance," 164–65.

265. Ristock, "Responding lesbian relationship violence," 102.

266. Merrill and Wolfe, "Battered Gay Men."

267. Gillum and DiFulvio, "'There's So Much'"; Perez-Darby, "Secret joy of accountability."

268. Perez-Darby, "The secret joy of accountability," 111.

269. Bornstein et al., "Understanding the experiences."

270. Cruz, "'Why Doesn't He'"; Merrill and Wolfe, "Battered Gay Men."

271. Merrill and Wolfe, "Battered Gay Men."

272. Alhusen, Lucea, and Glass, "Perceptions of and Experience"; Catherine Browning, "Silence"; Head and Milton, "Filling the Silence."

273. Leonard et al., *Coming Forward;* Merrill and Wolfe, "Battered Gay Men."

274. Leonard et al., *Coming Forward;* Meza-de-Luna et al., "Never to me!"; Ristock, "Responding lesbian relationship violence."

275. Kanuha, "'Relationships So Loving.'"

276. Kanuha, "'Relationships So Loving,'" 1187.

277. Alhusen, Lucea, and Glass, "Perceptions of and Experience"; Balsam, "Nowhere to Hide"; Head and Milton, "Filling the Silence"; McDonald, "Social context."

278. Balsam, "Nowhere to Hide," 30–31.

279. N. Brown, "Stories from Outside," 375.

280. Alhusen, Lucea, and Glass, "Perceptions of and Experience"; Glass et al., "Risk for reassault"; Turell and Herrmann, "'Family' support."

281. Balsam, "Nowhere to Hide."

282. Alhusen, Lucea, and Glass, "Perceptions of and Experience," 8.

283. Crenshaw, "Mapping the Margins."

284. Choudhury, "Violence that dares not"; Crenshaw, "Mapping the Margins."

285. Blenman, "Hand That Hits," 62.

286. Oswald, Fonseca, and Hardesty, "Lesbian Mothers' Counseling Experiences."

287. Oswald, Fonseca, and Hardesty, "Lesbian Mothers' Counseling Experiences."

288. Owen and Burke, "An exploration of prevalence."

289. Robinson, "There's a stranger."

290. Robinson, "There's a stranger."

291. Hardesty et al., "Lesbian/bisexual mothers," 39.

292. Oswald, Fonseca, and Hardesty, "Lesbian Mothers' Counseling Experiences."

293. Oswald, Fonseca, and Hardesty "Lesbian Mothers' Counseling Experiences."

294. McClennen, "Domestic violence between same-gender," 150.

295. Calton, Cattaneo, and Gebhard, "Barriers to help seeking."

296. St. Pierre and Senn, "External barriers to help-seeking."

297. GLBT Domestic Violence Coalition and Jane Doe Inc., "Shelter/housing needs."

298. Vidas, "Childhood sexual abuse."

299. Freedberg, "Health Care Barriers."

300. Guasp, *Gay and Bisexual Men's;* Hunt and Fish, "Prescription for change"; Mak, Chong, and Kwong, "Prevalence in Hong Kong"; Roch, Ritchie, and Morton, "Out of sight."

301. Catherine Browning, "Silence."

302. Catherine Browning, "Silence," 97.

303. Hester et al., "Exploring the service"; St. Pierre and Senn, "External barriers to help-seeking."

304. Glass et al., "Risk for reassault."

305. Turell and Herrmann, "Family' support."

306. Leonard et al., *Coming Forward;* McDonald, "Social context"; Roch, Ritchie, and Morton, "Out of sight"; St. Pierre and Senn, "External barriers to help-seeking."

307. St. Pierre and Senn, "External barriers to help-seeking."

308. Hardesty et al., "Lesbian/bisexual mothers."

309. Roch, Ritchie, and Morton, "Out of sight," 29.

310. Dolan-Soto, "Lesbian, gay, transgender."

311. Wolf et al., "Barriers to seeking police."

312. Bograd, "Strengthening domestic violence theories"; Chung and Lee, "Raising our voices"; Vidas, "Childhood sexual abuse"; Kanuha, "Compounding the triple jeopardy"; Sokoloff and Dupont, "Domestic violence at intersections."

313. Simpson and Helfrich, "Oppression and barriers."

314. Kanuha, "'Relationships So Loving'"; Robinson, "There's a stranger"; Simpson and Helfrich, "Oppression and barriers."

315. DiStefano, "Intimate partner violence."

316. Letellier, "Twin epidemics"; Russo, "Recognizing difference."

317. Letellier, "Twin epidemics," 71.

318. Ristock, "Decentering heterosexuality," 64.

319. Stanley et al., "Intimate violence."

320. Lie et al., "Lesbians in currently aggressive."

321. Lewis et al., "Sexual Minority Stressors"; Milletich et al., "Predictors of women's same-sex."

322. Coleman, "Treating the Lesbian Batterer"; Dutton, "Patriarchy and wife assault"; Collins, "Same-Sex Domestic Violence"; Letellier, "Gay and bisexual male."

323. M. Eaton, "Abuse by Any Other"; Lilith, "Reconsidering the abuse"; Merrill, "Ruling the exceptions."

324. Valentine et al., "Predictive Syndemic Effect."

325. Brennan et al., "Syndemic theory and HIV-related risk"; Mimiaga et al., "High prevalence multiple syndemic"; Mustanski et al., "Syndemic of psychosocial health"; Parsons et al., "Syndemic production"; Stall et al., "Association of co-occurring psychosocial"; Starks et al., "Syndemic factors"; Starks et al., "Linking Syndemic Stress"; Tulloch et al., "Retrospective reports."

326. Bornstein et al., "Understanding the experiences"; Cruz, "'Why Doesn't He'"; Gillum and DiFulvio, "'There's So Much'"; Girshick, Woman-to-Woman Sexual Violence; Hassouneh and Glass, "Influence of Gender-Role Stereotyping"; Island and Letellier, Men Who Beat Men; Merrill and Wolfe, "Battered Gay Men"; Patzel, "Lesbian partner abuse"; Walters, "Straighten Up."

327. Bornstein et al., "Understanding the experiences"; Cruz, "'Why Doesn't He'"; Ristock, "Cultural politics of abuse."

328. Braun et al., "'Risk' and sexual coercion"; Braun et al. "Sexual coercion"; Donovan and Hester, "'Because she was'"; Gavey et al., "Unsafe, Unwanted Sexual Coercion"; Kanuha, "'Relationships So Loving'"; Irwin, "(Dis) counted Stories"; Ristock, "Responding lesbian relationship violence."

329. Ball, "Gay men"; Ball and Hayes, "Same-sex intimate partner violence"; Jeffries and Ball, "Male same-sex intimate violence."

330. Balsam and Szymanski, "Relationship quality"; Bartholomew et al., "Correlates of partner abuse"; Edwards and Sylaska, "Perpetration of intimate partner"; Finneran et al., "Intimate partner violence"; Finneran and Stephenson, "Intimate partner violence, minority."

331. Herrick et al., "Adversity and syndemic production"; Finneran et al., "Intimate partner violence."

332. Balsam and Szymanski, "Relationship quality"; Carvalho et al., "Internalized sexual minority stressors"; Finneran and Stephenson, "Intimate partner violence, minority."

333. Carvalho et al., "Internalized sexual minority stressors"; Finneran et al., "Intimate partner violence"; Finneran and Stephenson, "Intimate partner violence, minority"; Herrick et al., "Adversity and syndemic production."

334. Edwards and Sylaska, "Perpetration of intimate partner"; Finneran et al., "Intimate partner violence."

335. Finneran et al., "Intimate partner violence."

336. Ristock, *No More Secrets,* 59.

337. Milletich et al., "Predictors of women's same-sex."

5. HOW CAN WE IMPROVE NONGOVERNMENTAL RESPONSES?

1. Giorgio, "Speaking silence," 1240.

2. Barnes, "'I'm Over It.'"

3. Alhusen, Lucea, and Glass, "Perceptions of and Experience"; Watkins, "Police perspective."

4. Alhusen, Lucea, and Glass, "Perceptions of and Experience," 10.

5. Giorgio, "Speaking silence"; Simpson and Helfrich, "Lesbian survivors."

6. Simpson and Helfrich, "Lesbian survivors," 49.

7. VanNatta, "Constructing the battered woman," 422.

8. Kaplan and Colbs, "Shattered Pride."

9. Farrell and Cerise, "Fair's fair"; Merrill and Wolfe, "Battered Gay Men"; Rachel Lanzerotti Consulting, "2005–06 Youth Relationship Violence"; Renzetti, "Building a second closet"; Ristock, "'And Justice for All?'"; Roch, Ritchie, and Morton, "Out of sight"; Scherzer, "Domestic violence, lesbian relationships"; Turell, "Seeking help."

10. Merrill and Wolfe, "Battered Gay Men."

11. Sylaska and Edwards, "Disclosure experiences."

12. Merrill and Wolfe, "Battered Gay Men"; Renzetti, "Building a second closet"; Ristock, "'And Justice for All?'"; Scherzer, "Domestic violence, lesbian relationships"; Turell, "Seeking help."

13. Rachel Lanzerotti Consulting, "2005–06 Youth Relationship Violence"; Roch, Ritchie, and Morton, "Out of sight."

14. Chesley, MacAulay, and Ristock, *Abuse in Lesbian Relationships;* Farrell and Cerise, "Fair's fair"; Henderson, "Prevalence of domestic violence"; Leonard et al., *Coming Forward;* Rachel Lanzerotti Consulting, "2005–06 Youth Relationship Violence"; Renzetti, "Building a second closet"; Ristock, "'And Justice for All?'"; St. Pierre and Senn, "External barriers to help-seeking"; Sylaska and Edwards, "Disclosure experiences"; Turell, "Seeking help."

15. St. Pierre and Senn, "External barriers to help-seeking."

16. Farrell and Cerise, "Fair's fair"; Rachel Lanzerotti Consulting, "2005–06 Youth Relationship Violence"; Renzetti, "Building a second closet"; Ristock, "'And Justice for All?'"; Sylaska and Edwards, "Disclosure experiences"; Turell, "Seeking help."

17. Rachel Lanzerotti Consulting, "2005–06 Youth Relationship Violence"; Renzetti, "Building a second closet"; Ristock, "'And Justice for All?'"; Turell, "Seeking help."

18. Chesley, MacAulay, and Ristock, *Abuse in Lesbian Relationships;* Farrell and Cerise, "Fair's fair"; Rachel Lanzerotti Consulting, "2005–06 Youth Relationship Violence"; Renzetti, "Building a second closet"; St. Pierre and Senn, "External barriers to help-seeking"; Turell, "Seeking help."

19. Chesley, MacAulay, and Ristock, *Abuse in Lesbian Relationships;* Renzetti, "Building a second closet"; Ristock, "'And Justice for All?'"; St. Pierre and Senn, "External barriers to help-seeking"; Turell, "Seeking help."

20. Renzetti, "Building a second closet"; Ristock, "'And Justice for All?'"

21. Farrell and Cerise, "Fair's fair"; Hunt and Fish, "Prescription for change"; Leonard et al., *Coming Forward;* Renzetti, "Building a second closet"; Ristock, "'And Justice for All?'"; St. Pierre and Senn, "External barriers to help-seeking"; Turell, "Seeking help."

22. Leonard et al., *Coming Forward;* St. Pierre and Senn, "External barriers to help-seeking."

23. Rachel Lanzerotti Consulting, "2005–06 Youth Relationship Violence"; Roch, Ritchie, and Morton, "Out of sight"; Turell, "Seeking help."

24. Rachel Lanzerotti Consulting, "2005–06 Youth Relationship Violence."

25. Kuehnle and Sullivan, "Gay and Lesbian Victimization"; McClennen, Summers, and Vaughan, "Gay men's domestic violence"; Merrill and Wolfe, "Battered Gay Men"; National Coalition of Anti-Violence Programs, *Lesbian, Gay, 2011.*

26. Scherzer, "Domestic violence, lesbian relationships."

27. McClennen, Summers, and Vaughan, "Gay men's domestic violence"; Merrill and Wolfe, "Battered Gay Men"; Scherzer, "Domestic violence, lesbian relationships."

28. McClennen, Summers, and Vaughan, "Gay men's domestic violence"; Merrill and Wolfe, "Battered Gay Men"; Scherzer, "Domestic violence, lesbian relationships."

29. McClennen, Summers, and Vaughan, "Gay men's domestic violence"; Merrill and Wolfe, "Battered Gay Men"; Scherzer, "Domestic violence, lesbian relationships."

30. Kuehnle and Sullivan, "Gay and Lesbian Victimization"; McClennen, Summers, and Vaughan, "Gay men's domestic violence"; Merrill and Wolfe, "Battered Gay Men"; National Coalition of Anti-Violence Programs, *Lesbian, Gay, 2011;* Scherzer, "Domestic violence, lesbian relationships."

31. Merrill and Wolfe, "Battered Gay Men."

32. Kuehnle and Sullivan, "Gay and Lesbian Victimization"; McClennen, Summers, and Vaughan, "Gay men's domestic violence"; Merrill and Wolfe, "Battered Gay Men."

33. Merrill and Wolfe, "Battered Gay Men"; Rachel Lanzerotti Consulting, "2005–06 Youth Relationship Violence"; Renzetti, "Building a second closet"; Ristock, "'And Justice for All?'"; Roch, Ritchie, and Morton, "Out of sight"; Scherzer, "Domestic violence, lesbian relationships"; Turell, "Seeking help."

34. Merrill and Wolfe, "Battered Gay Men"; Rachel Lanzerotti Consulting, "2005–06 Youth Relationship Violence"; Renzetti, "Building a second closet"; Ristock, "'And Justice for All?'"; Roch, Ritchie, and Morton, "Out of sight"; Scherzer, "Domestic violence, lesbian relationships"; Turell, "Seeking help."

35. St. Pierre and Senn, "External barriers to help-seeking"; Turell and Cornell-Swanson, "Not all alike."

36. St. Pierre and Senn, "External barriers to help-seeking."

37. Henderson, "Prevalence of domestic violence"; St. Pierre and Senn, "External barriers to help-seeking."

38. Langenderfer-Magruder et al., "Experiences of Intimate Partner."

39. Hunt and Fish, "Prescription for change"; McClennen, Summers, and Vaughan, "Gay men's domestic violence"; Merrill and Wolfe, "Battered Gay Men"; Renzetti, "Building a second closet"; Ristock, "'And Justice for All?'"

40. Turell, "Seeking help."

41. Turell, "Seeking help."

42. Merrill and Wolfe, "Battered Gay Men."

43. McClennen, Summers, and Vaughan, "Gay men's domestic violence"; Merrill and Wolfe, "Battered Gay Men"; Renzetti, "Building a second closet"; Ristock, "'And Justice for All?'"

44. McClennen, Summers, and Vaughan, "Gay men's domestic violence"; Merrill and Wolfe, "Battered Gay Men"; Renzetti, "Building a second closet"; Ristock, "'And Justice for All?'"

45. Hunt and Fish, "Prescription for change"; McClennen, Summers, and Vaughan, "Gay men's domestic violence"; Merrill and Wolfe, "Battered Gay Men"; Renzetti, "Building a second closet"; Ristock, "'And Justice for All?'"

46. McClennen, Summers, and Vaughan, "Gay men's domestic violence"; Renzetti, "Building a second closet"; Ristock, "'And Justice for All?'"

47. McClennen, Summers, and Vaughan, "Gay men's domestic violence"; Merrill and Wolfe, "Battered Gay Men"; Renzetti, "Building a second closet"; Ristock, "'And Justice for All?'"

48. McClennen, Summers, and Vaughan, "Gay men's domestic violence"; Renzetti, "Building a second closet."

49. Merrill and Wolfe, "Battered Gay Men."

50. McClennen, Summers, and Vaughan, "Gay men's domestic violence"; Renzetti, "Building a second closet"; Ristock, "'And Justice for All?'"

51. Renzetti, "Building a second closet"; Ristock, "'And Justice for All?'"

52. McClennen, Summers, and Vaughan, "Gay men's domestic violence"; Renzetti, "Building a second closet"; Ristock, "'And Justice for All?'"

53. McClennen, Summers, and Vaughan, "Gay men's domestic violence"; Merrill and Wolfe, "Battered Gay Men"; Renzetti, "Building a second closet"; Ristock, "'And Justice for All?'"

54. McClennen, Summers, and Vaughan, "Gay men's domestic violence"; Rachel Lanzerotti Consulting, "2005-06 Youth Relationship Violence."

55. Ristock, "'And Justice for All?'"; Renzetti, "Building a second closet"; Turell, "Seeking help."

56. Merrill and Wolfe, "Battered Gay Men."

57. Renzetti, "Building a second closet"; Turell, "Seeking help."

58. McClennen, Summers, and Vaughan, "Gay men's domestic violence."

59. Merrill and Wolfe, "Battered Gay Men."

60. Murray et al., "Same-sex intimate partner violence."

61. Turell and Cornell-Swanson, "Not all alike."

62. Sylaska and Edwards, "Disclosure experiences."

63. Merrill and Wolfe, "Battered Gay Men."

64. Merrill and Wolfe, "Battered Gay Men"; Rachel Lanzerotti Consulting, "2005-06 Youth Relationship Violence"; Renzetti, "Building a second closet"; Ristock, "'And Justice

for All?'"; Roch, Ritchie, and Morton, "Out of sight"; Scherzer, "Domestic violence, lesbian relationships"; Turell, "Seeking help."

65. Sylaska and Edwards, "Disclosure experiences."

66. Strasser et al., "Feasibility study, Atlanta, Georgia."

67. Roch, Ritchie, and Morton, "Out of sight."

68. Roch, Ritchie, and Morton, "Out of sight," 29.

69. Irwin, "(Dis) counted Stories"; Renzetti, "Building a second closet."

70. Bornstein et al., "Understanding the experiences."

71. McClennen, Summers, and Vaughan, "Gay men's domestic violence"; Merrill and Wolfe, "Battered Gay Men"; Renzetti, "Building a second closet"; Ristock, "'And Justice for All?'"

72. Ahmed, Aldén, and Hammarstedt, "Perceptions"; Harris and Cook, "Attributions about spouse abuse"; Russell, Chapleau, and Kraus, "When is it abuse?"; Seelau and Seelau, "Gender-Role Stereotypes"; Seelau, Seelau, and Poorman, "Gender and Role-Based Perceptions."

73. Sorenson and Thomas, "Views of Intimate Violence."

74. Renzetti, "Building a second closet."

75. Renzetti, "Building a second closet," 161.

76. Blenman, "Hand That Hits"; K. Davis and Taylor, "Voices from the margins."

77. Bornstein et al., "Understanding the experiences."

78. K. Davis and Glass, "Reframing the Heteronormative Constructions."

79. Kanuha, "'Relationships So Loving.'"

80. Bornstein et al., "Understanding the experiences."

81. Burk, "Think Re-think"; Turell and Herrmann, "'Family' support."

82. Merrill and Wolfe, "Battered Gay Men"; Rachel Lanzerotti Consulting, "2005–06 Youth Relationship Violence"; Renzetti, "Building a second closet"; Ristock, "'And Justice for All?'"; Roch, Ritchie, and Morton, "Out of sight"; Scherzer, "Domestic violence, lesbian relationships"; Turell, "Seeking help."

83. Renzetti, "Building a second closet."

84. McClennen, Summers, and Vaughan, "Gay men's domestic violence"; Merrill and Wolfe, "Battered Gay Men"; Renzetti, "Building a second closet"; Ristock, "'And Justice for All?'"

85. Walters, "Straighten Up."

86. Irwin, "(Dis) counted Stories"; Renzetti, "Building a second closet"; Walters, "Straighten Up."

87. Walters, "Straighten Up," 266.

88. L. A. Eaton et al., "Examining factors."

89. Ellison, "Setting the captives free."

90. Simpson and Helfrich, "Oppression and barriers."

91. Rachel Lanzerotti Consulting, "2005–06 Youth Relationship Violence"; Renzetti, "Building a second closet"; Ristock, "'And Justice for All?'"; Turell, "Seeking help."

92. Farrell and Cerise, "Fair's fair"; Merrill and Wolfe, "Battered Gay Men"; Renzetti, "Building a second closet"; Ristock, "'And Justice for All?'"; Scherzer, "Domestic violence, lesbian relationships"; Turell, "Seeking help."

93. Rachel Lanzerotti Consulting, "2005–06 Youth Relationship Violence"; Roch, Ritchie, and Morton, "Out of sight."

94. St. Pierre and Senn, "External barriers to help-seeking."

95. Farrell and Cerise, "Fair's fair"; Rachel Lanzerotti Consulting, "2005–06 Youth Relationship Violence"; Renzetti, "Building a second closet"; Ristock, "'And Justice for All?'"; Sylaska and Edwards, "Disclosure experiences"; Turell, "Seeking help."

96. Merrill and Wolfe, "Battered Gay Men."

97. Greene et al., "'Is This Normal?'"; Paroissien and Stewart, "Surviving lesbian abuse"; Vidas, "Childhood sexual abuse."

98. McClennen, Summers, and Vaughan, "Gay men's domestic violence"; Merrill and Wolfe, "Battered Gay Men"; Renzetti, "Building a second closet"; Ristock, "'And Justice for All?'"

99. McClennen, Summers, and Vaughan, "Gay men's domestic violence"; Renzetti, "Building a second closet"; Ristock, "'And Justice for All?'"

100. Gallopin and Leigh, "Teen perceptions," 19.

101. Tigert, "Power of shame," 74.

102. K. Davis and Taylor, "Voices from the margins"; Oswald, Fonseca, and Hardesty, "Lesbian Mothers' Counseling Experiences."

103. Wise and Bowman, "Comparison of Beginning Counselors."

104. Alhusen, Lucea, and Glass, "Perceptions of and Experience."

105. Oswald, Fonseca, and Hardesty, "Lesbian Mothers' Counseling Experiences."

106. Wise and Bowman, "Comparison of Beginning Counselors."

107. Alpert et al., "Family Violence"; NYS Office for the Prevention of Domestic Violence, "Domestic Violence in Lesbian."

108. Banks and Fedewa, "Counselors' Attitudes"; Mokonogho, Mittal, and Quitangon, "Treating the Transgender Homeless."

109. Ard and Makadon, "Addressing intimate partner violence"; Freedberg, "Health Care Barriers"; Hammond, "Lesbian victims"; Hancock, "Positive Counsellor Characteristics"; Hancock, McAuliffe, and Levingston, "Factors Impacting Counselor Competency."

110. Ard and Makadon, "Addressing intimate partner violence"; Sillman, "Diagnosis, screening, and counseling."

111. Weil, "Diagnosis and screening"; Weil, "Epidemiology and health consequences"; Weil, "Intervention and patient management."

112. Sollenberger et al., "Value of library."

113. Wise and Bowman, "Comparison of Beginning Counselors."

114. Freedberg, "Health Care Barriers."

115. Hancock, McAuliffe, and Levingston, "Factors Impacting Counselor Competency."

116. Seeman, "Sexual Minority Women"; Tigert, "Power of shame"; Vidas, "Childhood sexual abuse."

117. Tigert, "Power of shame," 74.

118. Chen, Jacobs, and Rovi, "Intimate partner violence"; Fern, "Domestic Violence"; Gentry, "Caring for lesbians"; Murray et al., "Same-sex intimate partner violence."

119. Chen, Jacobs, and Rovi, "Intimate partner violence"; Jablow, "Victims of abuse."

120. Freedberg, "Health Care Barriers"; St. Pierre and Senn, "External barriers to help-seeking"; C. M. West, "Lesbian intimate partner violence."

121. Gallopin and Leigh, "Teen perceptions"; Tigert, "Power of shame."

122. Alhusen, Lucea, and Glass, "Perceptions of and Experience."

123. Alhusen, Lucea, and Glass, "Perceptions of and Experience," 8; Freedberg, "Health Care Barriers."

124. Dietz, "Working."

125. Duke and Davidson, "Same-sex intimate partner violence"; Helfrich and Simpson, "Improving services"; St. Pierre and Senn, "External barriers to help-seeking."

126. Alhusen, Lucea, and Glass, "Perceptions of and Experience"; Ard and Makadon, "Addressing intimate partner violence"; Chen, Jacobs, and Rovi, "Intimate partner violence"; Freedberg, "Health Care Barriers"; Murray et al., "Same-sex intimate partner violence"; Senseman, "Screening for intimate violence"; St. Pierre and Senn, "External barriers to help-seeking"; C. M. West, "Lesbian intimate partner violence."

127. Freedberg, "Health Care Barriers."

128. Banks and Fedewa, "Counselors' Attitudes."

129. St. Pierre and Senn, "External barriers to help-seeking."

130. Banks and Fedewa, "Counselors' Attitudes."

131. Glass et al., "Risk for reassault"; Peterman and Dixon, "Domestic violence between same-sex"; SafeLives, "SafeLives Dash risk."

132. Ard and Makadon, "Addressing intimate partner violence"; Chen, Jacobs, and Rovi, "Intimate partner violence"; Fern, "Domestic Violence."

133. Freedberg, "Health Care Barriers."

134. Ramachandran et al., "Intimate partner violence."

135. Alexander, "Violence"; Banks and Fedewa, "Counselors' Attitudes"; Tigert, "Power of shame."

136. Ard and Makadon, "Addressing intimate partner violence"; Fern, "Domestic Violence"; Freedberg, "Health Care Barriers."

137. Alexander, "Violence," 97.

138. Ard and Makadon, "Addressing intimate partner violence"; Fern, "Domestic Violence"; Murray et al., "Same-sex intimate partner violence"; Quinn, "Open minds open doors."

139. Fern, "Domestic Violence"; Quinn, "Open minds open doors."

140. Leeder, *Treating abuse in families.*

141. St. Pierre and Senn, "External barriers to help-seeking."

142. Simpson and Helfrich, "Oppression and barriers."

143. Alhusen, Lucea, and Glass, "Perceptions of and Experience," 8.

144. Alhusen, Lucea, and Glass, "Perceptions of and Experience"; Chen, Jacobs, and Rovi, "Intimate partner violence"; Freedberg, "Health Care Barriers"; Murray et al., "Same-sex intimate partner violence"; Relf, "Battering and HIV"; Senseman, "Screening for intimate violence"; St. Pierre and Senn, "External barriers to help-seeking"; C. M. West, "Lesbian intimate partner violence."

145. Senseman, "Screening for intimate violence."

146. Chen, Jacobs, and Rovi, "Intimate partner violence," 30; Senseman, "Screening for intimate violence."

147. Ard and Makadon, "Addressing intimate partner violence."

148. Alhusen, Lucea, and Glass, "Perceptions of and Experience"; Chen, Jacobs, and Rovi, "Intimate partner violence"; Freedberg, "Health Care Barriers"; Murray et al., "Same-sex intimate partner violence"; Relf, "Battering and HIV"; Senseman, "Screening for intimate

violence"; St. Pierre and Senn, "External barriers to help-seeking"; C. M. West, "Lesbian intimate partner violence."

149. Chan and Cavacuiti, "Gay abuse screening protocol"; Donovan, "Redefining domestic violence"; Freedberg, "Health Care Barriers"; GLBTDVC, *Intimate Partner Abuse Screening;* Mravcak, "Primary care for lesbians"; Peterman and Dixon, "Domestic violence between same-sex."

150. Relf, "Battering and HIV."

151. Glass et al., "Risk for reassault."

152. Chan and Cavacuiti, "Gay abuse screening protocol"; Glass et al., "Risk for reassault."

153. Giorgio, "Speaking silence."

154. Blasko, Winek, and Bieschke, "Therapists' Prototypical Assessment."

155. Neilson, "Clinical Success, Political Failure?"

156. Murray et al., "Same-sex intimate partner violence."

157. Stanley et al., "Intimate violence."

158. Lie et al., "Lesbians in currently aggressive."

159. Bartholomew et al., "Correlates of partner abuse"; Carvalho et al., "Internalized sexual minority stressors"; B. C. Kelly et al. "Intersection of mutual violence"; Lie and Gentlewarrier, "Intimate violence in lesbian"; Lie et al., "Lesbians in currently aggressive"; Renner and Whitney, "Examining symmetry"; Renzetti, *Violent betrayal.*

160. Giorgio, "Speaking silence."

161. Perez-Darby, "Secret joy of accountability."

162. Giorgio, "Speaking silence."

163. Quinn, "Open minds open doors."

164. Fern, "Domestic Violence."

165. Ard and Makadon, "Addressing intimate partner violence"; Christine Browning, Reynolds, and Dworkin, "Affirmative psychotherapy"; Hanson, "Violence we face"; Horne and Hamilton, "Bisexuality and broken relationships"; Klinger, "Gay violence"; McClennen and Gunther, *Professional's Guide to Understanding;* Morrow and Hawxhurst, "Lesbian partner abuse"; Matthews and Lorah, "Domestic Violence in Same-Sex"; Murray et al., "Same-sex intimate partner violence"; Peterman and Dixon, "Domestic violence between same-sex"; Robinson, "There's a stranger"; C. M. West, "Leaving a second closet."

166. Peterman and Dixon, "Domestic violence between same-sex."

167. Fox, "Couples therapy"; Istar, "Couple assessment."

168. Blasko, "Prototypical Assessment"; Murray et al., "Same-sex intimate partner violence."

169. Wise and Bowman, "Comparison of Beginning Counselors."

170. Blasko, "Prototypical Assessment."

171. Wise and Bowman, "Comparison of Beginning Counselors."

172. Dietz, "Working"; Klinger, "Gay violence"; Klinger and Stein, "Impact of violence."

173. Kondas, "Existential explosion"; Oswald, Fonseca, and Hardesty, "Lesbian Mothers' Counseling Experiences"; Peterman and Dixon, "Domestic violence between same-sex."

174. Ard and Makadon, "Addressing intimate partner violence"; Murray et al., "Same-sex intimate partner violence."

175. Almeida et al., "Violence in the Lives."

176. Almeida et al., "Violence in the Lives"; Istar, "Couple assessment"; Kaplan and Colbs, "Shattered Pride"; Murray et al., "Same-sex intimate partner violence."

177. Hancock, McAuliffe, and Levingston, "Factors Impacting Counselor Competency."

178. Kaplan and Colbs, "Shattered Pride"; Murray et al., "Same-sex intimate partner violence."

179. Almeida et al., "Violence in the Lives."

180. Dietz, "Working"; Hancock, "Positive Counsellor Characteristics."

181. Hancock, "Positive Counsellor Characteristics."

182. Quinn, "Open minds open doors."

183. Banks and Fedewa, "Counselors' Attitudes"; Peterman and Dixon, "Domestic violence between same-sex."

184. Fern, "Domestic Violence."

185. Farley, "Establishing a safety plan"; FORGE, "Safety planning"; Peterman and Dixon, "Domestic violence between same-sex"; Quinn, "Open minds open doors," 48–49.

186. Farley, "Establishing a safety plan"; FORGE, "Safety planning."

187. Gentry, "Caring for lesbians."

188. Chen, Jacobs, and Rovi, "Intimate partner violence"; Fern, "Domestic Violence."

189. Heer et al., "Developing services."

190. Chen, Jacobs, and Rovi, "Intimate partner violence"; A. J. Miller, Bobner, and Zarski, "Sexual identity development"; Murray et al., "Same-sex intimate partner violence."

191. Chesley, MacAulay, and Ristock, *Abuse in Lesbian Relationships;* Farrell and Cerise, "Fair's fair"; Rachel Lanzerotti Consulting, "2005–06 Youth Relationship Violence"; Renzetti, "Building a second closet"; St. Pierre and Senn, "External barriers to help-seeking"; Turell, "Seeking help."

192. Chesley, MacAulay, and Ristock, *Abuse in Lesbian Relationships;* Renzetti, "Building a second closet"; Ristock, "'And Justice for All?'"; St. Pierre and Senn, "External barriers to help-seeking"; Turell, "Seeking help."

193. Rachel Lanzerotti Consulting, "2005–06 Youth Relationship Violence"; Roch, Ritchie, and Morton, "Out of sight"; Turell, "Seeking help."

194. Farrell and Cerise, "Fair's fair"; Rachel Lanzerotti Consulting, "2005–06 Youth Relationship Violence."

195. Cheung, Leung, and Tsui, "Asian male domestic violence."

196. Hines and Douglas, "Reported availability."

197. National Coalition of Anti-Violence Programs, *Lesbian, Gay, 2011.*

198. GLBT Domestic Violence Coalition and Jane Doe Inc., "Shelter/housing needs."

199. Colm, "Freedom & Strategy."

200. Greenberg, "Still hidden."

201. Stapel, "Falling to pieces."

202. Modi, Palmer, and Armstrong, "Role of Violence against."

203. U.S. Government Printing Office, "113th Congress Public Law."

204. U.S. Department of Justice, "Frequently Asked Questions."

205. Ristock, "Cultural politics of abuse"; Ristock, "Decentering heterosexuality."

206. Donnelly, Cook, and Wilson, "Provision and Exclusion"; Renzetti, "Poverty of services."

207. Simpson and Helfrich, "Lesbian survivors"; VanNatta, "Constructing the battered woman."

208. VanNatta, "Constructing the battered woman."

209. VanNatta, "Constructing the battered woman," 426.

210. VanNatta, "Constructing the battered woman," 427.

211. Quinn, "Open minds open doors."

212. Quinn, "Open minds open doors."

213. GLBT Domestic Violence Coalition and Jane Doe Inc., "Shelter/housing needs," 11.

214. U.S. Department of Justice, "Frequently Asked Questions."

215. Quinn, "Open minds open doors."

216. Ford et al., "Intimate Partner Violence Prevention."

217. Ristock, "Cultural politics of abuse."

218. Donovan and Hester, "'Because she was'"; Leonard et al., *Coming Forward*.

219. St. Pierre and Senn, "External barriers to help-seeking."

220. Irwin, "(Dis) counted Stories"; Kay and Jeffries, "Homophobia, heteronormativism"; Lindley, Friedman, and Struble, "Becoming Visible."

221. Lindley, Friedman, and Struble, "Becoming Visible."

222. Turell et al., "Lesbian, gay, bisexual."

223. Kay and Jeffries, "Homophobia, heteronormativism."

224. Holt, "Lesbian, gay, bisexual."

225. Simpson and Helfrich, "Oppression and barriers."

226. Alhusen, Lucea, and Glass, "Perceptions of and Experience"; Freedner et al., "Dating violence."

227. ACON, "Homelessness"; Goodmark, "Transgender people"; Greenberg, "Still hidden"; Mottet and Ohle, "Transitioning our shelters."

228. McClennen, Summers, and Vaughan, "Gay men's domestic violence"; Renzetti, "Building a second closet."

229. Merrill and Wolfe, "Battered Gay Men."

230. Renzetti, "Building a second closet"; Ristock, "'And Justice for All?'"

231. Merrill and Wolfe, "Battered Gay Men."

232. Heer et al., "Developing services"; Renzetti, "Poverty of services."

233. Heer et al., "Developing services."

234. Ford et al., "Intimate Partner Violence Prevention," 845.

235. Renzetti, "Poverty of services."

236. Harvey et al., "Barriers faced."

237. Girshick, "Organizing."

238. Girshick, "Organizing"; Heer et al., "Developing services."

239. Donnelly, Cook, and Wilson, "Provision and Exclusion"; Ford et al., "Intimate Partner Violence Prevention"; Heer et al., "Developing services."

240. Cheung, Leung, and Tsui, "Asian male domestic violence"; Ciarlante and Fountain, *Why It Matters;* Ford et al., "Intimate Partner Violence Prevention"; GLBT Domestic Violence Coalition and Jane Doe Inc., "Shelter/housing needs"; Harvey et al., "Barriers faced"; Heer et al., "Developing services"; Hines and Douglas, "Reported availability"; Renzetti, "Poverty of services."

241. Rooney, "Evolution of services."

242. Faulkner, "Lesbian abuse"; Quinn, "Open minds open doors"; Ristock, "Cultural politics of abuse"; Stowers, "Different model."

243. Holmes, "Destabilizing homonormativity"; J. M. Price, *Structural Violence*.

244. Renzetti, "Building a second closet"; Simpson and Helfrich, "Lesbian survivors."

245. Grant, Mottet, and Tanis, "Injustice at Every Turn."

246. Simpson and Helfrich, "Lesbian survivors," 53.

247. Simpson and Helfrich, "Lesbian survivors."

248. Giorgio, "Speaking silence," 1239.

249. GLBT Domestic Violence Coalition and Jane Doe Inc., "Shelter/housing needs," 14.

250. Alhusen, Lucea, and Glass, "Perceptions of and Experience"; Bornstein et al., "Understanding the experiences"; GLBTDVC, "Shelter/housing needs," 19; Quinn, "Open minds open doors."

251. GLBT Domestic Violence Coalition and Jane Doe Inc., "Shelter/housing needs", 19.

252. Quinn, "Open minds open doors," 9.

253. Simpson and Helfrich, "Lesbian survivors."

254. Donnelly, Cook, and Wilson, "Provision and Exclusion"; Simpson and Helfrich, "Lesbian survivors."

255. Alhusen, Lucea, and Glass, "Perceptions of and Experience," 9.

256. Ristock, "Cultural politics of abuse," 291.

257. Bordeleau and O'Brien, "Violence conjugale"; Burczycka and Cotter, "Shelters for abused women"; Ristock and Timbang, "Relationship violence"; Strickler and Drew, "Starting, Sustaining LGBTQ Antiviolence."

258. T. W. Burke, "Male-to-male gay domestic violence"; Heer et al., "Developing services"; Quinn, "Open minds open doors"; Renzetti, "Poverty of services."

259. Quinn, "Open minds open doors."

260. Quinn, "Open minds open doors."

261. Girshick, "Organizing."

262. Girshick, "Organizing," 91.

263. Giorgio, "Speaking silence," 1240; Helfrich and Simpson, "Improving services"; Quinn, "Open minds open doors"; Simpson and Helfrich, "Lesbian survivors"; VanNatta, "Constructing the battered woman."

264. Hammond, "Lesbian victims."

265. Quinn, "Open minds open doors."

266. Quinn, "Open minds open doors."

267. Ristock, "Cultural politics of abuse."

268. Simpson and Helfrich, "Lesbian survivors."

269. Simpson and Helfrich, "Lesbian survivors," 50.

270. Ford et al., "Intimate Partner Violence Prevention"; Senseman, "Screening for intimate violence."

271. Ard and Makadon, "Addressing intimate partner violence"; Chen, Jacobs, and Rovi, "Intimate partner violence"; Fern, "Domestic Violence."

272. Alhusen, Lucea, and Glass, "Perceptions of and Experience"; Chen, Jacobs, and Rovi, "Intimate partner violence"; Freedberg, "Health Care Barriers"; GLBT Domestic Violence Coalition and Jane Doe Inc., "Shelter/housing needs"; Murray et al., "Same-sex

intimate partner violence"; Relf, "Battering and HIV"; Ristock, "Cultural politics of abuse"; Senseman, "Screening for intimate violence"; Simpson and Helfrich, "Lesbian survivors"; St. Pierre and Senn, "External barriers to help-seeking"; Turell and Herrmann, "Family' support," 219; Warrier et al., "'Culturally Competent Responses'"; C. M. West, "Lesbian intimate partner violence."

273. Turell and Herrmann, "Family' support," 219.

274. Ard and Makadon, "Addressing intimate partner violence"; Fern, "Domestic Violence"; Murray et al., "Same-sex intimate partner violence"; Quinn, "Open minds open doors."

275. Giorgio, "Speaking silence"; Perez-Darby, "Secret joy of accountability"; Quinn, "Open minds open doors"; Scherzer, "Domestic violence, lesbian relationships"; Simpson and Helfrich, "Lesbian survivors."

276. Giorgio, "Speaking silence," 1248.

277. Bornstein et al., "Understanding the experiences."

278. Quinn, "Open minds open doors," 48.

279. Ard and Makadon, "Addressing intimate partner violence"; Christine Browning, Reynolds, and Dworkin, "Affirmative psychotherapy"; Hanson, "Violence we face"; Horne and Hamilton, "Bisexuality and broken relationships"; Klinger, "Gay violence"; McClennen and Gunther, *Professional's Guide to Understanding;* Morrow and Hawxhurst, "Lesbian partner abuse"; Matthews and Lorah, "Domestic Violence in Same-Sex"; Murray et al., "Same-sex intimate partner violence"; Peterman and Dixon, "Domestic violence between same-sex"; Robinson, "There's a stranger"; C. M. West, "Leaving a second closet."

280. Quinn, "Open minds open doors."

281. GLBT Domestic Violence Coalition and Jane Doe Inc., "Shelter/housing needs."

282. Banks and Fedewa, "Counselors' Attitudes"; Peterman and Dixon, "Domestic violence between same-sex."

283. Farley, "Establishing a safety plan"; FORGE, "Safety planning"; Peterman and Dixon, "Domestic violence between same-sex"; Quinn, "Open minds open doors," 48–49.

284. Farley, "Establishing a safety plan"; FORGE, "Safety planning."

285. Chen, Jacobs, and Rovi, "Intimate partner violence"; Fern, "Domestic Violence."

286. Rachel Lanzerotti Consulting, "2005–06 Youth Relationship Violence"; Renzetti, "Building a second closet"; Ristock, "'And Justice for All?'"; Roch, Ritchie, and Morton, "Out of sight"; St. Pierre and Senn, "External barriers to help-seeking"; Turell, "Seeking help."

287. Ciarlante and Fountain, *Why It Matters.*

288. Kay and Jeffries, "Homophobia, heteronormativism."

289. Quinn, "Open minds open doors"; Simpson and Helfrich, "Oppression and barriers."

290. Quinn, "Open minds open doors."

291. Mendez, "Serving gays and lesbians"; Simpson and Helfrich, "Oppression and barriers"; Waldron, "Lesbians of color."

292. Levy and Lobel, "Lesbian teens."

293. Quinn, "Open minds open doors"; Ristock, "Cultural politics of abuse."

294. Renzetti, "Building a second closet"; Simpson and Helfrich, "Lesbian survivors."

295. Quinn, "Open minds open doors."

296. Quinn, "Open minds open doors."

297. Quinn, "Open minds open doors."

298. Alhusen, Lucea, and Glass, "Perceptions of and Experience"; Bornstein et al., "Understanding the experiences"; GLBT Domestic Violence Coalition and Jane Doe Inc., "Shelter/housing needs", 19; Quinn, "Open minds open doors"; Renzetti, "Building a second closet"; Simpson and Helfrich, "Lesbian survivors."

299. Quinn, "Open minds open doors."

300. Quinn, "Open minds open doors."

301. Helfrich and Simpson, "Improving services"; Quinn, "Open minds open doors."

302. Ford et al., "Intimate Partner Violence Prevention."

303. Quinn, "Open minds open doors."

304. U.S. Government Printing Office, "113th Congress Public Law"; U.S. Department of Justice, "Frequently Asked Questions."

305. GLBT Domestic Violence Coalition and Jane Doe Inc., "Shelter/housing needs."

306. Duffy, "There's no pride"; Durish, "Documenting."

6. HOW CAN WE IMPROVE GOVERNMENT RESPONSES?

1. Alhusen, Lucea, and Glass, "Perceptions of and Experience," 11.

2. GLBT Domestic Violence Coalition and Jane Doe Inc., "Shelter/housing needs," 17.

3. Ventura and Davis, "Domestic violence court case."

4. Perez-Darby, "Secret joy of accountability."

5. Serra, "Queering International Human Rights."

6. Knauer, "Same-sex domestic violence."

7. Stapel, "Falling to pieces."

8. Stapel, "Falling to pieces."

9. Aulivola, "Outing Domestic Violence."

10. Aulivola, "Outing Domestic Violence."

11. Aulivola, "Outing Domestic Violence."

12. Aulivola, "Outing Domestic Violence."

13. A. West, "Prosecutorial activism."

14. Aulivola, "Outing Domestic Violence."

15. Franklin, "Closet Becomes Darker"; Goodmark, "Transgender people"; Jablow, "Victims of abuse"; Lundy, "Abuse that dare not"; Robson, "Lavender Bruises"; Robson, *Lesbian (Out) Law*; Murphy, "Queer justice"; Vickers, "Second closet."

16. Itaborahy and Zhu, *State-Sponsored Homophobia*.

17. United Kingdom Office of Public Sector Information, "Homosexual Offences."

18. Aulivola, "Outing Domestic Violence"; Pfeifer, "Out of the Shadows."

19. Associated Press, "12 states."

20. Itaborahy and Zhu, *State-Sponsored Homophobia*.

21. Trans Respect Versus Transphobia Worldwide, *Legal and Social Mapping*.

22. Turell and Herrmann, "'Family' support."

23. Human Rights Campaign, "Maps of State Laws."

24. Global Action for Trans Equality, "Gender Identity."

25. GLBT Domestic Violence Coalition and Jane Doe Inc., "Shelter/housing needs"; Quinn, "Open minds open doors."

26. Poirier, "Same-sex couples, 'exclusive commitment."

27. Masci, Sciupac, and Lipka, "Gay Marriage Around World."

28. Goodmark, "Transgender people."

29. National Coalition of Anti-Violence Programs, *Annual Report*.

30. da Luz, "Legal and Social Comparison."

31. WomensLaw.org, "Know the laws."

32. Girshick, "No Sugar, No Spice."

33. Collins, "Same-Sex Domestic Violence."

34. Serra, "Queering International Human Rights."

35. Serra, "Queering International Human Rights."

36. Bendery, "Violence Against Women Act."

37. Kapai, "Same Difference."

38. S. Little, "Challenging changing legal definitions," 259; Lorden, "Law of Unintended Consequences."

39. S. Little, "Challenging changing legal definitions," 259.

40. Collins, "Same-Sex Domestic Violence."

41. S. Little, "Challenging changing legal definitions"; Richardson v Easterling, 878 A2d 1212–16 (DC Cir 2005).

42. Hodges, "Trouble in Paradise"; S. Little, "Challenging changing legal definitions"; Lorden, "Law of Unintended Consequences."

43. Collins, "Same-Sex Domestic Violence."

44. Samons, "Same-Sex Domestic Violence."

45. Break the Cycle, "2010 State Law Report."

46. Home Office and Browne, "Extended definition."

47. Guadalupe-Diaz and Yglesias, "'Who's Protected?'"; Naidu and Mkhize, "Gender-based violence."

48. Naidu and Mkhize, "Gender-based violence."

49. Giorgio, "Speaking silence," 1240.

50. Stapel, "Falling to pieces."

51. Hunter, "Homosexuals as new class"; Stapel, "Falling to pieces."

52. Itaborahy and Zhu, *State-Sponsored Homophobia.*

53. Hunter, "Homosexuals as new class."

54. Stapel, "Falling to pieces," 276.

55. DeJong, Burgess-Proctor, and Elis, "Police officer perceptions," 695.

56. Walters, "Straighten Up," 261.

57. VanNatta, "Constructing the battered woman," 427.

58. National Coalition of Anti-Violence Programs, *Lesbian, Gay, in 2013.*

59. Bernstein and Kostelac, "Lavender and Blue."

60. Alhusen, Lucea, and Glass, "Perceptions of and Experience"; Amnesty International, "Stonewalled"; Blaney, "Police officers' views "; Glass et al., "Female-Perpetrated Femicide"; GLBT Domestic Violence Coalition and Jane Doe Inc., "Shelter/housing needs"; Ristock, "'And Justice for All?'"; Vidas, "Childhood sexual abuse"; Walters, "Straighten Up."

61. Younglove, Kerr, and Vitello, "Law Enforcement Officers' Perceptions."

62. McMullan, Carlan, and Nored, "Future law enforcement officers."

63. Alhusen, Lucea, and Glass, "Perceptions of and Experience."

64. Watkins, "Police perspective."

65. Chesley, MacAulay, and Ristock, *Abuse in Lesbian Relationships;* Henderson, "Prevalence of domestic violence"; Leonard et al., *Coming Forward;* Rachel Lanzerotti Consulting, "2005–06 Youth Relationship Violence"; Renzetti, "Building a second closet"; Ristock, "'And Justice for All?'"; St. Pierre and Senn, "External barriers to help-seeking"; Turell, "Seeking help."

66. Langenderfer-Magruder et al., "Experiences of Intimate Partner."

67. Alhusen, Lucea, and Glass, "Perceptions of and Experience"; Catherine Browning, "Silence"; T. W. Burke, Jordan, and Owen, "A cross-national comparison"; Finneran and Stephenson, "Gay and bisexual men's"; Goodmark, "Transgender people."

68. Hunt and Fish, "Prescription for change"; McClennen, Summers, and Vaughan, "Gay men's domestic violence"; Merrill and Wolfe, "Battered Gay Men"; Renzetti, "Building a second closet"; Ristock, "'And Justice for All?'"

69. Bernstein and Kostelac, "Lavender and Blue."

70. Pyles and Kim, "Multilevel approach."

71. Bernstein and Kostelac, "Lavender and Blue."

72. National Coalition of Anti-Violence Programs, *Lesbian, Gay, in 2013.*

73. National Coalition of Anti-Violence Programs, *Lesbian, Gay, in 2013.*

74. Alhusen, Lucea, and Glass, "Perceptions of and Experience"; Amnesty International, "Stonewalled"; DeJong, Burgess-Proctor, and Elis, "Police officer perceptions"; GLBT Domestic Violence Coalition and Jane Doe Inc., "Shelter/housing needs"; Renzetti, "Building a second closet"; Walters, "Straighten Up," 261.

75. Alhusen, Lucea, and Glass, "Perceptions of and Experience," 6.

76. DeJong, Burgess-Proctor, and Elis, "Police officer perceptions," 695.

77. Renzetti, "Building a second closet," 160.

78. Amnesty International, "Stonewalled," 84.

79. Walters, "Straighten Up," 261.

80. Amnesty International, "Stonewalled," 84.

81. Amnesty International, "Stonewalled," 87.

82. Renzetti, "Building a second closet."

83. Alhusen, Lucea, and Glass, "Perceptions of and Experience," 10

84. Stapel, "Falling to pieces."

85. A. West, "Prosecutorial activism."

86. National Coalition of Anti-Violence Programs, *Lesbian, Gay, in 2013.*

87. Leonard et al., *Coming Forward.*

88. Hirschel et al., "Explaining the prevalence"; Pattavina et al., "Comparison of police response."

89. Lipsky et al., "Impact of sexual orientation."

90. Jasinski and Mustaine, "Police response."

91. Chaffin, Chenoweth, and Letourneau, "Same-sex and race-based disparities."

92. Aulivola, "Outing Domestic Violence"; Klein and Orloff, "Protecting battered women."

93. Hirschel et al., "Explaining the prevalence."

94. Stanley et al., "Intimate violence."

95. Lie et al., "Lesbians in currently aggressive."

96. Archer, "Sex differences in aggression"; Straus, "Dominance and symmetry."

97. Carvalho et al., "Internalized sexual minority stressors"; Lie and Gentlewarrier, "Intimate violence in lesbian"; Renzetti, *Violent Betrayal*.

98. National Coalition of Anti-Violence Programs, *Lesbian, Gay, in 2013*.

99. National Coalition of Anti-Violence Programs, *Lesbian, Gay, in 2013*.

100. Goodmark, "Transgender people," 76.

101. Alhusen, Lucea, and Glass, "Perceptions of and Experience"; Giorgio, "Speaking silence"; Hassouneh and Glass, "Influence of Gender-Role Stereotyping."

102. Amnesty International, "Stonewalled."

103. Westbrook and Finn, "Community information."

104. Leonard et al., *Coming Forward*.

105. GLBT Domestic Violence Coalition and Jane Doe Inc., "Shelter/housing needs."

106. Tesch et al., "Same-sex domestic violence."

107. Alhusen, Lucea, and Glass, "Perceptions of and Experience."

108. C. M. West, "Lesbian intimate partner violence."

109. Kaplan and Colbs, "Shattered Pride"; C. M. West, "Lesbian intimate partner violence."

110. Rose, "Community interventions."

111. Amnesty International, "Stonewalled."

112. Tesch et al., "Same-sex domestic violence."

113. Amnesty International, "Stonewalled"; Tesch et al., "Same-sex domestic violence."

114. GLBT Domestic Violence Coalition and Jane Doe Inc., "Shelter/housing needs," 38.

115. Hunt and Fish, "Prescription for change"; Leonard et al., *Coming Forward*; Renzetti, "Building a second closet"; Ristock, "'And Justice for All?'"; St. Pierre and Senn, "External barriers to help-seeking"; Turell, "Seeking help."

116. McClennen, Summers, and Vaughan, "Gay men's domestic violence"; Renzetti, "Building a second closet"; Ristock, "'And Justice for All?'"

117. Goodmark, "Transgender people."

118. Lundy, "Equal Protection/Equal Safety," 43.

119. Goodmark, "Transgender people."

120. Poorman, Seelau, and Seelau, "Perceptions of Domestic Abuse."

121. Duthu, "Why doesn't anyone."

122. GLBT Domestic Violence Coalition and Jane Doe Inc., "Shelter/housing needs."

123. Alhusen, Lucea, and Glass, "Perceptions of and Experience"; Goodmark, "Transgender people."

124. Alhusen, Lucea, and Glass, "Perceptions of and Experience," 10.

125. Lundy, "Abuse that dare not," 273.

126. J. M. Price, *Structural Violence*.

127. Goodmark, "Transgender people."

128. Lynn, "Tool for attorneys."

129. Goodmark, "Transgender people."

130. Harada, "Comment."

131. Lazarus-Black, "Politics of place."

132. Goodmark, "Transgender people"; Ristock, "'And Justice for All?'"

133. Ristock, "'And Justice for All?'"

134. Goodmark, "Transgender people."

135. Goodmark, "Transgender people."

136. Goodmark, "Transgender people," 81.

137. Goodmark, "Transgender people."

138. Bricker, "Fatal defense"; Dupps, "Battered Lesbians"; M. Eaton, "Abuse by Any Other"; Ferraro, "Words Change"; Pertnoy, "Same Violence, Same Sex"; A. West, "Prosecutorial activism."

139. M. Eaton, "Abuse by Any Other"; Pertnoy, "Same Violence, Same Sex."

140. A. West, "Prosecutorial activism."

141. Bricker, "Fatal defense"; da Luz, "Legal and Social Comparison"; Dupps, "Battered Lesbians"; M. Eaton, "Abuse by Any Other"; Pertnoy, "Same Violence, Same Sex"; A. West, "Prosecutorial activism."

142. Pertnoy, "Same Violence, Same Sex."

143. Russell, Ragatz, and Kraus, "Does ambivalent sexism"; Russell, Ragatz, and Kraus, "Self-defense."

144. Hamberger, "Intervention in gay male."

145. Aulivola, "Outing Domestic Violence"; Klein and Orloff, "Protecting battered women."

146. Hirschel et al., "Explaining the prevalence."

147. Aulivola, "Outing Domestic Violence"; Klein and Orloff, "Protecting battered women."

148. Giorgio, "Speaking silence," 1242.

149. Sorenson and Shen, "Restraining Orders in California."

150. Duthu, "Why doesn't anyone"; Ristock, "'And Justice for All?'"

151. De Grace and Clarke, "Promising practices"; Leen et al., "Prevalence, dynamic risk factors"; Whitaker et al., "Critical review of interventions."

152. Alhusen, Lucea, and Glass, "Perceptions of and Experience"; Murray et al., "Same-sex intimate partner violence."

153. Potter, Fountain, and Stapleton, "Addressing sexual and relationship."

154. Holmes, "Troubling normalcy."

155. Bornstein et al., "Understanding the experiences"; Gillum and DiFulvio, "'There's So Much.'"

156. LGBT Youth Scotland, "Voices Unheard."

157. Kaplan and Colbs, "Shattered Pride"; Potter, Fountain, and Stapleton, "Addressing sexual and relationship."

158. Kaplan and Colbs, "Shattered Pride."

159. Ventura and Davis, "Domestic violence court case."

160. Chung and Lee, "Raising our voices"; Poorman and Seelau, "Lesbians who abuse."

161. Farley, "Tool for batterers."

162. Margolies and Leeder, "Violence at the Door."

163. Babcock et al., "Does batterers' treatment work?"

164. Babcock et al., "Does batterers' treatment work?"

165. Cannon and Buttell, "Illusion of inclusion"; K. Davis and Glass, "Reframing the Heteronormative Constructions."

166. Austin and Dankwort, "Standards for batterer programs."

167. Austin and Dankwort, "Standards for batterer programs."

168. Kernsmith and Kernsmith, "Treating female perpetrators."

169. B. J. Price and Rosenbaum, "Batterer intervention programs."

170. Austin and Dankwort, "Standards for batterer programs."

171. Donovan, Barnes, and Nixon, "Coral Project."

172. Maiuro and Eberle, "State standards."

173. Commonwealth of Massachusetts, "Pilot Program Specifications"; Mendoza and Dolan-Soto, "Running Same-Sex Batterer Groups."

174. Alhusen, Lucea, and Glass, "Perceptions of and Experience"; Murray et al., "Same-sex intimate partner violence."

175. Serra, "Queering International Human Rights."

7. CONCLUSIONS

1. Dulani, "Revolution Starts at Home," 14.

2. Barnett, Lee, and Thelen, "Gender differences"; Cascardi and Vivian, "Context for specific episodes"; DeKeseredy, "Future directions"; Hamberger, Lohr, and Bonge, "Intended function"; Kimmel, "'Gender Symmetry'"; Makepeace, "Gender differences in courtship"; Walters, Chen, and Breiding, *National Intimate Partner Survey.*

3. Ansara, "Exploring the patterns"; Barrett and St. Pierre, "Intimate partner violence"; Porter and Williams, "Intimate violence among underrepresented"; Walters, Chen, and Breiding, *National Intimate Partner Survey.*

4. Ansara, "Exploring the patterns"; Messinger, "Invisible victims"; K. A. McLaughlin et al., "Disproportionate exposure to early-life"; Porter and Williams, "Intimate violence among underrepresented"; Walters, Chen, and Breiding, *National Intimate Partner Survey.*

5. Brand and Kidd, "Frequency of physical aggression"; Dank et al., "Dating violence experiences"; L. A. Eaton et al., "Men who report"; Freedner et al., "Dating violence"; Reuter, Sharp, and Temple, "Exploratory study"; Zweig et al., *Technology, Teen Dating Violence.*

6. National Coalition of Anti-Violence Programs, *Lesbian, Gay, in 2013;* Nemoto, Bödeker, and Iwamoto, "Social support, exposure"; Pitts et al., *Private Lives;* Roch, Ritchie, and Morton, "Out of sight"; Scottish Transgender Alliance, "Transgender Experiences in Scotland"; Turell, "Descriptive analysis."

7. Alhusen, Lucea, and Glass, "Perceptions of and Experience," 8; Balsam, "Nowhere to Hide," 34; Blenman, "Hand That Hits."

8. Dragiewicz and DeKeseredy, "Claims about Women's Use"; Erbaugh, "Queering approaches"; Howe, *Sex, Violence and Crime;* Ristock, "Decentering heterosexuality," 66.

9. Bailey, "Treatment of domestic violence"; Bouchard, "*Abused men*"; Christensen, "Balancing the Approach"; Coleman, "Lesbian battering"; Coleman, "Treating the Lesbian Batterer"; Collins, "Same-Sex Domestic Violence"; Cook, *Abused Men;* Dutton, "Patriarchy and wife assault"; Dutton, Nicholls, and Spidel, "Female perpetrators"; Easton, "Family Violence"; Frieze, "Female violence"; George, "Riding the donkey backwards"; Gillis and Diamond, "Same-sex partner abuse"; Gillis and Diamond, "Dynamics of partner abuse";

Hamberger, "Domestic partner abuse"; Hamel, "Toward a gender-inclusive conception"; Koller, "'Ecological fallacy'"; Letellier, "Gay and bisexual male"; Malinen, "Thinking Woman-to-Woman Rape"; T. Martin, "What about Violence"; Merrill, "Ruling the exceptions"; Migliaccio, "Abused husbands"; Schneider, "Particularity and generality"; Vidas, "Childhood sexual abuse"; Westover, "Include All Forms."

10. Ahmed, Aldén, and Hammarstedt, "Perceptions"; Russell, Chapleau, and Kraus, "When is it abuse?"; Seelau and Seelau, "Gender-Role Stereotypes"; Seelau, Seelau, and Poorman, "Gender and Role-Based Perceptions"; Poorman, Seelau, and Seelau, "Perceptions of Domestic Abuse."

11. Wise and Bowman, "Comparison of Beginning Counselors."

12. Basow and Thompson, "Service Providers' Reactions"; Michael J. Brown and Groscup, "Perceptions."

13. Renzetti, "Building a second closet"; Walters, "Straighten Up."

14. Amnesty International, "Stonewalled"; Davis and Taylor, "Voices from the margins"; GLBT Domestic Violence Coalition and Jane Doe Inc., "Shelter/housing needs", 38; Oswald, Fonseca, and Hardesty, "Lesbian Mothers' Counseling Experiences"; Simpson and Helfrich, "Lesbian survivors"; VanNatta, "Constructing the battered woman"; Walters, "Straighten Up," 261.

15. Leonard et al., *Coming Forward;* Merrill and Wolfe, "Battered Gay Men."

16. Catherine Browning, "Silence"; Leonard et al., *Coming Forward;* McDonald, "Social context"; Roch, Ritchie, and Morton, "Out of sight"; St. Pierre and Senn, "External barriers to help-seeking"; Turell and Herrmann, "'Family' support."

17. Cruz, "'Why Doesn't He'"; Goodmark, "Transgender people"; McDonald, "Social context."

18. Bornstein et al., "Understanding the experiences"; Cruz, "'Why Doesn't He'"; Gillum and DiFulvio, "'There's So Much'"; Girshick, *Woman-to-Woman Sexual Violence;* Hassouneh and Glass, "Influence of Gender-Role Stereotyping"; Island and Letellier, *Men Who Beat Men;* Merrill and Wolfe, "Battered Gay Men"; Patzel, "Lesbian partner abuse"; Walters, "Straighten Up."

19. Dulani, "Revolution Starts at Home."

20. Masci, Sciupac, and Lipka, "Gay Marriage around the World."

21. Itaborahy and Zhu, *State-Sponsored Homophobia.*

22. Itaborahy and Zhu, *State-Sponsored Homophobia;* Trans Respect Versus Transphobia Worldwide, "Legal and Social Mapping."

23. Ortega and Busch-Armendariz, "In the Name of VAWA," 226.

24. Alhusen, Lucea, and Glass, "Perceptions of and Experience," 7.

25. Alhusen, Lucea, and Glass, "Perceptions of and Experience"; Quinn, "Open minds open doors."

26. Girshick, "Organizing."

APPENDIX

1. Courvant and Cook-Daniels, "Trans and intersex survivors"; FORGE, "Transgender sexual violence project."

BIBLIOGRAPHY

Abdale, Frank. "HIV-related violence." *Body Positive* 12, no. 10 (1999): 16–20.

Ackerman, Jeff, and Layton Field. "The Gender Asymmetric Effect of Intimate Partner Violence on Relationship Satisfaction." *Violence and Victims* 26, no. 6 (2011): 703–724.

Ahmed, Ali M., Lina Aldén, and Mats Hammarstedt. "Perceptions of Gay, Lesbian, and Heterosexual Domestic Violence among Undergraduates in Sweden," *International Journal of Conflict and Violence* 7, no. 2 (2013): 249–260.

AIDS Council of New South Wales (ACON). "Homelessness and Same Sex Domestic Violence in the Supported Accommodation Assistance Program." Sydney: ACON, October 2004. http://ssdv.acon.org.au/storage/HomelessnessSSDVinSAAP.pdf.

Alexander, Christopher J. "Violence in Gay and Lesbian Relationships." *Journal of Gay and Lesbian Social Services* 14, no. 1 (2002): 95–98.

Alhusen, Jeanne L., Marguerite B. Lucea, and Nancy Glass. "Perceptions of and Experience with System Responses to Female Same-Sex Intimate Partner Violence." Author manuscript. NIH Public Access. http://www.ncbi.nlm.nih.gov/pmc/articles/PMC3027223/pdf/nihms264652.pdf.

Almeida, Rhea V., Rosemary Woods, Theresa Messineo, Roberto J. Font, and Chris Heer. "Violence in the Lives of the Racially and Sexually Different: A Public and Private Dilemma." *Journal of Feminist Family Therapy* 5, nos. 3–4 (1994): 99–126.

Alpert, Elaine J., David Shannon, Alisa Velonis, Maura Georges, and Rachel A. Rich. "Family Violence and Public Health Education: A Call for Action." *Violence against Women* 8, no. 6 (2002): 746–778.

American College Health Association. *National College Health Assessment*. 2003. www.acha-ncha.org/docs/samplesurvey_acha-ncha_sp00-sp08.pdf.

Amnesty International. "Stonewalled: Police abuse and misconduct against lesbian, gay, bisexual and transgender people in the US." 2005.

Anderson, Kristin L. "Theorizing gender in intimate partner violence research." *Sex Roles* 52, no. 11–12 (2005): 853–865.

Anderson, Kristin L., and Debra Umberson. "Gendering Violence: Masculinity and Power in Men's Accounts of Domestic Violence." *Gender and Society* 15, no. 3 (2001): 358–380.

Andrasik, Michele P., Sarah E. Valentine, and David W. Pantalone. "'Sometimes You Just Have to Have a Lot of Bitter to Make It Sweet': Substance Abuse and Partner Abuse in the Lives of HIV-Positive Men Who Have Sex with Men." *Journal of Gay and Lesbian Social Services* 25, no. 3 (2013): 287–305.

Ansara, Donna L. "Exploring the patterns of intimate partner violence in Canada: A latent class approach." PhD diss., Johns Hopkins University, 2009.

Archer, John. "Sex differences in aggression between heterosexual partners: A meta-analytic review." *Psychological Bulletin* 126, no. 5 (2000): 651–681.

Ard, Kevin L., and Harvey J. Makadon. "Addressing intimate partner violence in lesbian, gay, bisexual, and transgender patients." *Journal of General Internal Medicine* 26, no. 8 (2011): 930–933.

Associated Press. "12 states still ban sodomy a decade after court ruling." *USA Today,* 2014. www.usatoday.com/story/news/nation/2014/04/21/12-states-ban-sodomy-a-decade-after-court-ruling/7981025/.

Aulivola, Michelle. "Outing Domestic Violence." *Family Court Review* 42, no. 1 (2004): 162–177.

Austin, Juliet B., and Juergen Dankwort. "Standards for batterer programs: A review and analysis." *Journal of Interpersonal Violence* 14, no. 2 (1999): 152–168.

Babcock, Julia C., Charles E. Green, and Chet Robie. "Does batterers' treatment work? A meta-analytic review of domestic violence treatment." *Clinical Psychology Review* 23, no. 8 (2004): 1023–1053.

Babcock, Julia C., Sarah A. Miller, and Cheryl Siard. "Toward a typology of abusive women: Differences between partner-only and generally violent women in the use of violence." *Psychology of Women Quarterly* 27, no. 2 (2003): 153–161.

Badenes-Ribera, Laura, Dolores Frias-Navarro, Amparo Bonilla-Campos, Gemma Pons-Salvador, and Hector Monterde-i-Bort. "Intimate partner violence in self-identified lesbians: A meta-analysis of its prevalence." *Sexuality Research and Social Policy* 12, no. 1 (2015): 47–59.

Bailey, G. R. "Treatment of domestic violence in gay and lesbian relationships." *Journal of Psychological Practice* 2, no. 2 (1996): 1–8.

Baker, Nancy L., Jessica D. Buick, Shari R. Kim, Sandy Moniz, and Khristina L. Nava. "Lessons from examining same-sex intimate partner violence." *Sex Roles* 69, nos. 3–4 (2013): 182–192.

Ball, Matthew J. "Gay men, intimate partner violence, and help-seeking: The incomprehensibility of being a victim." In *Queering Paradigms II: Interrogating Agendas,* edited by Burkhard Scherer and Matthew Ball, 313–330. Bern, Switzerland: Peter Lang, 2011.

Ball, Matthew J., and Sharon L. Hayes. "Same-sex intimate partner violence: Exploring the parameters." *Queering Paradigms* (2010): 161–177.

Balsam, Kimberly F. "Nowhere to Hide: Lesbian Battering, Homophobia, and Minority Stress." *Women and Therapy* 23, no. 3 (2001): 25–37.

Balsam, Kimberly F., Esther D. Rothblum, and Theodore P. Beauchaine. "Victimization over the life span: A comparison of lesbian, gay, bisexual, and heterosexual siblings." *Journal of Consulting and Clinical Psychology* 73, no. 3 (2005): 477.

Balsam, Kimberly F., and Dawn M. Szymanski. "Relationship quality and domestic violence in women's same-sex relationships: The role of minority stress." *Psychology of Women Quarterly* 29, no. 3 (2005): 258–269.

Banks, Jamye R., and Alicia L. Fedewa. "Counselors' Attitudes toward Domestic Violence in Same-Sex versus Opposite-Sex Relationships." *Journal of Multicultural Counseling and Development* 40, no. 4 (2012): 194–205.

Barnes, Rebecca. "'I Still Sort of Flounder Around in a Sea of Non-Language': The Constraints of Language and Labels in Women's Accounts of Woman-to-Woman Partner Abuse." In *Gender and Interpersonal Violence*, edited by Karen Throsby and Flora Alexander, 29–43. London: Palgrave Macmillan, 2008.

———. "'I'm Over It': Survivor Narratives after Woman-to-Woman Partner Abuse." *Partner Abuse* 4, no. 3 (2013): 380–398.

———. "'She Expected Her Women to be Pretty, Subservient, Dinner on the Table at Six': Problematising the Narrative of Egalitarianism in Lesbian Relationships through Accounts of Woman-to-Woman Partner Abuse." In *Mapping Intimacies: Relations, Exchanges, Affects*, edited by Tam Sanger and Yvette Taylor, 130–149. London: Palgrave Macmillan, 2013.

———. "'Suffering in a Silent Vacuum': Woman-to-Woman Partner Abuse as a Challenge to the Lesbian Feminist Vision." *Feminism and Psychology* 21, no. 2 (2011): 233–239.

Barnett, Ola W., Cheok Y. Lee, and Rose E. Thelen. "Gender differences in attributions of self-defense and control in interpartner aggression." *Violence against Women* 3, no. 5 (1997): 462–481.

Barrett, Betty Jo, and Melissa St. Pierre. "Intimate partner violence reported by lesbian-, gay-, and bisexual-identified individuals living in Canada: An exploration of within-group variations." *Journal of Gay and Lesbian Social Services* 25, no. 1 (2013): 1–23.

Barter, Christine. "In the name of love: Partner abuse and violence in teenage relationships." *British Journal of Social Work* 39, no. 2 (2009): 211–233.

Bartholomew, Kim, Katherine V. Regan, Doug Oram, and Monica A. White. "Correlates of partner abuse in male same-sex relationships." *Violence and Victims* 23, no. 3 (2008): 344–360.

Bartholomew, Kim, Katherine V. Regan, Monica A. White, and Doug Oram. "Patterns of abuse in male same-sex relationships." *Violence and victims* 23, no. 5 (2008): 617–636.

Basow, Susan A., and Janelle Thompson. "Service Providers' Reactions to Intimate Partner Violence as a Function of Victim Sexual Orientation and Type of Abuse." *Journal of Interpersonal Violence* 27, no. 7 (2012): 1225–1241.

Bendery, Jennifer. "Violence against Women Act Shouldn't Cover Same-Sex Couples, GOP Congresswoman Says." *Huffington Post*, 2012. www.huffingtonpost.com/2012/05/14/violence-against-women-act-same-sex-couples_n_1516281.html.

Bennhold, Katrin. "Is It Rape? It Depends on Who Is Asking." *New York Times*, 2010. www.nytimes.com/2010/12/29/world/europe/29iht-letter29.html?_r = 0.

Bernhard, Linda A. "Physical and sexual violence experienced by lesbian and heterosexual women." *Violence against Women* 6, no. 1 (2000): 68–79.

Bernstein, Mary, and Constance Kostelac. "Lavender and Blue: Attitudes about Homosexuality and Behavior toward Lesbians and Gay Men among Police Officers." *Journal of Contemporary Criminal Justice* 18, no. 3 (2002): 302–328.

Bimbi, David S., Nancy A. Palmadessa, and Jeffrey T. Parsons. "Substance use and domestic violence among urban gays, lesbians and bisexuals." *Journal of LGBT Health Research* 3, no. 2 (2008): 1–7.

Blair, Johnny. "A probability sample of gay urban males: The use of two-phase adaptive sampling." *Journal of Sex Research* 36, no. 1 (1999): 39–44.

Blaney, Elizabeth. "Police officers' views of specialized intimate partner violence training." *Policing: An International Journal of Police Strategies and Management* 33, no. 2 (2010): 354–375.

Blasko, Kelly A. "Prototypical Assessment of Same-Sex and Opposite-Sex Intimate Partner Violence Using a Control-Based Typology." Ph. D. diss., College of Education, Pennsylvania State University, 2008.

Blasko, Kelly A., Jon L. Winek, and Kathleen J. Bieschke. "Therapists' Prototypical Assessment of Domestic Violence Situations." *Journal of Marital and Family Therapy* 33, no. 2 (2007): 258–269.

Bledsoe, Linda K., and Bibhuti K. Sar. "Intimate partner violence control scale: Development and initial testing." *Journal of Family Violence* 26, no. 3 (2011): 171–184.

Blenman, Adrienne. "The Hand That Hits Is Not Always Male." *Canadian Woman Studies* 11, no. 4 (1991): 60–62.

Block, Carolyn Rebecca, and Antigone Christakos. "Intimate partner homicide in Chicago over 29 years." *Crime and Delinquency* 41, no. 4 (1995): 496–526.

Blosnich, John, and Robert Bossarte. "Comparisons of Intimate Partner Violence among Partners in Same-Sex and Opposite-Sex Relationships in the United States." *Research and Practice* 99, no. 12 (2009): 2182–2184.

———. "Drivers of disparity: Differences in socially based risk factors of self-injurious and suicidal behaviors among sexual minority college students." *Journal of American College Health* 60, no. 2 (2012): 141–149.

Boehmer, Ulrike. "Twenty years of public health research: Inclusion of lesbian, gay, bisexual, and transgender populations." *American Journal of Public Health* 92, no. 7 (2002): 1125–1130.

Bogart, Laura M., Rebecca L. Collins, William Cunningham, Robin Beckman, Daniela Golinelli, David Eisenman, and Chloe E. Bird. "The association of partner abuse with risky sexual behaviors among women and men with HIV/AIDS." *AIDS and Behavior* 9, no. 3 (2005): 325–333.

Bograd, Michele. "Strengthening domestic violence theories: Intersections of race, class, sexual orientation, and gender." *Journal of Marital and Family Therapy* 25, no. 3 (1999): 275–289.

Bordeleau, Suzie, and Karol O'Brien. "La violence conjugale chez les lesbiennes: L'expérience d'un groupe communautaire québécois." *Canadian Journal of Community Mental Health* 22, no. 2 (2009): 123–134.

Bornstein, Danica R., Jake Fawcett, Marianne Sullivan, Kirsten D. Senturia, and Sharyne Shiu-Thornton. "Understanding the experiences of lesbian, bisexual and trans survivors of domestic violence: A qualitative study." *Journal of Homosexuality* 51, no. 1 (2006): 159–181.

Bouchard, L. Jason. "*Abused Men: The Hidden Side of Domestic Violence,* by Philip W. Cook." *Everyman* 28 (1997): 52.

Bradford, Judith, Caitlin Ryan, and Esther D. Rothblum. "National Lesbian Health Care Survey: Implications for mental health care." *Journal of Consulting and Clinical Psychology* 62, no. 2 (1994): 228.

Brand, Pamela A., and Aline H. Kidd. "Frequency of physical aggression in heterosexual and female homosexual dyads." *Psychological Reports* 59, no. 3 (1986): 1307–1313.

Braun, Virginia, Johanna Schmidt, Nicola Gavey, and John Fenaughty. "Sexual coercion among gay and bisexual men in Aotearoa/New Zealand." *Journal of Homosexuality* 56, no. 3 (2009): 336–360.

Braun, Virginia, Gareth Terry, Nicola Gavey, and John Fenaughty. "'Risk' and sexual coercion among gay and bisexual men in Aotearoa/New Zealand: Key informant accounts." *Culture, Health and Sexuality* 11, no. 2 (2009): 111–124.

Break the Cycle. "2010 State Law Report Cards: A National Survey of Teen Dating Violence Laws." 2010. www.loveisrespect.org/sites/default/files/2010-State-Law-Report-Cards-Full-Report.pdf.

Brennan, Julia, Lisa M. Kuhns, Amy K. Johnson, Marvin Belzer, Erin C. Wilson, and Robert Garofalo. "Syndemic theory and HIV-related risk among young transgender women: The role of multiple, co-occurring health problems and social marginalization." *American Journal of Public Health* 102, no. 9 (2012): 1751–1757.

Bricker, Denise. "Fatal defense: An analysis of battered woman's syndrome expert testimony for gay men and lesbians who kill abusive partners." *Brooklyn Law Review* 58 (1992): 1379.

Brooks, Virginia R. *Minority Stress and Lesbian Women.* Lexington, MA: Lexington Books, 1981.

Brown, Michael J., and Jennifer Groscup. "Perceptions of Same-Sex Domestic Violence among Crisis Center Staff." *Journal of Family Violence* 24 (2009): 87–93.

Brown, Monique J., Julianne M. Serovich, and Judy A. Kimberly. "Depressive symptoms, substance use and partner violence victimization associated with HIV disclosure among men who have sex with men." *AIDS and Behavior* 20, no. 1 (2016): 184–192.

Brown, Nicola. "Holding tensions of victimization and perpetration: Partner abuse in trans communities." In *Intimate Partner Violence in LGBTQ Lives,* edited by Janice L. Ristock, 153–68. New York: Routledge, 2011.

———. "Stories from Outside the Frame: Intimate Partner Abuse in Sexual-Minority Women's Relationships with Transsexual Men." *Feminism and Psychology* 17, no. 3 (2007): 373–393.

Brown, Taylor N. T., and Jody L. Herman. "Intimate Partner Violence and Sexual Abuse among LGBT People." Los Angles: Williams Institute, 2015. http://williamsinstitute.law .ucla.edu/wp-content/uploads/Intimate-Partner-Violence-and-Sexual-Abuse-among-LGBT-People.pdf.

Browning, Catherine. "Silence on same-sex partner abuse." *Alternate Routes: A Journal of Critical Social Research* 12 (1995).

Browning, Christine, Amy L. Reynolds, and Sari H. Dworkin. "Affirmative psychotherapy for lesbian women." *Counseling Psychologist* 19, no. 2 (1991): 177–196.

Bucher, Jacob, and Michelle Manasse. "When screams are not released: A study of communication and consent in acquaintance rape situations." *Women and Criminal Justice* 21, no. 2 (2011): 123–140.

Bunge, Valerie Pottie. *National Trends in Intimate Partner Homicides, 1974–2000.* Ottawa: Canadian Centre for Justice Statistics, 2002.

Burczycka, Marta, and Adam Cotter. "Shelters for abused women in Canada, 2010." *Juristat* 31, no. 1 (2011).

Burk, Connie. "Think. Re-think: Accountable communities." In *The Revolution Starts at Home: Confronting Partner Abuse in Activist Communities,* edited by Ching-In Chen, Jai Dulani, and Leah Lakshmi Piepzna-Samarasinha, 264–279. Brooklyn, NY: South End Press, 2011.

Burke, Leslie K., and Diane R. Follingstad. "Violence in lesbian and gay relationships: Theory, prevalence, and correlational factors." *Clinical Psychology Review* 19, no. 5 (1999): 487–512.

Burke, Tod W. "Male-to-male gay domestic violence: The dark closet." *Violence in Intimate Relationships: Examining Sociological and Psychological Issues* (1998): 161–179.

Burke, Tod W., Michael L. Jordan, and Stephen S. Owen. "A cross-national comparison of gay and lesbian domestic violence." *Journal of Contemporary Criminal Justice* 18, no. 3 (2002): 231–257.

Butler, Judith. *Gender Trouble: Feminism and the Subversion of Identity.* New York: Routledge, 2010.

Calton, Jenna M., Lauren Bennett Cattaneo, and Kris T. Gebhard. "Barriers to help seeking for lesbian, gay, bisexual, transgender, and queer survivors of intimate partner violence." *Trauma, Violence, and Abuse* (2015): 1–16.

Cameron, Paul. "Domestic violence among homosexual partners." *Psychological Reports* 93, no. 2 (2003): 410–416.

Canadian Centre for Justice Statistics. "Family violence in Canada: A statistical profile, 2013." *Juristat* 34, no 1 (2015).

Cannon, C., and F. Buttell. "Illusion of inclusion: The failure of the gender paradigm to account for intimate partner violence in LGBT relationships." *Partner Abuse* 6, no. 1 (2015): 65–77.

Cannon, C., K. Lauve-Moon, and F. Buttell. "Re-Theorizing Intimate Partner Violence through Post-Structural Feminism, Queer Theory, and the Sociology of Gender." *Social Sciences* 4, no. 3 (2015): 668–687.

Cano, Annmarie, and Dina Vivian. "Life stressors and husband-to-wife violence." *Aggression and Violent behavior* 6, no. 5 (2001): 459–480.

Carlson, Bonnie E. "Questioning the party line on family violence." *Affilia* 7, no. 2 (1992): 94–110.

——. "Student Judgments about Dating Violence: A Factorial Vignette Analysis." *Research in Higher Education* 40, no. 2 (1999): 201–220.

Carvalho, Amana F., Robin J. Lewis, Valerian J. Derlega, Barbara A. Winstead, and Claudia Viggiano. "Internalized sexual minority stressors and same-sex intimate partner violence." *Journal of Family Violence* 26, no. 7 (2011): 501–509.

Cascardi, Michele, and Dina Vivian. "Context for specific episodes of marital violence: Gender and severity of violence differences." *Journal of Family Violence* 10, no. 3 (1995): 265–293.

Causby, Vickie, Lettie Lockhart, Barbara White, and Kathryn Greene. "Fusion and conflict resolution in lesbian relationships." *Journal of Gay and Lesbian Social Services* 3, no. 1 (1995): 67–82.

Centers for Disease Control. "Rates of diagnoses of HIV infection among adults and adolescents, by area of residence—United States." *HIV Surveillance Report* 23 (2011): 1–84.

Chaffin, Mark, Stephanie Chenoweth, and Elizabeth J. Letourneau. "Same-sex and race-based disparities in statutory rape arrests." *Journal of Interpersonal Violence* 31, no. 1 (2016): 26–48.

Chalabi, Mona, and John Burn-Murdoch. "McDonald's 34,492 Restaurants: Where Are They?" *Guardian*, 2013. www.theguardian.com/news/datablog/2013/jul/17/mcdonalds-restaurants-where-are-they.

Chan, Edward, and Chris Cavacuiti. "Gay abuse screening protocol (GASP): Screening for abuse in gay male relationships." *Journal of Homosexuality* 54, no. 4 (2008): 423–438.

Chen, Ping-Hsin, Abbie Jacobs, and Susan L. Rovi. "Intimate partner violence: IPV in the LGBT community." *FP Essentials* 412 (2013): 28–35.

Chesley, Laurie C., Donna MacAulay, and Janice Lynn Ristock. *Abuse in Lesbian Relationships: Information and Resources*. Edited by Cynthia Stewart. Ottawa: Health Canada, 1998.

Cheung, Monit, Patrick Leung, and Venus Tsui. "Asian male domestic violence victims: Services exclusive for men." *Journal of Family Violence* 24, no. 7 (2009): 447–462.

Cho, Hyunkag, and Dina J. Wilke. "Gender differences in the nature of the intimate partner violence and effects of perpetrator arrest on revictimization." *Journal of Family Violence* 25, no. 4 (2010): 393–400.

Chong, Eddie S. K., Winnie W. S. Mak, and Mabel M. F. Kwong. "Risk and protective factors of same-sex intimate partner violence in Hong Kong." *Journal of Interpersonal Violence* 28, no. 7 (2013): 1476–1497.

Choudhury, Prajna Paramita. "The violence that dares not speak its name: Invisibility in the lives of lesbian and bisexual South Asian American women." In *Body Evidence: Intimate Violence against South Asian Women in America*, edited by Shamita Das Dasgupta, 126–138. Piscataway, NJ: Rutgers University Press, 2007.

Christensen, Ferrel. "Balancing the Approach to Spouse Abuse." *Everyman* 1, no. 2 (1992): 4.

Chung, Cristy, and Summer Lee. "Raising our voices: Queer Asian women's response to relationship violence." San Francisco: Family Violence Prevention Fund, 1999. https://www.futureswithoutviolence.org/userfiles/file/ImmigrantWomen/Raising%20our%20Voices.pdf.

Ciarlante, Mitru, and Kim Fountain. *Why It Matters: Rethinking Victim Assistance for Lesbian, Gay, Bisexual, Transgender and Queer Victims of Hate Violence and Intimate Partner Violence*. Washington, DC: National Center for Victims of Crime; New York: National Coalition of Anti-Violence Programs, 2010.

Clements, Kristen, M. Katz, and R. Marx. "The transgender community health project: Descriptive results." San Francisco: San Francisco Department of Public Health, 1999. http://hivinsite.ucsf.edu/InSite?page=cftg-02-02.

Coker, Ann L., Paige H. Smith, Lesa Bethea, Melissa R. King, and Robert E. McKeown. "Physical health consequences of physical and psychological intimate partner violence." *Archives of Family Medicine* 9, no. 5 (2000): 451.

Coleman, Vallerie E. "Lesbian battering: The relationship between personality and the perpetration of violence." *Violence and Victims* 9, no. 2 (1994): 139–152.

———. "Treating the Lesbian Batterer: Theoretical and Clinical Considerations; A Contemporary Psychoanalytic Perspective." *Journal of Aggression, Maltreatment and Trauma* 7, nos. 1–2 (2003): 159–205.

Collins, Mary Beth D. "Same-Sex Domestic Violence: Addressing the Issues for the Proper Protection of Victims." *Journal of Law in Society* 4 (2002): 99.

Colm, Timothy. "Freedom and Strategy / Trauma and Resistance." In *The Revolution Starts at Home: Confronting Partner Abuse in Activist Communities,* edited by Ching-In Chen, Jai Dulani, and Leah Lakshmi Piepzna-Samarasinha, 174–184. Brooklyn, NY: South End Press, 2011.

Commonwealth of Massachusetts. "Pilot Program Specifications for Intervention with Gay, Lesbian, Bisexual and Transgender Perpetrators of Intimate Partner Violence." 1999. www.mass.gov/eohhs/docs/dph/com-health/violence/bi-guidelines-glbt.pdf.

Connell, Robert W. *Gender and Power.* Stanford, CA: Stanford University Press, 1987.

Cook, Philip W. *Abused Men: The Hidden Side of Domestic Violence.* Westport, CT: ABC-CLIO, 2009.

Cook-Daniels, Loree. "Intimate Partner Violence in Transgender Couples: 'Power and Control' in a Specific Cultural Context." *Partner Abuse* 6, no. 1 (2015): 126–139.

Cooper, Alexia, and Erica L. Smith. "Homicide trends in the United States, 1980–2008." Washington, DC: Bureau of Justice Statistics, 2011. www.bjs.gov/content/pub/pdf/htus8008.pdf.

Cornelius, Tara L., Ryan C. Shorey, and Stacy M. Beebe. "Self-reported communication variables and dating violence: Using Gottman's marital communication conceptualization." *Journal of Family Violence* 25, no. 4 (2010): 439–448.

Courvant, Diana, and Loree Cook-Daniels. "Trans and intersex survivors of domestic violence: Defining terms, barriers, and responsibilities." SurvivorProject.org, 1998. www.survivorproject.org/defbarresp.html.

Craft, Shonda M., and Julianne M. Serovich. "Family-of-origin factors and partner violence in the intimate relationships of gay men who are HIV positive." *Journal of Interpersonal Violence* 20, no. 7 (2005): 777–791.

Craft, Shonda M., Julianne M. Serovich, Patrick C. McKenry, and Ji-Young Lim. "Stress, attachment style, and partner violence among same-sex couples." *Journal of GLBT Family Studies* 4, no. 1 (2008): 57–73.

Crenshaw, Kimberle. "Mapping the Margins: Intersectionality, Identity Politics, and Violence against Women of Color." *Stanford Law Review* 43, no. 6 (1991): 1241–1299.

Cruz, J. Michael. "Gay male domestic violence and the pursuit of masculinity." *Gay Masculinities* 12 (2000): 66.

———. "'Why Doesn't He Just Leave?': Gay Male Domestic Violence and the Reasons Victims Stay." *Journal of Men's Studies* 11, no. 3 (2003): 309–323.

Cruz, J. Michael, and Juanita M. Firestone. "Exploring violence and abuse in gay male relationships." *Violence and Victims* 13, no. 2 (1998): 159–173.

Cruz, J. Michael, and Robert L. Peralta. "Family violence and substance use: The perceived effects of substance use within gay male relationships." *Violence and Victims* 16, no. 2 (2001): 161–172.

Cunradi, Carol B., Genevieve M. Ames, and Michael Duke. "The Relationship of Alcohol Problems to the Risk for Unidirectional and Bidirectional Intimate Partner Violence among a Sample of Blue-Collar Couples." *Violence and Victims* 26, no. 2 (2011): 147.

Cusack, Carmen, and Matthew Waranius. "Nonconsensual insemination and pornography: The relationship between sex roles, sex crimes, and STRT, Gay, and Shemale films on Youporn. com." *Journal of Research in Gender Studies* 2 (2012): 15.

da Luz, Carla M. "A Legal and Social Comparison of Heterosexual and Same-Sex Domestic Violence: Similar Inadequacies in Legal Recognition and Response." *Southern California Review of Law and Women's Studies* 4 (1994): 251–293.

Dank, Meredith, Pamela Lachman, Janine M. Zweig, and Jennifer Yahner. "Dating violence experiences of lesbian, gay, bisexual, and transgender youth." *Journal of Youth and Adolescence* 43, no. 5 (2014): 846–857.

Dauvergne, Mia. "Homicide in Canada, 2001." *Juristat* 22, no. 7 (2002).

David, Deborah Sarah, and Robert Brannon, eds. *The Forty-Nine Percent Majority: The Male Sex Role.* Reading, MA: Addison-Wesley, 1976.

Davis, Alissa, John Best, Chongyi Wei, Juhua Luo, Barbara Van Der Pol, Beth Meyerson, Brian Dodge, Matthew Aalsma, Joseph Tucker, and Social Entrepreneurship for Sexual Health Research Group. "Intimate Partner Violence and Correlates with Risk Behaviors and HIV/STI Diagnoses among Men Who Have Sex with Men and Men Who Have Sex with Men and Women in China: A Hidden Epidemic." *Sexually Transmitted Diseases* 42, no. 7 (2015): 387–392.

Davis, Kierrynn, and Nel Glass. "Reframing the Heteronormative Constructions of Lesbian Partner Violence." In *Intimate Partner Violence in LGBTQ Lives,* edited by Janice L. Ristock, 13–36. New York: Routledge, 2011.

Davis, Kierrynn, and Bev Taylor. "Voices from the margins: Mapping the narratives of rural lesbian domestic violence." Paper Presented at the "Expanding Our Horizons: Understanding the Complexities of Violence against Women" Conference, Sidney, Australia, 2002. http://citeseerx.ist.psu.edu/viewdoc/download?doi=10.1.1.542.508&rep=rep1&type=pdf.

De Grace, Alyssa, and Angela Clarke. "Promising practices in the prevention of intimate partner violence among adolescents." *Violence and Victims* 27, no. 6 (2012): 849–859.

DeJong, Christina, Amanda Burgess-Proctor, and Lori Elis. "Police officer perceptions of intimate partner violence: An analysis of observational data." *Violence and Victims* 23, no. 6 (2008): 683–696.

DeKeseredy, Walter S. "Future directions." *Violence against Women* 12, no. 11: 1078–1085.

DeKeseredy, Walter S., Daniel G. Saunders, Martin D. Schwartz, and Shahid Alvi. "The meanings and motives for women's use of violence in Canadian college dating relationships: Results from a national survey." *Sociological Spectrum* 17, no. 2 (1997): 199–222.

DeKeseredy, Walter S., and Martin D. Schwartz. "Measuring the extent of woman abuse in intimate heterosexual relationships: A critique of the Conflict Tactics Scales." Washington, DC: US Department of Justice, Violence against Women Grants Office Electronic Resources, 1998. www.vawnet.org/Assoc_Files_VAWnet/AR_ctscrit.pdf.

Descamps, Monica J., Esther Rothblum, Judith Bradford, and Caitlin Ryan. "Mental health impact of child sexual abuse, rape, intimate partner violence, and hate crimes in the National Lesbian Health Care Survey." *Journal of Gay and Lesbian Social Services* 11, no. 1 (2000): 27–55.

De Smet, Olivia, Kasia Uzieblo, Tom Loeys, Ann Buysse, and Thomas Onraedt. "Unwanted pursuit behavior after breakup: Occurrence, risk factors, and gender differences." *Journal of Family Violence* 30, no. 6 (2015): 753–767.

Diamond, Deborah L., and Sharon C. Wilsnack. "Alcohol abuse among lesbians: A descriptive study." *Journal of Homosexuality* 4, no. 2 (1979): 123–142.

Dietz, Christine. "Working with lesbian, gay, bisexual and transgendered abuse survivors." *Journal of Progressive Human Services* 12, no. 2 (2002): 27–49.

Dillman, Don A., Glenn Phelps, Robert Tortora, Karen Swift, Julie Kohrell, Jodi Berck, and Benjamin L. Messer. "Response rate and measurement differences in mixed-mode surveys using mail, telephone, interactive voice response (IVR) and the Internet." *Social Science Research* 38, no. 1 (2009): 1–18.

DiStefano, Anthony S. "Intimate partner violence among sexual minorities in Japan: Exploring perceptions and experiences." *Journal of Homosexuality* 56, no. 2 (2009): 121–146.

Dobash, R. Emerson, and Russell P. Dobash. *Women, Violence and Social Change.* Boston: Routledge, 2003.

Dolan-Soto, Diane R. "Lesbian, gay, transgender and bisexual (LGTB) domestic violence in New York City." New York: New York City Gay and Lesbian Anti-Violence Project, 2001. www.ncavp.org/common/document_files/Reports/1999nycdvrpt.pdf.

Donnelly, Denise A., Kimberly J. Cook, and Linda A. Wilson. "Provision and Exclusion: The Dual Face of Services to Battered Women in Three Deep South States." *Violence against Women* 5, no. 7 (1999): 710–741.

Donovan, Catherine. "Redefining domestic violence and abuse: unintended consequences of risk assessment." In *Constructing Risky Identities in Policy and Practice,* edited by Jeremy Kearney and Catherine Donovan, 109–126. London: Palgrave Macmillan, 2013.

———. "Tackling Inequality in the Intimate Sphere: Problematizing Love and Violence in Same-Sex Relationships." In *After Legal Equality: Family, Sex, and Kinship,* edited by Robert Leckey, 167–183. Oxford: Routledge, 2015.

Donovan, Catherine, Rebecca Barnes, and Catherine Nixon. "The Coral Project: Exploring Abusive Behaviours in Lesbian, Gay, Bisexual and/or Transgender Relationships Interim Report September 2014." Sunderland, England: University of Sunderland; Leicester, England: University of Leicester, 2014. http://thecoralproject.pbworks.com/w/file/fetch/86606782/Coral%20Project_Interim%20Report_Exec%20Summary_Final.pdf.

Donovan, Catherine, and Marianne Hester. "'Because she was my first girlfriend, I didn't know any different': Making the case for mainstreaming same-sex sex/relationship education." *Sex Education* 8, no. 3 (2008): 277–287.

———. *Domestic Violence and Sexuality: What's Love Got to Do with It?* Bristol, UK: Policy Press, 2015.

———. "Exploring emotion work in domestically abusive relationships." In *Intimate Partner Violence in LGBTQ Lives,* edited by Janice L. Ristock, 81–101. New York: Routledge, 2011.

———. "'I Hate the Word "Victim"': An Exploration of Recognition of Domestic Violence in Same Sex Relationships." *Social Policy and Society* 9, no. 2 (2010): 279–289.

———. "Seeking help from the enemy: Help-seeking strategies of those in same-sex relationships who have experienced domestic abuse." *Child and Family Law Quarterly* 23, no. 1 (2011): 26–40.

Donovan, Catherine, Marianne Hester, Jonathan Holmes, and Melanie McCarry. "Comparing domestic abuse in same sex and heterosexual relationships." Bristol, UK: University of Bristol, 2006. www.equation.org.uk/wp-content/uploads/2012/12/Comparing-Domestic-Abuse-in-Same-Sex-and-Heterosexual-relationships.pdf.

Douglas, Emily M., and Denise A. Hines. "The helpseeking experiences of men who sustain intimate partner violence: An overlooked population and implications for practice." *Journal of Family Violence* 26, no. 6 (2011): 473–485.

Dragiewicz, Molly, and Walter S. DeKeseredy. "Claims about Women's Use of Non-fatal Force in Intimate Relationships: A Contextual Review of Canadian Research." *Violence against Women* 18, no. 9 (2012): 1008–1026.

Drijber, Babette C., Udo J. L. Reijnders, and Manon Ceelen. "Male victims of domestic violence." *Journal of Family Violence* 28, no. 2 (2013): 173–178.

Duffy, Kate. "There's no pride in domestic violence: The Same Sex Domestic Violence Interagency, Sydney, Australia." In *Intimate Partner Violence in LGBTQ Lives*, edited by Janice L. Ristock, 258–273. New York: Routledge, 2011.

Duke, Alysondra, and M. Meghan Davidson. "Same-sex intimate partner violence: Lesbian, gay, and bisexual affirmative outreach and advocacy." *Journal of Aggression, Maltreatment and Trauma* 18, no. 8 (2009): 795–816.

Dulani, Jai. "The Revolution Starts at Home: Pushing through the Fear." In *The Revolution Starts at Home: Confronting Partner Abuse in Activist Communities*, edited by Ching-In Chen, Jai Dulani, and Leah Lakshmi Piepzna-Samarasinha, 10–14. Oakland, CA: zine, 2008.

Dunkle, Kristin L., Frank Y. Wong, Eric J. Nehl, Lavinia Lin, Na He, Jennifer Huang, and Tony Zheng. "Male-on-male intimate partner violence and sexual risk behaviors among money boys and other men who have sex with men in Shanghai, China." *Sexually Transmitted Diseases* 40, no. 5 (2013): 362–365.

Dupps, David S. "Battered Lesbians: Are They Entitled to a Battered Woman Defense." *Journal of Family Law* 29 (1990): 879.

Durish, Patricia. "Documenting the Same Sex Abuse Project, Toronto, Canada." In *Intimate Partner Violence in LGBTQ Lives*, edited by Janice L. Ristock, 232–257. New York: Routledge, 2011.

Durso, Laura E., and Gary J. Gates. "Serving Our Youth: Findings from a National Survey of Services Providers Working with Lesbian, Gay, Bisexual and Transgender Youth Who Are Homeless or at Risk of Becoming Homeless." Los Angeles: Williams Institute with True Colors Fund and The Palette Fund, 2012. http://williamsinstitute.law.ucla.edu/wp-content/uploads/Durso-Gates-LGBT-Homeless-Youth-Survey-July-2012.pdf.

Duthu, Kathleen Finley. "Why doesn't anyone talk about gay and lesbian domestic violence." *Thomas Jefferson Law Review* 18 (1996): 23.

Dutton, Donald G. "Patriarchy and wife assault: The ecological fallacy." *Violence and Victims* 9, no. 2 (1994): 167–182.

Dutton, Donald G., Tonia L. Nicholls, and Alicia Spidel. "Female perpetrators of intimate abuse." *Journal of Offender Rehabilitation* 41, no. 4 (2005): 1–31.

Dyer, Typhanye Penniman, Steve Shoptaw, Thomas E. Guadamuz, Michael Plankey, Uyen Kao, David Ostrow, Joan S. Chmiel, Amy Herrick, and Ron Stall. "Application of syndemic theory to black men who have sex with men in the Multicenter AIDS Cohort Study." *Journal of Urban Health* 89, no. 4 (2012): 697–708.

Easton, Steven. "Family Violence: What You Haven't Heard." *Everyman* 8 (1994): 4.

Eaton, Lisa A., Michelle Kaufman, Andrea Fuhrel, Demetria Cain, Charsey Cherry, Howard Pope, and Seth C. Kalichman. "Examining factors co-existing with interpersonal violence in lesbian relationships." *Journal of Family Violence* 23, no. 8 (2008): 697–705.

Eaton, Lisa A., Eileen V. Pitpitan, Seth C. Kalichman, Kathleen J. Sikkema, Donald Skinner, Melissa H. Watt, and Desiree Pieterse. "Men who report recent male and female sex partners in Cape Town, South Africa: An understudied and underserved population." *Archives of Sexual Behavior* 42, no. 7 (2013): 1299–1308.

Eaton, Mary. "Abuse by Any Other Name: Feminism." In *The Public Nature of Private Violence: The Discovery of Domestic Abuse,* edited by Martha A. Fineman and Roxanne Mykitiuk, 195–223. New York: Routledge, 1994.

Edwards, Katie M., and Kateryna M. Sylaska. "The perpetration of intimate partner violence among LGBTQ college youth: The role of minority stress." *Journal of Youth and Adolescence* 42, no. 11 (2013): 1721–1731.

Edwards, Katie M., Kateryna M. Sylaska, Johanna E. Barry, Mary M. Moynihan, Victoria L. Banyard, Ellen S. Cohn, Wendy A. Walsh, and Sally K. Ward. "Physical Dating Violence, Sexual Violence, and Unwanted Pursuit Victimization: A Comparison of Incidence Rates among Sexual-Minority and Heterosexual College Students." *Journal of Interpersonal Violence* 30, no. 4 (2015): 580–600.

Elliott, Pam. "Shattering illusions: Same-sex domestic violence." In *Violence in Gay and Lesbian Domestic Partnerships,* edited by Claire M. Renzetti and Charles Harvey Miley, 1–8. Binghampton, NY: Harrington Park Press, 1996.

Ellison, M. "Setting the captives free: Same sex domestic violence and the justice loving church." In *The Spirituality of Men: Sixteen Christians Write about Their Faith,* edited by Philip L. Culbertson, 145–162. Minneapolis: Fortress Press, 2002.

Ellsberg, Mary, and Lori Heise. *Researching Violence against Women: A Practical Guide for Researchers and Activists.* Washington, DC: World Health Organization, PATH, 2005.

Elze, Diane E. "Against all odds: The dating experiences of adolescent lesbian and bisexual women." *Journal of Lesbian Studies* 6, no. 1 (2002): 17–29.

Erbaugh, Elizabeth B. "Queering approaches to intimate partner violence." In *Gender Violence: Interdisciplinary Perspectives,* 2nd ed., edited by Laura L. O'Toole, Jessica R. Schiffman, and Margie L. Kiter Edwards, 451–459. New York: NYU Press, 2007.

Farley, Ned. "A survey of factors contributing to gay and lesbian domestic violence." *Journal of Gay and Lesbian Social Services* 4, no. 1 (1996): 35–42.

———. "Same-sex domestic violence: Establishing a safety plan with victims." In *The Therapist's Notebook for Lesbian, Gay, and Bisexual Clients: Homework, Handouts, and Activities for Use in Psychotherapy,* edited by Joy S. Whitman and Cynthia J. Boyd, 229–233. London: Routledge, 2013.

———. "Same-sex domestic violence: A tool for batterers." In *The Therapist's Notebook for Lesbian, Gay, and Bisexual Clients: Homework, Handouts, and Activities for Use in Psychotherapy,* edited by Joy S. Whitman and Cynthia J. Boyd, 234–237. London: Routledge, 2013.

Farrell, J., and S. Cerise. "Fair's fair: A snapshot of violence and abuse in Sydney LGBT relationships." Sydney, Australia: AIDS Council of NSW and the Same Sex Domestic Violence Interagency and Working Group, 2006. http://static1.1.sqspcdn.com/static/f/471667/8241404/1282546269423/SSDV_A4Report.pdf?token=4nqa4IJDiP11MNSs9iMFtJCddtU%3D.

Faulkner, Ellen. "Lesbian abuse: The social and legal realities." *Queen's Law Journal* 16 (1991): 261.

Federal Bureau of Investigation. *Crime in the United States: 2011.* [Table 42]. Accessed January 2016. https://www.fbi.gov/about-us/cjis/ucr/crime-in-the-u.s/2011/crime-in-the-u.s.-2011/tables/table-42.

Feitz, Antonia. "Demonizing men." *Everyman* 58 (2002): 52.

Feldman, Matthew B., Rafael M. Díaz, Geoffrey L. Ream, and Nabila El-Bassel. "Intimate partner violence and HIV sexual risk behavior among Latino gay and bisexual men." *Journal of LGBT Health Research* 3, no. 2 (2007): 9–19.

Feldman, Matthew B., Geoffrey L. Ream, Rafael M. Díaz, and Nabila El-Bassel. "Intimate partner violence and HIV sexual risk behavior among Latino gay and bisexual men: The role of situational factors." *Journal of LGBT Health Research* 3, no. 4 (2007): 75–87.

Felson, Richard B., and Paul-Philippe Paré. "The reporting of domestic violence and sexual assault by nonstrangers to the police." *Journal of Marriage and Family* 67, no. 3 (2005): 597–610.

Fern, Richard S. "Domestic Violence in Same-Sex Couples: Epidemiology, Assessment, and Intervention." *Advanced Emergency Nursing Journal* 20, no. 4 (1998): 30–39.

Ferraro, Kathleen J. "The Words Change, But the Melody Lingers: The Persistence of the Battered Woman Syndrome in Criminal Cases Involving Battered Women." *Violence against Women* 9, no. 1 (2003): 110–129.

Finneran, Catherine, Anna Chard, Craig Sineath, Patrick Sullivan, and Rob Stepheneon. "Intimate partner violence and social pressure among gay men in six countries." *Western Journal of Emergency Medicine* 13, no. 3 (2012): 260–271.

Finneran, Catherine, and Rob Stephenson. "Antecedents of intimate partner violence among gay and bisexual men." *Violence and Victims* 29, no. 3 (2014): 422.

——. "Gay and bisexual men's perceptions of police helpfulness in response to male-male intimate partner violence." *Western Journal of Emergency Medicine* 14, no. 4 (2013).

——. "Intimate partner violence among men who have sex with men: A systematic review." *Trauma, Violence, and Abuse* 14, no. 2 (2013): 168–185.

——. "Intimate partner violence, minority stress, and sexual risk-taking among US men who have sex with men." *Journal of Homosexuality* 61, no. 2 (2014): 288–306.

Fisher, Robert J. "Social desirability bias and the validity of indirect questioning." *Journal of Consumer Research* (1993): 303–315.

Follingstad, Diane R., and Maryanne Edmundson. "Is psychological abuse reciprocal in intimate relationships? Data from a national sample of American adults." *Journal of Family Violence* 25, no. 5 (2010): 495–508.

Follingstad, Diane R., and M. Jill Rogers. "Validity concerns in the measurement of women's and men's report of intimate partner violence." *Sex Roles* 69, nos. 3–4 (2013): 149–167.

Ford, Chandra L., Terra Slavin, Karin L. Hilton, and Susan L. Holt. "Intimate Partner Violence Prevention Services and Resources in Los Angeles: Issues, Needs, and Challenges for Assisting Lesbian, Gay, Bisexual, and Transgender Clients." *Health Promotion Practice* (2012): 841–849.

FORGE. "Safety planning with transgender clients FAQ." FORGE, 2013. http://forge-forward.org/wp-content/docs/FAQ-01-2013-safety-planning.pdf.

———. "Trans-specific power and control tactics." FORGE, 2013. http://forge-forward.org /wp-content/docs/power-control-tactics-categories_FINAL.pdf.

———. "Transgender sexual violence project." FORGE, 2005. https://web.archive.org /web/20101221150537/http://forge-forward.org/transviolence/docs/FINAL_Graphs.pdf.

Fortunata, Blaise, and Carolynn S. Kohn. "Demographic, psychosocial, and personality characteristics of lesbian batterers." *Violence and Victims* 18, no. 5 (2003): 557–568.

Fox, Lisa J. "Couples therapy for gay and lesbian couples with a history of domestic violence." In *A Professional Guide to Understanding Gay and Lesbian Domestic Violence: Understanding Practice Interventions*, edited by Joan C. McClennen and John Gunther, 107–126. Lewiston, NY: Edwin Mellen Press, 1999.

Frankland, Andrew, and Jac Brown. "Coercive control in same-sex intimate partner violence." *Journal of Family Violence* 29, no. 1 (2014): 15–22.

Franklin, Marnie J. "The Closet Becomes Darker for the Abused: A Perspective on Lesbian Partner Abuse." *Cardozo Women's Law Journal* 9 (2002): 299.

Freedberg, Pauline. "Health Care Barriers and Same-Sex Intimate Partner Violence: A Review of the Literature." *Journal of Forensic Nursing* 2, no. 1 (2006): 15–25.

Freedner, Naomi, Lorraine H. Freed, Y. Wendy Yang, and S. Bryn Austin. "Dating violence among gay, lesbian, and bisexual adolescents: Results from a community survey." *Journal of Adolescent Health* 31, no. 6 (2002): 469–474.

Friedman, Mark S., Michael P. Marshal, Ron Stall, JeeWon Cheong, and Eric R. Wright. "Gay-related development, early abuse and adult health outcomes among gay males." *AIDS and Behavior* 12, no. 6 (2008): 891–902.

Friedman, Susan Hatters, Sana Loue, Emily L. Goldman Heaphy, and Nancy Mendez. "Intimate partner violence victimization and perpetration by Puerto Rican women with severe mental illnesses." *Community Mental Health Journal* 47, no. 2 (2011): 156–163.

Frieze, Irene Hanson. "Female violence against intimate partners: An introduction." *Psychology of Women Quarterly* 29, no. 3 (2005): 229–237.

Frosch, Dan. "Death of a Transgender Woman Is Called a Hate Crime." *New York Times*, 2008.

———. "Murder and hate verdict in transgender case." *New York Times*, 2009.

Gallopin, Colleen, and Laila Leigh. "Teen perceptions of dating violence, help-seeking, and the role of schools." *Prevention Researcher* 16, no. 1 (2009): 17–21.

Galvan, Frank H., Rebecca Collins, David E. Kanouse, M. Audrey Burnam, Susan M. Paddock, Robin Beckman, and Steve R. Mitchell. "Abuse in the close relationships of people with HIV." *AIDS and Behavior* 8, no. 4 (2004): 441–451.

Gannoni, Alexandra, and Tracy Cussen. "Same-sex intimate partner homicide in Australia." Canberra: Australian Institute of Criminology, Australian Government, 2014. www.aic .gov.au/media_library/publications/tandi_pdf/tandi469.pdf.

García, Martha Lucia. "A 'New Kind' of Battered Woman." In *Same-Sex Domestic Violence: Strategies for Change*, edited by Beth Levanthal and Sandra E. Lundy, 165. Thousand Oaks, CA: SAGE, 1999.

Gates, Gary. J. *How Many People Are Lesbian, Gay, Bisexual, and Transgender?* Los Angeles: Williams Institute, 2011.

———. *Sexual Minorities in the 2008 General Social Survey: Coming Out and Demographic Characteristics*. Los Angeles: Williams Institute, 2010.

Gavey, Nicola, Johanna Schmidt, Virginia Braun, John Fenaughty, and Maia Eremin. "Unsafe, Unwanted Sexual Coercion as a Barrier to Safer Sex among Men Who Have Sex with Men." *Journal of Health Psychology* 14, no. 7 (2009): 1021–1026.

Gentry, Susan E. "Caring for lesbians in a homophobic society." *Health Care for Women International* 13, no. 2 (1992): 173–180.

George, Malcolm J. "Riding the donkey backwards: Men as the unacceptable victims of marital violence." *Journal of Men's Studies* 3, no. 2 (1994): 137.

Gilberg, Jenny, Jeremy NeVilles-Sorell, Tina Olson, Beryl Rock, Babette Sandman, Barry Skye, Rebecca St. George, and Victoria Ybanez. *Addressing Domestic Violence in Native Communities: Introductory Manual.* Duluth, MN: Mending the Sacred Hoop—Technical Assistance Project, 2003.

Gilfus, Mary E., Nicole Trabold, Patricia O'Brien, and Ann Fleck-Henderson. "Gender and intimate partner violence: Evaluating the evidence." *Journal of Social Work Education* 46, no. 2 (2010): 245–263.

Gillis, J. Roy, and Shaindl Diamond. "Dynamics of partner abuse in sexual and gender minority communities." In *Cruel but Not Unusual: Violence in Canadian Families: A Sourcebook for Educators and Practitioners,* 2nd ed., edited by Ramona Alaggia and Cathy Vine, 213–234. Waterloo, Ontario, Canada: Wilfrid Laurier University Press, 2012.

———. "Same-sex partner abuse: Challenges to the existing paradigms of intimate violence theory." In *Cruel but Not Unusual: Violence in Canadian Families,* edited by Ramona Alaggia and Cathy Vine, 127–144. Waterloo, Ontario, Canada: Wilfrid Laurier University Press, 2006.

Gillum, Tameka L., and Gloria T. DiFulvio. "Examining dating violence and its mental health consequences among sexual minority youth." In *Handbook of LGBT Communities, Crime, and Justice,* edited by Dana Peterson and Vanessa R. Panfil, 431–448. New York: Springer, 2014.

———. "'There's So Much at Stake': Sexual Minority Youth Discuss Dating Violence." *Violence against Women* 18, no. 7 (2012): 725–745.

Giorgio, Grace. "Speaking silence: Definitional dialogues in abusive lesbian relationships." *Violence against Women* 8, no. 10 (2002): 1233–1259.

Girshick, Lori B. "No Sugar, No Spice: Reflections on Research on Woman-to-Woman Sexual Violence." *Violence against Women* 8, no. 12 (2002): 1500–1520.

———. "Organizing in the lesbian community to confront lesbian battering." *Journal of Gay and Lesbian Social Services* 9, no. 1 (1999): 83–92.

———. *Woman-to-Woman Sexual Violence: Does She Call It Rape?* Lebanon, NH: University Press of New England, 2002.

Glass, Nancy, Jane Koziol-McLain, Jacquelyn Campbell, and Carolyn Rebecca Block. "Female-Perpetrated Femicide and Attempted Femicide: A Case Study." *Violence against Women* 10, no. 6 (2004): 606–625.

Glass, Nancy, Nancy Perrin, Ginger Hanson, Tina Bloom, Emily Gardner, and Jacquelyn C. Campbell. "Risk for reassault in abusive female same-sex relationships." *American Journal of Public Health* 98, no. 6 (2008): 1021–1027.

GLBT Domestic Violence Coalition and Jane Doe Inc. "Shelter/housing needs for gay, lesbian, bisexual and transgender (GLBT) victims of domestic violence." 2005. www.ncdsv.org/images/shelterhousingneedsforglbtvictimsdv.pdf.

GLBTDVC. *Intimate Partner Abuse Screening Tool for Gay, Lesbian, Bisexual and Transgender (GLBT) Relationships.* Boston, MA: Gay, Lesbian, Bisexual and Transgender Domestic Violence Coalition, 2003.

Global Action for Trans Equality. "Gender Identity and Human Rights." Accessed January 2015. http://transactivists.org/resources/documents/.goldberg, Joshua Mira, and Caroline White. "Reflections on approaches to trans anti-violence education." In *Intimate Partner Violence in LGBTQ Lives,* edited by Janice L. Ristock, 56–77. New York: Routledge, 2011.

Goldberg, Naomi G., and Ilan H. Meyer. "Sexual orientation disparities in history of intimate partner violence results from the California Health Interview Survey." *Journal of Interpersonal Violence* 28, no. 5 (2013): 1109–1118.

Gonzalez-Guarda, Rosa M., Joseph P. De Santis, and Elias P. Vasquez. "Sexual orientation and demographic, cultural, and psychological factors associated with the perpetration and victimization of intimate partner violence among Hispanic men." *Issues in Mental Health Nursing* 34, no. 2 (2013): 103–109.

Goodenow, Carol, Laura A. Szalacha, Leah E. Robin, and Kim Westheimer. "Dimensions of sexual orientation and HIV-related risk among adolescent females: Evidence from a statewide survey." *American Journal of Public Health* 98, no. 6 (2008): 1051–1058.

Goodman, Peggy E. "The relationship between intimate partner violence and other forms of family and societal violence." *Emergency Medicine Clinics of North America* 24, no. 4 (2006): 889–903.

Goodmark, Leigh. "Transgender people, intimate partner abuse, and the legal system." *Harvard Civil Rights–Civil Liberties Law Review* 48 (2013): 51–104.

Graham, Kathryn, Sharon Bernards, Andrea Flynn, Paul F. Tremblay, and Samantha Wells. "Does the relationship between depression and intimate partner aggression vary by gender, victim–perpetrator role, and aggression severity?" *Violence and Victims* 27, no. 5 (2012): 730–743.

Graham-Kevan, Nicola, and John Archer. "Control tactics and partner violence in heterosexual relationships." *Evolution and Human Behavior* 30, no. 6 (2009): 445–452.

Grant, Jaime M., Lisa A. Mottet, and Justin Tanis. "Injustice at Every Turn: A Report from the National Transgender Discrimination Survey." Washington, DC: National Center for Transgender Equality and National Gay and Lesbian Task Force, 2011. www.thetaskforce.org/static_html/downloads/reports/reports/ntds_full.pdf.

Greenberg, Kae. "Still hidden in the closet: Trans women and domestic violence." *Berkeley Journal of Gender, Law and Justice.* 27 (2012): 198.

Greene, George J., Kimberly A. Fisher, Laura Kuper, Rebecca Andrews, and Brian Mustanski. "'Is This Normal? Is This Not Normal? There Is No Set Example': Sexual Health Intervention Preferences of LGBT Youth in Romantic Relationships." *Sexuality Research and Social Policy* 12, no. 1 (2015): 1–14.

Greenwood, Gregory L., Michael V. Relf, Bu Huang, Lance M. Pollack, Jesse A. Canchola, and Joseph A. Catania. "Battering victimization among a probability-based sample of men who have sex with men." *American Journal of Public Health* 92, no. 12 (2002): 1964–1969.

Gruber, James E., and Susan Fineran. "Comparing the impact of bullying and sexual harassment victimization on the mental and physical health of adolescents." *Sex Roles* 59, nos. 1–2 (2008): 1–13.

Guadalupe-Diaz, Xavier L. "An Exploration of Differences in the Help-Seeking of LGBQ Victims of Violence by Race, Economic Class and Gender." *Gay and Lesbian Issues and Psychology Review* 9, no. 1 (2013): 15.

Guadalupe-Diaz, Xavier L., and Jonathan Yglesias. "'Who's Protected?' Exploring Perceptions of Domestic Violence Law by Lesbians, Gays, and Bisexuals." *Journal of Gay and Lesbian Social Services* 25, no. 4 (2013): 465–485.

Guasp, April. *Gay and Bisexual Men's Health Survey.* London: Stonewall, 2012.

Gundlach, Ralph H. "Sexual molestation and rape reported by homosexual and heterosexual women." *Journal of Homosexuality* 2, no. 4 (1977): 367–384.

Halberstam, Judith. *Female Masculinity.* Durham, NC: Duke University Press, 1998.

Halpern, Carolyn Tucker, Mary L. Young, Martha W. Waller, Sandra L. Martin, and Lawrence L. Kupper. "Prevalence of partner violence in same-sex romantic and sexual relationships in a national sample of adolescents." *Journal of Adolescent Health* 35, no. 2 (2004): 124–131.

Hamberger, L. Kevin. "Domestic partner abuse: Expanding paradigms for understanding and intervention." *Violence and Victims* 9, no. 2 (1994): 91.

———. "Female offenders in domestic violence: A look at actions in their context." *Journal of Aggression, Maltreatment and Trauma* 1, no. 1 (1997): 117–129.

———. "Intervention in gay male intimate violence requires coordinated efforts on multiple levels." *Journal of Gay and Lesbian Social Services* 4, no. 1 (1996): 83–91.

———. "Men's and women's use of intimate partner violence in clinical samples: Toward a gender-sensitive analysis." *Violence and Victims* 20, no. 2 (2005): 131–151.

Hamberger, L. Kevin, and Clare E. Guse. "Men's and women's use of intimate partner violence in clinical samples." *Violence against Women* 8, no. 11 (2002): 1301–1331.

Hamberger, L. Kevin, Jeffrey M. Lohr, and Dennis Bonge. "The intended function of domestic violence is different for arrested male and female perpetrators." *Family Violence and Sexual Assault Bulletin* 10, nos. 3–4 (1994): 40–44.

Hamby, Sherry, and Amy Jackson. "Size does matter: The effects of gender on perceptions of dating violence." *Sex Roles* 63, nos. 5–6 (2010): 324–331.

Hamel, John. "Toward a gender-inclusive conception of intimate partner violence research and theory: Part 1—Traditional perspectives." *International Journal of Men's Health* 6, no. 1 (2007): 36–53.

Hammond, Nancy. "Lesbian victims of relationship violence." *Women and Therapy* 8, nos. 1–2 (1989): 89–105.

Han, Sohyun C., Matthew W. Gallagher, Molly R. Franz, May S. Chen, Fabiana M. Cabral, and Brian P. Marx. "Childhood sexual abuse, alcohol use, and PTSD symptoms as predictors of adult sexual assault among lesbians and gay men." *Journal of Interpersonal Violence* 28, no. 12 (2013): 2505–2520.

Hancock, Ryan. "Positive Counsellor Characteristics with Sexual Minority Intimate Partner Violence Victims." *Canadian Journal of Counselling and Psychotherapy/Revue canadienne de counseling et de psychothérapie* 48, no. 2 (2014).

Hancock, Ryan, Garrett McAuliffe, and Kathleen Levingston. "Factors Impacting Counselor Competency with Sexual Minority Intimate Partner Violence Victims." *Journal of LGBT Issues in Counseling* 8, no. 1 (2014): 74–94.

Hanson, Bea. "The violence we face as lesbians and gay men: The landscape both outside and inside our communities." *Journal of Gay and Lesbian Social Services* 4, no. 2 (1996): 95–113.

Harada, Satoko. "Comment: Additional Barriers to Breaking the Silence: Issues to Consider When Representing a Victim of Same-Sex Domestic Violence." *University of Baltimore Law Forum* 41, no. 2 (2011): 4.

Hardesty, Jennifer L., Ramona F. Oswald, Lyndal Khaw, and Carol Fonseca. "Lesbian/bisexual mothers and intimate partner violence: Help seeking in the context of social and legal vulnerability." *Violence against Women* 17, no. 1 (2011): 28–46.

Hardesty, Jennifer L., Ramona F. Oswald, Lyndal Khaw, Carol Fonseca, and Grace H. Chung. "Lesbian mothering in the context of intimate partner violence." *Journal of Lesbian Studies* 12, nos. 2–3 (2008): 191–210.

Harms, Bradley Lee. "Domestic violence in the gay male community." Master's thesis, San Francisco State University, Department of Psychology, 1995.

Harned, Melanie S. "Abused women or abused men? An examination of the context and outcomes of dating violence." *Violence and Victims* 16, no. 3 (2001): 269–285.

———. "A multivariate analysis of risk markers for dating violence victimization." *Journal of Interpersonal Violence* 17, no. 11 (2002): 1179–1197.

Harris, Richard Jackson, and Cynthia A. Cook. "Attributions about spouse abuse: It matters who the batterers and victims are." *Sex Roles* 30, nos. 7–8 (1994): 553–565.

Harvey, Shannon, Martin Mitchell, Jasmin Keeble, C. McNaughton Nicholls, and Nilufer Rahim. "Barriers faced by lesbian, gay, bisexual and transgender people in accessing domestic abuse, stalking and harassment, and sexual violence services." Cardiff, Wales: Welsh Government, 2014.

Harway, Michele, and James M. O'Neil, eds. *What Causes Men's Violence against Women?* Thousand Oaks, CA: Sage Publications, 1999.

Hassouneh, Dena, and Nancy Glass. "The Influence of Gender-Role Stereotyping on Women's Experiences of Female Same-Sex Intimate Partner Violence." *Violence against Women* 14, no. 3 (2008): 310–325.

Head, Sarah, and Martin Milton. "Filling the Silence: Exploring the Bisexual Experience of Intimate Partner Abuse." *Journal of Bisexuality* 14, no. 2 (2014): 277–299.

Heer, Christine, Eileen Grogan, Sandra Clark, and Lynda Marie Carson. "Developing services for lesbians in abusive relationships: A macro and micro approach." In *Battered Women and Their Families: Intervention Strategies and Treatment Programs*, 2nd ed., edited by Albert R. Roberts, 365. New York: Springer, 1998.

Helfrich, Christine A., and Emily K. Simpson. "Improving services for lesbian clients: What do domestic violence agencies need to do?" *Health Care for Women International* 27, no. 4 (2006): 344–361.

Hellemans, Sabine, Tom Loeys, Ann Buysse, Alexis Dewaele, and Olivia De Smet. "Intimate partner violence victimization among non-heterosexuals: Prevalence and associations with mental and sexual well-being." *Journal of Family Violence* 30, no. 2 (2015): 171–188.

Hellmuth, Julianne C., Katherine W. Follansbee, Todd M. Moore, and Gregory L. Stuart. "Reduction of intimate partner violence in a gay couple following alcohol treatment." *Journal of Homosexuality* 54, no. 4 (2008): 439–448.

Henderson, Laurie. "Prevalence of domestic violence among lesbians and gay men. Data report to Flame TV." London: Sigma Research, 2003. http://sigmaresearch.org.uk/files /report2003.pdf.

Herrick, Amy L., Sin How Lim, Michael W. Plankey, Joan S. Chmiel, Thomas T. Guadamuz, Uyen Kao, Steven Shoptaw, Adam Carrico, David Ostrow, and Ron Stall. "Adversity and syndemic production among men participating in the multicenter AIDS cohort study: A life-course approach." *American Journal of Public Health* 103, no. 1 (2013): 79–85.

Hester, Marianne, and Catherine Donovan. "Researching domestic violence in same-sex relationships: A feminist epistemological approach to survey development." *Journal of Lesbian Studies* 13, no. 2 (2009): 161–173.

Hester, Marianne, Catherine Donovan, and Eldin Fahmy. "Feminist epistemology and the politics of method: Surveying same sex domestic violence." *International Journal of Social Research Methodology* 13, no. 3 (2010): 251–263.

Hester, Marianne, Emma Williamson, Linda Regan, Mark Coulter, Khatidja Chantler, Geetanjali Gangoli, Rebecca Davenport, and Lorraine Green. "Exploring the service and support needs of male, lesbian, gay, bi-sexual and transgendered and black and other minority ethnic victims of domestic and sexual violence (Report prepared for Home Office)." Bristol, UK: University of Bristol, 2012.

Hickson, Ford C. I., Peter M. Davies, Andrew J. Hunt, Peter Weatherburn, Thomas J. McManus, and Anthony P. M. Coxon. "Gay men as victims of nonconsensual sex." *Archives of Sexual Behavior* 23, no. 3 (1994): 281–294.

Hiebert-Murphy, Diane, Janice L. Ristock, and D. Brownridge. "The meaning of 'risk' for intimate partner violence among women in same-sex relationships." In *Intimate Partner Violence in LGBTQ Lives,* edited by Janice L. Ristock, 37–55. New York: Routledge, 2011.

Hill, Nicholle A., Kamilah M. Woodson, Angela D. Ferguson, and Carlton W. Parks Jr. "Intimate partner abuse among African American lesbians: Prevalence, risk factors, theory, and resilience." *Journal of Family Violence* 27, no. 5 (2012): 401–413.

Hines, Denise A., and Emily M. Douglas. "The reported availability of US domestic violence services to victims who vary by age, sexual orientation, and gender." *Partner Abuse* 2, no. 1 (2011): 3–30.

Hipwell, A. E., Stephanie D. Stepp, K. Keenan, A. Allen, A. Hoffmann, L. Rottingen, and R. McAloon. "Examining links between sexual risk behaviors and dating violence involvement as a function of sexual orientation." *Journal of Pediatric and Adolescent Gynecology* 26, no. 4 (2013): 212–218.

Hirschel, David, E. Buzawa, A. Pattavina, D. Faggiani, and M. Reuland. *Explaining the prevalence, context, and consequences of dual arrest in intimate partner cases.* Washington: U.S. Department of Justice, National Institute of Justice, 2007. https://www.ncjrs.gov /pdffiles1/nij/grants/218355.pdf.

Hirschel, David, Ira W. Hutchison, and Meaghan Shaw. "The interrelationship between substance abuse and the likelihood of arrest, conviction, and re-offending in cases of intimate partner violence." *Journal of Family Violence* 25, no. 1 (2010): 81–90.

Hochstetler, Andy, Heith Copes, and J. Patrick Williams. "'That's Not Who I Am': How Offenders Commit Violent Acts and Reject Authentically Violent Selves." *Justice Quarterly* 27, no. 4 (2010): 492–516.

Hodges, Krisana M. "Trouble in Paradise: Barriers to Addressing Domestic Violence in Lesbian Relationships." *Law and Sexuality: A Review of Lesbian, Gay, Bisexual and Transgender Legal Issues* 9 (1999–2000): 311.

Hoffman, Sam. *Old Jews Telling Jokes: 5,000 Years of Funny Bits and Not-So-Kosher Laughs.* New York: Villard Books, 2010.

Holmes, Cindy. "Destabilizing homonormativity and the public/private dichotomy in North American lesbian domestic violence discourses." *Gender, Place and Culture* 16, no. 1 (2009): 77–95.

———. "Troubling normalcy: Examining 'healthy relationships' discourses in lesbian domestic violence prevention." In *Intimate Partner Violence in LGBTQ Lives,* edited by Janice L. Ristock, 209–231. New York: Routledge, 2011.

Holt, Susan. "Lesbian, gay, bisexual, and transgender intimate partner violence: The California report." Los Angeles: LA Gay and Lesbian Center STOP Partner Abuse/Domestic Violence Program, 2011.

Holtzworth-Munroe, Amy. "Female perpetration of physical aggression against an intimate partner: A controversial new topic of study." *Violence and Victims* 20, no. 2 (2005): 251–259.

Home Office and Jeremy Browne. "Extended definition of domestic violence takes effect." United Kingdom Home Office. Accessed January 2016. www.gov.uk/government/news/extended-definition-of-domestic-violence-takes-effect.

Horne, Sharon G., and Shana V. Hamilton. "Bisexuality and broken relationships." In *Becoming Visible: Counseling Bisexuals across the Lifespan,* edited by Beth Λ. Firestein, 153. New York: Columbia University Press, 2007.

Houston, Eric, and David J. McKirnan. "Intimate partner abuse among gay and bisexual men: Risk correlates and health outcomes." *Journal of Urban Health* 84, no. 5 (2007): 681–690.

Howe, Adrian. *Sex, Violence and Crime: Foucault and the "Man" Question.* Oxford: Routledge, 2008.

Htun, Mala, and S. Laurel Weldon. "The civic origins of progressive policy change: Combating violence against women in global perspective, 1975–2005." *American Political Science Review* 106, no. 3 (2012): 548–569.

Human Rights Campaign. "Maps of State Laws and Policies." 2015. www.hrc.org/state_maps.

Hunt, Ruth, and Julie Fish. "Prescription for change: Lesbian and bisexual women's health check." London: Sigma Research, 2008. https://www.stonewall.org.uk/sites/default/files/Prescription_for_Change__2008_.pdf.

Hunter, Mac D. "Homosexuals as a new class of domestic violence subjects under the New Jersey Prevention of Domestic Violence Act of 1991." *University of Louisville Journal of Family Law* 31 (1992): 557.

Irwin, Jude. "(Dis) counted Stories: Domestic Violence and Lesbians." *Qualitative Social Work* 7, no. 2 (2008): 199–215.

Island, David, and Patrick Letellier. *Men Who Beat the Men Who Love Them: Battered Gay Men and Domestic Violence.* Binghamton, NY: Haworth Press, 1991.

Istar, Arlene S. "Couple assessment: Identifying and intervening in domestic violence in lesbian relationships." *Journal of Gay and Lesbian Social Services* 4, no. 1 (1996): 93–106.

Itaborahy, Lucas Paoli, and Jingshu Zhu. *State-Sponsored Homophobia: A World Survey of Laws: Criminalisation, Protection and Recognition of Same-Sex Love.* Geneva: International Lesbian, Gay, Bisexual, Trans and Intersex Association, 2014. http://old.ilga.org /Statehomophobia/ILGA_SSHR_2014_Eng.pdf.

Jablow, Pamela M. "Victims of abuse and discrimination: Protecting battered homosexuals under domestic violence legislation." *Hofstra Law Review* 28 (1999): 1095–1143.

Jackson, Nicky Ali. "Same-Sex Domestic Violence: Myths, Facts, Correlates, Treatment, and Prevention Strategies." In *Battered Women and Their Families: Intervention Strategies and Treatment Programs,* 3rd ed., edited by Albert R. Roberts, 451–470. New York: Springer, 2007.

Jacobson, Lamerial, Andrew P. Daire, and Eileen M. Abel. "Intimate Partner Violence: Implications for Counseling Self-Identified LGBTQ College Students Engaged in Same-Sex Relationships." *Journal of LGBT Issues in Counseling* 9, no. 2 (2015): 118–135.

Jasinski, Jana L., and Elizabeth Ehrhardt Mustaine. "Police response to physical assault and stalking victimization: A comparison of influential factors." *American Journal of Criminal Justice* 26, no. 1 (2001): 23–41.

Jeffries, Samantha, and Matthew Ball. "Male same-sex intimate partner violence: A descriptive review and call for further research." *eLaw Journal* 15 (2008): 134.

Johnson, Jeanne J. "Same-sex domestic violence: Testing the cycle theory of violence." PhD diss., Alliant International University, 2004. Dissertation Abstracts International, 66, 556.

Johnson, Michael P. "Patriarchal terrorism and common couple violence: Two forms of violence against women." *Journal of Marriage and the Family* (1995): 283–294.

JokeIndex.com. *Driving the Wrong Way.* Accessed May 2015. www.jokeindex.com/joke .asp?Joke = 1940.

Jones, Cassandra A., and Chitra Raghavan. "Sexual orientation, social support networks, and dating violence in an ethnically diverse group of college students." *Journal of Gay and Lesbian Social Services* 24, no. 1 (2012): 1–22.

Kalichman, Seth C., Eric Benotsch, David Rompa, Cheryl Gore-Felton, James Austin, Webster Luke, Kari DiFonzo, Jeff Buckles, Florence Kyomugisha, and Dolores Simpson. "Unwanted sexual experiences and sexual risks in gay and bisexual men: Associations among revictimization, substance use, and psychiatric symptoms." *Journal of Sex Research* 38, no. 1 (2001): 1–9.

Kalichman, Seth C., Cheryl Gore-Felton, Eric Benotsch, Marjorie Cage, and David Rompa. "Trauma symptoms, sexual behaviors, and substance abuse: Correlates of childhood sexual abuse and HIV risks among men who have sex with men." *Journal of Child Sexual Abuse* 13, no. 1 (2004): 1–15.

Kalichman, Seth C., and David Rompa. "Sexually coerced and noncoerced gay and bisexual men: Factors relevant to risk for human immunodeficiency virus (HIV) infection." *Journal of Sex Research* 32, no. 1 (1995): 45–50.

Kalokhe, Ameeta S., Anuradha Paranjape, Christine E. Bell, Gabriel A. Cardenas, Tamy Kuper, Lisa R. Metsch, and Carlos Del Rio. "Intimate partner violence among HIV-infected crack cocaine users." *AIDS Patient Care and STDs* 26, no. 4 (2012): 234–240.

Kanuha, Valli. "Compounding the triple jeopardy: Battering in lesbian of color relationships." *Women and Therapy* 9, nos. 1–2 (1990): 169–184.

————. "'Relationships So Loving and So Hurtful': The Constructed Duality of Sexual and Racial/Ethnic Intimacy in the Context of Violence in Asian and Pacific Islander Lesbian and Queer Women's Relationships." *Violence against Women* 19, no. 9 (2013): 1175–1196.

Kapai, Puja. "The Same Difference: Protecting Same-Sex Couples under the Domestic Violence Ordinance." *Asian Journal of Comparative Law* 4 (2009): 1–33.

Kaplan, Claire N., and Sandy L. Colbs. "Shattered Pride: Resistance and Intervention Strategies in Cases of Sexual Assault, Relationship Violence, and Hate Crimes Against Lesbian, Gay, Bisexual, and Transgender Students." In *Towards Acceptance: Sexual Orientation Issues on Campus,* edited by Vernon A. Wall and Nancy J. Evans, 215–244. Lanham, MD: University Press of America, 2000.

Kaschak, Ellyn, ed. *Intimate Betrayal: Domestic Violence in Lesbian Relationships.* New York: Haworth Press, Routledge, 2001.

Katz-Wise, Sarah L. and Janet S. Hyde. "Victimization Experiences of Lesbian, Gay, and Bisexual Individuals: A Meta-Analysis." *Journal of Sex Research* 49, nos. 2–3 (2012): 142–167.

Kay, Melissa, and Samantha Jeffries. "Homophobia, heteronormativism and hegemonic masculinity: Male same-sex intimate violence from the perspective of Brisbane service providers." *Psychiatry, Psychology and Law* 17, no. 3 (2010): 412–423.

Kelley, Michelle L., Robin J. Lewis, and Tyler B. Mason. "Discrepant Alcohol Use, Intimate Partner Violence, and Relationship Adjustment among Lesbian Women and Their Same-Sex Intimate Partners." *Journal of Family Violence* 30, no. 8 (2015): 977–986.

Kelley, Michelle L., Robert J. Milletich, Robin J. Lewis, Barbara A. Winstead, Cathy L. Barraco, Miguel A. Padilla, and Courtney Lynn. "Predictors of Perpetration of Men's Same-Sex Partner Violence." *Violence and Victims* 29, no. 5 (2014): 784–796.

Kelly, Brian C., Hubert Izienicki, David S. Bimbi, and Jeffrey T. Parsons. "The intersection of mutual partner violence and substance use among urban gays, lesbians, and bisexuals." *Deviant Behavior* 32, no. 5 (2011): 379–404.

Kelly, C., and L. Warshafsky. "Partner abuse in gay male and lesbian relationships." Paper presented at the Third National Family Violence Research Conference, Durham, NH, 1987.

Kelly, Liz. "When does the speaking profit us? Reflections on the challenges of developing feminist perspectives on abuse and violence by women." In *Women, Violence and Male Power: Feminist Activism, Research and Practice,* edited by Marianne Hester, Liz Kelly, and Jill Radford, 34–49. Buckingham, England: Open University Press, 1996.

Kernsmith, Poco, and Roger Kernsmith. "Treating female perpetrators: State standards for batterer intervention services." *Social Work* 54, no. 4 (2009): 341–349.

Keuroghlian, Alex S., Sari L. Reisner, Jaclyn M. White, and Roger D. Weiss. "Substance use and treatment of substance use disorders in a community sample of transgender adults." *Drug and Alcohol Dependence* 152 (2015): 139–146.

Kimmel, Michael S. "'Gender Symmetry' in Domestic Violence: A Substantive and Methodological Research Review." *Violence against Women* 8, no. 11 (2002): 1332–1363.

Klein, Catherine F., and Leslye E. Orloff. "Protecting battered women: Latest trends in civil legal relief." *Women and Criminal Justice* 10, no. 2 (1999): 29–47.

Klinger, Rochelle L. "Gay violence." *Journal of Gay and Lesbian Psychotherapy* 2, no. 3 (1996): 119–134.

Klinger, Rochelle L., and Terry S. Stein. "Impact of violence, childhood sexual abuse, and domestic violence and abuse on lesbians, bisexuals, and gay men." In *Textbook of Homosexuality and Mental Health,* edited by Robert P. Cabaj and Terry S. Stein, 801–818. Washington: American Psychiatric Press, 1996.

Klitzman, Robert L., Jason D. Greenberg, Lance M. Pollack, and Curtis Dolezal. "MDMA ('ecstasy') use, and its association with high risk behaviors, mental health, and other factors among gay/bisexual men in New York City." *Drug and Alcohol Dependence* 66, no. 2 (2002): 115–125.

Knauer, Nancy J. "Same-sex domestic violence: Claiming a domestic sphere while risking negative stereotypes." *Temple Political and Civil Rights Law Review* 8 (1998): 325.

Koblin, Beryl A., L. Torian, Gengsheng Xu, V. Guilin, H. Makki, D. Mackellar, and L. Valleroy. "Violence and HIV-related risk among young men who have sex with men." *AIDS Care* 18, no. 8 (2006): 961–967.

Koeppel, Maria D. H., and Leana A. Bouffard. "Sexual orientation and the effects of intimate partner violence." *Women and Criminal Justice* 24, no. 2 (2014): 126–150.

Koller, Jürgen. "'The ecological fallacy' (Dutton 1994) revised." *Journal of Aggression, Conflict and Peace Research* 5, no. 3 (2013): 156–166.

Kondas, Dorian. "Existential explosion and Gestalt therapy for gay male survivors of domestic violence." *Gestalt Review: A Publication of the Gestalt International Study Center* 12, no. 1 (2008): 58–74.

Krahé, Barbara, Stephan Schütze, Immo Fritsche, and Eva Waizenhöfer. "The prevalence of sexual aggression and victimization among homosexual men." *Journal of Sex Research* 37, no. 2 (2000): 142–150.

Krestan, Jo-Ann, and Claudia S. Bepko. "The problem of fusion in the lesbian relationship." *Family Process* 19, no. 3 (1980): 277–289.

Kubicek, Katrina, Miles McNeeley, and Shardae Collins. "'Same-Sex Relationship in a Straight World': Individual and Societal Influences on Power and Control in Young Men's Relationships." *Journal of Interpersonal Violence* 30, no. 1 (2015): 83–109.

———. "Young Men Who Have Sex with Men's Experiences with Intimate Partner Violence." *Journal of Adolescent Research* 31, no. 2 (2016): 143–175.

Kuehnle, Kristen, and Anne Sullivan. "Gay and Lesbian Victimization Reporting Factors in Domestic Violence and Bias Incidents." *Criminal Justice and Behavior* 30, no. 1 (2003): 85–96.

Kulkin, Heidi S., June Williams, Heath F. Borne, Dana de la Bretonne, and Judy Laurendine. "A review of research on violence in same-gender couples: A resource for clinicians." *Journal of Homosexuality* 53, no. 4 (2007): 71–87.

Kurz, Demie. "Physical assaults by husbands: A major social problem." *Current Controversies on Family Violence* (1993): 88–103.

Landers, Stewart J., and Paola Gilsanz. "The health of lesbian, gay, bisexual and transgender (LGBT) persons in Massachusetts: A survey of health issues comparing LGBT persons with their heterosexual and non-transgender counterparts." Boston: Massachusetts Department of Public Health, 2009. www.masstpc.org/wp-content/uploads/2012/10/DPH-2009-lgbt-health-report.pdf.

Landolt, Monica A., and Donald G. Dutton. "Power and personality: An analysis of gay male intimate abuse." *Sex Roles* 37, nos. 5–6 (1997): 335–359.

Langenderfer-Magruder, Lisa, N. Eugene Walls, Darren L. Whitfield, Samantha M. Brown, and Cory M. Barrett. "Partner Violence Victimization among Lesbian, Gay, Bisexual, Transgender, and Queer Youth: Associations among Risk Factors." *Child and Adolescent Social Work Journal* 33, no. 1 (2016): 55–68.

Langenderfer-Magruder, Lisa N., Darren L. Whitfield, N. Eugene Walls, Shanna K. Kattari, and Daniel Ramos. "Experiences of Intimate Partner Violence and Subsequent Police Reporting among Lesbian, Gay, Bisexual, Transgender, and Queer Adults in Colorado: Comparing Rates of Cisgender and Transgender Victimization." *Journal of Interpersonal Violence* 31, no. 5 (2016): 855–871.

Lauritsen, Janet L., Karen Heimer, and James P. Lynch. "Trends in the gender gap in violent offending: New evidence from the National Crime Victimization Survey." *Criminology* 47, no. 2 (2009): 361–399.

Lazarus-Black, Mindie. "The politics of place: Practice, process, and kinship in domestic violence courts." *Human Organization* 65, no. 2 (2006): 140–155.

Leeder, Elaine. *Treating Abuse in Families: A Feminist and Community Approach.* New York: Springer, 1994.

Leen, Eline, Emma Sorbring, Matt Mawer, Emma Holdsworth, Bo Helsing, and Erica Bowen. "Prevalence, dynamic risk factors and the efficacy of primary interventions for adolescent dating violence: An international review." *Aggression and Violent Behavior* 18, no. 1 (2013): 159–174.

Leonard, William, Anne Mitchell, Sunil Patel, and Christopher Fox. *Coming Forward: The Underreporting of Heterosexist Violence and Same Sex Partner Abuse in Victoria.* Monograph Series no. 69. Melbourne: Australian Research Centre in Sex, Health and Society, La Trobe University, 2008.

Letellier, Patrick. "Gay and bisexual male domestic violence victimization: Challenges to feminist theory and responses to violence." *Violence and Victims* 9, no. 2 (1994): 95–106.

———. "Twin epidemics: Domestic violence and HIV infection among gay and bisexual men." *Journal of Gay and Lesbian Social Services* 4, no. 1 (1996): 69–81.

Leung, Patrick, Monit Cheung, and Thang D. Luu. "Hardships and interpersonal relationships among Asian-Americans with same-sex partners." *Journal of GLBT Family Studies* 9, no. 3 (2013): 288–301.

Leventhal, Beth, and Sandra Lundy, eds. *Same-Sex Domestic Violence: Strategies for Change.* Thousand Oaks, CA: Sage Publications, 1999.

Levy, Barry, and Kerry Lobel. "Lesbian teens in abusive relationships." In *Dating violence: Young Women in Danger,* edited by Barrie Levy, 203–208. Seattle: Seal Press, 1991.

Lewis, Robin J., Robert J. Milletich, Valerian J. Derlega, and Miguel A. Padilla. "Sexual Minority Stressors and Psychological Aggression in Lesbian Women's Intimate Relationships: The Mediating Roles of Rumination and Relationship Satisfaction." *Psychology of Women Quarterly* 38, no. 4 (2014): 535–550.

Lewis, Robin J., Robert J. Milletich, Michelle L. Kelley, and Alex Woody. "Minority stress, substance use, and intimate partner violence among sexual minority women." *Aggression and Violent Behavior* 17, no. 3 (2012): 247–256.

Lewis, Robin J., Miguel A. Padilla, Robert J. Milletich, Michelle L. Kelley, Barbara A. Winstead, Cathy Lau-Barraco, and Tyler B. Mason. "Emotional distress, alcohol use, and bidirectional partner violence among lesbian women." *Violence against Women* 21, no. 8 (2015): 917–938.

LGBT Youth Scotland. "Voices Unheard: LGBT domestic abuse and gender based violence: an educational resource with a focus on lesbian, gay, bisexual and transgender young people's experiences of domestic abuse and other forms of gender based violence." 2014. www.lgbtyouth.org.uk/files/documents/Voices_Unheard_report.pdf.

Li, Ying, Joseph J. Baker, Valeriy R. Korostyshevskiy, Rebecca S. Slack, and Michael W. Plankey. "The association of intimate partner violence, recreational drug use with HIV seroprevalence among MSM." *AIDS and Behavior* 16, no. 3 (2012): 491–498.

Lie, Gwat-Yong, and Sabrina Gentlewarrier. "Intimate violence in lesbian relationships: Discussion of survey findings and practice implications." *Journal of Social Service Research* 15, nos. 1–2 (1991): 41–59.

Lie, Gwat-Yong, Rebecca Schilit, Judy Bush, Marilyn Montagne, and Lynn Reyes. "Lesbians in currently aggressive relationships: How frequently do they report aggressive past relationships?" *Violence and Victims* 6, no. 2 (1991): 121–135.

Lilith, Ryiah. "Reconsidering the abuse that dare not speak its name: A criticism of recent legal scholarship regarding same-gender domestic violence." *Michigan Journal of Gender and Law* 7 (2000): 181.

Lindley, Lisa L., Daniela B. Friedman, and Corrie Struble. "Becoming Visible: Assessing the Availability of Online Sexual Health Information for Lesbians." *Health Promotion Practice* 13, no. 4 (2012): 472–480.

Lipsky, Sherry, Antoinette Krupski, Peter Roy-Byrne, Alice Huber, Barbara A. Lucenko, and David Mancuso. "Impact of sexual orientation and co-occurring disorders on chemical dependency treatment outcomes." *Journal of Studies on Alcohol and Drugs* 73, no. 3 (2012): 401–412.

Little, Betsi, and Cheryl Terrance. "Perceptions of domestic violence in lesbian relationships: Stereotypes and gender role expectations." *Journal of Homosexuality* 57, no. 3 (2010): 429–440.

Little, Shannon. "Challenging changing legal definitions of family in same-sex domestic violence." *Hastings Women's Law Journal* 19 (2008): 259.

Livia, Anna, and Kira Hall, eds. *Queerly Phrased: Language, Gender, and Sexuality.* New York: Oxford University Press, 1997.

Lloyd, Sally A. "The darkside of courtship: Violence and sexual exploitation." *Family Relations* (1991): 14–20.

Lobel, Kerry. *Naming the Violence: Speaking Out about Lesbian Battering (Report of the National Coalition against Domestic Violence Lesbian Task Force).* Seattle: Seal Press, 1986.

Lockhart, Lettie L., Barbara W. White, Vicki Causby, and Alicia Isaac. "Letting out the secret: Violence in lesbian relationships." *Journal of Interpersonal Violence* 9, no. 4 (1994): 469–492.

Long, Susan M., Sarah E. Ullman, LaDonna M. Long, Gillian E. Mason, and Laura L. Starzynski. "Women's experiences of male-perpetrated sexual assault by sexual orientation." *Violence and Victims* 22, no. 6 (2007): 684–701.

Lorden, C. Susie. "The Law of Unintended Consequences: The Far-Reaching Effects of Same-Sex Marriage Ban Amendments." *Quinnipiac Law Review,* Fall 2006.

Lundy, Sandra E. "Abuse that dare not speak its name: Assisting victims of lesbian and gay domestic violence in Massachusetts." *New England Law Review* 28 (1993): 273.

———. "Equal Protection/Equal Safety." *Same-Sex Domestic Violence: Strategies for Change* (1999): 43.

Luo, Feijun, Deborah M. Stone, and Andra T. Tharp. "Physical dating violence victimization among sexual minority youth." *American Journal of Public Health* 104, no. 10 (2014): e66–e73.

Lupri, Eugen. "Institutional resistance to acknowledging intimate male abuse." Paper presented at the Counter-Roundtable Conference on Domestic Violence, Calgary, Alberta, Canada, May 7, 2004.

Lynn, Morgan. "Tool for attorneys working with lesbian, gay, bisexual, and transgender (LGBT) survivors of domestic violence." *American Bar Association and The National LGBT Bar Association* (n.d.). Accessed January 2016. https://static1.squarespace.com/static/566c7foc 2399a3bdabb57553/t/566ca3d32399a3bdabb6e1e5/1449960403057/2011-ABA-Tool-for-Attorneys-working-with-LGBT-Survivors-of-DV.pdf.

Lyons, Thomas, Amy K. Johnson, and Robert Garofalo. "'What Could Have Been Different': A Qualitative Study of Syndemic Theory and HIV Prevention among Young Men Who Have Sex with Men." *Journal of HIV/AIDS and Social Services* 12, nos. 3–4 (2013): 368–383.

Macmillan, Ross, and Rosemary Gartner. "When she brings home the bacon: Labor-force participation and the risk of spousal violence against women." *Journal of Marriage and the Family* (1999): 947–958.

Madera, Sheilla Rodríguez, and José Toro-Alfonso. "Description of a domestic violence measure for Puerto Rican gay males." *Journal of Homosexuality* 50, no. 1 (2005): 155–173.

Mahony, Tina Hotton. "Police-reported dating violence in Canada, 2008." *Juristat* 30, no. 2 (2010).

Maiuro, Roland D., and Jane A. Eberle. "State standards for domestic violence perpetrator treatment: Current status, trends, and recommendations." *Violence and Victims* 23, no. 2 (2008): 133–155.

Mak, Winnie W. S., E. S. K. Chong, and M. M. F. Kwong. "Prevalence of same-sex intimate partner violence in Hong Kong." *Public Health* 124, no. 3 (2010): 149–152.

Makepeace, James M. "Gender differences in courtship violence victimization." *Family Relations* 35, no. 3 (1986): 383–388.

Malinen, KelleyAnne. "Thinking Woman-to-Woman Rape: A Critique of Marcus's 'Theory and Politics of Rape Prevention.'" *Sexuality and Culture* 17, no. 2 (2013): 360–376.

Margolies, Liz, and Elaine Leeder. "Violence at the Door: Treatment of Lesbian Batterers." *Violence against Women* 1, no. 2 (1995): 139–157.

Marrujo, Becky, and Mary Kreger. "Definition of roles in abusive lesbian relationships." *Journal of Gay and Lesbian Social Services* 4, no. 1 (1996): 23–34.

Martin, Brittny A., Ming Cui, Koji Ueno, and Frank D. Fincham. "Intimate partner violence in interracial and monoracial couples." *Family Relations* 62, no. 1 (2013): 202–211.

Martin, Del. *Battered Wives.* Volcano, CA: Volcano Press, 1981.

Martin, Trevor. "What about Violence against Men?" *Everyman* 28 (1997): 24.

Martin-Storey, Alexa. "Prevalence of dating violence among sexual minority youth: Variation across gender, sexual minority identity and gender of sexual partners." *Journal of Youth and Adolescence* 44, no. 1 (2015): 211–224.

Masci, David, Elizabeth Sciupac, and Michael Lipka. "Gay Marriage around the World, Updated June 26, 2015." Washington, DC: Pew Research Center, 2015. www.pewforum .org/2013/12/19/gay-marriage-around-the-world-2013/.

Mason, Tyler B., Robin J. Lewis, Robert J. Milletich, Michelle L. Kelley, Joseph B. Minifie, and Valerian J. Derlega. "Psychological aggression in lesbian, gay, and bisexual individuals' intimate relationships: A review of prevalence, correlates, and measurement issues." *Aggression and Violent Behavior* 19, no. 3 (2014): 219–234.

Massachusetts Department of Education. *2005 Massachusetts Youth Risk Behavior Survey Results.* Boston, 2006.

Matte, Melody, and Marie-France Lafontaine. "Validation of a measure of psychological aggression in same-sex couples: Descriptive data on perpetration and victimization and their association with physical violence." *Journal of GLBT Family Studies* 7, no. 3 (2011): 226–244.

Matthews, Connie R., and Peggy Lorah. "Domestic Violence in Same-Sex Relationships." In *Casebook for Counseling Lesbian, Gay, Bisexual, and Transgender Persons and Their Families,* edited by Sari H. Dworkin and Mark Pope, 307–317. Alexandria, VA: American Counseling Association, 2012.

McAdams, Dan P. "The psychology of life stories." *Review of General Psychology* 5, no. 2 (2001): 100.

McCarry, Melanie, Marianne Hester, and Catherine Donovan. "Researching same sex domestic violence: Constructing a survey methodology." *Sociological Research Online* 13, no. 1 (2008): 8.

McCarthy, Justin. "Nearly 3 in 10 Worldwide See Their Areas as Good for Gays." Gallup. Accessed January 2015. www.gallup.com/poll/175520/nearly-worldwide-areas-good-gays.aspx.

McClennen, Joan C. "Domestic violence between same-gender partners: Recent findings and future research." *Journal of Interpersonal Violence* 20, no. 2 (2005): 149–154.

———. "Prevailing theories regarding same-gender partner abuse: Proposing the feminist social-psychological model." In *A Professional Guide to Understanding Gay and Lesbian Domestic Violence: Understanding Practice Interventions,* edited by Joan C. McClennen and John Joseph Gunther, 3–12. Lewiston, NY: Edwin Mellen Press, 1999.

———. "Researching gay and lesbian domestic violence: The journey of a non-LGBT researcher." *Journal of Gay and Lesbian Social Services* 15, nos. 1–2 (2003): 31–45.

McClennen, Joan C., and John Joseph Gunther, eds. *A Professional's Guide to Understanding Gay and Lesbian Domestic Violence: Understanding Practice Interventions.* Lewiston, NY: Edwin Mellen Press, 1999.

McClennen, Joan C., Anne B. Summers, and James G. Daley. "The lesbian partner abuse scale." *Research on Social Work Practice* 12, no. 2 (2002): 277–292.

McClennen, Joan C., Anne B. Summers, and Charles Vaughan. "Gay men's domestic violence: Dynamics, help-seeking behaviors, and correlates." *Journal of Gay and Lesbian Social Services* 14, no. 1 (2002): 23–49.

McDonald, Courtney. "The social context of woman-to-woman intimate partner abuse (WWIPA)." *Journal of Family Violence* 27, no. 7 (2012): 635–645.

McKenry, Patrick C., Julianne M. Serovich, Tina L. Mason, and Katie Mosack. "Perpetration of gay and lesbian partner violence: A disempowerment perspective." *Journal of Family Violence* 21, no. 4 (2006): 233–243.

McLaughlin, Erin M., and Patricia D. Rozee. "Knowledge about heterosexual versus lesbian battering among lesbians." *Women and Therapy* 23, no. 3 (2001): 39–58.

McLaughlin, Katie A., Mark L. Hatzenbuehler, Ziming Xuan, and Kerith J. Conron. "Disproportionate exposure to early-life adversity and sexual orientation disparities in psychiatric morbidity." *Child Abuse and Neglect* 36, no. 9 (2012): 645–655.

McMullan, Elizabeth C., Philip E. Carlan, and Lisa S. Nored. "Future law enforcement officers and social workers: Perceptions of domestic violence." *Journal of Interpersonal Violence* 25, no. 8 (2010): 1367–1387.

McNeely, Robert L., Philip W. Cook, and José B. Torres. "Is domestic violence a gender issue, or a human issue?" *Journal of Human Behavior in the Social Environment* 4, no. 4 (2001): 227–251.

Mena, Felipe Reyes, José R. Rodríguez, and Sarah Malavé. "Manifestaciones de la violencia doméstica en una muestra de hombres homosexuales y mujeres lesbianas puertorriqueñas" [Domestic violence manifestations in a sample of gay Puerto Rican men and lesbian women]. *Revista interamericana de psicología/Interamerican Journal of Psychology* 39, no. 3 (2005): 449–456.

Mendez, Juan M. "Serving gays and lesbians of color who are survivors of domestic violence." *Journal of Gay and Lesbian Social Services* 4, no. 1 (1996): 53–60.

Mendoza, Jesmen. "The impact of minority stress on gay male partner abuse." In *Intimate Partner Violence in LGBTQ Lives,* edited by Janice L. Ristock, 169–181. New York: Routledge, 2011.

Mendoza, Jesmen, and Diane R. Dolan-Soto. "Running Same-Sex Batterer Groups." In *Intimate Partner Violence in LGBTQ Lives,* edited by Janice L. Ristock, 274–300. New York: Routledge, 2011.

Merlis, Suzanne R., and Deanna Linville. "Exploring a community's response to lesbian domestic violence through the voices of providers: A qualitative study." *Journal of Feminist Family Therapy* 18, nos. 1–2 (2006): 97–136.

Merrill, Gregory S. "Ruling the exceptions: Same-sex battering and domestic violence theory." *Journal of Gay and Lesbian Social Services* 4, no. 1 (1996): 9–22.

———. "Understanding domestic violence among gay and bisexual men." In *Issues in intimate violence,* edited by Raquel Kennedy Bergen, 129–141. Thousand Oaks, CA: SAGE, 1998.

Merrill, Gregory S., and Valerie A. Wolfe. "Battered Gay Men: An Exploration of Abuse, Help Seeking, and Why They Stay." *Journal of Homosexuality* 39, no. 2 (2000): 1–30.

Messinger, Adam M. "Invisible victims: Same-sex IPV in the national violence against women survey." *Journal of Interpersonal Violence* 26, no. 11 (2011): 2228–2243.

———. "Marking 35 Years of Research on Same-Sex Intimate Partner Violence: Lessons and New Directions." In *Handbook of LGBT Communities, Crime, and Justice,* edited by Dana Peterson and Vanessa R. Panfil, 65–85. New York: Springer Science+Business Media, 2014.

Meyer, Ilan H. "Prejudice, social stress, and mental health in lesbian, gay, and bisexual populations: Conceptual issues and research evidence." *Psychological Bulletin* 129, no. 5 (2003): 674.

Meyer, Ilan H., Jessica Dietrich, and Sharon Schwartz. "Lifetime prevalence of mental disorders and suicide attempts in diverse lesbian, gay, and bisexual populations." *American Journal of Public Health* 98, no. 6 (2008): 1004–1006.

Meyer, Ilan H., Sharon Schwartz, and David M. Frost. "Social patterning of stress and coping: Does disadvantaged social statuses confer more stress and fewer coping resources?" *Social Science and Medicine* 67, no. 3 (2008): 368–379.

Meyer, Ilan H., and Patrick A. Wilson. "Sampling lesbian, gay, and bisexual populations." *Journal of Counseling Psychology* 56, no. 1 (2009): 23–31.

Meza-de-Luna, M. E., M. L. Cantera-Espinosa, P. Westendarp-Palacios, and P. Palacios-Sierra. "Never to me! Concealment of intimate partner violence in Queretaro, Mexico." *Trames: A Journal of the Humanities and Social Sciences* 19, no. 2 (2015): 155.

Migliaccio, Todd A. "Abused husbands: A narrative analysis." *Journal of Family issues* 23, no. 1 (2002): 26–52.

Miller, Amy J., Ronald F. Bobner, and John J. Zarski. "Sexual identity development: A base for work with same-sex couple partner abuse." *Contemporary Family Therapy* 22, no. 2 (2000): 189–200.

Miller, Diane Helene, Kathryn Greene, Vickie Causby, Barbara W. White, and Lettie L. Lockhart. "Domestic violence in lesbian relationships." *Women and Therapy* 23, no. 3 (2001): 107–127.

Miller, Jody, and Norman A. White. "Gender and adolescent relationship violence: A contextual examination." *Criminology* 41, no. 4 (2003): 1207–1248.

Miller, Susan L. "Expanding the boundaries: Toward a more inclusive and integrated study of intimate violence." *Violence and Victims* 9, no. 2 (1994): 183.

Milletich, Robert J., Leslie A. Gumienny, Michelle L. Kelley, and Gabrielle M. D'Lima. "Predictors of women's same-sex partner violence perpetration." *Journal of Family Violence* 29, no. 6 (2014): 653–664.

Mimiaga, Matthew J., Katie B. Biello, Angela M. Robertson, Catherine E. Oldenburg, Joshua G. Rosenberger, Conall O'Cleirigh, David S. Novak, Kenneth H. Mayer, and Steven A. Safren. "High prevalence of multiple syndemic conditions associated with sexual risk behavior and HIV infection among a large sample of Spanish-and Portuguese-speaking men who have sex with men in Latin America." *Archives of Sexual Behavior* 44, no. 7 (2015): 1869–1878.

Mize, Krystal D., and Todd K. Shackelford. "Intimate partner homicide methods in heterosexual, gay, and lesbian relationships." *Violence and Victims* 23, no. 1 (2008): 98–114.

Modi, Monica N., Sheallah Palmer, and Alicia Armstrong. "The role of Violence Against Women Act in addressing intimate partner violence: A public health issue." *Journal of Women's Health* 23, no. 3 (2014): 253–259.

Mokonogho, Josephine, Sukriti Mittal, and Gertie Quitangon. "Treating the Transgender Homeless Population: Experiences During Residency Training." *Journal of Gay and Lesbian Mental Health* 14, no. 4 (2010): 346–354.

Moore, C. D., and Caroline K. Waterman. "Predicting self-protection against sexual assault in dating relationships among heterosexual men and women, gay men, lesbians, and bisexuals." *Journal of College Student Development* 40, no. 2 (1999): 132–140.

Moore, Todd M., and Gregory L. Stuart. "A Review of the Literature on Masculinity and Partner Violence." *Psychology of Men and Masculinity* 6, no. 1 (2005): 46.

Moradi, Bonnie, Jonathan J. Mohr, Roger L. Worthington, and Ruth E. Fassinger. "Counseling psychology research on sexual (orientation) minority issues: Conceptual and methodological challenges and opportunities." *Journal of Counseling Psychology* 56, no. 1 (2009): 5–22.

Morris, Jessica F., and Kimberly F. Balsam. "Lesbian and bisexual women's experiences of victimization: Mental health, revictimization, and sexual identity development." *Journal of Lesbian Studies* 7, no. 4 (2003): 67–85.

Morrison, Adele M. "Queering Domestic Violence to 'Straighten Out' Criminal Law: What Might Happen When Queer Theory and Practice Meet Criminal Law's Conventional Responses to Domestic Violence." *Southern California Review of Law and Women's Studies* 13 (2003): 81.

Morrow, Susan L., and Donna M. Hawxhurst. "Lesbian partner abuse: Implications for therapists." *Journal of Counseling and Development* 68, no. 1 (1989): 58–62.

Mottet, Lisa, and John Ohle. "Transitioning our shelters: Making homeless shelters safe for transgender people." *Journal of Poverty* 10, no. 2 (2006): 77–101.

Mravcak, Sally A. "Primary care for lesbians and bisexual women." *Screening* 100, no. 10 (2006): 12–15.

Murphy, Nancy E. "Queer justice: Equal protection for victims of same-sex domestic violence." *Valparaiso University Law Review* 30 (1995): 335.

Murray, Christine E., and A. Keith Mobley. "Empirical research about same-sex intimate partner violence: A methodological review." *Journal of Homosexuality* 56, no. 3 (2009): 361–386.

Murray, Christine E., A. Keith Mobley, Anne P. Buford, and Megan M. Seaman-DeJohn. "Same-sex intimate partner violence: Dynamics, social context, and counseling implications." *Journal of LGBT Issues in Counseling* 1, no. 4 (2007): 7–30.

Mustanski, Brian, Rebecca Andrews, Amy Herrick, Ron Stall, and Phillip W. Schnarrs. "A syndemic of psychosocial health disparities and associations with risk for attempting suicide among young sexual minority men." *American Journal of Public Health* 104, no. 2 (2014): 287–294.

Mustanski, Brian, Robert Garofalo, Amy Herrick, and Geri Donenberg. "Psychosocial health problems increase risk for HIV among urban young men who have sex with men: Preliminary evidence of a syndemic in need of attention." *Annals of Behavioral Medicine* 34, no. 1 (2007): 37–45.

N. "A sliding stance." In *The Revolution Starts at Home: Confronting Partner Abuse in Activist Communities,* edited by Ching-In Chen, Jai Dulani, and Leah Lakshmi Piepzna-Samarasinha, 162–166. Brooklyn, NY: South End Press, 2011.

Naidu, Evashnee, and Nonhlanhla Mkhize. "Gender-based violence: The lesbian and gay experience." *Agenda* 19, no. 66 (2005): 34–38.

National Coalition of Anti-Violence Programs. *Lesbian, Gay, Bisexual, Transgender, Queer and HIV-Affected Intimate Partner Violence, 2011.* New York: National Coalition of Anti-Violence Programs, 2012.

———. *Lesbian, Gay, Bisexual, Transgender, Queer and HIV-Affected Intimate Partner Violence in 2013.* New York: National Coalition of Anti-Violence Programs, 2014.

———. *Annual Report on Lesbian, Gay, Bisexual, Transgender Domestic Violence.* New York, NY: National Coalition of Anti-Violence Programs, 1998.

National Institutes of Health. "Research on the Health of LGBTI Populations [R01]." Call for proposals, National Institute of Child Health and Human Development, National Institutes of Health. Accessed January 2016. http://grants.nih.gov/grants/guide/pa-files /PA-12-111.html.

Nava, Michael. "The Shadow Within: Internalized Homophobia in Gay Men and Same-Sex Domestic Violence." PhD diss., Pacifica Graduate Institute, 2008.

Neilson, Jacqueline. "Clinical Success, Political Failure? Reflections on the 'Interiority' of Abusive Lesbian Relations." *Journal of Lesbian Studies* 8, nos. 1–2 (2004): 107–121.

Nemoto, Tooru, Birte Bödeker, and Mariko Iwamoto. "Social support, exposure to violence and transphobia, and correlates of depression among male-to-female transgender women with a history of sex work." *American Journal of Public Health* 101, no. 10 (2011): 1980–1988.

Nickel, Robin S. "Children witnessing abuse between their same-gender caregivers." In *A Professional's Guide to Understanding Gay and Lesbian Domestic Violence: Understanding Practice Interventions,* edited by Joan C. McClennen and John Gunther, 145–164. Lewiston, NY: Edwin Mellon Press, 1999.

Nicolas, Gandalf, and Allison Louise Skinner. "'That's So Gay!' Priming the General Negative Usage of the Word *Gay* Increases Implicit Anti-Gay Bias." *Journal of Social Psychology* 152, no. 5 (2012): 654–658.

Nieves-Rosa, Luis E., Alex Carballo-Dieguez, and Curtis Dolezal. "Domestic abuse and HIV-risk behavior in Latin American men who have sex with men in New York City." *Journal of Gay and Lesbian Social Services* 11, no. 1 (2000): 77–90.

Nowinski, Sabrina N., and Erica Bowen. "Partner violence against heterosexual and gay men: Prevalence and correlates." *Aggression and Violent Behavior* 17, no. 1 (2012): 36–52.

NYS Office for the Prevention of Domestic Violence. "Domestic Violence in Lesbian, Gay, Bisexual and Transgender Communities Trainers Manual." 2010. www.vawnet.org /Assoc_Files_VAWnet/LGTBManual.pdf.

Ofreneo, Mira Alexis P., and Cristina Jayme Montiel. "Positioning theory as a discursive approach to understanding same-sex intimate violence." *Asian Journal of Social Psychology* 13, no. 4 (2010): 247–259.

Oldenburg, Catherine E., Amaya G. Perez-Brumer, Katie B. Biello, Stewart J. Landers, Joshua G. Rosenberger, David S. Novak, Kenneth H. Mayer, and Matthew J. Mimiaga. "Transactional Sex among Men Who Have Sex with Men in Latin America: Economic, Sociodemographic, and Psychosocial Factors." *American Journal of Public Health* 105, no. 5 (2015): e95-e102.

Oliffe, John L., Christina Han, Estephanie Sta Maria, Maria Lohan, Terry Howard, Donna E. Stewart, and Harriet MacMillan. "Gay men and intimate partner violence: A gender analysis." *Sociology of Health and Illness* 36, no. 4 (2014): 564–579.

Olson, Loreen N., and Sally A. Lloyd. "'It depends on what you mean by starting': An exploration of how women define initiation of aggression and their motives for behaving aggressively." *Sex Roles* 53, nos. 7–8 (2005): 603–617.

Oringher, Jonathan, and Kristin W. Samuelson. "Intimate partner violence and the role of masculinity in male same-sex relationships." *Traumatology* 17, no. 2 (2011): 68–74.

Ortega, Debora, and Noël Busch-Armendariz. "In the Name of VAWA." *Affilia* 28, no. 3 (2013): 225–228.

Oswald, Ramona F., Carol A. Fonseca, and Jennifer L. Hardesty. "Lesbian Mothers' Counseling Experiences in the Context of Intimate Partner Violence." *Psychology of Women Quarterly* 34, no. 3 (2010): 286–296.

Owen, Stephen S., and Tod W. Burke. "An exploration of prevalence of domestic violence in same-sex relationships." *Psychological Reports* 95, no. 1 (2004): 129–132.

Pantalone, David W., Danielle M. Hessler, and Jane M. Simoni. "Mental health pathways from interpersonal violence to health-related outcomes in HIV-positive sexual minority men." *Journal of Consulting and Clinical Psychology* 78, no. 3 (2010): 387.

Pantalone, David W., Keith J. Horvath, Trevor A. Hart, Sarah E. Valentine, and Debra L. Kaysen. "Traumatic revictimization of men who have sex with men living with HIV/AIDS." *Journal of Interpersonal Violence* 30, no. 9 (2014): 1459–1477.

Pantalone, David W., K. Lehavot, J. M. Simoni, and K. L. Walters. "I ain't never been a kid: Early violence exposure and other pathways to partner violence for sexual minority men with HIV." In *Intimate Partner Violence in LGBTQ Lives*, edited by Janice L. Ristock, 185–208. New York: Routledge, 2011.

Pantalone, David W., Karen L. Schneider, Sarah E. Valentine, and Jane M. Simoni. "Investigating partner abuse among HIV-positive men who have sex with men." *AIDS and Behavior* 16, no. 4 (2012): 1031–1043.

Paroissien, Karen, and Penny Stewart. "Surviving lesbian abuse: Empowerment groups for education and support." *Women Against Violence: An Australian Feminist Journal* 9 (2000): 33.

Parsons, Jeffrey T., Christian Grov, and Sarit A. Golub. "Sexual compulsivity, co-occurring psychosocial health problems, and HIV risk among gay and bisexual men: further evidence of a syndemic." *American Journal of Public Health* 102, no. 1 (2012): 156–162.

Parsons, Jeffrey T., H. Jonathon Rendina, Raymond L. Moody, Ana Ventuneac, and Christian Grov. "Syndemic production and sexual compulsivity/hypersexuality in highly sexually active gay and bisexual men: Further evidence for a three group conceptualization." *Archives of Sexual Behavior* 44, no. 7 (2015): 1903–1913.

Pascoe, Cheri Jo. "'Dude, you're a fag': Adolescent masculinity and the fag discourse." *Sexualities* 8, no. 3 (2005): 329–346.

Pathé, Michele T., Paul E. Mullen, and Rosemary Purcell. "Same-gender stalking." *Journal of the American Academy of Psychiatry and the Law Online* 28, no. 2 (2000): 191–197.

Pathela, Preeti, and Julia A. Schillinger. "Sexual behaviors and sexual violence: Adolescents with opposite-, same-, or both-sex partners." *Pediatrics* 126, no. 5 (2010): 879–886.

Pattavina, April, David Hirschel, Eve Buzawa, Don Faggiani, and Helen Bentley. "A comparison of the police response to heterosexual versus same-sex intimate partner violence." *Violence against Women* 13, no. 4 (2007): 374–394.

Patzel, Brenda. "Lesbian partner abuse: Differences from heterosexual victims of abuse; A review from the literature." *Kansas Nurse* 80, no. 9 (2005): 7–8.

Paul, Jay P., Joseph Catania, Lance Pollack, and Ronald Stall. "Understanding childhood sexual abuse as a predictor of sexual risk-taking among men who have sex with men: The Urban Men's Health Study." *Child Abuse and Neglect* 25, no. 4 (2001): 557–584.

Paulozzi, Leonard J., Linda E. Saltzman, Martie P. Thompson, and Patricia Holmgreen. "Surveillance for homicide among intimate partners: United States, 1981–1998." *Morbidity and Mortality Weekly Report (MMWR) Surveillance Summaries* 50 (2001): 1–16.

Peplau, Letitia A., and Adam W. Fingerhut. "The close relationships of lesbians and gay men." *Annual Review of Psychology* 58 (2007): 405–424.

Peplau, Letitia A., Rosemary C. Veniegas, and Susan Miller Campbell. "Gay and lesbian relationships." In *The Lives of Lesbians, Gays, and Bisexuals: Children to Adults*, edited by Ritch C. Savin-Williams and Kenneth M. Cohen, 250–273. Fort Worth, TX: Harcourt Brace College Publishers, 1996.

Pepper, Bonnie I., and Shara Sand. "Internalized Homophobia and Intimate Partner Violence in Young Adult Women's Same-Sex Relationships." *Journal of Aggression, Maltreatment and Trauma* 24, no. 6 (2015): 656–673.

Peralta, Robert L., and Jodi Ross. "Understanding the complexity of alcohol-related intimate partner violence in the lives of Hispanic men who have sex with men: Methodological issues and considerations." *Gender Issues* 26, no. 1 (2009): 85–104.

Perez-Darby, Shannon. "The secret joy of accountability: Self-accountability as a building block for change." In *The Revolution Starts at Home: Confronting Partner Abuse in Activist Communities*, edited by Ching-In Chen, Jai Dulani, and Leah Lakshmi Piepzna-Samarasinha, 100–113. Brooklyn, NY: South End Press, 2011.

Perreault, Samuel. "Homicide in Canada, 2011." *Juristat* 32, no. 1 (2012).

Pertnoy, Leonard. "Same Violence, Same Sex, Different Standard: An Examination of Same-Sex Domestic Violence and the Use of Expert Testimony on Battered Woman's Syndrome in Same-Sex Domestic Violence Cases." *St. Thomas Law Review* 24, no. 3 (2012): 2013–04.

Peterman, Linda M., and Charlotte G. Dixon. "Domestic violence between same-sex partners: Implications for counseling." *Journal of Counseling and Development: JCD* 81, no. 1 (2003): 40.

Pfeifer, Tara R. "Out of the Shadows: The Positive Impact of Lawrence v. Texas on Victims of Same-Sex Domestic Violence." *Penn State Law Review* 109 (2004): 1251.

Phillips, Gregory, II, Manya Magnus, Irene Kuo, Anthony Rawls, James Peterson, Luz Montanez, Tiffany West-Ojo, Yujiang Jia, Jenevieve Opoku, and Alan E. Greenberg. "Childhood sexual abuse and HIV-related risks among men who have sex with men in Washington, DC." *Archives of Sexual Behavior* 43, no. 4 (2014): 771–778.

Pitts, Marian, Anthony Smith, Anne Mitchell, and Sunil Patel. *Private Lives: A Report on the Health and Wellbeing of GLBTI Australians*. Melbourne, Australia: Australian Research Centre in Sex, Health and Society, La Trobe University, 2006.

Poirier, Marc R. "Same-sex couples and the 'exclusive commitment': untangling the issues and consequences: piecemeal and wholesale approaches towards marriage equality in New Jersey; Is *Lewis v. Harris* a dead end or just a detour?" *Rutgers Law Review* 59 (2007): 291–917.

Poon, Colleen S., and Elizabeth M. Saewyc. "Out yonder: Sexual-minority adolescents in rural communities in British Columbia." *American Journal of Public Health* 99, no. 1 (2009): 118–124.

Poon, Maurice Kwong-Lai. "Beyond good and evil: The social construction of violence in intimate gay relationships." In *Intimate Partner Violence in LGBTQ Lives*, edited by Janice L. Ristock, 102–130. New York: Routledge, 2011.

———. "Inter-racial same-sex abuse: The vulnerability of gay men of Asian descent in relationships with Caucasian men." *Journal of Gay and Lesbian Social Services* 11, no. 4 (2000): 39–67.

Poorman, Paula B. "Forging community links to address abuse in lesbian relationships." *Women and Therapy* 23, no. 3 (2001): 7–24.

Poorman, Paula B., and Sheila M. Seelau. "Lesbians who abuse their partners: Using the FIRO-B to assess interpersonal characteristics." *Women and Therapy* 23, no. 3 (2001): 87–105.

Poorman, Paula B., Eric P. Seelau, and Sheila M. Seelau. "Perceptions of Domestic Abuse in Same-Sex Relationships and Implications for Criminal Justice and Mental Health Responses." *Violence and Victims* 18, no. 6 (2003): 659–669.

Porter, Judy Lee, and LaVerne McQuiller Williams. "Intimate violence among underrepresented groups on a college campus." *Journal of Interpersonal Violence* 26, no. 16 (2011): 3210–3224.

Potter, Sharyn J., Kim Fountain, and Jane G. Stapleton. "Addressing sexual and relationship violence in the LGBT community using a bystander framework." *Harvard Review of Psychiatry* 20, no. 4 (2012): 201–208.

Price, Bethany J., and Alan Rosenbaum. "Batterer intervention programs: A report from the field." *Violence and Victims* 24, no. 6 (2009): 757–770.

Price, Joshua M. *Structural Violence: Hidden Brutality in the Lives of Women.* Albany, NY: SUNY Press, 2012.

Pruitt, Kaitlyn L., Darcy White, Jason W. Mitchell, and Rob Stephenson. "Sexual agreements and intimate-partner violence among male couples." *International Journal of Sexual Health* 27, no. 4 (2015): 429–441.

Purcell, David W., Christopher H. Johnson, Amy Lansky, Joseph Prejean, Renee Stein, Paul Denning, Zaneta Gau, Hillard Weinstock, John Su, and Nicole Crepaz. "Estimating the Population Size of Men Who Have Sex with Men in the United States to Obtain HIV and Syphilis Rates." *Open AIDS Journal* 6, no. 1 (2012).

Puzone, Carol A., Linda E. Saltzman, Marcie-Jo Kresnow, Martie P. Thompson, and James A. Mercy. "National Trends in Intimate Partner Homicide United States, 1976–1995." *Violence against Women* 6, no. 4 (2000): 409–426.

Pyles, Loretta, and Kyung Mee Kim. "A multilevel approach to cultural competence: A study of the community response to underserved domestic violence victims." *Families in Society: The Journal of Contemporary Social Services* 87, no. 2 (2006): 221–229.

Pyra, Maria, Kathleen Weber, Tracey E. Wilson, Jennifer Cohen, Lynn Murchison, Lakshmi Goparaju, and Mardge H. Cohen. "Sexual minority status and violence among HIV infected and at-risk women." *Journal of General Internal Medicine* 29, no. 8 (2014): 1131–1138.

Quinn, Mary-Elizabeth. "Open minds open doors: Transforming domestic violence programs to include LGBTQ survivors." Boston: The Network/La Red, 2010. www.ncdsv .org/images/TheNetworkLaRed_OpenMindsOpenDoors_2010.pdf.

Rachel Lanzerotti Consulting. "2005–06 Youth Relationship Violence Survey Findings." San Francisco: Love and Justice Project of Community United against Violence, 2006. www.cuav.org/wp-content/uploads/2012/08/1725_L+JRelationshipViolenceReport.pdf.

Ramachandran, Shruti, Michael A. Yonas, Anthony J. Silvestre, and Jessica G. Burke. "Intimate partner violence among HIV-positive persons in an urban clinic." *AIDS Care* 22, no. 12 (2010): 1536–1543.

Randle, Anna A., and Cynthia A. Graham. "A review of the evidence on the effects of intimate partner violence on men." *Psychology of Men and Masculinity* 12, no. 2 (2011): 97–111.

Regan, Katherine V., Kim Bartholomew, Doug Oram, and Monica A. Landolt. "Measuring

Physical Violence in Male Same-Sex Relationships: An Item Response Theory Analysis of the Conflict Tactics Scales." *Journal of Interpersonal Violence* 17, no. 3 (2002): 235–252.

Reisner, Sari L., Kathryn L. Falb, Aimee Van Wagenen, Chris Grasso, and Judith Bradford. "Sexual orientation disparities in substance misuse: The role of childhood abuse and intimate partner violence among patients in care at an urban community health center." *Substance Use and Misuse* 48, no. 3 (2013): 274–289.

Relf, Michael V. "Battering and HIV in men who have sex with men: A critique and synthesis of the literature." *Journal of the Association of Nurses in AIDS Care* 12, no. 3 (2001): 41–48.

Relf, Michael V., Bu Huang, Jacquelyn Campbell, and Joe Catania. "Gay identity, interpersonal violence, and HIV risk behaviors: An empirical test of theoretical relationships among a probability-based sample of urban men who have sex with men." *Journal of the Association of Nurses in AIDS Care* 15, no. 2 (2004): 14–26.

Renner, Lynette M., and Stephen D. Whitney. "Examining symmetry in intimate partner violence among young adults using socio-demographic characteristics." *Journal of Family Violence* 25, no. 2 (2010): 91–106.

Rennison, Callie Marie. "Intimate partner violence and age of victim, 1993–1999 (NCJ Publication no. 187635)." Washington, DC: US Department of Justice, 2001.

Renzetti, Claire M. "Building a second closet: Third party responses to victims of lesbian partner abuse." *Family Relations* (1989): 157–163.

———. "On dancing with a bear: Reflections on some of the current debates among domestic violence theorists." *Violence and Victims* 9, no. 2 (1994): 195.

———. "The poverty of services for battered lesbians." *Journal of Gay and Lesbian Social Services* 4, no. 1 (1996): 61–68.

———. "Violence and abuse in lesbian relationships." In *Issues in Intimate Violence,* edited by Raquel Kennedy Bergen, 117–127. Thousand Oaks, CA: SAGE, 1998.

———. "Violence in lesbian relationships." In *Battering and Family Therapy: A Feminist Perspective,* edited by Marsali Hansen and Michele Harway, 188–199. Newbury Park, CA: SAGE, 1993.

———. "Violence in Lesbian Relationships: A Preliminary Analysis of Causal Factors." *Journal of Interpersonal Violence* 3, no. 4 (1988): 381–399.

———. *Violent betrayal: Partner abuse in lesbian relationships.* Newbury Park, CA: Sage Publications, 1992.

Renzetti, Claire M., and Charles H. Miley. *Violence in Gay and Lesbian Domestic Partnerships.* New York: Haworth Press, 1996.

Reuter, Tyson R., Carla Sharp, and Jeff R. Temple. "An exploratory study of teen dating violence in sexual minority youth." *Partner Abuse* 6, no. 1 (2015): 8–28.

Rhodes, Scott D., Thomas P. McCoy, Aimee M. Wilkin, and Mark Wolfson. "Behavioral risk disparities in a random sample of self-identifying gay and non-gay male university students." *Journal of Homosexuality* 56, no. 8 (2009): 1083–1100.

Richards, Andrew, Nathalie Noret, and Ian Rivers. "Violence and abuse in same-sex relationships: A review of the literature." Social Inclusion and Diversity Paper no. 5, "Research into Practice." York, England: York St. John College, 2003.

Ricks, Janice L., Carol Vaughn, and Sophia F. Dziegielewski. "Domestic violence among lesbian couples." In *Handbook of Domestic Violence Intervention Strategies: Policies,*

Programs, and Legal Remedies, edited by Albert R. Roberts, 451–463. Oxford: Oxford University Press, 2002.

Risser, Jan M. H., Andrea Shelton, Sheryl McCurdy, John Atkinson, Paige Padgett, Bernardo Useche, Brenda Thomas, and Mark Williams. "Sex, Drugs, Violence, and HIV Status Among Male-to-Female Transgender Persons in Houston, Texas." *International Journal of Transgenderism* 8, nos. 2–3 (2005): 67–74.

Ristock, Janice L. "'And Justice for All?' . . . The Social Context of Legal Responses to Abuse in Lesbian Relationships." *Canadian Journal of Women and the Law* 7 (1994): 415–430.

——. "Beyond ideologies: Understanding violence in lesbian relationships." *Canadian Woman Studies/Les Cahiers de la Femme* 12 (1991): 74–79.

——. "The cultural politics of abuse in lesbian relationships: Challenges for community action." In *Subtle Sexism: Current Practice and Prospects for Change,* edited by Nijole V. Benokraitis, 279–296. Thousand Oaks, CA: SAGE, 1997.

——. "Decentering heterosexuality: Responses of feminist counselors to abuse in lesbian relationships." *Women and Therapy* 23, no. 3 (2001): 59–72.

——, ed. *Intimate Partner Violence in LGBTQ Lives.* New York: Routledge, 2011.

——. *No More Secrets: Violence in lesbian Relationships.* New York: Psychology Press, 2002.

——. "Responding to lesbian relationship violence: An ethical challenge." In *Reclaiming Self: Issues and Resources for Women Abused by Intimate Partners,* edited by Leslie M. Tutty and Carolyn Goard, 98–116. Halifax, Nova Scotia, Canada: Fernwood, 2002.

Ristock, Janice L., and Norma Timbang. "Relationship violence in lesbian/gay/bisexual /transgender/queer [LGBTQ] communities: Moving beyond a Gender Based Framework." Violence against Women Online Resources, 2005.

Roberts, Andrea L., S. Bryn Austin, Heather L. Corliss, Ashley K. Vandermorris, and Karestan C. Koenen. "Pervasive trauma exposure among US sexual orientation minority adults and risk of posttraumatic stress disorder." *American Journal of Public Health* 100, no. 12 (2010): 2433–2441.

Roberts, Jeffrey A. "An integrative review of intimate partner violence among men who have sex with men: Correlates of victimization and development of a conceptual framework." *Humanity and Society* 29, no. 2 (2005): 126–136.

Robinson, Amorie. "There's a stranger in this house: African American lesbians and domestic violence." *Women and Therapy* 25, nos. 3–4 (2002): 125–132.

Robson, Ruthann. "Lavender Bruises: Intra-Lesbian Violence, Law and Lesbian Legal Theory." *Golden Gate University Law Review* 20 (1990): 567–591.

——. *Lesbian (Out) Law: Survival under the Rule of Law.* Ithaca, NY: Firebrand Books, 1992.

Roch, Amy, Graham Ritchie, and James Morton. *Out of Sight, out of mind? Transgender People's Experiences of Domestic Abuse.* Edinburgh: LGBT Youth Scotland and the Scottish Transgender Alliance, 2010. https://www.lgbtyouth.org.uk/files/documents /DomesticAbuseResources/transgender_DA.pdf.

Rohrbaugh, Joanna Bunker. "Domestic violence in same-gender relationships." *Family Court Review* 44, no. 2 (2006): 287–299.

Rooney, Margaux. "The evolution of services for male domestic violence victims at WEAVE." *Partner Abuse* 1, no. 1 (2010): 117–124.

Rose, Suzanna M. "Community interventions concerning homophobic violence and partner violence against lesbians." *Journal of Lesbian Studies* 7, no. 4 (2003): 125–139.

Rothman, Emily Faith, Deinera Exner, and Allyson L. Baughman. "The prevalence of sexual assault against people who identify as gay, lesbian, or bisexual in the United States: A systematic review." *Trauma, Violence, and Abuse* 12, no. 2 (2011): 55–66.

Rowlands, James. *Domestic Abuse among Gay and Bisexual Men: An Exploratory Study in South Wales.* Norwich, England: School of Social Work and Psychosocial Studies, University of East Anglia, 2006.

Royko, Mike. "500,000 Gay Men Don't Have to Take Abuse from Partner." *Chicago Tribune,* 1996. http://articles.chicagotribune.com/1996-12-10/news/9612100232_1_spousal-abuse-gay-men-issue-of-same-sex-marriage.

Russell, Brenda. "Bridging the Gap in Knowledge about Partner Abuse in LGBTQ Populations." *Partner Abuse* 6, no. 1 (2015): 3–7.

Russell, Brenda, Kristine M. Chapleau, and Shane W. Kraus. "When is it abuse? How assailant gender, sexual orientation, and protection orders influence perceptions of intimate partner abuse." *Partner Abuse* 6, no. 1 (2015): 47–64.

Russell, Brenda, Laurie Ragatz, and Shane Kraus. "Does ambivalent sexism influence verdicts for heterosexual and homosexual defendants in a self-defense case?" *Journal of Family Violence* 24, no. 3 (2009): 145–157.

———. "Self-defense and legal decision making: The role of defendant and victim gender and gender-neutral expert testimony of the battered partner's syndrome." *Partner Abuse* 1, no. 4 (2010): 399–419.

Russo, Ann. "Lesbian and bisexual women's battering: Homophobia, heterosexism, and violence." in *Taking Back Our Lives: A Call to Action for the Feminist Movement,* edited by Ann Russo, 57–80. New York: Routledge, 2001.

———. "Recognizing difference: Exploring violence in lesbian relationships." *Psychology of Women Quarterly* 27, no. 1 (2003): 86–88.

Sabidó, Meritxell, Ligia Regina Franco Sansigolo Kerr, Rosa Salani Mota, Adele Schwartz Benzaken, Adriana de A. Pinho, Mark D. C. Guimaraes, Ines Dourado, Edgar Merchan-Hamman, and Carl Kendall. "Sexual Violence against Men Who Have Sex with Men in Brazil: A Respondent-Driven Sampling Survey." *AIDS and Behavior* 19, no. 9 (2015): 1630–1641.

SafeLives. "SafeLives Dash risk checklist: Quick start guidance." Accessed January 2016. www.safelives.org.uk/sites/default/files/resources/Dash%20risk%20checklist%20quick%20start%20guidance%20FINAL.pdf.

Samons, Christina. "Same-Sex Domestic Violence: The Need for Affirmative Legal Protections at All Levels of Government." *Southern California Review of Law and Social Justice* 22 (2012): 417.

Santaya, Pedro O. Téllez, and Andrew S. Walters. "Intimate partner violence within gay male couples: Dimensionalizing partner violence among Cuban gay men." *Sexuality and Culture* 15, no. 2 (2011): 153–178.

Santos, Ana Cristina. "'Between two women it does not happen': An exploratory study into lesbian conjugal violence." *Journal of Critical Social Sciences* 98 (2012): 3–24.

Sarantakos, Sotirios. "Same-sex couples: Problems and prospects." *Journal of Family Studies* 2, no. 2 (1996): 147–163.

Scherzer, Teresa. "Domestic violence in lesbian relationships: Findings of the lesbian relationships research project." *Journal of Lesbian Studies* 2, no. 1 (1998): 29–47.

Schilit, Rebecca, Gwat-Yong Lie, and Marilyn Montagne. "Substance use as a correlate of violence in intimate lesbian relationships." *Journal of Homosexuality* 19, no. 3 (1990): 51–66.

Schilit, Rebecca, Gwat-Yong Lie, Judy Bush, Marilyn Montagne, and Lynn Reyes. "Intergenerational transmission of violence in lesbian relationships." *Affilia* 6, no. 1 (1991): 72–87.

Schneider, Elizabeth M. "Particularity and generality: Challenges of feminist theory and practice in work on woman-abuse." *New York University Law Review* 67 (1992): 520.

Schwartz, Martin D. "Methodological issues in the use of survey data for measuring and characterizing violence against women." *Violence against Women* 6, no. 8 (2000): 815–838.

Scottish Transgender Alliance. "Transgender Experiences in Scotland: Research Summary." Equality Network, 2008. www.scottishtrans.org/wp-content/uploads/2013/03/staexperiences summary03082.pdf.

Sears, Heather A., E. Sandra Byers, John J. Whelan, and Marcelle Saint-Pierre. "'If it hurts you, then it is not a joke': Adolescents' ideas about girls' and boys' use and experience of abusive behavior in dating relationships." *Journal of Interpersonal Violence* 21, no. 9 (2006): 1191–1207.

Seelau, Eric P., Sheila M. Seelau, and Paul B. Poorman. "Gender and Role-Based Perceptions of Domestic Abuse: Does Sexual Orientation Matter?" *Behavioral Sciences and the Law* 21 (2003): 199–214.

Seelau, Sheila M., and Eric P. Seelau. "Gender-Role Stereotypes and Perceptions of Heterosexual, Gay and Lesbian Domestic Violence." *Journal of Family Violence* 20, no. 6 (2005): 363–371.

Seeman, Mary V. "Sexual Minority Women in Treatment for Serious Mental Illness: A Literature Review." *Journal of Gay and Lesbian Mental Health* 19, no. 3 (2015): 303–319.

Senseman, Rachel L. "Screening for intimate partner violence among gay and lesbian patients in primary care." *Clinical Excellence for Nurse Practitioners* 6, no. 4 (2002): 27–32.

Serra, Natalie E. "Queering International Human Rights: LGBT Access to Domestic Violence Remedies." *Journal of Gender, Social Policy and the Law* 21 (2012): 583.

Shelton, Andrea J., J. Atkinson, Jan M. H. Risser, S. A. McCurdy, B. Useche, and P. M. Padgett. "The prevalence of partner violence in a group of HIV-infected men." *AIDS Care* 17, no. 7 (2005): 814–818.

Sheridan, Lorraine P., Adrian C. North, and Adrian J. Scott. "Experiences of stalking in same-sex and opposite-sex contexts." *Violence and Victims* 29, no. 6 (2014): 1014–1028.

Siemieniuk, Reed A. C., Hartmut B. Krentz, Jessica A. Gish, and M. John Gill. "Domestic violence screening: Prevalence and outcomes in a Canadian HIV population." *AIDS Patient Care and STDs* 24, no. 12 (2010): 763–770.

Siemieniuk, Reed A. C., P. Miller, K. Woodman, K. Ko, H. B. Krentz, and M. J. Gill. "Prevalence, clinical associations, and impact of intimate partner violence among HIV-infected gay and bisexual men: A population-based study." *HIV Medicine* 14, no. 5 (2013): 293–302.

Sigurvinsdottir, Rannveig, and Sarah E. Ullman. "The role of sexual orientation in the victimization and recovery of sexual assault survivors." *Violence and Victims* 30, no. 4 (2015): 636–648.

Sillman, Jane S. "Diagnosis, screening, and counseling for domestic violence." UpToDate, 2010. www.uptodate.com.

Simpson, Emily K., and Christine A. Helfrich. "Lesbian survivors of intimate partner violence: Provider perspectives on barriers to accessing services." *Journal of Gay and Lesbian Social Services* 18, no. 2 (2007): 39–59.

————. "Oppression and barriers to service for Black, lesbian survivors of intimate partner violence." *Journal of Gay and Lesbian Social Services* 26, no. 4 (2014): 441–465.

Singh, Anneliese, and Vel S. McKleroy. "'Just getting out of bed is a revolutionary act': The resilience of transgender people of color who have survived traumatic life events." *Traumatology* (2010): 34–44.

Sinha, Maire. "Family violence in Canada: A statistical profile, 2010." *Juristat* 32, no. 1 (2012).

Smith, Carrol. "Women Who Abuse Their Female Intimate Partners." In *Intimate Partner Violence in LGBTQ Lives,* edited by Janice L. Ristock, 131–152. New York: Routledge, 2011.

Smollin, Leandra M. "Lesbian, gay, bisexual, transgender, and queer adolescent dating violence: a review and discussion of research and theory." *Rutgers Journal of Sociology* 1 (2011): 133–164.

Sokoloff, Natalie J., and Ida Dupont. "Domestic violence at the intersections of race, class, and gender: Challenges and contributions to understanding violence against marginalized women in diverse communities." *Violence against Women* 11, no. 1 (2005): 38–64.

Sollenberger, Julia, Susan K. Cavanaugh, Kathleen Burr Oliver, and Cheryl A. Thompson. "The value of library and information services in patient care: results of a multisite study." *Journal of the Medical Library Association* 101, no. 1 (2013): 38.

Sorenson, Susan B., and Haikang Shen. "Restraining Orders in California: A Look at Statewide Data." *Violence against Women* 11, no. 7 (2005): 912–933.

Sorenson, Susan B. and Kristie A. Thomas, "Views of Intimate Partner Violence in Same- and Opposite-Sex Relationships," *Journal of Marriage and Family* 71 (2009): 337–352.

Sprigg, Peter, "Questions and Answers: What's Wrong with Letting Same-Sex Couples 'Marry'?" Family Research Council. Accessed January 2015. www.frc.org/whats-wrong-with-letting-same-sex-couples-marry.

St. Pierre, Melissa, and Charlene Y. Senn. "External barriers to help-seeking encountered by Canadian gay and lesbian victims of intimate partner abuse: An application of the barriers model." *Violence and Victims* 25, no. 4 (2010): 536–552.

Stall, Ron, Thomas C. Mills, John Williamson, Trevor Hart, Greg Greenwood, Jay Paul, Lance Pollack, Diane Binson, Dennis Osmond, and Joseph A. Catania. "Association of co-occurring psychosocial health problems and increased vulnerability to HIV/AIDS among urban men who have sex with men." *American Journal of Public Health* 93, no. 6 (2003): 939–942.

Stanley, Jessica L., Kim Bartholomew, Tracy Taylor, Doug Oram, and Monica Landolt. "Intimate violence in male same-sex relationships." *Journal of Family Violence* 21, no. 1 (2006): 31–41.

Stapel, Sharon. "Falling to pieces: New York State civil legal remedies available to lesbian, gay, bisexual, and transgender survivors of domestic violence." *New York Law School Law Review* 52 (2007): 247.

Starks, Tyrel J., Brett M. Millar, Jeremy J. Eggleston, and Jeffrey T. Parsons. "Syndemic factors associated with HIV risk for gay and bisexual men: Comparing latent class and latent factor modeling." *AIDS and Behavior* 18, no. 11 (2014): 2075–2079.

Starks, Tyrel J., Andrew N. Tuck, Brett M. Millar, and Jeffrey T. Parsons. "Linking Syndemic Stress and Behavioral Indicators of Main Partner HIV Transmission Risk in Gay Male Couples." *AIDS and Behavior* 20, no. 2 (2015): 439–448.

Statistiska centralbyran [Statistics Sweden]. "Befolkningsstatistik [Population Statistics]." Accessed January 2015. www.scb.se/en_/Finding-statistics/Statistics-by-subject-area /Population/Population-composition/Population-statistics/.

Stephenson, Robert, Alex de Voux, and Patrick S. Sullivan. "Intimate partner violence and sexual risk-taking among men who have sex with men in South Africa." *Western Journal of Emergency Medicine* 12, no. 3 (2011).

Stephenson, Robert, and Catherine Finneran. "The IPV-GBM scale: A new scale to measure intimate partner violence among gay and bisexual men." *PloS One* 8, no. 6 (2013): 1–10.

Stephenson, Robert, Casey D. Hall, Whitney Williams, Kimi N. Sato, and Catherine Finneran. "Towards the development of an intimate partner violence screening tool for gay and bisexual men." *Western Journal of Emergency Medicine* 14, no. 4 (2013): 390–400.

Stephenson, Robert, Marisa Hast, Catherine Finneran, and Craig R. Sineath. "Intimate partner, familial and community violence among men who have sex with men in Namibia." *Culture, Health and Sexuality* 16, no. 5 (2014): 473–487.

Stephenson, Robert, Christine Khosropour, and Patrick Sullivan. "Reporting of intimate partner violence among men who have sex with men in an on-line survey." *Western Journal of Emergency Medicine* 11, no. 3 (2010).

Stephenson, Robert, Christopher Rentsch, Laura F. Salazar, and Patrick S. Sullivan. "Dyadic characteristics and intimate partner violence among men who have sex with men." *Western Journal of Emergency Medicine* 12, no. 3 (2011).

Stephenson, Robert, Kimi Noe Sato, and Cathrine Finneran. "Dyadic, partner, and social network influences on intimate partner violence among male-male couples." *Western Journal of Emergency Medicine* 14, no. 4 (2013).

Stevens, Sally, Josephine D. Korchmaros, and Delaina Miller. "A comparison of victimization and perpetration of intimate partner violence among drug abusing heterosexual and lesbian women." *Journal of Family Violence* 25, no. 7 (2010): 639–649.

Stiles-Shields, Colleen, and Richard A. Carroll. "Same-sex domestic violence: Prevalence, unique aspects, and clinical implications." *Journal of Sex and Marital Therapy* 41, no. 6 (2015): 636–648.

Stoddard, Joel P., Suzanne L. Dibble, and Norman Fineman. "Sexual and physical abuse: A comparison between lesbians and their heterosexual sisters." *Journal of Homosexuality* 56, no. 4 (2009): 407–420.

Stoffelen, J., G. Kok, H. Hospers, and L. M. G. Curfs. "Homosexuality among people with a mild intellectual disability: An explorative study on the lived experiences of homosexual people in the Netherlands with a mild intellectual disability." *Journal of Intellectual Disability Research* 57, no. 3 (2013): 257–267.

Stowers, Genie N. L. "A different model: Alternative service delivery for today's diverse communities." *Journal of Health and Human Services Administration* (1999): 174–195.

Strand, Susanne, and Troy E. McEwan. "Same-gender stalking in Sweden and Australia." *Behavioral Sciences and the Law* 29, no. 2 (2011): 202–219.

Strasser, Sheryl M., Megan Smith, Danielle Pendrick-Denney, Sarah Boos-Beddington, Ken Chen, and Frances McCarty. "Feasibility study of social media to reduce intimate partner violence among gay men in metro Atlanta, Georgia." *Western Journal of Emergency Medicine* 13, no. 3 (2012).

Straus, Murray A. "The controversy over domestic violence by women." In *Violence in intimate relationships,* edited by Ximena B. Arriaga and Stuart Oskamp, 17–44. Thousand Oaks, CA: SAGE, 1999.

———. "Dominance and symmetry in partner violence by male and female university students in 32 nations." *Children and Youth Services Review* 30, no. 3 (2008): 252–275.

———. "Future research on gender symmetry in physical assaults on partners." *Violence against Women* 12, no. 11 (2006): 1086–1097.

———. "Measuring intrafamily conflict and violence: The conflict tactics (CT) scales." *Journal of Marriage and the Family* (1979): 75–88.

Straus, Murray A., Sherry L. Hamby, Sue Boney-McCoy, and David B. Sugarman. "The revised conflict tactics scales (CTS2): Development and preliminary psychometric data." *Journal of Family Issues* 17, no. 3 (1996): 283–316.

Strickler, Edward, Jr., and Quillin Drew. "Starting and Sustaining LGBTQ Antiviolence Programs in a Southern State." *Partner Abuse* 6, no. 1 (2015): 78–106.

Stuart, Gregory L., Todd M. Moore, Julianne C. Hellmuth, Susan E. Ramsey, and Christopher W. Kahler. "Reasons for intimate partner violence perpetration among arrested women." *Violence against Women* 12, no. 7 (2006): 609–621.

Sugarman, David B., and Gerald T. Hotaling. "Intimate violence and social desirability: A meta-analytic review." *Journal of Interpersonal Violence* 12, no. 2 (1997): 275–290.

Swan, Suzanne C., and David L. Snow. "Behavioral and psychological differences among abused women who use violence in intimate relationships." *Violence against Women* 9, no. 1 (2003): 75–109.

Sykes, Gresham M., and David Matza. "Techniques of neutralization: A theory of delinquency." *American Sociological Review* 22, no. 6 (1957): 664–670.

Sylaska, Kateryna M., and Katie M. Edwards. "Disclosure experiences of sexual minority college student victims of intimate partner violence." *American Journal of Community Psychology* 55, nos. 3–4 (2015): 326–335.

Sylaska, Kateryna M., and Andrew S. Walters. "Testing the extent of the gender trap: College students' perceptions of and reactions to intimate partner violence." *Sex Roles* 70, nos. 3–4 (2014): 134–145.

Talicska, Joshua D. "Out of One Closet and into Another: Why Abused Homosexual Males Refrain from Reporting Their Abuse and What to Do about It." *Modern American* 8 (2012): 21–30.

Tark, Jongyeon, and Gary Kleck. "Resisting Rape: The Effects of Victim Self-Protection on Rape Completion and Injury." *Violence against Women* 20, no. 3 (2014): 270–292.

Taylor, C., and Janice L. Ristock. "We are all treaty people: An anti-oppressive research ethics of solidarity with Indigenous Two-Spirit and LGBTQ people living with partner violence." In *Intimate Partner Violence in LGBTQ Lives,* edited by Janice L. Ristock, 301–320. New York: Routledge, 2011.

Taylor, Paul. "A survey of LGBT Americans: Attitudes, experiences and values in changing times." Washington, DC: Pew Research Center, 2013. http://www.pewsocialtrends.org /files/2013/06/SDT_LGBT-Americans_06-2013.pdf.

Tesch, Brian Peter, and Debra A. Bekerian. "Hidden in the Margins: A Qualitative Examination of What Professionals in the Domestic Violence Field Know about Transgender Domestic Violence." *Journal of Gay and Lesbian Social Services* 27, no. 4 (2015): 391–411.

Tesch, Brian Peter, Debra A. Bekerian, Peter English, and Evan Harrington. "Same-sex domestic violence: Why victims are more at risk." *International Journal of Police Science and Management* 12 (2010): 526–535.

Thompson, Carleen M., Susan M. Dennison, and Anna Stewart. "Are female stalkers more violent than male stalkers? Understanding gender differences in stalking violence using contemporary sociocultural beliefs." *Sex Roles* 66, nos. 5–6 (2012): 351–365.

Tigert, Leanne M. "The power of shame: Lesbian battering as a manifestation of homophobia." *Women and Therapy* 23, no. 3 (2001): 73–85.

Tjaden, Patricia Godeke, and Nancy Thoennes. *Extent, Nature, and Consequences of Intimate Partner Violence: Findings from the National Violence against Women Survey.* Washington, DC: National Institute of Justice/Centers for Disease Control and Prevention, 2000.

Todd, Megan. "Blue Rinse Blues? Older Lesbians' Experiences of Domestic Violence." In *Mapping Intimacies,* edited by Tam Sanger and Yvette Taylor, 150–168. London: Palgrave Macmillan, 2013.

Toro-Alfonso, José. "Domestic Violence among Same Sex Partners in Puerto Rico." *Journal of Gay and Lesbian Social Services* 9, no. 1 (1999): 69–78.

Toro-Alfonso, José, and Sheilla Rodríguez-Madera. "Sexual coercion in a sample of Puerto Rican gay males." *Journal of Gay and Lesbian Social Services* 17, no. 1 (2004): 47–58.

Tran, Alvin, Lavinia Lin, Eric J. Nehl, Colin L. Talley, Kristin L. Dunkle, and Frank Y. Wong. "Prevalence of substance use and intimate partner violence in a sample of A/PI MSM." *Journal of Interpersonal Violence* 29, no 11 (2014): 2054–2067.

Trans Respect versus Transphobia Worldwide. "Legal and Social Mapping—World #1." Accessed October 2015. http://transrespect.org/wp-content/uploads/2015/08/web_tvt_mapping_1_EN1.pdf.

Tulloch, Tyler G., Nooshin K. Rotondi, Stanley Ing, Ted Myers, Liviana M. Calzavara, Mona R. Loutfy, and Trevor A. Hart. "Retrospective reports of developmental stressors, syndemics, and their association with sexual risk outcomes among gay men." *Archives of Sexual Behavior* 44, no. 7 (2015): 1879–1889.

Tully, Carol Thorpe. *Lesbians, Gays, and the Empowerment Perspective.* New York: Columbia University Press, 2000.

———. "Domestic violence: The ultimate betrayal of human rights." *Journal of Gay and Lesbian Social Services* 13, nos. 1–2 (2001): 83–98.

Turell, Susan C. "A descriptive analysis of same-sex relationship violence for a diverse sample." *Journal of Family Violence* 15, no. 3 (2000): 281–293.

———. "Seeking help for same-sex relationship abuses." *Journal of Gay and Lesbian Social Services* 10, no. 2 (1999): 35–49.

Turell, Susan C., and La Vonne Cornell-Swanson. "Not all alike: Within-group differences in seeking help for same-sex relationship abuses." *Journal of Gay and Lesbian Social Services* 18, no. 1 (2006): 71–88.

Turell, Susan C., and Molly M. Herrmann. "'Family' support for family violence: Exploring community support systems for lesbian and bisexual women who have experienced abuse." *Journal of Lesbian Studies* 12, nos. 2–3 (2008): 211–224.

Turell, Susan C., Molly L. Herrmann, Gary Hollander, and Carol Galletly. "Lesbian, gay, bisexual, and transgender communities' readiness for intimate partner violence prevention." *Journal of Gay and Lesbian Social Services* 24, no. 3 (2012): 289–310.

United Kingdom Office of Public Sector Information. "The Homosexual Offences (Northern Ireland) Order 1982 (No. 1536 (N.I. 19))." *The UK Statute Law Database* (1982). Accessed January 2010. www.legislation.gov.uk/nisi/1982/1536/contents.

United Nations. "UNiTE to End Violence against Women." YouTube video, 1:55. Accessed January 2015. www.un.org/en/women/endviolence/.

U.S. Census Bureau. "Quick Facts: United States." Accessed January 2016. www.census.gov /quickfacts/table/PST045215/00.

U.S. Department of Justice. "Frequently Asked Questions: Nondiscrimination Grant Condition in the Violence Against Women Reauthorization Act of 2013." (2014). Accessed January 2016. https://www.justice.gov/sites/default/files/ovw/legacy/2014/06/20/faqs-ngc-vawa.pdf.

U.S. Government Printing Office. "113th Congress Public Law 4: Violence Against Women Act Reauthorization of 2013." (2013). Accessed January 2016. https://www.gpo.gov/fdsys /pkg/PLAW-113publ4/html/PLAW-113publ4.htm.

Valentine, Sarah E., Steven Elsesser, Chris Grasso, Steven A. Safren, Judith B. Bradford, Ethan Mereish, and Conall O'Cleirigh. "The Predictive Syndemic Effect of Multiple Psychosocial Problems on Health Care Costs and Utilization among Sexual Minority Women." *Journal of Urban Health* 92, no. 6 (2015): 1092–1104.

Valentine, Sarah E., and David W. Pantalone. "Correlates of perceptual and behavioral definitions of abuse in HIV-positive sexual minority men." *Psychological Trauma: Theory, Research, Practice, and Policy* 5, no. 5 (2013): 417–425.

VanNatta, Michelle. "Constructing the battered woman." *Feminist Studies* 31, no. 2 (2005): 416–443.

Ventura, Lois A., and Gabrielle Davis. "Domestic violence court case conviction and recidivism." *Violence against Women* 11, no. 2 (2005): 255–277.

Vickers, Lee. "The second closet: Domestic violence in lesbian and gay relationships; A Western Australian perspective." *Murdoch University Electronic Journal of Law* 3, no. 4 (1996): 11–26.

Vidas, Michael De. "Childhood sexual abuse and domestic violence: A support group for Latino gay men and lesbians." *Journal of Gay and Lesbian Social Services* 10, no. 2 (1999): 51–68.

Waldner-Haugrud, Lisa K., and Linda V. Gratch. "Sexual coercion in gay/lesbian relationships: Descriptives and gender differences." *Violence and Victims* 12, no. 1 (1997): 87–98.

Waldner-Haugrud, Lisa K., Linda V. Gratch, and Brian Magruder. "Victimization and perpetration rates of violence in gay and lesbian relationships: Gender issues explored." *Violence and Victims* 12, no. 2 (1997): 173–184.

Waldron, Charlene M. "Lesbians of color and the domestic violence movement." *Journal of Gay and Lesbian Social Services* 4, no. 1 (1996): 43–52.

Walker, Julia K. "Investigating trans people's vulnerabilities to intimate partner violence/ abuse." *Partner Abuse* 6, no. 1 (2015): 107–125.

Walker, Lenore E. *The Battered Woman.* New York: Harper Perennial, 1979.

Wallace, Harvey. *Family Violence: Legal, Medical, and Social Perspectives.* 4th ed. Boston: Pearson Education, 2005.

Walmsley, Roy. "World female imprisonment list." 2nd ed. London: International Centre for Prison Studies, 2012. www.prisonstudies.org/sites/default/files/resources/downloads /wfil_2nd_edition.pdf.

Walters, Mikel L. "Straighten Up and Act like a Lady: A Qualitative Study of Lesbian Survivors of Intimate Partner Violence, *Journal of Gay and Lesbian Social Services,* 23 (2011): 250–270.

Walters, Mikel L., Jieru Chen, and Matthew J. Breiding. *The National Intimate Partner and Sexual Violence Survey (NISVS): 2010 Findings on Victimization by Sexual Orientation.* Atlanta: National Center for Injury Prevention and Control, Centers for Disease Control and Prevention, 2013.

Warrier, Sujata, Beverly Williams-Wilkins, Emily Pitt, Robert M. Reece, Betsy Mcalister Groves, Alicia F. Lieberman, and Margaret Mcnamara. "'Culturally Competent Responses' and 'Children: Hidden Victims': Excerpts from Day 2 Plenary Sessions." *Violence against Women* 8, no. 6 (2002): 661–686.

Waterman, Caroline K., Lori J. Dawson, and Michael J. Bologna. "Sexual coercion in gay male and lesbian relationships: Predictors and implications for support services." *Journal of Sex Research* 26, no. 1 (1989): 118–124.

Watkins, Phillip. "Police perspective: Discovering hidden truths in domestic violence intervention." *Journal of Family Violence* 20, no. 1 (2005): 47–54.

Weil, Amy. "Intimate partner violence: Diagnosis and screening." UpToDate, 2015. www .uptodate.com.

———. "Intimate partner violence: Epidemiology and health consequences." UpToDate, 2015. www.uptodate.com.

———. "Intimate partner violence: Intervention and patient management." UpToDate, 2015. www.uptodate.com.

Weldon, S. Laurel. *Protest, Policy, and the Problem of Violence against Women: A Cross-National Comparison.* Pittsburgh: University of Pittsburgh Press, 2002.

Welles, Seth L., Theodore J. Corbin, John A. Rich, Elizabeth Reed, and Anita Raj. "Intimate partner violence among men having sex with men, women, or both: Early-life sexual and physical abuse as antecedents." *Journal of Community Health* 36, no. 3 (2011): 477–485.

West, Angela. "Prosecutorial activism: Confronting heterosexism in a lesbian battering case." *Harvard Women's Law Journal* 15 (1992): 249–271.

West, Candace, and Don H. Zimmerman. "Doing gender." *Gender and Society* 1, no. 2 (1987): 125–151.

West, Carolyn M. "Leaving a second closet: Outing partner violence in same-sex couples." In *Partner Violence: A Comprehensive Review of 20 Years of Research,* edited by Jana L. Jasinski and Linda M. Williams, 163–183. Thousand Oaks, CA: SAGE, 1998.

———. "Lesbian intimate partner violence: Prevalence and dynamics." *Journal of Lesbian Studies* 6, no. 1 (2002): 121–127.

———. "Partner abuse in ethnic minority and gay, lesbian, bisexual, and transgender populations." *Partner Abuse* 3, no. 3 (2012): 336–357.

Westbrook, Lynn, and Jeanine Finn. "Community information as boundary object: Police responsibility for abuse survivors." *Journal of Documentation* 68, no. 6 (2012): 806–825.

Weston, Rebecca, Linda L. Marshall, and Ann L. Coker. "Women's motives for violent and nonviolent behaviors in conflicts." *Journal of Interpersonal Violence* 22, no. 8 (2007): 1043–1065.

Westover, Gary. "Include All Forms of Domestic Violence." *Everyman* 46 (2001): 35.

Whitaker, Daniel J., Shannon Morrison, Christine Lindquist, Stephanie R. Hawkins, Joyce A. O'Neil, Angela M. Nesius, Anita Mathew, and Le'Roy Reese. "A critical review of interventions for the primary prevention of perpetration of partner violence." *Aggression and Violent Behavior* 11, no. 2 (2006): 151–166.

Williams, John K., Leo Wilton, Manya Magnus, Lei Wang, Jing Wang, Typhanye Penniman Dyer, Beryl A. Koblin, et al. "Relation of childhood sexual abuse, intimate partner violence, and depression to risk factors for HIV among black men who have sex with men in 6 US cities." *American Journal of Public Health* 105, no. 12 (2015): 2473–2481.

Wise, Amy J., and Sharon L. Bowman. "Comparison of Beginning Counselors' Responses to Lesbian vs. Heterosexual Partner Abuse." *Violence and Victims* 12, no. 2 (1997): 127–135.

Wolf, Marsha E., Uyen Ly, Margaret A. Hobart, and Mary A. Kernic. "Barriers to seeking police help for intimate partner violence." *Journal of Family Violence* 18, no. 2 (2003): 121–129.

Wolfe, David A., Claire C. Crooks, Debbie Chiodo, and Peter Jaffe. "Child maltreatment, bullying, gender-based harassment, and adolescent dating violence: Making the connections." *Psychology of Women Quarterly* 33, no. 1 (2009): 21–24.

Wolfe, David A., Katreena Scott, Deborah Reitzel-Jaffe, Christine Wekerle, Carolyn Grasley, and Anna-Lee Straatman. "Development and validation of the conflict in adolescent dating relationships inventory." *Psychological Assessment* 13, no. 2 (2001): 277–293.

WomensLaw.org. "Know the laws: South Carolina: Orders of Protection." Accessed October 2015. www.womenslaw.org/laws_state_type.php?id = 584&state_code = SC&open_id = 11688#content-12905.

Wong, Carolyn F., George Weiss, George Ayala, and Michele D. Kipke. "Harassment, discrimination, violence and illicit drug use among young men who have sex with men." *AIDS Education and Prevention: Official Publication of the International Society for AIDS Education* 22, no. 4 (2010): 286.

Woodin, Erica M., Alina Sotskova, and K. Daniel O'Leary. "Intimate partner violence assessment in an historical context: Divergent approaches and opportunities for progress." *Sex Roles* 69, nos. 3–4 (2013): 120–130.

Worcester, Nancy. "Women's Use of Force: Complexities and Challenges of Taking the Issue Seriously." *Violence against Women* 8, no. 11 (2002): 1390–1415.

World Health Organization. "Prevention of intimate partner and sexual violence (violence against women)." Accessed January 2015. www.who.int/violence_injury_prevention /violence/sexual/en/.

Wright, Margaret O'Dougherty, Dana L. Norton, and Jill Anne Matusek. "Predicting verbal coercion following sexual refusal during a hookup: Diverging gender patterns." *Sex Roles* 62, nos. 9–10 (2010): 647–660.

Wu, Elwin, Nabila El-Bassel, L. Donald McVinney, Leona Hess, Mark V. Fopeano, Hyesung G. Hwang, Mahnaz Charania, and Gordon Mansergh. "The association between substance use and intimate partner violence within Black male same-sex relationships." *Journal of Interpersonal Violence* 30, no. 5 (2014): 762–781.

Younglove, Jane A., Marcee G. Kerr, and Corey J. Vitello. "Law Enforcement Officers' Perceptions of Same Sex Domestic Violence: Reasons for Cautious Optimism," *Journal of Interpersonal Violence* 17, no. 7 (2002): 760–772.

Yu, Yong, Shuiyuan Xiao, and Kirin Qilin Liu. "Dating violence among gay men in China." *Journal of Interpersonal Violence* 28, no. 12 (2013): 2491–2504.

Zahnd, Elaine, David Grant, May Jawad Aydin, Jenny Y. Chia, and Imelda D. Padilla-Frausto. "Nearly four million California adults are victims of intimate partner violence." Los Angeles: UCLA Center for Health Policy Research, 2010.

Zweig, Janine M., Meredith Dank, Pamela Lachman, and Jennifer Yahner. *Technology, Teen Dating Violence and Abuse, and Bullying: Final Report.* Washington, DC: Urban Institute, 2013. https://www.ncjrs.gov/pdffiles1/nij/grants/243296.pdf.

Zweig, Janine M., Pamela Lachman, Jennifer Yahner, and Meredith Dank. "Correlates of cyber dating abuse among teens." *Journal of Youth and Adolescence* 43, no. 8 (2014): 1306–1321.

INDEX

adoption, 19, 175–176

age, impact on LGBTQ IPV, 63–65, 70–72, 74, 77–79, 100–101

AIDS. *See* HIV, AIDS, and STIs

alcohol. *See* substance use

anonymity, 57. *See also* research, challenges in defining and sampling population for; sampling

antidiscrimination policies in nations, lack of. *See* discrimination against LGBTQ people, not IPV-specific; discriminatory attitudes against LGBTQ people; government policies, impact on LGBTQ IPV

antidiscrimination training. *See* training

anti-sodomy policies. *See* government policies, impact on LGBTQ IPV

attachment, as a degree of dependency. *See* LGBTQ IPV, causes of perpetration

attorneys/lawyers. *See* courts

barriers to escape, 114; challenges in seeking help (and role of discrimination), 121–123; fear of harm, outing, and stigma, 13–15, 91, 119–122; financial dependence, emotional dependence, and love, 117–119; not recognizing IPV, 7–8, 114–117. *See also* help-seeking among LGBTQ IPV victims

battered woman's syndrome (BWS), 187–188. *See also* courts

battered women's movement, impact on societal responses to LGBTQ IPV, 15, 173

batterer-intervention programs (BIPs): defined, 12; effectiveness of, 13, 190; cognitive behavioral therapy (CBT) in, 12, 190–191; Duluth model in, 12, 190–191; tailored to LGBTQ IPV, 191; one-size-fits-all approach, 11–13, 190–191. *See also* interventions

bidirectional LGBTQ IPV, 88; misinterpreting time-frame data as evidence of relationship-level "mutual battering," 42-43, 87-89; self-defense in, 89. *See also* LGBTQ IPV, directionality

biphobia. *See* discrimination against LGBTQ people, not IPV-specific; discriminatory attitudes against LGBTQ people

bisexual sexual orientation, 22

book methodology, 199–201

bystanders, 135, 163–164, 189. *See also* friends; interventions

causes of LGBTQ IPV. *See* LGBTQ IPV, causes of perpetration

child abuse: as predictor of LGBTQ IPV, 98–99; perpetrated by same-gender parents, 99;

children: percentage of same-gender couples with, 99; used to control victims, 65–66, 121

cisgender, 2, 22